P9-DMT-440

ARTTALK

Title Page Credit:
Henri-Charles Manguin. *Port Saint Tropez, le 14 Julliet.* Oil on canvas. 61.3 x 50.2 cm (24 ⅛ x 19 ¾").
The Museum of Fine Arts, Houston, Texas. The John A. and Audrey Jones Beck Collection.

ARTTALK

SECOND EDITION

Rosalind Ragans, Ph. D.
Associate Professor Emerita
Georgia Southern University

GLENCOE
McGraw-Hill

New York, New York Columbus, Ohio Mission Hills, California Peoria, Illinois

Contributors and Reviewers

Thomas Beacham
Art Teacher
Telfair County High School
McRae, GA

Leilani Calzada
Art Teacher
Burges High School
El Paso, TX

Sherry Christensen
Art Teacher
Lee High School
San Antonio, TX

Ron Durham
Art Coordinator
Arlington I.S.D.
Arlington, TX

Nell Elam
Art Teacher
Starkville High School
Starkville, MS

Joyce Hearne
English/Art Teacher
El Paso High School
El Paso, TX

Larry Hurt
Art Teacher
Ben Davis High School
Indianapolis, IN

Audrey Komroy
Art Teacher
Akron High School
Akron, NY

Ann Krone
Art Coordinator
Wichita USD 259
Wichita, KS

David McIntyre
Visual Arts Facilitator
El Paso Independent School District
El Paso, TX

Elaine McMichael
Supervisor of Art Education
Somerville High School
Somerville, MA

Sandra H. Moore
Art Specialist
John Sevier Middle School
Kingsport, TN

Virginia Neff
Art Teacher
Shawnee Mission
Shawnee Mission, KS

Christine Peña
Art Teacher
USC Magnet
Los Angeles, CA

Carlyne Seegraves
Elementary Art Teacher
Woodcliff Arts Center
East Grand Rapids Public Schools
Grand Rapids, MI

Becky Schopfner
Art Teacher
Chaffin Junior High School
Fort Smith, AR

Barbara Stodola
Executive Director
The John G. Blank Center for the Arts
Michigan City, IN

Send all inquiries to:
GLENCOE/McGraw-Hill
936 Eastwind Drive
Westerville, Ohio 43081

ISBN 0-02-640295-5

Printed in the United States

4 5 6 7 8 9 AGK 00 99 98 97 96 95

Studio Lesson Consultants

The author wishes to express her gratitude to the following art teachers who participated in field testing the Studio Lessons with their students:

Karen Anable-Nichols
Reseda High School
Reseda, CA

Thomas Beacham
Telfair County High School
Helena, GA

Pam Bergman
Hume-Fogg Academic High School
Nashville, TN

Wendy Bull
Colonial Junior High School
Memphis, TN

Craig Burkhalter
Southeast High School
Macon, GA

Barbara Cox
Glencliff High School
Nashville, TN

Maggie Davis
Northwestern Senior High School
Miami, FL

Marsha Hogue
Lake Highlands High School
Dallas, TX

Sandra H. Moore
John Sevier Middle School
Kingsport, TN

Bunyan Morris
Marvin Pittman Laboratory School
Statesboro, GA

PerriAnn C. Morris
Jenkins County High School
Millen, GA

Ted Oliver
Fannin County High School
Blue Ridge, GA

Kelly Pasman
Parkview Junior High School
New Castle, IN

David Sebring
Dobson High School
Mesa, AZ

Margaret M. Shearouse
Harlem High School
Harlem, GA

Rosanne Stutts
Davidson Fine Arts School
Augusta, GA

Nancy Walker
Colonial Junior High School
Memphis, TN

Student Contributors

The following students contributed exemplary work for the Studio Lesson pages:

Dobson High School, Mesa, AZ: Joel Switzer 5.36A, Lyle Kinlicheenie 10.34A, Jacob Marx 11.32A; Reseda High School, Reseda, CA: Wesley Ashcraft 7.39A, Dago Chavarria 9.27A; Douglas Anderson High School, Jacksonville, FL: Jessica Erickson 9.8; Northwestern Senior High School, Miami FL: Manuel Cuellar 10.33A; Davidson Fine Arts School, Augusta, GA: Heather Story 7.40A, Therese Turman 9.28A; Fannin County High School, Blue Ridge, GA: Amy Jones 5.38A; Harlem High School, Harlem, GA: Josh Menefee 12.28A; Jenkins County High School, Millen, GA: Kristen Leonard 5.35A, Genie Wiggins 8.28A, Melissa Hurst 8.30A, Erin Reeves, Stephanie McMillan, Nimesh Solanki, Krystal Boyd 9.29A; Joy Crocket, Martha Pierce 9.30A; Marvin Pittman Laboratory School, Statesboro, GA: Sean Sanders 6.24, Eddie Dinello, 6.41, Dana Van Tassel 6.42, 6.43; Marian Puckett 7.9; Elisabeth Adams, Meg Chandler, Eric DeLoach, John Dewey, Nichalos Gordon, Christi Groover, Chrissy Joiner, Ashley MacCaughelty, Marco Marchionni, Katie J. Olliff, Shaana Perkins, Alison Powell, Elizabeth Price, Chad Prosser, Dawn Ross, Jenny Smith, Kelly Smith, Anna Woodyard, all 7.38A; Elizabeth Ariail 8.14; Dawn Ross 8.29A; Marissa MacCaughelty 9.21; Maggie Moore 9.22; Trip Healy 10.10; Maggie Horne 11.34A; Southeast High School, Macon, GA: Jennifer Maddox 12.27A; Telfair County High School, Helena, GA: Rebecca Renew 5.37A; Ware County High School, Waycross, GA: Dorothy Robbins 12.29A; Parkview Junior High School, New Castle, IN: Kevin Swiegart 7.37A; John Sevier Middle School, Kingsport, TN: Sarah Rains 8.8; Colonial Junior High School, Memphis, TN: Alexandria Hare 6.44A, Carey Arnett 6.46A; Glencliff High School, Nashville, TN: Jason Swafford 8.27A; Hume-Fogg Academic High School, Nashville, TN: Karianne Mattox 6.16; Dede Bacon 6.45A; Lake Highlands High School, Dallas, TX: Chip Cullum 10.31A; Ginna Ladd 10.32A; Rogher Jeri 11.33A.

Credits for the art details found throughout the Table of Contents are listed below. Following the credit information in parentheses are the figure number and the page on which the full work of art can be found.

viiT: Margareta Haverman. *A Vase of Flowers*. Detail. 1716. Oil on wood. 79.4 × 60.3 cm (31¼ × 23¾″). The Metropolitan Museum of Art, New York, New York. Purchase, 1871. (Figure 2.6, page 31.)

viiB: Andrew Wyeth. *Christina's World*. Detail. 1948. Tempera on gessoed panel. 81.9 × 121.3 cm (32¼ × 47¾″). The Museum of Modern Art, New York, New York. Purchase. (Figure 2.8, page 33.)

viii: Lilla Cabot Perry. *Lady with a Bowl of Violets*. Detail. 1910. Oil on canvas. 102 × 76.2 cm (40¼ × 30″). National Museum of Women in the Arts, Washington, D.C. The Holladay Collection (Figure 3.35, page 66.)

ix: Louise Nevelson. *Dawn*. Detail. 1962. Wood painted gold. 323 × 240 × 19 cm (127 × 94½ × 7½″). The Pace Gallery, New York, New York. (Figure 2.9, page 36.)

x: Sandro Botticelli. *The Adoration of the Magi*. Detail. c. 1481-82. Tempera on wood. 70.1 × 104.1 cm (27⅝ × 41″). National Gallery of Art, Washington, D.C. Andrew W. Mellon Collection, 1937. (Figure 6.25, page 135.)

xi: Northwestern Plains Indian, *Feather Bonnet*. Detail. c. 1890. Rooster hackles, wood rods, porcupine hair, ermine skins, horsehair, buckskin, glass beads. 84 × 68.6 cm (33 × 27″). Buffalo Bill Historical Center, Cody, Wyoming. Chandler-Pohrt Collection. (Figure 8.1, page 190.)

xii: Juan Gris. *Guitar and Flowers*. Detail. 1912. Oil on canvas. 112.1 × 70.2 cm (44⅛ × 27⅝″). The Museum of Modern Art, New York, New York. Bequest of Anna Erickson Levene in memory of her husband, Dr. Phoebus Aaron Theodor Levene. (Figure 12.24, page 332.)

xiii: Albrecht Dürer. *An Oriental Ruler Seated on His Throne*. Detail. c. 1495. Pen and black ink. 30.6 × 19.7 cm (12 × 7¾″). National Gallery of Art, Washington, D.C. Ailsa Mellon Bruce Fund. (Figure 6.23, page 134.)

CONTENTS

CHAPTER 3 *Art History* 40

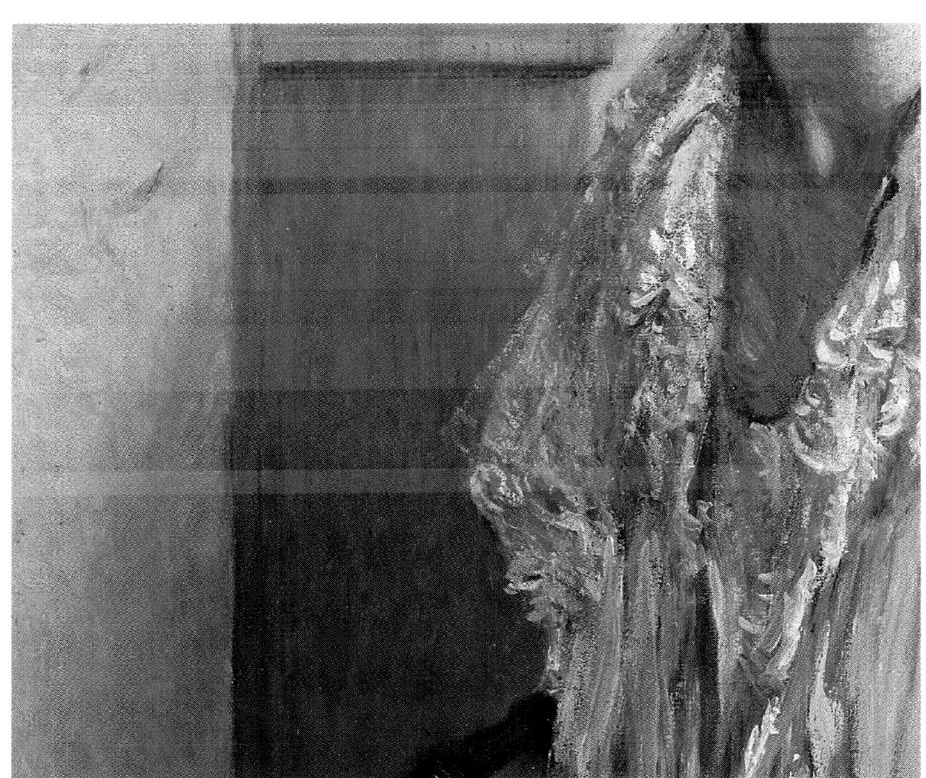

CHAPTER 6

UNIT 4

TECHNIQUE TIPS HANDBOOK 346

Features

Art Criticism in Action

Meet the Artist

Activities

Listing of Studio Lessons by Media

Jan Steen. *The Dancing Couple.* (Detail.) 1663. Oil on canvas. 102.5 × 142.5 cm (40⅜ × 56⅛″). National Gallery of Art, Washington, D.C. Widener collection.

APPRECIATING THE VISUAL ARTS

In *ArtTalk* you will be learning about the visual arts. These are the arts that produce images and objects to look at. The visual arts include all objects created for visual appeal—including those that serve a useful purpose.

Why should you read about and learn how to make visual arts? Because they satisfy human needs for display, celebration, personal expression, and communication. We use the visual arts to enhance our visual environment, to express our innermost feelings, and to communicate ideas.

In the first unit of *ArtTalk* you will learn about the language of visual art. You will begin to learn how to look at art in new ways and to make judgments about its artistic merit. You will also learn about the many different kinds of art created throughout history and the career opportunities in art today. After completing Unit 1, you will be ready to begin creating your own art. You will also be on your way toward developing a fuller appreciation for the visual arts and for the natural art that surrounds you in the environment.

FIGURE 1.1 Grant Wood was an American artist who chose to paint the people and the landscapes of mid-twentieth-century Iowa in the realistic style he learned by studying the art of fifteenth-century German artists. His paintings are still popular today because they make people feel they are looking at America's "good old days."

Grant Wood. *Return from Bohemia*. 1935. Colored crayon, gouache, and pencil on brown paper. 59.7 x 51 cm (23½ x 20"). The Regis Collection, Minneapolis, Minnesota.

CHAPTER 1

The Language of Art

When you talk to someone or write a letter, you *communicate*. You share your ideas and feelings with that person. You use words—either spoken or written—to communicate a message.

You can also communicate through the arts. They are languages for expressing ideas and feelings that everyday words cannot explain. The arts talk in ways that go beyond simply describing something or telling a story.

The arts can cross the language barriers of different countries. Someone who cannot speak English can understand what is happening in the painting by Grant Wood (Figure 1.1). Mikhail Baryshnikov may speak English with a Russian accent, but when he dances, the language of his movement is understood all around the world.

The arts may even help us communicate with beings from other worlds. In 1972 scientists of the National Aeronautics and Space Administration (NASA) attached a special plaque to *Pioneer 10*, the first exploratory vessel designed to leave our solar system. This spacecraft is out beyond our planets today, carrying this plaque, which has drawings of a human man and woman and a diagram of our solar system. The NASA scientists thought these visual symbols were the best way to try to communicate with any beings *Pioneer 10* might encounter.

FIRST IMPRESSIONS

In *Return from Bohemia* (Figure 1.1 on the opposite page) Grant Wood has shown himself at work on a painting. What is your first reaction to this work of art? What questions come to mind as you look at this group portrait? Does Wood use the concealed canvas and the title to help tell more than a simple story? How does he communicate to you?

Objectives

After completing this chapter, you will be able to:

- Identify the elements of art and the principles of design.
- Describe the media used in drawing and painting.
- Explain how you can improve your perceptual skills.
- List the processes used in printmaking and sculpture.
- Name and identify the subject, composition, and content in a work of art.

Words to Know

composition
content
credit line
edition
elements of art
freestanding
medium
nonobjective art
perception
photography
principles of design
printmaking
relief
subject
symbol

THE ELEMENTS AND PRINCIPLES

You know that the people in our world speak many different languages. Spanish, Swahili, Japanese, Hindi, French, English, and Apache are only a few of the three thousand different languages that have been spoken on this planet Earth.

Each language has its own system of words and rules of grammar. To learn a new language you need to learn new words and a new set of rules for putting those words together.

The language of visual art also has its own system. All of the objects you look at in a work of art are made up of certain common elements. They are arranged according to basic principles. As you learn these basic elements and principles, you will learn the language of art.

Being able to use the language of visual art will help you in many ways. It will increase your ability to understand, appreciate, and enjoy art. It will increase your ability to express yourself clearly when discussing art. It will even help you improve your ability to produce artworks.

The Elements of Art

A **symbol** is *something that stands for, or represents, something else*. In a spoken language words are symbols. The word *chair* stands for a piece of furniture that has a seat, legs, a back, and sometimes arms. In the language of art we use visual symbols to communicate ideas.

The *basic visual symbols in the language of art* are known as the **elements of art**. Just as there are basic kinds of words—such as nouns, verbs, adjectives, and adverbs—there are basic kinds of art elements. These are *line, shape* and *form, space, color, value*, and *texture*. The elements are the visual building blocks that the artist puts together to create a work of art. No matter how a work is made, it will contain some or all of these elements.

When you are looking at a visual image, it is difficult to separate one element from another. For example, when you look at a painting, you may see a rough, red square outlined with a black line. However, rather than seeing the elements of texture (rough), color (red), shape (square), and line (black) separately, you see them all at once. You see the object as a whole. You visually "read" the elements together.

Sometimes the differences between the elements are not clear-cut. A line may be so wide that it looks like a shape, or an artist may manipulate light and dark values to indicate different surface textures. Look at the variety of textures Janet Fish has created in *Fallen Vase* (Figure 1.2).

When you first learned to read, you did not begin with a full-length novel. You learned by reading one word at a time. That is how you will start to read the language of art: one element at a time.

The Principles of Design

After you have learned to recognize the elements of art, you will learn the ways in which the elements can be organized for different effects. When you learn a language, you learn the rules of grammar by which words are organized into sentences and paragraphs. Without these rules people would find it very difficult to communicate.

Visual images are also organized according to rules. The *rules that govern how artists organize the elements of art* are called the **principles of design**. They also help artists organize the elements for specific effects. The principles of design have a strong influence on the way art communicates, and they are the subject of the last four chapters in *ArtTalk*. The principles you will learn about are *rhythm, movement, balance, proportion, variety, emphasis, harmony*, and *unity*. In Figure 1.3 on page 8, the artist Julio Larraz has created a mysterious mood by the way he has used the principles of design to organize the elements in his painting *Papiamento*.

THE MEDIA AND PROCESSES OF ART

The *material used to make art* is called a **medium**. Tempera is an opaque medium used for painting. A medium can be something as ordinary as a crayon or as exotic as gold. You need to know that the word *medium* has an unusual plural form. It is **media**. Clay, wood, and marble are media used for sculpting.

Janet Fish. *Fallen Vase.* 1987. Oil on canvas. 178 × 101.6 cm (70 × 40″). Robert Miller Gallery, New York, New York.

LOOKING CLOSELY

FIGURE 1.2 Look closely at the different ways that Fish has used light values to indicate different surfaces. The transparent red glass bowl has different highlights than the slightly less shiny ceramic lamp base. Now notice the different way she uses light to show highlights on the soft, sheer curtains. How is the light different on the fruit than it is on the fallen vase? How has light been used to indicate that there is a lit lightbulb inside the translucent lamp shade? Look at the green leaves in the window and the leaves on the trees on the distant hill. What has the artist done with the edges of shapes to indicate distance?

texture.
-roughness.
-smoothness

Just as the artist's choice of how to arrange the elements of art using the principles of design affects the look of the finished work, so do the medium and the process the artist chooses. A watercolor painting of an outdoor scene will look very different from an oil painting of the same scene. During your art class you will use many art media to make art. The following describes some of the most familiar media and processes that you will use and read about.

Drawing

Drawing is the process of moving a pointed instrument over a smooth surface to leave a mark. That mark is a line. Line is the most important element of art in drawing.

The most popular drawing media are graphite pencils, colored pencils, marking pens, charcoal, crayons, pastels, and colored chalk. Pen and ink, pen and brush, and brushes with watercolors are also used to make drawings.

FIGURE 1.3 Julio Larraz has camouflaged the figure of the woman in this painting by placing her against the textured trunk of the palm tree, using active lines for the palm fronds, and painting the water an intense blue. Why do you think the artist arranged the picture this way? What kind of mood did he create by using these techniques? Now that you have looked closely at the painting, what question do you think the artist wanted to raise in the viewer's mind?

Julio Larraz. *Papiamento.* 1987. Oil on canvas. 143.5 × 209.5 cm (56½ × 82½″). Nohra Haime Gallery, New York, New York.

There are many different purposes for drawing. Some of the most important are to develop perception, to record ideas, to help plan projects, and to make finished artworks. The drawing *Preacher* by Charles White is an example of a finished work of art drawn with pen and ink (Figure 1.4).

To an artist, looking and perceiving are not the same thing. Looking is simply noticing and labeling an object. **Perception** is *the act of looking at something carefully and thinking deeply about what is seen.* Developing perception requires that you really study the object being observed and that you notice every detail carefully. Through drawing, artists become better at perceiving.

Many artists use sketchbooks to record their surroundings and to study objects. Artists also record ideas and impressions in these sketchbooks that can be used later. The Renaissance artist Leonardo da Vinci (lay-oh-**nar**-doh da **vin**-chee) filled more than one hundred sketchbooks with his perceptions and ideas. He made visual drawings and added written notes. His sketchbooks included everything from perceptions of people to his notations on the movement of water (Figure 1.5) and his plans for flying machines.

Drawing is usually the first step in completing many paintings and other art projects. Rough sketches, or studies, are almost always done before creating a work in another medium such as paint or clay. Fashion designers draw their ideas for new styles long before any fabric is cut. Many creative people, such as stage designers, graphic designers,

FIGURE 1.4 The artist has built up the dark areas in this drawing by carefully applying layers of lines that cross each other in different directions. It is easy to see the lines in the gray shadows, but some areas appear totally black.

Charles White. *Preacher.* 1952. Ink on cardboard. 54 × 75 cm (21⅜ × 29⅜″). Collection of Whitney Museum of American Art, New York, New York.

FIGURE 1.5 Da Vinci's observations of moving water could not be verified until this century, when we had cameras that could capture the movement of water in a photograph. Da Vinci filled his notebooks with sketches and notes that could be read only when held up to a mirror.

Leonardo da Vinci. Page from his sketchbook showing movement of water. Royal Library, Windsor Castle, London, England. The Royal Collection 1993, Her Majesty Queen Elizabeth II.

and architects, must show presentation drawings for a client's approval. Figure 1.6 is an architect's loose perspective drawing that presents an exciting feeling about a new building. This kind of drawing is very different from the precise blueprints that an architect must prepare before the actual construction of a building can begin.

Throughout this book you will be asked to make several sketches and select the best one to carry out an assignment. You will also be asked to make perception drawings. You will be asked to keep all these sketches and drawings in a sketchbook. This sketchbook will be a record of your experiences in this class.

Testing Your Knowledge

1. Applying Your Skills. Draw an arrangement of three everyday objects in your sketchbook. You will look back at this later to see how your work has improved.

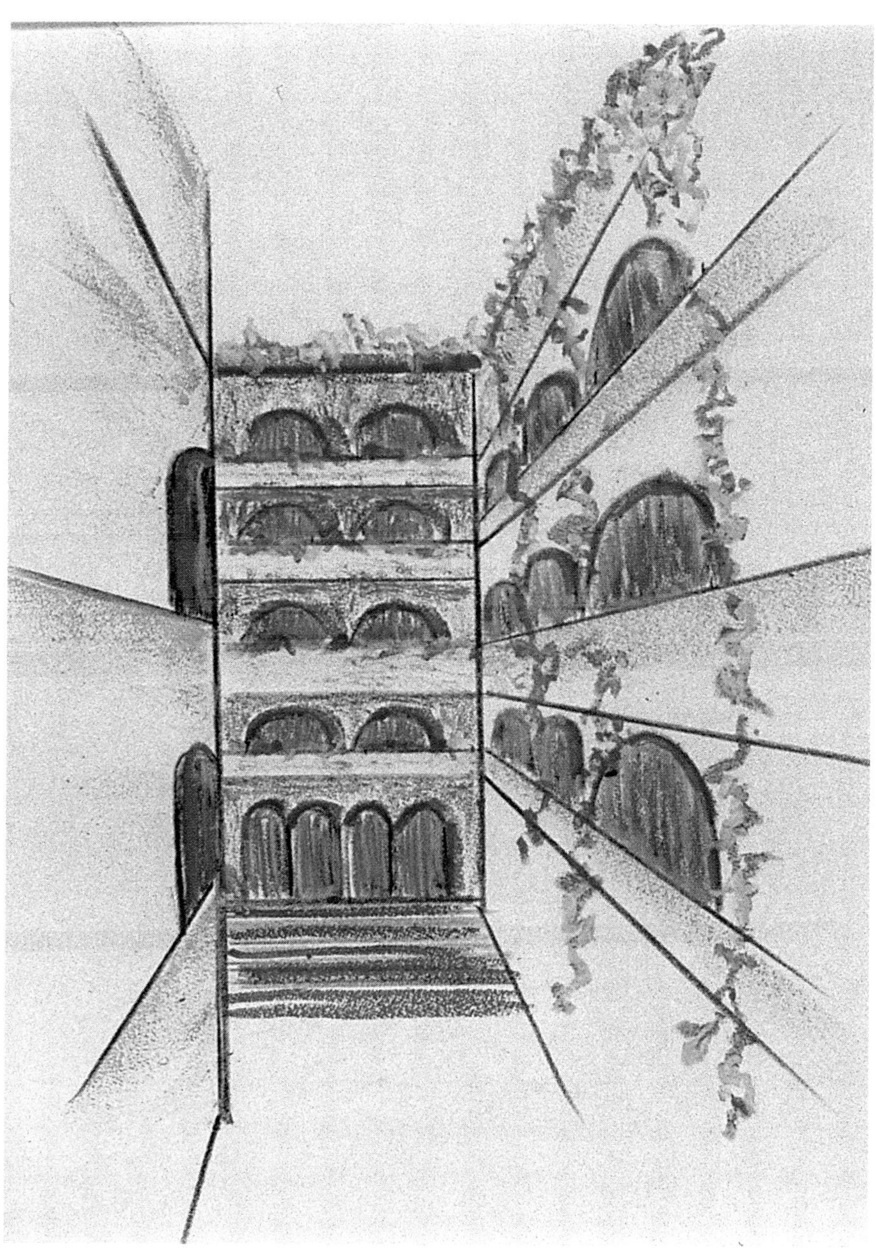

FIGURE 1.6 Notice how the architect has indicated the features with a minimum of lines.

2. Further Challenge. Add two objects to the arrangement, placing one in the foreground and one in the background.

3. Computer Option. In the center of your screen, draw one rectangle and two circles of different sizes. You may use colors or patterns. The shapes in the center of your screen should not touch. Use Copy and Paste tools to create four different arrangements using all three shapes. The shapes in these arrangements may overlap. Save this file for future reference.

Painting

Painting is the process of applying color to a surface using tools such as a brush, a painting knife, a roller, or even fingers. Some paints can be diluted and blown as a fine mist onto a surface with an airbrush. The surface is the material to which the paint is applied. Canvas, paper, and wood are three examples of material. The look of a finished painting has much to do with the combination of media, tools, and the surface the artist chooses. In Figures 1.7 and 1.8 on page 12, you can see how Winslow Homer has created two images that are almost exactly alike. Figure 1.7 is made with thin, wet, flowing watercolor on white paper. The white in that painting is the white of the paper. Figure 1.8 is painted with thick, creamy oil paint on canvas, and the white in the oil painting is opaque white paint.

All paints have three basic ingredients: pigment, binder, and solvent. The *pigment* is a finely ground powder that gives every paint its color. Pigments are produced by chemical processes or by grinding up some kind of earth, stone, or mineral. The *binder*, sometimes called the vehicle, is a liquid that holds together the grains of pigment in a form that can be spread over a surface, where it is allowed to dry. The *solvent* is the material used to thin the binder.

The binder for oil paint is linseed oil, and the solvent is turpentine. The binder for watercolor is gum arabic, and the solvent is water. Acrylic paint, which first appeared in the 1950s, uses an acrylic polymer as a binder. When acrylic paint is wet, water is used as the solvent. Once acrylic is dry, it is waterproof.

Exploring Paints

1. Applying Your Skills. Gather as many different kinds of paint of the same color as you can. For example, look for red watercolor, red tempera paint, and red acrylic. On a piece of paper, draw one shape for each kind of paint. Paint each shape with a different kind of paint. Display your results alongside those done by your classmates. Discuss the similarities and differences you observe.

2. Further Challenge. Follow the directions above but draw two shapes for each kind of paint. Paint one of each shape with thick paint; dilute the paint with the proper solvent to fill the second shape. Compare the results obtained with thick and thinned paint.

Printmaking

In printmaking the artist makes multiple original images. **Printmaking** is *a process in which an artist repeatedly transfers an original image from one prepared surface to another.* Paper is often the surface to which the printed image is transferred.

Notice that a print is not the same as a reproduction of an artwork such as those you see on the pages of this book. The making of a reproduction is a photographic process. Confusing original prints with reproductions is a mistake many people make because reproductions are often called prints. All prints made by the printmaking process are made using three basic steps:

- ***Creating the printing plate.*** A *printing plate* is a surface onto or into which the image is placed. In creating a plate, the artist makes a mirror image of the final print.
- ***Inking the plate.*** The artist applies ink to the plate. This is done with a *brayer,* a roller with a handle. For a multicolor print, one plate must be made for each color.
- ***Transferring the image.*** The paper or other material is pressed against the inked plate, and the ink is transferred to the new surface. Sometimes this is done by hand. At other times a printing press is used.

FIGURE 1.7 Winslow Homer. *Sketch for Hound and Hunter.* 1892. Watercolor. 35.4 x 50.3 cm (13⅞ × 19⅞″). National Gallery of Art, Washington, D.C. Gift of Ruth K. Henschel in memory of her husband, Charles R. Henschel.

FIGURES 1.7 AND 1.8 The images you see in these two works by Winslow Homer are almost exactly alike. The difference is that one is painted with thin, wet, flowing watercolor paint, while the other is painted with thick, creamy oil paint. Can you describe the different effects these two materials have on the same subject?

FIGURE 1.8 Winslow Homer. *Hound and Hunter.* 1892. Oil on canvas. 71.8 x 122.3 cm (28¼ × 48⅛″). National Gallery of Art, Washington, D.C. Gift of Stephen C. Clark.

A series of identical prints made from the same plate is called an **edition**. The printmaker writes his or her name, the title of the work, and the number of each print, in pencil in the bottom margin. The number 10/20 indicates that you are looking at the tenth of twenty prints that were made from the same plate.

There are four main techniques artists use for making prints. They are relief, intaglio, lithography, and screen printing.

Relief printing. In this method the artist cuts away the sections of a surface not meant to hold ink. The image to be printed is, as a result, raised from the background. In Figure 1.9 Elizabeth Catlett has controlled the light and dark areas of her linoleum-cut relief print by the amount she has cut away. Notice that the white lines are wider in the very light area.

Intaglio. This name comes from the Italian word meaning "to cut into." Intaglio is a process in which ink is forced to fill lines that have been cut or etched into a metal surface, while the plate's surface is wiped clean. When the prints have been made, you can actually feel the lines of raised ink.

Lithography. This printmaking process is based on the principle that grease and water do not mix. In lithography the image to be printed is drawn on limestone, zinc, or aluminum with a special greasy crayon. When the drawing is completed, the surface is chemically treated with a nitric-acid solution to clean it, and it is rinsed with water. Then, when the surface is inked, the greasy area alone holds the ink.

Screen printing. This is the newest method for making prints. It was developed in the United States during this century. This technique makes

FIGURE 1.9 Catlett has devoted her artistic career to a socially conscious art that represents the struggles of African Americans.

Elizabeth Catlett. *Sharecropper.* 1970. Linoleum cut on paper. 45.2 × 43 cm ($17^{13}/_{16} \times 16^{15}/_{16}$"). National Museum of American Art, Washington, D.C.

use of a stencil that is placed on a fabric screen stretched across a frame. The screen is placed flat on the printing surface, and a squeegee is used to press ink through the porous fabric areas not covered by the stencil. A screen print that has been handmade by an artist is called a *serigraph*. If more than one color is used, a separate screen is made for each color. How many screens do you think Miroslav Sutej used to create his serigraph in Figure 1.10?

Making a Printing Plate

1. Applying Your Skills. A printmaker must think in reverse. The printing plate must be a mirror image of the final print. In your sketchbook make a small design using your initials. The design should be less than 1 inch (2.5 cm) square. Copy this design onto a sheet of thin paper. Place the thin paper over a thick pad of newsprint. Draw over the initials, pressing down hard. Turn the paper over and you will see your initials in reverse.

2. Further Challenge. Make a stamp print of your initials. See Technique Tip 14 on page 354 in the Handbook for directions.

3. Computer Option. Use the Text tool to type your name. Use the Select and Flip tools to produce a mirror image. You may also experiment with flipping a simple drawing to produce a mirror image.

Photography

Photography is *a technique of capturing optical images on light-sensitive surfaces*. Everyone can take a photograph. All you have to do is point a camera, trip the shutter, and you have a snapshot. To make a work of art using photography, however, one

FIGURE 1.10 This work has no recognizable objects as subject matter. The artist has created a work that is very interesting by emphasizing the elements of color and shape.

Miroslav Sutej. *Ultra AB*. 1966. Color silkscreen. 49.2 × 45 cm (19⅓ × 17¾″). Library of Congress, Washington, D. C. Pennell Fund, 1970.

FIGURE 1.11 Look closely at this work. What does it tell you about the financial condition of these people?

Dorothea Lange. *Migrant Mother.* 20.3 × 25.4 cm (8 × 10″). Courtesy of the Library of Congress, Washington, D.C.

must make decisions regarding the subject, composition, light conditions, lens opening, and shutter speed. Photography as an art also involves scientific control of what happens in the darkroom to control the look of the final image.

Dorothea Lange was a photojournalist who made the world aware of the problems of migrant workers during the Depression. She was a reporter who worked with a camera. Look closely at this work (Figure 1.11). What does it tell you about the financial status of these people? How many children are in the photo? Even though her face is creased with worry lines, the mother's posture tells you her relationship to the family.

Today, technology is changing the way photographs are made, but it still takes the artist's eye to *see* and the artist's technical skills to *make* a work of art.

Composing a Photograph

1. Applying Your Skills. With an automatic camera, you can make a photograph that looks more like art than a snapshot. Look carefully through the viewing lens. Try to frame your composition so that the object relates well to the background. If you take a picture of a person, come in close enough to catch the mood of the person. Bring your photos to class and compare your best shots with those of your classmates.

2. Further Challenge. Take a carefully composed photograph of a building or a landscape scene. Include some nearby foliage on one side of your viewing lens but focus on the distant objects. Discover what happens visually when your film is developed.

Sculpture

Sculpture takes up space. *Vaquero*, by Luis Jimenez (Figure 1.12), stands in front of the National Museum of American Art in Washington, D.C. As you walk toward the museum and then up the steps, you see the cowboy on his horse from changing points of view. This work is an example of sculpture in the round, or freestanding sculpture. **Freestanding** means *surrounded on all sides by space*. This kind of sculpture can be viewed from all sides.

FIGURE 1.12 Which elements has Jimenez used to make the sculpture so unusual?

Luis Jimenez. *Vaquero*. Modeled 1980, cast 1990. Fiberglass and epoxy. 5 m (16′6″) high. National Museum of American Art, Washington, D.C.

Some sculpture is attached to a background, such as the wall of a building. That is called relief sculpture. **Relief** is *a type of sculpture in which forms project from a flat background*. Relief sculptures are designed to be viewed only from the front.

Artists use a variety of techniques and materials to create sculpture. The processes include modeling, carving, casting, and assembly.

Modeling. This is a process in which a soft, pliable material is built up and shaped. Materials such as clay, wax, and plaster are used in modeling. Because the sculptor gradually adds more and more material to build a form, modeling is referred to as an *additive* process.

Carving. Here the sculptor cuts or chips a form from a mass of material to create a sculpture. Carving is a *subtractive* process. Material is removed until the sculpture is completed. Wood and stone are materials that can be carved.

Casting. In this process melted metal or another liquid substance is poured into a mold to harden. This method allows the artist to duplicate something originally created in wax, clay, or plaster using a more permanent material. Just as with printmaking, an edition of sculptures can be made from the same mold. Once the edition is complete, the mold is destroyed.

Assembly. Assembly is a modern technique. In this process the artist gathers and joins together a variety of different materials to construct a sculpture. One assembly process involves welding together pieces of metal. Nancy Graves used a combination of casting and assembly to create *Zaga* (Figure 1.13).

Crafts

Before machines were invented, people made everything by hand. Fabric for clothing was woven by hand. Plates, bowls, and pots in which to cook were made by hand. Today, artists are still making one-of-a-kind items by hand. Some objects are created for practical use, and others are made purely for decorative purposes. Art made to be experienced visually is called *fine art*. Art made to be functional as well as visually pleasing is called *applied art*. Some crafts are considered fine art if they are made solely for decorative purposes.

Today, artists are creating both functional and decorative craft objects. Weavings are made from

FIGURE 1.13 Graves collects natural objects and casts them in bronze. Then she assembles the pieces of bronze to create new forms and paints them. Can you name some of the objects that were used to create this sculpture?

Nancy Graves. *Zaga*. 1983. Cast bronze with polychrome chemical patination. 182.9 × 124.5 × 81.4 cm (72 × 49 × 32″). Nelson-Atkins Museum of Art, Kansas City, Missouri. © Nancy Graves/VAGA, New York 1994.

natural wool, linen, silk, cotton, and manufactured fibers. Quilts are stitched from fine fabrics to be hung on the wall like paintings. Baskets are woven from reeds and wood slats as well as manufactured fibers. Pottery is made with clay from the earth. Handmade glass objects are formed by forcing air through a tube to shape globs of melted glass. Jewelry is crafted using expensive materials such as precious stones and gold, but it can also be made using paper. As wonderful as technology has become, we still appreciate having an object that is one-of-a-kind and made by hand.

THE WORK OF ART

Works of art may be defined by three basic properties, or features. These properties are *subject, composition*, and *content*.

The Subject

The **subject** is *the image viewers can easily identify in a work of art*. The subject may be one person or many people. It may be a thing, such as a boat. It may be an event, such as a dance. The subjects in John Trumbull's painting (Figure 1.14 on page 18) are easily recognized. The subjects are the soldiers, the white flag in the distance, and the sky.

In recent years some artists have chosen to create nonobjective artwork. **Nonobjective art** is *art that has no recognizable subject matter*. Figure 1.10 on page 14 is such a work.

The Composition

The second property of a work of art is the composition of the work. The **composition** is *the way the principles of design are used to organize the elements*. Notice how Trumbull has organized the lines, values, shapes, and color to lead your eyes to the center of interest: the two figures lying on the ground.

The Content

The third property of a work of art is the content. The **content** is *the message the work communicates*. The message may be an idea or a theme, such as patriotism or family togetherness. It may be an emotion, such as pride, love, or loneliness.

In the 1960s NASA recorded every step of the space program with photographs. However, NASA officials felt that they needed artists to communicate to the people of the future the wonder and excitement that everyone felt about leaving the bonds of earth and venturing into space. They asked the artists to come to Cape Canaveral in Florida, observe everything that was going on, and capture the emotions of the time. All the artists painted the same subject matter, but the

FIGURE 1.14 This large historical painting records one event in the siege of Gibraltar when the British defended the huge rock from the Spaniards in 1784. Everyone is carefully posed to create a scene of dignity.

John Trumbull. *The Sortie Made by the Garrison of Gibraltar.* 1789. Oil on canvas. 180.3 × 271.8 cm (71 × 107″). The Metropolitan Museum of Art, New York, New York. Purchase, Pauline V. Fullerton Bequest; Mr. and Mrs. James Walter Carter and Mr. and Mrs. Raymond J. Horowitz Gifts; Erving Wolf Foundation and Vain and Harry Fish Foundation, Inc. Gifts; Gift of Hanson K. Corning, by exchange; and Maria DeWitt Jesup and Morris K. Jesup Funds, 1976.

emotions the artists put into their individual works were different. The emotions the artists put into the paintings made up the content. Three of these paintings are shown in Figures 1.15, 1.16, and 1.17.

THE CREDIT LINE

Look at Figure 1.15. The credit line appears beneath the caption. A **credit line** is *a list of important facts about a work of art.* Every artwork in this book has a credit line.

Decoding a Credit Line

Most credit lines contain six or more facts. They are as follows:

- ***Name*** of the artist.
- ***Title*** of the work. This always appears in italics.
- ***Year*** the work was created. Sometimes, in the case of older works, "c." appears before the year. This is an abbreviation for *circa*, which means "around" or "about" in Latin.
- ***Medium*** used by the artist. If more than one medium is used, the credit line may read "mixed media."
- ***Size*** of the work. The first number is always the height, the second number is the width, and if the work is three-dimensional, the third number indicates the depth.
- ***Location*** of the work. Location names the gallery, museum, or collection in which the work is housed and the city, state, and country. The names of the donors may also be included.

Using Credit Information

1. Applying Your Skills. Who is the artist of the work in Figure 1.9 on page 13? What is the title of the painting by Grant Wood (Figure 1.1, page 4)? Which work in this chapter was completed most recently?

2. Further Challenge. Which two works by the same artist have almost the same title and are created using two different media? Which is the largest work in this chapter? Which work in this chapter is not housed in the United States?

FIGURE 1.15 Kingman interpreted the subject in terms of his Oriental heritage. He transformed the rocket into a pagoda form. Why do you think he included the birds, a hot air balloon, helicopter, and single-engine plane? Notice the many areas of clear white paper.

Dong Kingman. *Higher, Faster, and Farther.* 1969. Watercolor on paper. 71.1 × 91.4 cm (28 × 36″). Courtesy of NASA.

FIGURE 1.16 Fernandes saw the launch as a graceful leap from the earth's surface. He bathed his work in the glowing colors of the morning sun. If you look closely, you can see the audience along the bank of the Banana River, almost hidden in the brilliance of the light.

Julio Fernandes. *Apollo 11.* 1969. Watercolor on paper. 34.3 × 40.6 cm (13½ × 16″). Courtesy of NASA.

FIGURE 1.17 Dodd captures the glowing Saturn rocket encased in its web of red supports. He sees beyond the mechanical forms to portray for us the effect it has on his emotions.

Lamar Dodd. *Night Before Launch.* 1969. Oil on canvas. 127.5 × 91.4 cm (50 × 36″). Courtesy of NASA.

ART CRITICISM IN ACTION

FIGURE 1.18 Henry Moore. *Family Group.* 1948-49. Bronze (cast 1950). 150.5 × 118.1 cm (59¼ × 46½"). The Museum of Modern Art, New York, New York. A. Conger Goodyear Fund.

CRITIQUING THE WORK

1. **Credit Line** Read the credit line for *Family Group* (Figure 1.18). List the following: the artist's name, the date the artwork was created, the medium used, the size, and the location of the work. If you were standing in front of *Family Group*, how would the level of your head relate to the heads of the people?
2. **Subject** What is the subject of *Family Group?* Can you easily identify the subject in this sculpture?
3. **Composition** Look at the shapes and forms of the people, including their posture and body language. How has Moore linked the figures? What has he done with the vertical and horizontal lines to provide a unified composition?
4. **Content** Looking at the composition of the sculpture, what message do you receive? How has Moore conveyed his message? Do you think he was successful in communicating his view? Why or why not?

COMPARING THE WORKS

Now look at *The Tragedy* by Pablo Picasso (Figure 1.19). Look at the credit line information. Note the date, medium used, the size of the work, and its location. If *The Tragedy* were hanging on the door to your classroom, how much of the door would it cover?

Compare the amount of realistic detail the artist uses in each work. Compare the space the artist has placed between the people. Compare the colors. Compare the surface textures of the people. Which work has real-looking texture, and which work shows the texture of the medium? How have the differences in composition affected the message of the artworks? Write a brief paragraph about the message each work communicates.

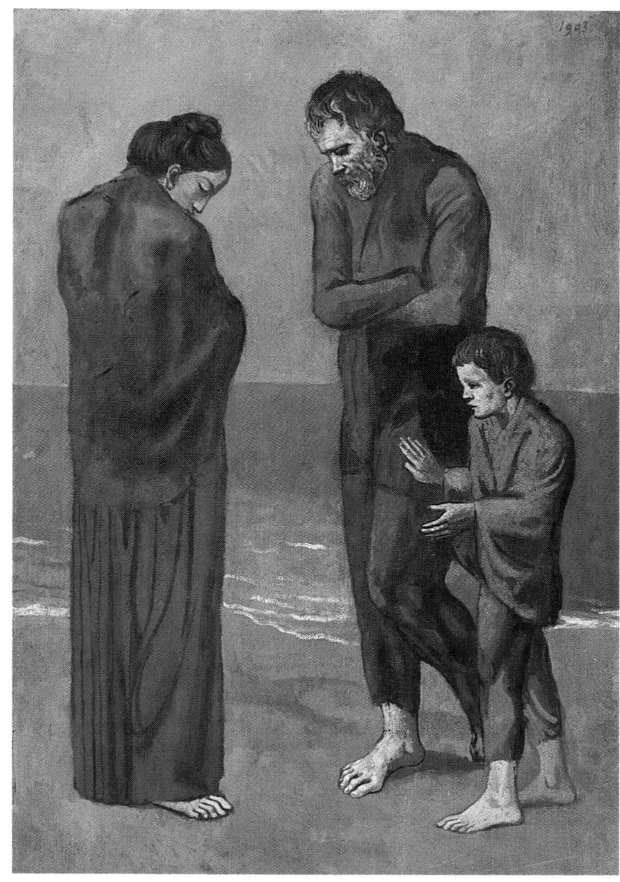

FIGURE 1.19 Pablo Picasso. *The Tragedy.* 1903. Oil paint on wood. 105.4 × 69 cm (41½ × 27⅛"). National Gallery of Art, Washington, D.C. Chester Dale Collection.

FYI Henry Moore was not easily discouraged. When he was asked to create a massive sculpture for the UNESCO (United Nations Educational, Scientific, and Cultural Organization) building, he searched the marble quarries in Italy until he found the perfect piece. There was only one problem—it weighed more than 60 tons (54 metric tons). Not to be defeated by the fact that he could not move the mountain of marble, Moore brought his tools to the quarry and carved for a year. When he had reduced the work to a movable size, it was transported to Paris so Moore could finish it in place. That work is the simplest and largest of Moore's reclining figures.

MEET THE ARTIST

HENRY MOORE

English, 1898–1986

Henry Moore created sculptures that were completely unique. He made images in stone that retained the look of natural stone. When he worked with wood, it seemed as if the rain and wind had worn the wood down to the shape he gave it. When he worked with metals such as lead and bronze, his figures took on the shapes of the molten flow of the metal.

The year 1940 was a turning point for him. England was at war, and Moore became an official war artist. His sensitive, abstract drawings of Londoners huddled in subway tunnels to escape the Nazi bombing established him as a leading English artist.

Moore's work focused on three themes: the family, the reclining female figure, and the abstract form within a form. The motivation for *Family Group* (Figure 1.18) was the pending birth of his daughter. He was obsessed with the idea of family.

When Moore's sculptures came back from the foundry, they were shiny, like new pennies. He wanted them to be a dull green so that they would look older and softer. To do this he coated them with acids. Then he rubbed them down so that they looked like thousands of hands had been touching them for years.

Henry Moore is recognized as one of the greatest and most innovative sculptors of the twentieth century. His work can be seen in collections of modern art throughout the world.

MORE PORTFOLIO IDEAS

Hold a piece of clay behind your back and model and smooth it into a rounded but uneven form having at least one opening that goes completely through it. Keep turning the clay as you work so that every surface is affected. When you are finished, the form should look like a rock that has been worn down by the forces of nature.

Follow the above instructions. Then bring the work in front of you. Use clay modeling tools to refine the form. When the clay has become leather-hard (damp but unmovable), polish some of the surfaces with a smooth river rock or the back of a spoon to create a surface texture variation.

CHAPTER 1 REVIEW

Building Vocabulary

On a separate sheet of paper, write the term that best matches each definition given below.

1. Something that stands for, or represents, something else.
2. The basic visual symbols in the language of art.
3. The rules that govern how artists organize the elements of art.
4. A material used to make art.
5. The act of looking at something carefully and thinking deeply about what is seen.
6. A process in which an artist repeatedly transfers an original image from one prepared surface to another.
7. A series of identical prints made from the same plate.
8. A technique of capturing optical images on light-sensitive surfaces.
9. Surrounded on all sides by space.
10. Sculpture in which forms project from a flat background.
11. The image viewers can easily identify in a work of art.
12. Art that has no recognizable subject matter.

Reviewing Art Facts

Answer the following questions using complete sentences.

1. Name the elements of art.
2. List the principles of design.
3. Name at least four of the most popular media used in drawing.
4. What are the three basic ingredients common to all paints?
5. What three basic steps are used in the printmaking process?
6. What printmaking process is best suited to printing on fabric?
7. Name a subtractive process an artist can use to create a sculpture.
8. Select a work of art in this chapter and name the subject.
9. Read the credit-line information of an artwork from any chapter and list the figure number, the title, the year the work was created, and the medium.
10. In what way do you think increasing your perception skills will enrich your everyday experiences?

Thinking Critically About Art

1. **Analyze.** List all the art media you have used. Which media do you prefer? Write a brief paragraph including two or more reasons for your personal preference.
2. **Compare and contrast.** Study Figures 1.15, 1.16, and 1.17 on page 19. List the similarities you find in all three paintings. Then identify the qualities that make each of the paintings unique and different.
3. **Analyze.** Compare Figure 1.19 on page 21 to Figure 11.27 on page 297. List the similarities and differences. Find at least two facts in the credit lines of the two works that account for the similarities. Explain the importance of these facts.

Making Art Connections

1. **Science.** In addition to being a master artist, Leonardo da Vinci was a man of many other talents. He designed machines that could not work during his time because things such as the internal combustion engine had not been invented yet. Hold Figure 1.5 up to a mirror and transcribe some of the notes he wrote. Find someone who can translate the notes and discover what Leonardo was communicating in his sketchbook.
2. **Music and Dance.** Find out how the arts of music and dance communicate without words. Is there a language of music? Is there a language of dance? Look up these art forms in the library or interview an expert such as your music teacher or a dance instructor. Write a report in which you discuss the "words" and "grammar" of either of these art forms.

FIGURE 2.1 Cassatt is famous for the inventive way she created paintings and prints on one theme: the relationship between mother and child. She presented them in everyday settings without making them look sentimental or trite.

Mary Cassatt. *Baby Reaching for an Apple.* 1893. Oil on canvas. 100.3 × 65.4 cm (39½ × 25¾″). Virginia Museum of Fine Arts, Richmond, Virginia. Museum purchase with funds provided by an anonymous donor.

CHAPTER 2

Art Criticism and Aesthetic Judgment

Have you ever been so involved in watching a movie that you felt as if you were part of the action? Have you ever watched a favorite movie so many times that you knew the dialogue by heart? If so, you have been deeply involved with a work of art.

After you see a new TV program, you probably discuss it with your friends. You might recommend that they watch the next episode—or advise them not to waste their time. In either case you are judging the show and making decisions about why it was a failure or success. You are acting like a critic.

There are professional critics who appear on television and write reviews in newspapers or magazines. They tell you about new movies, TV shows, videos, and books. They tell you something about the plot, the quality of the acting and directing, and their opinion of the work as a whole. You don't always agree with their opinion because your **criteria**, or *standards of judgment*, may be very different from those of the professional critics.

In this chapter you will learn about **art criticism**, *an organized system for studying a work of art*. You will also learn about **aesthetics** (es-**thet**-iks), *the philosophy or study of the nature of beauty and art*. After you have learned the steps of art criticism, you will be able to criticize works of art yourself. When you have learned the different aesthetic theories for judging the merits of an artwork, you will be able to form your own opinions about works of art with self-confidence.

First Impressions

Mary Cassatt belonged to a group of painters called Impressionists. They painted outdoors to capture the effects of sunlight on their subjects. What do you see in Cassatt's painting (Figure 2.1) that indicates it was painted outside? Look for areas of the painting in which the artist shows the effects of sunlight. How has she used brushstrokes to give the impression of filtered light? Notice the way the woman is holding the child. What does this say to you about the relationship between the woman and the child?

Objectives

After completing this chapter, you will be able to:

- Explain the purpose of art criticism.
- Use the steps of art criticism.
- Begin to criticize works of art yourself.
- Explain the aesthetic theories of art: Imitationalism, Formalism, and Emotionalism.
- Know what to look for when judging functional objects.

Words to Know

aesthetic experience
aesthetics
analysis
art criticism
criteria
description
design qualities
Emotionalism
expressive qualities
Formalism
Imitationalism
interpretation
judgment
literal qualities

WHY STUDY ART CRITICISM?

What do you think of when you hear the word *criticism*? Do you think it means saying something negative? This is not true. A criticism can be a positive statement. When you shop for clothes, you try on many things. You act as a critic using personal criteria to determine which pieces of clothing look good on you and which pieces do not suit you. You have developed your own criteria for choosing clothing through personal experience.

When you look at Nancy Graves's *Rheo* (Figure 2.2) you may be confused. You may not have had enough experience to develop a set of criteria to judge this work. If you are like most people, you don't know what to say. You may be afraid that you will say the wrong thing.

Art criticism is not difficult. In fact, it can be a lot of fun. At the very least, it can make the study of art less mysterious and more logical.

Art criticism is an organized system for looking at and talking about art. Anyone can do it. You do not need to be an expert on art. All you really need are your eyes to see and a brain to think about what you are seeing.

If you look at art without thinking, nothing can happen. If you think carefully about what you see, however, you will build your perceptual skills and learn a great deal.

Your own life experiences will help you understand each work of art. No one has done or seen exactly the same things you have, so no one will see exactly what you see in a work of art. No one can think exactly the way you think. You may see ideas in a work of art that were never dreamed of by the artist. This does not mean that you are wrong; it simply means that the work of art is so powerful that it has a special meaning for everybody.

Learning art criticism will help you interpret a work of art. It will give you the confidence to discuss a work of art without worrying about what other people might think. It will help you to organize your thoughts. You will develop the courage to speak your mind and make sound aesthetic

Nancy Graves. *Rheo*. 1975. Acrylic, oil, and gold leaf on canvas. 162.5 × 162.5 cm (64 × 64″). National Museum of Women in the Arts, Washington, D.C. Gift of Wallace and Wihelmina Holladay. © Nancy Graves/VAGA 1994.

LOOKING CLOSELY

FIGURE 2.2 At first glance this seems to be a painting of simple shapes, lines, and color. Look again. What kind of shapes do you see? What sizes are they? What colors do you see? Where are they? There are different kinds of lines. Describe them and tell what colors they are. What kinds of textures are painted on the small shapes? Do they remind you of anything? Notice how the small shapes are arranged. They seem to be floating over the others and yet there are no shadows. Can you discover how Graves created this illusion?

judgments. It will help you develop a better understanding and appreciation for all types and styles of art.

As you learn the language of art, you will be able to "dig deeper" into each art object. The deeper you dig, the more important your feelings for that work of art will become. This will make your **aesthetic experience**, or your *personal interaction with a work of art*, more meaningful and memorable. The work will then become a permanent part of your memory. From that point on it will affect the way you react to other visual images.

Testing Personal Responses

1. Applying Your Skills. Show the painting of the cat in Figure 2.3 to at least three people outside of class. Ask each person to think about and interpret this work of art. Then ask how he or she feels about cats. Did the judgment each one made match his or her feelings about cats?

2. Further Challenge. Record the responses you received. Ask those people who did not think this work of art was aesthetically pleasing to give you their reasons. Report your findings during the class discussion.

FIGURE 2.3 If you are a cat lover, you will have a positive reaction to the tiger cat resting luxuriously on the cushion. If you do not like cats, however, you will probably have a completely different response to this work.

Théophile-Alexandre Steinlen. *Winter: Cat on a Cushion.* Date unknown. Color lithograph. 50.8 × 61 cm (20 × 24″). The Metropolitan Museum of Art, New York, New York. Gift of Henry J. Plantin, 1950.

How to Criticize a Work of Art

Critiquing an artwork is like playing detective. You must assume the artist has a secret message hidden within the work. Your job is to find the message and solve the mystery.

In this chapter you will learn a special four-step system that will help you find the hidden messages in art. The four steps, which must be taken in order, are **Description, Analysis, Interpretation**, and **Judgment**. By taking these steps you will be able to answer the following questions:

- What do I see? (Description)
- How is the work organized? (Analysis)
- What is the artist saying? (Interpretation)
- Is this a successful work of art? (Judgment)

As you go through the steps of *description* and *analysis*, you will collect facts and clues. When you get to *interpretation*, you will make guesses about what you think the artist is trying to say. Finally, during *judgment*, you will make your own decisions, both personal and objective, about the artistic merit of the work.

Step One: Description (What do I see?)

In the first step in art criticism, **description**, you carefully *make a list of all the things you see in the work*. This step is meant to slow your pace. Slowing down helps you notice things you might otherwise miss. It keeps you from making a judgment before you have studied all the details.

Every description should include the size of the work and the medium used. You will find these facts in the credit line. This information will help you visualize the real size and the look of the work. Notice that Figure 3.31 on page 62 and Figure 3.36 on page 67 are about the same size in this book. Read the credit line to see which work is the larger.

Look at the sculpture by Sir Jacob Epstein called *The Visitation* (Figure 2.4). Notice that the figure is 66 inches, or 5 feet 6 inches (167.6 cm), tall. How does that compare to your own height? If you were standing on the same level as the sculpture, how would the level of the woman's eyes relate to yours?

The medium of the sculpture is cast bronze. Do you know what bronze looks like when it is new? Do you know what happens to bronze when it is exposed to weather?

During the description step you must be objective. You must list only the facts. For example, if you are describing Figure 2.1 on page 24, *Baby Reaching for an Apple* by Mary Cassatt, you can say that you see a woman holding a child. Do not say that you see a mother holding her own child. That would be a guess. You do not know if the woman is the child's mother. Save your guesses for the interpretation step. If you see distant figures and you cannot tell whether they are women or men, simply list them as people.

Look at Figure 2.2 on page 26. It is difficult to identify objects in this work. This is a nonobjective work. In this work the elements become the subject matter.

FIGURE 2.4 Imagine standing next to this figure. How would it look? What do you think your first reaction would be?

Sir Jacob Epstein. *The Visitation.* 1926. Bronze. 165.3 × 53.1 × 47.9 cm (65⅛ × 20⅞ × 18⅞"). Hirshhorn Museum and Sculpture Garden, Smithsonian Institution, Washington, D.C. Gift of Joseph H. Hirshhorn, 1966.

ACTIVITY Practicing Description

1. Applying Your Skills. Watch a sports program on television. Pretend you are an explorer from another planet and do not know anything about the game. Describe in writing what the athletes are doing, but remember you know none of the terms related to the sport or the people. Read your description to the class. Can your classmates guess what kind of game you were watching?

2. Further Challenge. Sketch two figures participating in a popular sport. Do not show any uniforms or equipment that would give away the name of the sport. Try to capture the gestures and action that describe the sport. Can your friends guess what sport you are describing with figures alone?

Step Two: Analysis (How is the work organized?)

During Step Two you are still collecting facts. Now, however, you will pay attention to the elements and principles, which you read about in Chapter 1. In **analysis** you *discover how the work is organized.* This is where the artist creates the secret message, the mood or idea, by the way he or she organizes the elements using the principles.

For example, look again at Figure 2.4. Notice the *shape* of the figure; the *lines* formed by the folds in the skirt; the surface *texture* of her hair, skin, and fabric; and so on. Shape, lines, and texture are elements of art. Look for other elements. In this step you will list the way the artist has used all the elements. You will also note the way the elements are organized using rhythm, movement, balance, proportion, variety, emphasis, and unity. Of course, you will learn more about both the elements and principles later in this book.

FIGURE 2.5 What is your interpretation of this painting? If you were to show it to others, do you think their interpretations would be the same as yours?

Leo Twiggs. *The Blue Wall.* 1969. Batik painting. 61 × 76.2 cm (24 × 30″). Private collection.

Step Three: Interpretation (What is the artist saying?)

During Step Three you will answer the question "What is the artist saying to me?" In **interpretation** you will *explain or tell the meaning or mood of the work.* It is here that you can make guesses.

Interpretation can be the most difficult step in art criticism, because you must dare to be different. It can also be the most creative and the most rewarding step.

You must use your intelligence, imagination, and courage. You must not be afraid to make an interpretation that is different from someone else's. After all, you are different from other people. Your interpretation will depend on what you have experienced and seen in your life.

Your interpretation must be based on the facts and clues you collected during your first two steps. Your interpretation can be based on your feelings, but your feelings must be backed up by observation of what you actually see in the artwork.

Interpreting a Work

1. Applying Your Skills. Show *The Blue Wall* by Leo Twiggs, Figure 2.5, to three people outside of class. Ask them what they think is the meaning of this painting. Tell them it doesn't matter whether they like the work or not. You just want to know what they think it means. Then write a few sentences telling what each person said. Compare your results with those of your classmates. Are there any similar answers? Do adults see different meanings than people your age?

2. Further Challenge. When you decide on your own interpretation of the work, write a story about the boys that explains the message you have received from the work. What happened before this scene, what are they thinking at the moment depicted in this painting, and what will happen next? Explain why the wall is important in their lives.

Step Four: Judgment (Is this a successful work of art?)

In Step Four you will judge whether or not the work is successful. In **judgment** you *determine the degree of artistic merit*. This is the time to give your opinions. No one can ever tell you what to like or dislike. You must make up your own mind. To make a good judgment, you need to be honest with yourself. You need to know why you feel the way you do. For example, look back at Figure 2.3 on page 27. How do you feel about this picture? The artist loved cats. Do you? How do you think the way you feel about cats might affect your reaction to this work?

The chief goal of aesthetics is to answer the question "What is successful art?" In their search for an answer, aestheticians have put forth different views on what is important in a work of art. These ideas, or schools of thought, on what to look for in works of art are called aesthetic theories.

You can also make an objective judgment that does not depend entirely on your personal feelings. You can turn to aesthetic theories to answer the question "Is this a successful work of art?" This is an aesthetic question.

AESTHETIC THEORIES AND QUALITIES OF ART

The aesthetic qualities that are discussed most often by aestheticians are the literal qualities, the design qualities, and the expressive qualities. These are directly related to the properties of art that were discussed in Chapter 1 on page 17: subject, composition, and content. The **literal qualities**, are *the realistic qualities that appear in the subject of the work*. For instance, if the artist depicts a realistic figure of a man on a horse, the literal quality of the work is the image of a man on a horse. The **design qualities**, or *how well the work is organized*, are found when you look at the composition of the work. Does it look balanced; is there a rhythmic quality; is there variety? Has the artist made a unified work of art? The **expressive qualities**, or *those qualities that communicate ideas and moods,* are those you notice when you study the content of a work. Is there something in the work that makes you feel a certain emotion or conveys an idea to you? The three aesthetic theories are most commonly referred to as Imitationalism, Formalism, and Emotionalism.

Imitationalism and Literal Qualities

Some critics think that the most important thing about a work of art is the realistic presentation of subject matter. It is their opinion that a work is successful if it looks like and reminds the viewer of what he or she sees in the real world. People with this point of view feel that an artwork should imitate life, that it should look lifelike before it can be considered successful. This aesthetic theory, called **Imitationalism**, *focuses on realistic presentation.*

Formalism and Design Qualities

Other critics think that composition is the most important factor in a work of art. This aesthetic theory, called **Formalism**, *places emphasis on the design qualities*, the arrangement of the elements of art using the principles of design.

Emotionalism and Expressive Qualities

This theory is concerned with the content of the work of art. Some critics claim that no object can be considered art if it fails to send a message to the viewer. The expressive quality is most important to them. Their theory, called **Emotionalism**, *requires a strong communication of feelings, moods, or ideas* from the work to the viewer.

Look at Margareta Haverman's painting *A Vase of Flowers* (Figure 2.6). You may like it because the

Margareta Haverman. *A Vase of Flowers.* 1716. Oil on wood. 79.4 × 60.3 cm (31¼ × 23¾″). The Metropolitan Museum of Art, New York, New York. Purchase, 1871.

LOOKING CLOSELY

FIGURE 2.6 There is much more to this painting than its obvious realistic beauty. Notice that the flower at the top of the painting is a tulip, which blooms in the spring. The flowers in the center are summer flowers. Observe how the roses near the bottom are fading and drooping. At the lower edge of the painting you see autumn fruits. This painting is a *vanitas* painting. The word *vanitas* is a Latin word meaning vain and empty. These paintings are meant to remind people that time passes and things change, and that people shouldn't put too much emphasis on material things.

artist has painted everything very realistically (Imitationalism). You can see drops of water sparkling on the leaves and a snail crawling on a leaf in the lower-left corner. Someone else may like this painting because of the arrangement of the flowers and how light is used to sweep from the top flower to the grapes at the bottom (Formalism). A third person may like the painting simply because he or she likes flowers (Emotionalism).

You can judge art using just one aesthetic theory or more than one, depending on the type of art and your own purposes. If you limit yourself to using only one theory, however, you may miss some exciting discoveries in a work. Perhaps the best method is to use all three. Then you will be able to discover as much as possible about a particular piece of art.

Judging Functional Objects

You can use art criticism to make aesthetic judgments about functional objects as well as objects of fine art. The object in Figure 2.7, on page 32, is an example. In criticizing functional objects, you follow the first two steps, description and analysis, as described earlier. During interpretation you must consider the purpose of the object as its meaning. In the judgment phase you consider how the object

FIGURE 2.7 Sitting on this beautiful chair would make you feel as if you were sitting on a pedestal, but the chair would not be considered a well-designed chair unless you were comfortable.

Eero Saarinen. *Armchair.* 1957. Molded plastic reinforced with fiberglass; painted aluminum base. 81.3 cm (32″) high. Collection, The Museum of Modern Art, New York, New York. Gift of Knoll Associates, Inc.

works when it is used. A chair may look beautiful, but if it is not comfortable to sit in, it does not function properly and you must judge it to be unsuccessful.

Someone may buy a car based on looks alone. Someone else may buy a piece of clothing without regard for the way it looks on his or her body. Neither person is making a wise choice. When judging functional objects, attention must be given to function as well as aesthetic qualities.

Judging Your Own Work

Art criticism will help you analyze your own works of art. The four steps of art criticism will help you be as honest and unbiased as possible. The analysis step may be the most useful. It will help you perceive how you have organized the elements using the principles of design. By looking carefully at each element and reviewing how you have used it, you will see your work in a new way. By observing how you have organized the elements, you will gain insight into your decision-making process. When you apply all four of the steps of art criticism to your work, you should find out why your work either needs improvement or is a success.

Classifying Aesthetic Theories

1. Applying Your Skills. Select one large work of art in this book. Show the picture to at least three people outside of class. Ask them whether they like the work. Then ask them to tell you why they like or dislike the work. Classify their answers according to the three aesthetic theories of art: Imitationalism, Formalism, or Emotionalism.

2. Further Challenge. Find a work that fits each of the aesthetic theories in this chapter. List the title of each work, the theory that best applies to the work, and why you think that theory is most applicable.

ART CRITICISM: GETTING STARTED

There is only one way to learn art criticism: by doing it. This is why you will be given many opportunities throughout *ArtTalk* to develop your criticism skills.

At the end of each chapter you will be given questions to help you criticize a work of art. The evaluation questions at the end of each major Studio Lesson will also take you through the art-criticism steps to help you study your own artworks.

To help you begin, we will look at and criticize *Christina's World* by Andrew Wyeth (Figure 2.8).

Description

Look at the credit line below Figure 2.8. Record the size of the painting and the medium. Imagine the size of the work as if it were hanging on a wall in front of you.

FIGURE 2.8 Andrew Wyeth. *Christina's World.* 1948. Tempera on gesso panel. 81.9 × 121.3 cm (32¼ × 47¾″). Collection, The Museum of Modern Art, New York, New York. Purchase.

Now look at the reproduction of the painting very carefully. List everything you see. Try to be objective. Don't make guesses, and don't let your feelings about the work influence you during this step. Write down every fact you can observe, even the small details.

When you finish describing the work, read through the following questions and statements. They will show you the details you might have missed. Don't feel upset if you missed some of the details. Remember, this is your first attempt at art criticism.

What facts about the female's dress did you list? Did you notice the faded pink quality? Does the dress look new? Do you think the fabric is heavy or light? Look at the folds. What do they tell you about the fabric? What does the belt look like? What color is it?

What matches the belt color? Her hair. Look at her hair. Notice all the individual hairs? Does the way she fixes her hair match the style of her dress? What about those strands of hair flying loosely around her head?

Next, notice her shoes. What do you think was used to make them? Is there any sign of wear on the bottom of the shoes? Look closely at her legs. What color are they? Is the color quality the same as that of her arms? Do you notice anything unusual about her arms and her hands? Look carefully at her left hand. Is it at the same level as the rest of her body?

Imitate her posture. Study the picture closely as you do this. Where is all your weight resting?

Where is the female located? What facts can you gather by studying the ground and the rest of the background? What colors do you see? Notice the individual blades of grass. Do they bend in a special direction? What is the difference between the area where she is located and the top of the hill? Did you see the road? Did you notice what kind of a road it is?

How many buildings do you see? How are they different? What material was used to build them? What color are they? Do you see the birds flying around one building?

What color is the sky? From what direction is the light coming? Let the shadows help you. How much of the picture is sky and how much is ground? Was the artist looking down from above or up from below the scene?

Try to avoid making guesses. Save your written clues to help you during interpretation.

Analysis

This is the step that reveals the artist's message, or idea. For now we will move on to interpretation. Later, when you know more about the language of art, come back and look at *Christina's World* again. You will uncover many clues about the work that you may have missed at this point.

Interpretation

Review the clues you have collected. What do you think the artist is trying to say about the relationship between the female and her environment?

Hold a ruler along the left slope of the roof of the largest building. Do you see how that line leads your eyes to the woman? Notice how she is straining toward the house. She is wearing faded colors, and the house looks unpainted and weathered. What does that tell you about her and the house? Why do you think so much of the space in the work is taken up by the ground? Why has the artist shown separate blades of grass? When you acted out the woman's pose, did you feel pressure on your arms and hands? Did you feel the tension? Did you notice that your legs were not carrying any weight?

Have you guessed what the artist is trying to say about the relationship between the woman and the house? Did you sense any special feelings?

Other than the title that has been given, can you think of a word or phrase that describes this work? What title would you give it?

Try to go beyond the events that appear to be taking place in this painting. Search for the general idea, or theme, that you believe the artist was trying to express. If you add the facts you discovered during description to your personal ideas, you will discover what the painting means to you.

Remember, your interpretation may be different from your classmates'. You may all have collected the same facts from the work, but the memories of life that you bring to this experience are uniquely your own. The message that this work communicates to you is influenced by your own life experiences.

Judgment

Now you are ready to make an aesthetic judgment about *Christina's World*.

Would an aesthetician who embraces the theory of Imitationalism judge this to be a successful work? Why or why not?

Would an aesthetician who believes Formalism is the correct theory consider this a successful work? Has Wyeth done a successful job of organizing the elements of art using the principles of design? Why or why not?

Would an aesthetician who believes Emotionalism to be the most important theory consider this work a success? Has the work communicated a message to you, the viewer? Why or why not?

What do *you* think? Does the painting make you think? Would you like to be able to look at it every day? Why or why not?

Do you think one of the three aesthetic theories is more important in judging this work than the others? Explain your answer.

STUDENTS PRACTICE ART CRITICISM

Look at *Dawn* by Louise Nevelson (Figure 2.9 on page 36).

Students studying art criticism have written about this work. During description they noticed that the work is very large, almost 8 feet (2.4 m) tall, and that it was made of wood painted gold. It is made of forty-nine rectangular boxes. At first

FIGURE 2.8A Andrew Wyeth. *Christina's World.* (Detail) 1948. Tempera on gessoed panel. 81.9 × 121.3 cm (32¼ × 47¾″). Collection, The Museum of Modern Art, New York, New York.

they thought it was nonobjective, but as they studied it they saw pieces of recognizable objects in the boxes such as banisters, gun stocks, baseball bats, rolling pins, musical instruments, carved leaves, dumbbells, and bedposts. They also observed both free-form and geometric shapes in the work.

During interpretation each student had different ideas. One said "This work is about people. The total work looks static, with free-form shapes in their own individual containers. The space seems crammed full of things. This makes me think of society. The geometric shapes represent the normal, everyday people. The free-form shapes are the eccentric, rebellious people in life. The many individual compartments are the many individual social groups of today."

Another student commented, "It shows the bad and good of human nature, all existing in the same world. The guns and bats represent violence. The musical instruments and the finely carved pieces of furniture seem to express education and culture. No two people are alike, but all are united in one world represented by the unified boxes in this sculpture."

A third student felt this work was very nostalgic. "I think that this work should be called 'America.' The rifle stock reminds me of being out in the wilderness hunting with my grandpa. The banisters make me think of my house and how important our houses are to us in America. The rolling pin reminds me of Mom and my grandma cooking in the kitchen on a hot summer day and of eating under the shade tree at the picnic table."

Although this work has many strong formal qualities, when the students reached the judgment step, many of them felt that this work evoked powerful emotional responses!

"I like this work because it evokes emotions in me about how I think America should be, not the reality of how it really is."

"I like this sculpture because it uses Emotionalism, because it gives me certain feelings about society."

"It looks very emotional. It has too many feelings crammed into one piece of art!"

These students were not afraid to reveal their thoughts and feelings during interpretation and judgment. Now it is your turn to study Nevelson's *Dawn*. Even though you have read what other students said about this work, study it yourself. Turn the page. You may see things they never noticed.

ART CRITICISM IN ACTION

FIGURE 2.9 Louise Nevelson. *Dawn.* 1962. Wood painted gold. 323 × 240 × 19 cm (127 × 94½ × 7½″). The Pace Gallery, New York, New York.

CRITIQUING THE WORK

1. **Describe** Read the credit line and record the important information. Would this work fit on a wall in your classroom? Look over all the small parts and list the things you find.
2. **Analyze** How is the work organized? What has Louise Nevelson done to make the different found objects look like they belong together? Does the work look crowded or empty? What affect does the use of a single color have on the piece?
3. **Interpret** What kind of message is the artist making about your world with this sculpture? Write a paragraph explaining your interpretation. Then create a new title for the work that fits your interpretation.
4. **Judge** You have now had a "conversation" with a work of art that does not convey an obvious story. Do you feel more comfortable with nonobjective art? Do you think this is a successful work? Which of the aesthetic theories would you use to judge this work?

FIGURE 2.10 Lorenzo Ghiberti. *Gates of Paradise.* (Detail). 1425–52. Gilt bronze. Baptistry of Florence, Italy.

COMPARING THE WORKS

Look at *Dawn* (Figure 2.9) and the panel from the *Gates of Paradise* by Lorenzo Ghiberti (Figure 2.10). Identify the similarities and differences between the two works. Compare your interpretation of the Nevelson wall to the theme of the Ghiberti panel. Do you find a connection between the two themes? Explain. Decide which of these works you find more interesting. Use one or more of the aesthetic theories to defend your judgment in a class discussion.

FYI Nevelson joined the brand-new Pace Gallery in 1964. The director, Arnold Glimcher, believed in her and did a good job of presenting her work to collectors. By 1967 she had become financially secure. She appreciated wealth for the obvious reasons, but she also saw it as an indication of the value of her work. In 1969 she told a *Houston Chronicle* reporter that she enjoyed the fact that a woman artist in America could collect wooden scraps from the street, put them together, and sell them to the Rockefellers for one hundred thousand dollars.

MEET THE ARTIST

LOUISE NEVELSON

Born in Kiev, Ukraine
American citizen, 1899–1988

Louise Nevelson was the glamorous, fascinating person that everyone imagines an artist should be. Art was the dominating force in her life. She claimed that by the time she was seven she knew she would be a sculptor.

In 1920 Nevelson moved to New York City. By 1929 she was a full-time student at the Art Students' League, seriously studying with some of the best teachers of the time. She knew she was destined to spend the rest of her life creating art. Inspired by Cubism, pre-Columbian art, and the creative drive within herself, Nevelson continued her studies in Europe.

During the 1940s she experimented with all art media. She lived near a neighborhood that was being renovated, and the discarded wood scraps from the demolished buildings inspired her first three-dimensional assemblage, or assembled sculpture.

Nevelson painted each assemblage a solid color. She started out painting all her work black. Later she experimented with solid white. She even painted a few pieces, like *Dawn*, gold.

In the 1970s she experimented with new media such as Cor-ten steel, Lucite, and aluminum. These strong materials enabled her to produce gigantic outdoor pieces.

Today there is a square in New York City named for Louise Nevelson. It contains seven of her mammoth, freestanding, steel sculptures that are about 90 feet (30 m) high. Like many other great artists, she led a very self-centered life, but she has left the world a magnificent collection of uniquely powerful sculptures.

MORE PORTFOLIO IDEAS

Collect small found objects. Arrange them in a small box, no larger than a shoe box, in the manner of Nevelson. You may create nonobjective shapes with scraps of cardboard to help your composition. Glue your final arrangement into the box. Paint everything one color.

Select a story or poem as a theme for your box. Do the above activity, but collect objects to fit your theme. You may have to create some objective shapes as well as nonobjective shapes to enhance your theme.

Select five objects at random from clip art. Arrange them in an interesting manner inside a rectangle, adding geometric shapes to the composition. Use only one hue to color all the shapes, but change the intensity or value of the hue to indicate depth.

CHAPTER 2 REVIEW

Building Vocabulary

On a separate sheet of paper, write the term that best matches each definition given below.

1. Standards of judgment.
2. An organized system for studying a work of art.
3. The philosophy or study of the nature of beauty and art.
4. Personal interaction with a work of art.
5. The art-criticism step in which you make a list of all the things you see in a work.
6. The art-criticism step in which you discover how the work is organized.
7. The art-criticism step in which you explain or tell the meaning or mood of the work.
8. The art-criticism step in which you determine the degree of artistic merit of the work.
9. The realistic qualities that appear in the subject of the work.
10. The qualities that indicate how well the work is organized.
11. The qualities that communicate ideas and moods.
12. The aesthetic theory that focuses on realistic presentation.
13. The aesthetic theory that places emphasis on the design qualities.
14. The aesthetic theory that requires a communication of feelings, moods, or ideas.

Reviewing Art Facts

Answer the following questions using complete sentences.

1. What will learning the steps of art criticism help you develop?
2. Name the four steps of art criticism in the order in which they must be followed.
3. In which step would you list the size of the work and the medium used?
4. Name the three aesthetic theories.
5. If the organization of an artwork is most important to an art critic, which aesthetic theory would he or she hold?
6. When criticizing functional objects, what must you consider during interpretation besides beauty?

Thinking Critically About Art

1. **Apply.** Select something from your home that is used solely for aesthetic purposes. Critique it using the four steps of art criticism. When you are finished, ask yourself if the object seems different than it did before. Has your opinion of the object changed?
2. **Analyze.** Find a movie critic's review of a current film in a newspaper or magazine. Read it carefully. Try to find statements that fit each of the four steps of art criticism.
3. **Extend.** Do you think you can appreciate the qualities of a work of art even though you don't like it? Explain your conclusions.

Making Art Connections

1. **Mathematics.** Look at the art of M. C. Escher. It utilizes geometric concepts to convey its messages. Pay attention to the use of literal qualities in unusual settings. Do the literal qualities and design qualities play equally important parts in Escher's work? Critique an Escher work using the four steps of art criticism.
2. **Science.** Some say that the four steps of art criticism parallel the four steps of the scientific method. Research information about the scientific method. Do you think the two methods are similar or different? Explain your conclusions.
3. **Social Studies.** Research the work of Mexican Muralists such as Diego Rivera and David Alfaro Siqueiros. Much of their art focused on the social struggles of the Mexican working class and was meant to bring about social change. Can you identify the aesthetic theories in this chapter that apply to art movements that concern social protest? Bring your findings to class for discussion.

FIGURE 3.1 Hayden's self-portrait is symbolic rather than realistic. He tells us about his life without telling us what he really looked like. Hayden exhibited his work in the Harmon Foundation shows; he also worked as a janitor in the Harmon Foundation's office building to support himself. The Foundation was an organization that promoted and supported the work of African-American artists from the 1920s through the 1960s.

Palmer Hayden. *The Janitor Who Paints.* c. 1937. Oil on canvas. 99.4 × 83.5 cm (39⅛ × 32⅞"). National Museum of American Art, Washington, D.C.

CHAPTER 3

Art History

Ever since there have been human beings, there has been art. The need to create has always been a part of human nature. Before people kept written records, they made paintings, drawings, sculpture, and objects to adorn their bodies, and they decorated functional objects with attractive designs.

You can look at visual images from the past to learn what the people who lived before us were like. The art they made reveals a great deal about their feelings, their beliefs, their ideas, and the way they lived. Someday in the future people will learn about our lives by studying the art objects we are producing now.

Art history is the record of art from past to present. Art historians look at changes that occur in the field of art over time. They also look at differences in the way art is made from place to place.

The history of visual art is as broad and complex as the history of the world. This chapter is just a peek into the treasure chest that makes up your visual heritage. It will help you understand how works of art are related.

First Impressions

What is your first impression of the three people in *The Janitor Who Paints* by Palmer Hayden (Figure 3.1)? Can you use the visual clues to collect information about that artist and his world? How does he support himself? Can you guess when this work was painted by looking at the objects in the room and at the people's clothing? Can you guess where this room might be located?

Objectives

After completing this chapter, you will be able to:

- Explain the value of art history.
- Use a four-step system to learn about a work of art.
- Understand how historical events influence artists' work.
- Briefly discuss movements in the history of art, from prehistoric through modern times.

Words to Know

Baroque
Byzantine
Cubism
dynasty
Expressionism
Gothic
Impressionism
linear perspective
mobile
Realism
Regionalist
Renaissance
Rococo
Romanesque
style
Surrealism

LEARNING ABOUT WORKS OF ART

In the last chapter you learned the four steps of *art criticism*, an organized system for getting information from a work of art. There is also a four-step system for organizing the way you gather information about the history of a work of art. The labels for these four steps are the same: Description, Analysis, Interpretation, and Judgment. This time, however, there are different definitions for the terms, and different questions to be answered.

- When, where, and by whom was the work done? (Description)
- What is the style of the work, and does the work fit into an art movement? (Analysis)
- How did time and place affect the artist's style and subject matter? (Interpretation)
- Does the work of art make an important contribution to the history of art? (Judgment)

Step One: Description

During this step you are collecting facts, just as you did during art criticism. This time you are looking for information *about* the work of art. You want to know who did it, when, and where it was done. If you were looking at an original work of art, you would look for the artist's signature and the date on the work. In this book, since the works have been reduced in size, you probably will not be able to see the artist's signature or date on the work itself. You will find the name of the artist and the date the work was created, however, in the credit line. If you look at the credit line for Figure 3.1, you will discover that the name of the artist is Palmer Hayden, and that the work was painted sometime between 1930 and 1940. To learn where it was painted, you can look back to the section called Artists and Their Works on pages 366–370. There you can find Hayden's nationality as well as the time he lived.

Step Two: Analysis

During analysis you will be looking for the artist's style. Style is like handwriting: No two people have exactly the same handwriting, and no two artists have exactly the same style. Individual **style** is *the artist's personal way of using the elements of art and principles of design to express feelings and ideas.* To analyze the style of one artist, you will need to see several works by the same artist. Look at *Marisol* by Alice Neel (Figure 3.2). Notice the blue lines that outline the figure and the chair. Observe that the clothing is painted in rough, loose brushstrokes but the face and hands are modeled carefully with a heavy buildup of paint. Study the intense expression of the eyes. The blue lines and the concentration on the intensely expressive hands and face are part of Neel's unique style.

FIGURE 3.2 In this portrait Neel communicates her feelings about her friend as well as what Marisol looks like. Notice the posture of the sculptor. Her torso is as rigid as one of her sculptures. See Figure 6.1, page 118.

Alice Neel. *Marisol.* 1981. Oil on canvas. 107 × 61 cm (42 × 24″). Collection of the Honolulu Academy of Art. Hawaii, Robert Miller Gallery, New York, New York. © The estate of Alice Neel.

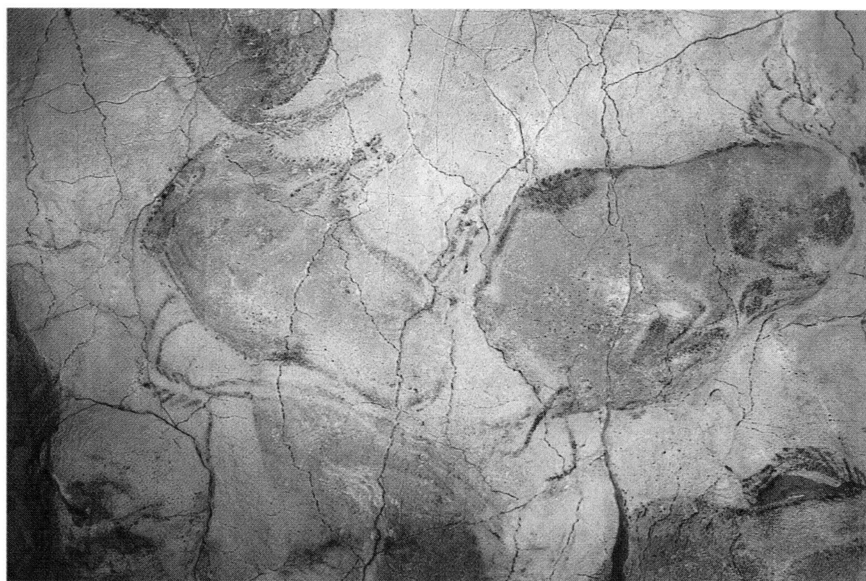

FIGURE 3.3 An amateur archaeologist excavated in this low-roofed cave for four years before his daughter, who was small enough to stand up straight in the cave and look up, discovered these paintings of sleeping, galloping, and crouching animals.

The Hall of the Bulls. c. 15,000 B.C. Altamira Caves, Spain.

Step Three: Interpretation

In order to do the interpretation step, you will need to do some research to find out how time and place have affected the artist's style and subject matter. An art historian would tell you that Alice Neel was an American artist who painted only people in whom she was interested. The rise of an abstract art style after World War II left her on the outside. Neel believed that the abstract elements were important, but she felt strongly that people and psychological truths were even more important. She remained independent of all styles and movements, and her work was not recognized by the Establishment until 1970.

Step Four: Judgment

Once again you must turn to research to find out this work's importance in the history of art. Did the work introduce a new style, or is it an outstanding example of an existing style? When you check the date it was painted and the birth date of Neel in Artists and Their Works on page 369, you find that it was painted when Neel was eighty-one years old and at the height of her career. As you read you will find out that historians consider her a great American portrait painter. You will also learn that *Marisol* is a portrait of an important American sculptor. Since this work was done at the height of Neel's career, you can conclude that it is an outstanding example of her unique style.

Now that you have become familiar with the system for gathering information about the history of a work of art, we will take a journey back into time. As early as 15,000 B.C. artists were drawing pictures reflecting their life and times.

ART OF EARLIEST TIMES

The art presented in this section was produced over a period of many thousands of years. The artworks produced during those ancient times tell us a great deal about the earliest cultures and civilizations of our world.

Prehistoric Cultures

Prehistoric means before history, or before written records were kept. That is why the art and artifacts from that period are so important. They are all that remains to tell us about the people who lived during those times.

Figure 3.3 is one of many paintings left by Stone Age cave dwellers. The colors are so bright and the animals so realistic that, for a long time, experts refused to believe paintings such as these were really created by prehistoric artists.

To this day no one knows the purpose of the paintings. They were found deep inside caves, far from the entrances and living areas. Because of

FIGURE 3.4 Notice how the sculptor has followed the rules of Egyptian art, showing each part of the body from the most visible view. The symbols around the figures are hieroglyphs, picture symbols that stand for words.

Methethy with His Daughter and a Son. c. 2450 B.C. Polychromed limestone relief. 143 × 76 cm (56¼ × 30″). Nelson-Atkins Museum of Art, Kansas City, Missouri. Purchase, Nelson Trust.

their location, we know they were not created for decoration. Some people believe the paintings were part of a hunting ritual. They may have been created by a shaman, or medicine man, who believed that the magical image of the animal could help hunters capture the animal. The paintings may also have been visual prayers for animals to appear during the next hunt. Another theory is that the paintings were created by cave dwellers to celebrate a successful hunt.

Ancient River Valleys

The ancient civilizations of Egypt, Mesopotamia, China, and India each developed in a river valley. Each civilization had a monarchy and a religion based on nature.

Egypt. Ancient Egypt developed along the banks of the Nile River more than three thousand years before the birth of Christ. The Egyptian civilization continued for almost three thousand years after that. The arts of Ancient Egypt express the endurance and solidity of that culture.

Religion influenced every part of Egyptian life. The *pharaohs,* or rulers, were worshiped as gods and held complete authority over the kingdom. Egyptians believed in life after death and preserved bodies of the dead in preparation for the afterlife. The famous pyramids of Egypt were built as the tombs of the pharaohs.

Egyptian artists who decorated temples and tombs had to follow very strict rules set forth by the rulers. The rules required that each part of the body be shown from the most visible angle. Thus, in relief wall sculpture and painting, figures were represented in an unusual way. Look at Figure 3.4. You can see that the heads, arms, legs, and feet are shown in profile. The shoulders and eyes are seen from a frontal view.

We have learned a great deal about life in Egypt from the paintings found on the walls inside the tombs. Scenes from the life of the person buried in the tomb were depicted. These scenes were intended to remind the spirit of its life on earth.

Mesopotamia. The culture of Mesopotamia was more the culture of a region than of a people. The region was the fertile crescent of land between the Tigris and Euphrates rivers. The people lived in city-states, and each city had its own monarch. Today this land is shared by Syria and Iraq.

The first important group to dominate the area were the Sumerians. They were the first people to have a system of writing. Called *cuneiform,* this writing system was made up of wedge-shaped characters. Sumerian artwork was more realistic than that of the Egyptians. In Figure 3.5 you see a small sculpture showing details of dress and facial features. Other cultures that later became important were those of Babylon and Assyria.

China. The Yellow River valley was the site of the ancient Chinese civilization. This civilization

FIGURE 3.5 This figure was placed in the temple as a substitute for the worshiper. The large eyes, hands clasped in prayer, and realistic detail are typical of Sumerian sculpture.

Statua di Donna. c. 2700–2600 B.C. Marble. The Iraq Museum, Baghdad, Iraq.

FIGURE 3.6 This vessel was used in a ceremony to ensure harmony with the spirits of deceased ancestors. Notice the large eyes and beak of an owl on the lower part of the vessel. Can you find other animals in the designs that cover this container?

Ancient China. *Ritual Wine Container.* Shang dynasty. Thirteenth century B.C. Bronze. 76.4 × 31 × 31.8 cm (30 × 12⅛ × 12½″). Arthur M. Sackler Gallery, Smithsonian Institution, Washington, D.C.

still exists today. It boasts the oldest continuous culture in the history of the world.

The history of China, until modern times, was divided into dynasties. A **dynasty** was *a period of time during which a single family provided a succession of rulers.* Dynasties are named for ruling families. The first of these was the Shang dynasty. The lasting achievement from that time period was the cast-bronze work. The ritual wine vessel in Figure 3.6 is an example of the beautiful work done at that time: the thirteenth century B.C.

India. The culture of ancient India remained a legend until modern times. In 1865 railroad workers laying track in the Indus River valley discovered a hill of crumbling fired-clay bricks near the city of Harappa. The bricks date back to 2500 B.C.

In 1922 a second city was found in the same area. Its name is Mohenjo-Daro. The architectural remains of the city indicate that it was a major commercial center. Wide, open streets divided the city into large blocks, multistoried houses of fired brick and wood, and elaborate drainage systems (Figure 3.7 on page 46). Other ancient sites have also been uncovered in India.

FIGURE 3.7 Mohenjo-Daro is an early example of urban planning. The city was a center of commerce and trade and is believed to have had a population of 35,000 people.

Mohenjo-Daro, India. c. 2500 B.C.

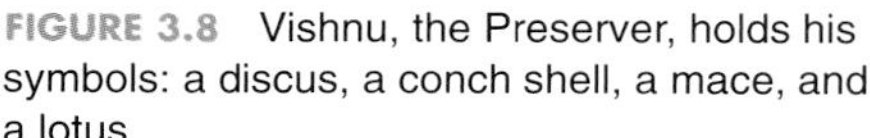

FIGURE 3.8 Vishnu, the Preserver, holds his symbols: a discus, a conch shell, a mace, and a lotus.

South Indian. *Standing Vishnu.* Early Chola period, tenth century. Bronze. 85.7 × 35.6 cm (33¾ × 14″). The Metropolitan Museum of Art, New York, New York. Purchase, 1962. Mr. and Mrs. John D. Rockfeller gift.

FIGURE 3.9 The layout of this temple was designed to create a solar calendar by which the summer and winter solstices and the spring and fall equinoxes could be fixed. Why was this important in an agricultural society?

Southeast Asia. Temple at Angkor Wat, Kampuchea (Cambodia). 1113–50.

ART OF ASIA

The cultures of India, Indochina, China, and Japan have all produced exciting art forms. One way in which the art of these cultures is different from European art is that it is based on different philosophies and religious beliefs.

India

The art of India has been strongly influenced by the Hindu and Buddhist religions. Buddhism had a strong influence over the country from the third century B.C. to the sixth century A.D. After that time Hinduism became dominant. Hinduism combined several different beliefs and practices that developed over a long period of time. In Hinduism there are three primary processes in life and in the universe: creation, preservation, and destruction. The three main Hindu gods reflect this belief. They are Brahma, the Creator; Vishnu, the Preserver (Figure 3.8); and Shiva, the Destroyer. In Hinduism both humans and animals are believed to have souls. Reincarnation is a purification process in which the soul lives in many bodies in many lifetimes until it becomes one with Brahma, the great soul.

India exported its religions to the rest of Asia. In Cambodia many temples were built of stone in the Indian style. The temple at Angkor Wat (Figure 3.9) was originally a Hindu temple built between the years 1113 and 1150. Dedicated to Vishnu by its builder, it represents the Hindu view of the universe.

China

China adopted Buddhism during the Han dynasty, which lasted from 206 B.C. to A.D. 220. Buddhism and the other Chinese religions stressed the oneness of human beings with nature. Chinese artists found that long periods of meditation enabled them to perceive the beauty of an object or a scene. This made them better able to capture the beauty of the subject in their painting. (See Figure 3.10.) Many Chinese paintings were made on a scroll. The scroll is a long roll of parchment or silk. Some were hung on walls; others were meant to be unrolled a little at a time and read like a book.

FIGURE 3.10 Notice how small a space on the scroll is taken up by the people. The hut blends into the natural setting. The fine handwriting in the upper right corner is an important part of the composition. The busy lines of the writing balance the busy lines of the autumn leaves below.

Hua Yen. *Conversation in Autumn.* 1762. Ink and color on paper. 115.3 × 39.7 cm (45⅜ × 15⅝″). The Cleveland Museum of Art, Cleveland, Ohio. The John L. Severance Fund.

The Chinese also produced sculpture for religious purposes and to the honor the dead. During the Sung dynasty porcelain objects were made of fine-grained white clay called kaolin. Work in porcelain reached its highest point during the Ming dynasty. Today tombs full of clay sculptures are being discovered.

FIGURE 3.11 The woodcut print has long been a work of art that even the poorest person could afford. The printmaker is able to make many inexpensive original works from the wooden printing plates. In this print the great pine tree of Karasaki is seen in a drenching rain. The artist, Hiroshige, was a great landscape print artist.

Andō Hiroshige. *Evening Rain on the Karasaki Pine* (from the series Eight Views of Omi Province). Nineteenth century. Woodblock print. 26 × 38.1 cm (10¼ × 15"). The Metropolitan Museum of Art, New York, New York. H. O. Havemeyer Collection. Bequest of Mrs. H. O. Havemeyer, 1929.

Japan

Japan also adopted Buddhism as its major religion. Until the end of the ninth century, Japanese artists copied the art styles of China and other Asian countries. Then Japanese artists began to develop a style uniquely their own. Many different subjects are shown in Japanese painting and printmaking. Some of the subjects are stories of war, everyday scenes, court life, and nature. The demands for artwork were great. To meet those demands, Japanese artists perfected a technique that had been invented in China—woodblock printing. Using this technique the artist could produce many inexpensive prints of one image (Figure 3.11).

ART OF GREECE AND ROME

Greece was the birthplace of Western civilization. The influence of ancient Greek culture can still be seen today. Almost every city in our country has at least one building with features that resemble the architecture of the classic Greek temple.

The Greeks built temples in honor of their gods. The most outstanding example is the Parthenon in Athens. Inside was a huge statue of the goddess Athena in ivory and gold.

The Greeks believed in a logical, harmonious world. They sought perfect proportions in buildings, sculpture, and music by following formulas. Their artists produced statues that represented the Greek ideal of a perfect body. According to one story, athletes used these statues, like the one shown in Figure 3.12, as models for building up their own muscle structure.

When they were new, Greek temples and statues were not the pure white they are today. The Greeks loved color, and they painted their buildings and sculpture various hues. Time has since worn the paint away.

Even though the Romans conquered Greece in 146 B.C., they did not conquer Greek culture. The Romans adopted Greek culture and changed it to suit their own needs. Greek sculptors, painters, architects, philosophers, and teachers had a great influence on the Roman Empire.

Earlier, the Romans had absorbed the culture of the Etruscans in Italy. Two outstanding Etruscan developments that the Romans adopted were a system of drainage and an improved use of the arch in the construction of buildings. What we call Roman art is a blend of the ideal Greek and the practical Etruscan arts.

The Romans added much to what they adopted. They used the arch and concrete to build large-scale structures, including huge vaulted and domed inner spaces. The Romans also developed beautiful interior decoration, excellent roads, and realistic rather than idealized portrait sculpture (Figure 3.13).

Before the fourth century, Christians were not allowed to practice their religion in public. After the Roman emperor Constantine legalized Christianity, the Christians were able to build their own churches. Their churches were based on Roman design, and the interiors were decorated with mosaics. These were pictures made by arranging small pieces of colored glass. The pieces of glass were set unevenly into the wall so that they glittered in the reflected light of church candles.

FIGURE 3.13 The Romans were not concerned with the Greek ideal of human perfection. They wanted accurate, realistic portraits that looked like the people they represented. Notice the wrinkles and loose skin of the man in this portrait.

Greco-Roman. *Man of the Republic*. c. 50 B.C. Terra cotta. 35.7 cm (14″) high, face 18 cm (7″) long. Courtesy of the Museum of Fine Arts, Boston, Massachusetts. Contribution, purchase of E. P. Warren.

FIGURE 3.12 Many of the original sculptures by the great Greek artists have been lost. This is a copy made by a Roman sculptor.

Myron. *Discobolus (Discus Thrower)*. c. 450 B.C. Roman copy of a bronze original. Life-size. Italy. Palazzo Vecchio, Florence, Italy.

In the eastern part of the Roman Empire, a new style of art developed. This style thrived around the city of Constantinople (now Istanbul) and spread to towns such as Ravenna in Italy. Named after the city of Byzantium, **Byzantine** art used *very rich colors and figures that were flat and stiff* (Figure 3.14 on page 50). These artworks blended Greek, Roman, and Asian styles and usually had a religious theme.

Analyzing Architecture

1. Applying Your Skills. Find a building in your community that uses the style of one of the ancient cultures discussed on the previous pages. Write the location, the culture from which the style was adopted, the purpose of the building, and anything else you can learn about it.

2. Further Challenge. Make a sketch of the same building in your sketchbook. List the ancient culture and describe the features that match the style of the ancient culture.

ART OF THE MIDDLE AGES IN EUROPE

The Middle Ages began with the conquest of Rome in A.D. 476 by invaders from the north and lasted about one thousand years. This period of time was also called the *Age of Faith* because the Christian religion was such an important force. Monasteries, or buildings that housed persons under religious vows, grew in number, and the monks who lived in them created finely decorated religious manuscripts. Churches grew in size and political importance.

At the beginning of this period, new churches were built in western Europe. The style of architecture, named after the Roman style, was called **Romanesque** and *featured massive size; solid, heavy walls; wide use of the rounded Roman arch; and many sculptural decorations.*

In the twelfth century, more and more European people moved from the countryside into towns. Workers such as stone carvers and carpenters organized into craft guilds (unions), and apprentices learned their craft from the masters in these guilds. A wealthy new middle class, city pride, and religious faith led to the building of huge cathedrals. Two developments—the pointed arch and the flying buttress—brought about changes in architecture. This new style, called **Gothic**, *featured churches that soared upward,* like the cathedral shown in Figure 3.15. The Gothic cathedrals became the world's largest architectural structures since the Egyptian pyramids.

By using stained-glass windows, Gothic builders changed the light that entered the churches into rich, glowing color. Gothic sculpture and painting took on less stylized, more realistic qualities. Religious scenes were painted on church altarpieces with egg tempera paint and gold leaf.

FIGURE 3.14 This painting is a good example of the Byzantine blending of Western realism and Asian decorative patterns. The heads and graceful hands are shaded to give the illusion of roundness. The Oriental influence is seen in the flat bodies and the patterns of the gold lines.

Byzantine. *Madonna and Child on Curved Throne.* 1480. Tempera on wood. 81.5 × 49 cm (32⅛ × 19⅜"). National Gallery of Art, Washington, D.C. Andrew W. Mellon Collection.

The Gothic Style

1. Applying Your Skills. Find a book in the library about cathedrals built in the Gothic style. List the names of three of the cathedrals in your sketchbook and tell where and when they were built.

2. Further Challenge. Draw a diagram in your sketchbook of the cross section of a Gothic cathedral. Identify and label the pointed arch and the flying buttresses.

FIGURE 3.15 Notice the use of pointed arches, stained-glass windows, and realistic sculptures in this Gothic cathedral.

Reims Cathedral. Reims, France. 1225–99.

ART OF THE RENAISSANCE IN EUROPE

By the beginning of the fifteenth century, the Middle Ages were waning. The invention of the printing press and the European exploration of the Americas and the Pacific were two factors that indicated the beginning of a new era. As you would expect, the art of Europe also went through many changes.

Renaissance (**ren**-uh-sahns) is a French word that means "rebirth." In Italy the fifteenth century brought new interest, a rebirth, in the philosophy and art of ancient Greece and Rome. The **Renaissance** is *the name given to the period of awakening at the end of the Middle Ages.*

The Renaissance in Italy, and later in northern Europe, was much more than a rebirth of ancient ways. It was a complete change in human awareness. People became more aware of the world around them and realized that each person had an important part to play in it. Kings and church leaders had to make way at the top of the power structure for bankers and merchants.

During the Middle Ages artists had worked not for themselves but for the Church. They had been members of the working class. During the Renaissance, however, great artists such as Leonardo da Vinci (**vin**-chee), Michelangelo (my-kel-**an**-jay-loh), and Raphael (**rah**-fah-yell) mingled socially with nobles and kings.

In both painting and sculpture the solid, realistic appearance of people and objects became very important (Figure 3.16 on page 52). To show people and objects accurately, Italian artists studied the classical art of Greece and Rome as well as the natural world around them. Leonardo studied many subjects in depth. He left more than 120 notebooks filled with observation drawings and notes on subjects that range from human anatomy to plans for machines.

An architect named Filippo Brunelleschi (fee-**leep**-poh brew-nell-**less**-key) developed a technique called **linear perspective,** *a graphic system that creates the illusion of depth and volume on a flat surface.* Perspective provided a set of rules that

FIGURE 3.16 Notice how realistically Michelangelo carved the features of this head of the Virgin Mary. You will find the full sculpture in Figure 11.37, page 309.

Michelangelo. *Pietà*. (Detail) c. 1500. Marble. 174 cm (5′ 8½″) high; base 195 cm (6′4¾″) high. Vatican, St. Peter's Basilica, Rome, Italy.

enabled artists to show figures and objects in space. The rules of perspective made the placement of objects, and the depiction of their mass, measurable and exact. This gave an exciting illusion of reality to works of art.

The changes in painting seen in Renaissance Italy came later to northern European countries such as Flanders and Germany. Northern artists like Jan van Eyck (yahn van ike) concentrated mainly on symbols and the surface details of objects (Figure 7.42, page 187). The invention of oil painting (usually credited to van Eyck) allowed artists to work on fine details while the paint was still wet. Later, northern artists combined this attention to detail with an emotional style.

ART OF ISLAM

One thousand years earlier in the Middle East, an event took place that had a major effect on both the religious beliefs and the art of the area. Muhammad was born in Mecca in A.D. 570. He grew up and became an Arab merchant, and he believed that he received personal revelations that challenged him to change the current religion of the Arabs who worshiped many idols. He taught that there was only one god, Allah, and his followers were called Muslims. Muhammad became their prophet, and after his death his teachings were assembled into the Koran, the holy scripture; and Islam was the name given to the religious faith of the Muslims.

Islamic art, the art of the Muslim world, is decorative. The interior of a mosque, a Muslim place of worship, was decorated with ornate calligraphy (beautiful writing), geometric patterns, and stylized plants and flowers. Art depicting people or animals was not permitted in mosques.

Book illustrators, however, were not limited by the same restrictions. They depicted people and animals in everyday scenes such as banquets, hunting scenes, and incidents inspired by popular romantic stories. They filled their illustrations with beautiful, decorative patterns. The illustration shown in Figure 3.17 was completed in 1525, just

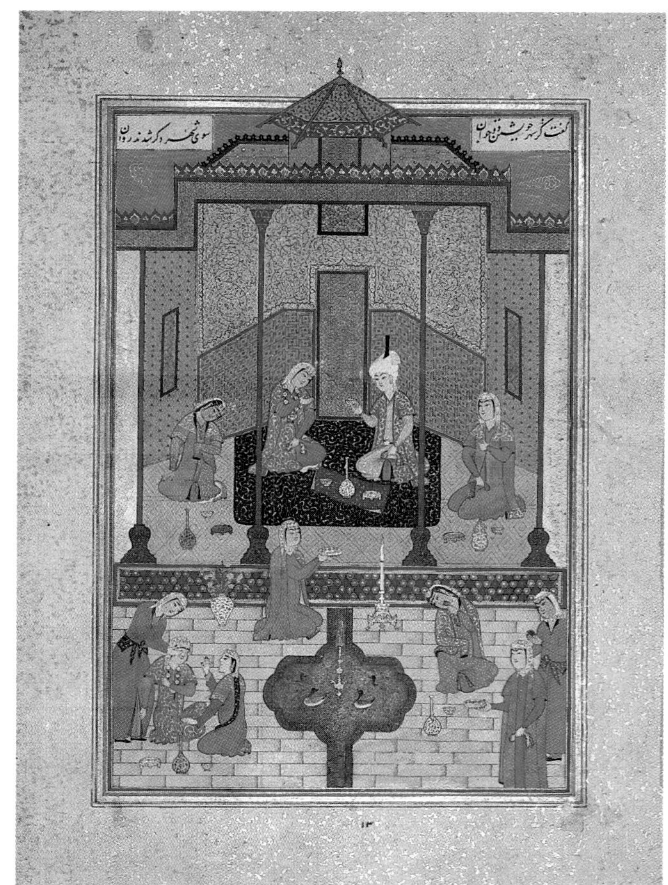

FIGURE 3.17 This is a scene from a book about court life in Iran.

Nizami. *Khamseh: Bahram Gur and the Chinese Princess in the Sandalwood Pavilion on Thursday*. 1524–25. Colors and gilt on paper. 32.4 × 22.2 cm (12¾ × 8¾″). The Metropolitan Museum of Art, New York, New York. Gift of Alexander Smith Cochran, 1913.

twenty-five years after Michelangelo created *Pietà*, shown on page 309. Only eight years earlier, Christopher Columbus left on a trip that was to culminate in an unexpected discovery.

ART OF NATIVE AMERICANS

The people of North, Central, and South America had well-organized civilizations by the time the Europeans arrived on these continents in 1492. Any culture before the Europeans arrived is considered pre-Columbian, or prior to Columbus. There were over twenty million people living in two thousand different groups. Each group had its own unique language, traditions, rituals, and art forms. Some groups remained hunters, some became farmers, and some built and lived in complex cities. The arts were an integral part of their sacred rituals and daily living.

FIGURE 3.19 This mask was woven with corn husks. What does that tell you about the people who used the mask?

Iroquois. *Corn Husk Mask.* Ontario, Canada, Grand River Reservation. c. 1900. Woven corn husks. 31 cm (12″). Milwaukee Public Museum, Milwaukee, Wisconsin.

FIGURE 3.18 This figure represents a participant in a game that served as a religious ceremony. The player had to bounce a ball off the band that encircled his waist and into a hoop on a wall. The winners received many gifts from the audience, while the losers were sacrificed to the gods.

Gulf Coast, Mexico. *Figurine (Ballplayer).* Late Classic period, c. A.D. 900. Hollow, mold-made ceramic. Height 17 cm (6¾″). Width, 7.6 cm (3″). Albany Museum of Art, Albany, Georgia.

The statue in Figure 3.18 comes from pre-Columbian Mexico and represented a participant in an elaborate ritual that was carried out in the manner of a ball game.

The corn-husk mask shown in Figure 3.19 was worn by the Iroquois of North America during ceremonies in which bountiful crops were predicted in the year to come. The men's leggings shown in Figure 6.5 (page 121) and Figure 6.6 (page 121) also come from North America. The glass beads used to decorate the leggings tell us that they were made after the arrival of the Europeans.

ART OF EUROPE IN THE SEVENTEENTH THROUGH THE NINETEENTH CENTURY

The European world was growing through exploration and scientific discoveries. Both the telescope and the microscope were changing the way people saw the universe. The new worldview was reflected in the arts.

The Seventeenth Century

By the beginning of the seventeenth century, artists were creating dramatic, theatrical works that seemed to burst with energy and strong emotions. The art style that developed was called **Baroque** and *emphasized movement, strong value contrast, and variety.*

The forms and figures in Baroque art turn, twist, and spiral into space. Baroque artists refined perspective to the point where they could make figures seem to move off the canvas toward the viewer. They opened up space in the distance toward infinity. In addition to all this movement, they added dramatic lighting effects using dark, mysterious shadows and brightly lit areas. (Figure 3.20).

The Eighteenth Century

In the eighteenth century, Baroque art evolved into a more relaxed style called **Rococo**, which *stressed free graceful movement, a playful use of line, and delicate colors.* Rococo art was used to decorate the homes of the French aristocracy, and their luxurious and carefree life was often depicted in the paintings.

FIGURE 3.20 Judith Leyster was a Dutch woman who dared to break rules. Women artists of her time were expected to paint delicate still lifes, but Leyster chose to do portraits and subjects from everyday life.

Judith Leyster. *Self-Portrait.* c. 1635. Oil on canvas. 72.3 × 65.3 (29⅜ × 25⅝″). National Gallery of Art, Washington, D.C. Gift of Mr. and Mrs. Robert Woods Bliss.

Analyzing a Work

1. Applying Your Skills. Select one work of art from the Renaissance or the Baroque period. Use the four steps of the art-history method to tell about the work. You may need to research the work of art and the artist in an encyclopedia or a book about the artist. Write your findings in your sketchbook.

2. Further Challenge. In your sketchbook, make a pencil sketch of the work you studied in the above assignment. Next to the sketch, list the title of the work, the artist, and the style in which it was done.

The Nineteenth Century

The industrial and democratic revolutions of the late eighteenth century brought about a new, faster way of life. Change was the only thing that was certain. New styles of art developed quickly as a rebellion against the styles of earlier artists.

Neoclassicism. The French Revolution abandoned the Rococo style because it mirrored the life of the aristocracy. Academies, which replaced the old apprentice system, taught a new style of art that better suited the new society. This style was based on the look of Greek and Roman art and was called *Neoclassic* ("new classic"). The Neoclassic style was severely realistic and unemotional. An outstanding artist of this style was Jacques Louis David (zjahk loo-**ee** dah-**veed**). See *Death of Socrates* by David (Figure 5.40, page 115).

Romanticism. *Romanticism* was a reaction to the unemotional Neoclassic style. The Romantic artists disliked the many rules and lack of emotion in the Neoclassic style of art. Romanticists such as Rosa Bonheur painted emotional scenes of action with brilliant colors. (See *The Horse Fair*, Figure 9.4, page 224.) The Romanticists believed that the artist's personal impression of an event was more interesting than an accurate, historical report.

Realism. Another group of artists felt that they should portray political, social, and moral issues. They rejected the rules of Neoclassicism and the

FIGURE 3.21 Eakins was so concerned with learning to draw realistically that he left the Pennsylvania Academy of Fine Arts, where students drew from plaster casts, and attended classes at a medical school to learn anatomy.

Thomas Eakins. *Baseball Players Practicing.* 1875. Watercolor. 27.6 × 32.7 cm (10⅞ × 12⅞"). Museum of Art, Rhode Island School of Design, Providence, Rhode Island. Jesse Metcalf and Walter H. Kimball Funds.

drama of Romanticism. They believed that peasants and factory workers shown in a realistic style were suitable subjects for artistic study. This style, called **Realism**, *presented familiar scenes as they actually were.* In Spain, the art of Francisco Goya (fran-**seese**-koh **goh**-yah) took a realistic turn as he recorded the ugly truth of war during the Spanish Revolution. American artists such as Thomas Eakins also painted everyday subjects realistically.

Impressionism. The Realists had taken a hard look at the real world. Another group of artists also were interested in the world outside the studio and, in fact, did much of their painting outdoors. Scientific discoveries about light and color led this group to emphasize the effects of sunlight on objects. They concentrated on reflected light rather than on the form of objects. These artists broke up solid forms and blurred edges by applying paint to the canvas in small dabs of pure color. The dabs were blended together in the eye of the viewer. The style, **Impressionism**, *captured everyday subjects and emphasized the momentary effects of sunlight.* If you stand too close to an Impressionist's painting, all you will see are colorful dabs and dots. You have to step back to allow your vision to blend the colors. In Figure 3.22 on page 56 the camera has done the blending for you.

Post-Impressionism. Gradually some artists who had started as Impressionists became dissatisfied. They wanted to produce something more meaningful. Some wanted to express feelings, intuitions, and ideas. Others wanted to show more structure and form in their work, like that shown in the house depicted in Figure 3.23 on page 56. The most outstanding of these *Post-Impressionists* were Paul Cézanne (say-**zahn**), Vincent van Gogh (goh), and Paul Gauguin (goh-**gan**). Each expanded his style to create something so unusual that the styles themselves led to important developments in the art of the twentieth century.

Analyzing a Style

1. Applying Your Skills. Choose one of the styles of the nineteenth century. Find a picture of an artwork in that style in another chapter of this book. Tell the class why you think your example represents that style.

2. Further Challenge. Find a book about Impressionism in the library. List at least four Impressionist works of art, each one painted by a different artist. Select one of the four works. Use the four steps of art history to write about the work.

FIGURE 3.22 In this work, Monet dissolves all edges and lines in variations of color. The buildings and the water seem to melt together into dabs and dots of flickering violet and blue.

Claude Monet. *Palazzo da Mula, Venice.* 1908. Oil on canvas. 62 × 81.1 cm (24½ × 31⅞″). National Gallery of Art, Washington, D.C. Chester Dale Collection.

FIGURE 3.23 Cézanne was concerned with the structure of objects. He used small brushstrokes like little building blocks to make forms look like geometric solids. Notice how the foliage looks as solid as the rocks.

Paul Cézanne. *Le Chateau Noir.* 1900–04. Oil on canvas. 73.7 × 96.6 cm (29 × 38″). National Gallery of Art, Washington, D.C. Gift of Eugene and Agnes E. Meyer.

ART OF AFRICA

The huge continent of Africa has a population of millions that is subdivided into about one thousand culture groups. The arts are as varied as the peoples. Africa has hundreds of ancient Neolithic rock painting sights. The paintings and rock engravings are more recent than those found in Europe, but they have the same subject matter. They depict humans, animals, and nonobjective symbolic designs.

Most of the African art you see in museums today has been made within the last century. Older wooden or fabric pieces have been destroyed by the damp climate and by insects such as the wood-eating white ant. As early as the sixteenth century, however, artists of the Benin kingdom produced metal sculptures that displayed an outstanding command of metal-casting techniques (Figure 6.45, page 146).

The arts of Africa were, and still are, interwoven into the religious and everyday lives of the many nations, kingdoms, and culture groups on that continent. Africans do not see art as a separate activity unrelated to their everyday lives. Everything, from the paintings that women apply to the mud walls of their homes (Figure 7.30, page 172) to the ancestral figure made by the Bamum peoples of Cameroon (Figure 3.24), serves a practical function. Ceremonial canes, combs for the hair, stools, chairs, pipes, and spoons are carved with the same care and craftsmanship as an ancestral mask.

Weaving is widespread. Traditionally women weave everyday fabrics, while the ceremonial weavings such as Kente cloth was reserved for men alone (Figure 9.11 page 228, and Figure 9.29 on page 242).

Sculpture is regarded as one of Africa's greatest contributions to the world's cultural heritage. It inspired the development of Cubism in Europe at the beginning of the twentieth century. African wood carvings include figures and masks. The figures are ancestral figures, power figures, and funeral figures. They all have proportions that reflect cultural concepts rather than realism and an enlarged head to indicate its importance as the center of reason and wisdom. See the wood carving shown in Figure 3.25 on page 58.

FIGURE 3.24 As trade with Europeans increased, African artists incorporated new materials into traditional art. The imported glass beads used to decorate the surface of this royal figure denote wealth and power.

Bamum peoples, Fumban, Grassfields region, Cameroon. *Male Figure.* 1908 or earlier. Wood, brass, glass beads, cowrie shells. Height, 160 cm (63"). National Museum of African Art, Smithsonian Institution, Washington, D.C. Gift of Evelyn A. J. Hall and John Friede.

FIGURE 3.25 This sculpture represents a magician who can travel between the spirit world and the real world. Notice how his posture, with his shoulders back and his chest thrust forward, captures the dignity and pride of a man who speaks with spirits.

Africa, Ivory Coast, Senufo Tribe. *Equestrian Figure.* Nineteenth to twentieth centuries. Wood, patination. 32.5 × 7.3 × 22.3 cm (12¾ × 3 × 8¾"). Dallas Museum of Art, Dallas, Texas. Gustav and Franyo Schindler Collection. Gift of the McDermott Foundation in honor of Eugene McDermott.

THE BEGINNING OF THE TWENTIETH CENTURY

During the first half of the twentieth century, the range of art styles grew, and the speed at which changes occurred increased. The influence of rules and the Academy were dead. Artists were free to experiment and explore. It became impossible to separate artists into neat categories. Increased travel and new ways of communication helped artists compare ideas. One individual or group could influence another. Some artists who lived a long life, such as Matisse and Picasso, changed their own styles several times.

European Art

In general, art in Europe moved in three major directions. One direction was primarily concerned with expressing emotions. Another emphasized structure, or composition. Still another stressed imagination and dreamlike inventions. Artists experimented with subject matter as well as with composition and style.

At the beginning of the twentieth century, a group of young French painters expressed emotion by creating works that exploded with brilliant colors, bold distortions, and loose brushstrokes. They were called *Fauves*, which is French for "wild beasts." The Fauves continued the expressive ideas of Vincent van Gogh and Paul Gauguin. The leader of this group, Henri Matisse (ahn-**ree** mah-**tees**), was concerned with expressing the feeling he had for life. He insisted that his work had but one purpose: to give pleasure.

A different sort of feeling characterized the work of the German artists. A movement began that was called **Expressionism**, in which *artists tried to*

FIGURE 3.26 Kollwitz devoted her art to describing the plight of the poor and denouncing the atrocities of war. She was concerned with the human condition and believed she could best express this concern through printmaking.

Käthe Kollwitz. *Self-Portrait.* 1921. Etching. 21.6 × 26.7 cm (8½ × 10½"). National Museum of Women in the Arts, Washington, D.C. Museum Purchase: The Member's Acquisition Fund.

FIGURE 3.27 Picasso has changed the traditional view of the human form using a style known as Analytical Cubism. We see hints of geometric shapes with transparent openings through which colors melt and flow. Can you see how the atomic theory of matter in motion has influenced this stage of Picasso's work?

Pablo Picasso. *Nude Woman.* 1910. Oil on canvas. 187.3 × 61 cm (73¾ × 24″). National Gallery of Art, Washington, D.C. Ailsa Mellon Bruce Fund.

communicate their strong emotional feelings and which stressed personal feelings rather than composition. The German Expressionists experienced the terrible economic and social conditions in Germany before and after World War I. Their emotional subjects ranged from fear and anger to concern with death. Käthe Kollwitz (**kah**-teh **kohl**-vits) (Figure 3.26) was one Expressionist who was concerned with poverty and war. She produced many moving images of mothers grieving for dead children. Her work was based on personal experience: She lost her eldest son during World War I.

Another group of artists created work that went in a different direction. **Cubism** is *a style that emphasizes structure and design.* Three different things influenced the Cubists. The first was an idea: All shapes in nature are based on geometric solids. The second was a scientific discovery: All matter is made up of atoms that are constantly in motion. The third was art from another culture: the structure of African sculpture that had recently been brought to Paris. The Cubists tried to paint three-dimensional objects as if they could be seen from many different points of view at the same time. The painting in Figure 3.27 is an early Cubist work.

A group of Italian artists, the *Futurists,* took Cubism a step farther. They placed lines and shapes in a composition to suggest motion. Their paintings and sculpture seem to come to life. (See Figure 9.24 on page 236.)

In Holland, an artist named Piet Mondrian created nonobjective art using only vertical and horizontal black lines; black, white, and gray rectangles; and the three primary colors. His style was the exact opposite of Expressionism. (See Figure 7.35, page 176.)

A third group of artists introduced fantasy into their subject matter. Fantasy has always been a part of art. It can be traced back to Greek mythology and to the monsters and gargoyles of the Middle Ages. After World War I, the *Dadaists* used fantasy to take aim at the culture they thought had failed them. Their works featured strange objects such as fur-lined teacups.

Another movement offered a slightly saner version of the Dada philosophy. **Surrealism** was *a style in which dreams, fantasy, and the subconscious served as inspiration for artists.* Surrealists presented very realistic, almost photographic images but

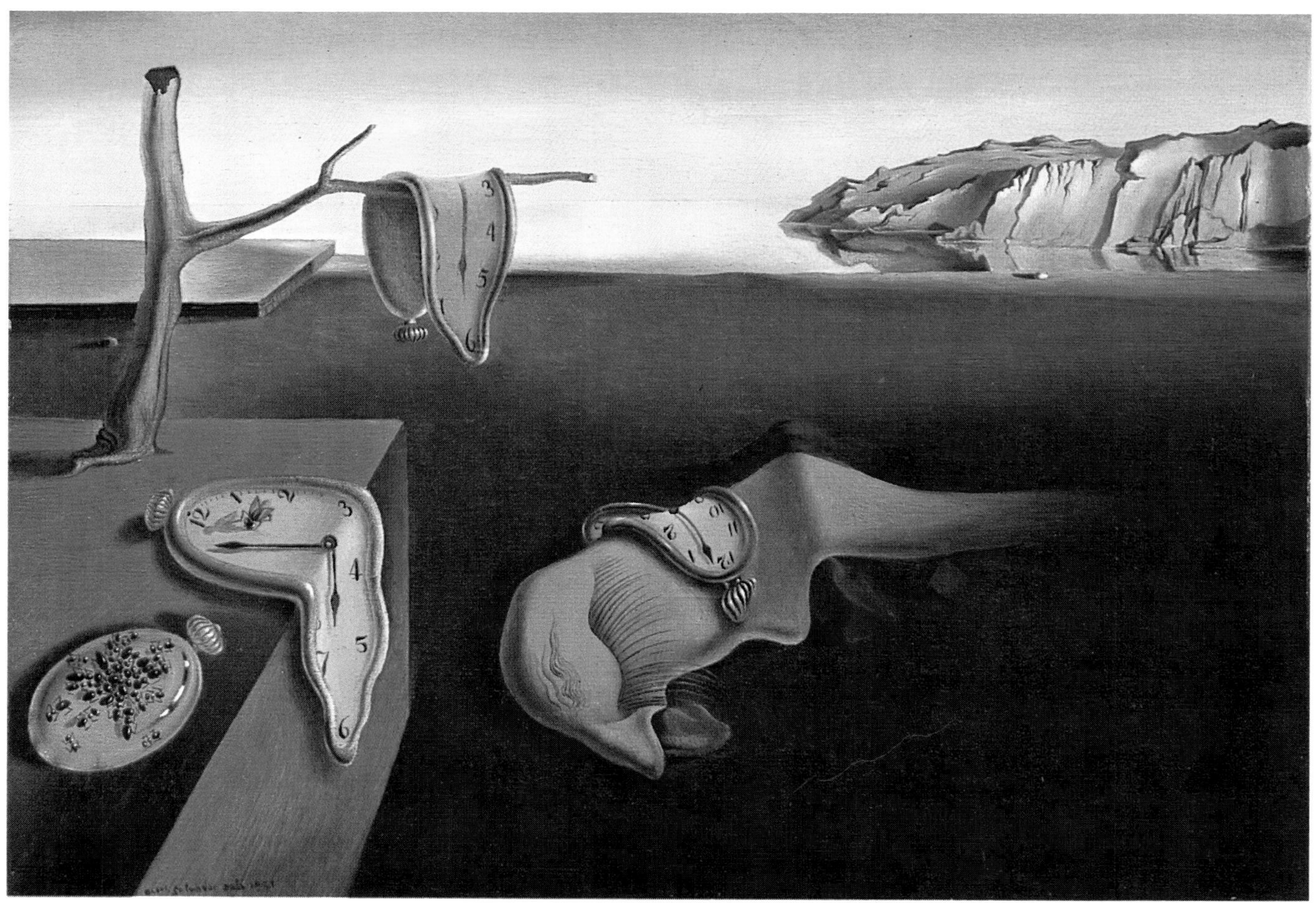

FIGURE 3.28 Dali has created a strange world in which metal objects that should be firm seem to melt. Realistic details, such as the ants, add to the nightmare quality of the scene. Can you recognize the object lying on the ground in the center of the picture?

Salvador Dali. *The Persistence of Memory.* 1931. Oil on canvas. 24.1 × 33 cm (9½ × 13″). Collection, The Museum of Modern Art, New York, New York. Given anonymously.

combined objects that didn't belong together. Figure 3.28 is an example. The work of the Surrealists is strange and dreamlike. Some paintings are like nightmares, some are funny, and some are mysterious and frightening. No Surrealist work is supposed to make sense to the viewer, however.

North American Art

At the beginning of the twentieth century, a group of young artists in the United States turned to the harsh realities of the city for subject matter. They called themselves The Eight and organized an exhibition in 1908. Their original name was forgotten when they were quickly labeled the Ashcan School by critics who were shocked by the subject matter of their work: stark tenement buildings, crowded city streets, and poor working people.

An even greater impact on the American art world was made when the Armory Show of 1913 was held. This show introduced Americans to the new art being created in Europe. Most of the American public was confused by what they saw, but many artists were challenged by the daring exhibition and took their first steps toward making modern art in America.

However, there was one group of artists with whom Americans felt comfortable. The **Regionalists** were *artists who painted the farmlands and cities of America realistically*, as in Figure 3.29. Each artist had a slightly different style, but their messages were more upbeat than the messages of the Ashcan

LOOKING CLOSELY

FIGURE 3.29 Benton painted his American scenes larger than life. His subject was a nation filled with restless people, surging industrial forces, and landscapes full of a barely controllable power. This mural was a combination of biographical and historical information blended with artistic invention. Can you identify the musical instruments depicted in this mural? How many sources of country music can you find? What other clues can you find that reveal the time and place portrayed in this mural? How did Benton achieve the vitality conveyed by the work?

Thomas Hart Benton. *The Sources of Country Music.* 1975. Acrylic on canvas. 1.8 x 3 m (6 x 10'). The Country Music Hall of Fame and Museum, Nashville, Tennessee. © T. H. Benton and R.P. Benton Testamentary Trusts/VAGA, New York 1994.

School. They focused on the vast expanse, beauty, productivity, and abundance of America. The people in their paintings were shown as happy and hardworking.

Most sculptors at this time worked with traditional materials using traditional methods. A few then began experimenting with the new materials of the twentieth century. The most exciting step was taken by Alexander Calder (Figure 9.26, page 237), who made sculpture move by arranging wire and sheet metal into a balanced arrangement that stayed in motion. He called these moving sculptures *mobiles* (**moh**-beels).

The twentieth century also saw big changes in architecture. New materials and new demands led to the development of skyscrapers. Functional structures with steel frames that emphasized simplicity of form replaced heavy, decorated structures. Frank Lloyd Wright believed that form should follow function, and he designed buildings that were in harmony with the environment (Figure 3.30 on page 62).

FIGURE 3.30 Frank Lloyd Wright designed this house to be functional as well as to blend in with the environment.

Frank Lloyd Wright. *The David Wright House.* Scottsdale, Arizona. 1951.

The strong emotions of the time were also revealed in the art of a group of Mexican artists. As the twentieth century started, Mexico was deeply troubled. The tension erupted into the Mexican Revolution. Some Mexican artists developed a style with which to express their feelings about the plight of the people. They were referred to as the *Mexican Muralists*, because they covered walls and ceilings with their murals about Mexican history, the suffering of the peasants, and the immoral behavior of the ruling class (Figure 3.31). They combined the solid forms of ancient Mexican art with the powerful colors of European Expressionism. The work of José Clemente Orozco shown in Figure 3.31 is an example of the vigorous style and social-protest subject matter protrayed by the Mexican Muralists.

FIGURE 3.31 Orozco captures the raw emotion of the Mexican peasants fighting to hold their position. Notice how the artist has exaggerated the muscles to show how the men are tensed for combat.

José Clemente Orozco. *Barricade.* 1931. Oil on canvas. 140 × 114.3 cm (55 × 45″). The Museum of Modern Art, New York, New York. Given anonymously.

Analyzing a Style

1. Applying Your Skills. Choose one of the styles from the beginning of the twentieth century. Find a picture of an artwork in that style in another chapter of this book. Tell the class why you think your example represents that style.

2. Further Challenge. Go to the library and find a book about one of the artists who worked during the first half of the twentieth century. Select one work of art in that book and use the four steps of art history to write about it.

FROM THE FIFTIES TO THE FUTURE

After World War II the European art world was disorganized. Paris was no longer the center of creativity. Many artists who had fled Hitler's Germany settled in New York City. They began teaching there, and by the 1950s they and their students established a new center for the arts.

What happened next took place with breathtaking speed. During the last fifty years there have been more changes in artistic style and technique than there have been since prehistoric times. To begin with, a variety of art forms once considered minor art found a place as equals to painting and sculpture, and their creators are exploring new frontiers. These arts include printmaking, weaving, ceramics, and jewelry.

There are also more artists working today than ever before, all over the world. With new developments in travel and communication, no place is far from the mainstream of art. Artists in mainland China are creating oil paintings in the style of the old European masters. Sculptors in Africa who have studied art history are creating individual sculptures that are not tied to community traditions. Because of increased opportunity and changing attitudes, more women and minority artists have been able to study, exhibit, and gain recognition.

The following is a brief description of some of the major movements that have occurred.

Abstract Expressionism

Abstract Expressionism was the first new style to arrive on the scene in New York in the years following World War II. It was *abstract* because it emphasized the elements and principles of art as its subject matter. It was *expressive* because it stressed feelings and emotions rather than planned design (See Figure 3.32, page 64).

Pop and Op Art

During the early 1960s artists turned to the mass media, and especially to advertising, for subject matter. *Pop* artists portrayed images of popular culture, such as Coke bottles, soup cans, Brillo boxes, giant hamburgers, and comic strips, in a variety of art forms. Sculptors worked with the neon tubing of signs. These artists made people take a new look at everyday objects. (See Figure 12.28, page 336.)

People have always been fascinated by illusions. They enjoy looking at pictures that fool the eye. *Op*, or optical art, uses scientific knowledge about vision to create optical illusions of movement. Op art has hard edges and smooth surfaces, and every element is carefully planned. (See Figure 7.6, page 158.)

Color-Field Painting

Color-field painting is concerned only with flat fields of color. It is done without the precision of Op art, and it is without emotion. It is color for the pure sensation of color. One example is the work of Mark Rothko. His color areas have hazy edges that seem to float in space. (See Figure 7.20, page 166.)

New Realism

Americans have a love for realism, and some American artists continue to portray subjects in a realistic style. Andrew Wyeth, whose work you studied in Chapter 2, is one example. Sculpture made by Duane Hanson is so real that it once

FIGURE 3.32 Hofmann came to New York from Germany and opened an art school. He was the father of the Abstract Expressionist style that grew in New York. He is best known for his heavy use of brilliant colors. In this work, two sharply-defined rectangles seem to float over a background of loosely brushed but heavily built-up colors, which suggest water and flowers.

Hans Hofmann. *Flowering Swamp*. 1957. Oil on wood. 122 × 91.5 cm (48⅛ × 36⅛"). Hirshhorn Museum and Sculpture Garden, Smithsonian Institution, Washington, D.C. Gift of the Joseph H. Hirshhorn Foundation, 1966.

fooled a gallery security guard (Figure 3.33). One of Hanson's motionless, seated figures looked so real that the guard thought it was ill and called for an ambulance. This style has several names: *Photo-Realism*, *Hyper-Realism*, and *Super-Realism*.

Other Styles

Minimalists reduced their works to a minimum of elements. Sculpture was reduced to a minimum of geometric forms; paintings were reduced to one color. Some artists created gigantic earthworks that made the public more aware of the environment. Today critics are calling some artists *Postmodern*. The art world is changing so fast that you need to look at a current monthly art magazine to know what the newest movements are.

Directions in Architecture

As with every other visual form, architecture has not followed just one direction. Some buildings, like the glass and metal boxes that fill the cities, are still being designed for function. Some buildings are shaped to take advantage of solar power. Architects are also designing buildings that are asymmetrical and decorative (Figure 3.34). Landscape architects are teaming up with city architects and planners to create cities that help solve urban-living problems. Other teams are redesigning the centers of cities to make them more attractive places to live in and to visit.

Applying the Steps

1. Applying Your Skills. Look through this book to find five paintings that were created since 1950. For each, list the name of the artist, the title of the work, and the style in which the work was painted.

2. Further Challenge. Select a work of art, other than a painting, that was created since 1950. Use the four steps of art history to write about the work. You may have to go to the library to find the information you need.

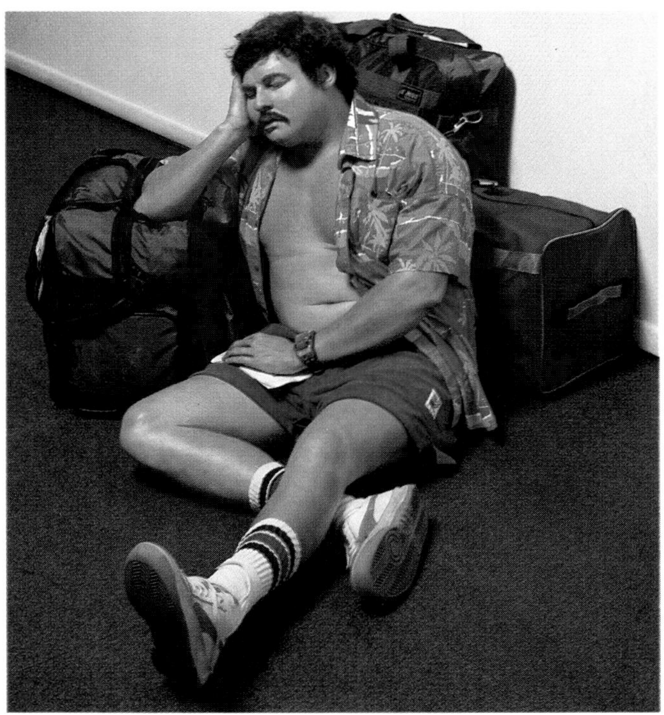

FIGURE 3.33 Hanson's sculpture is an example of the New Realism. If you observed this figure in an art gallery, would you mistake him for a real person?

Duane Hanson. *Traveler with Sunburn.* 1986. Bronze, oil paint, and mixed media. Life-size. Private collection.

FIGURE 3.34 Spear says that her firm seeks to capture the spirit of time and place in its architecture. This building is a center for the development of innovative technology and software production. Do you think the form, which seems to defy the forces of gravity, fits the purpose of the building?

Laurinda Spear of the architectural firm of Arquitectonica International, Miami. *Centre for Innovative Technology.* Fairfax and Louden counties, Virginia.

ART CRITICISM IN ACTION

FIGURE 3.35 Lilla Cabot Perry. *Lady with a Bowl of Violets.* 1910. Oil on canvas. 102 × 76.2 cm (40¼ × 30″). National Museum of Women in the Arts, Washington, D.C. The Holladay Collection. Gift of Wallace and Wilhelmina Holladay.

CRITIQUING THE WORK

1. **Describe** Study the painting *Lady with a Bowl of Violets* by Lilla Cabot Perry (Figure 3.35). Read the credit line. Notice the size of the painting and the medium. Now describe everything you see in the painting. Observe the woman's clothing, her hairstyle, her posture, and the expression on her face. Notice the furniture and the objects in the background. Collect facts and clues only.
2. **Analyze** Look at the colors. Do you see any unusual lighting effects? What has the artist done to create the luminous quality in the subject's dress?

FIGURE 3.36 Leonardo da Vinci. *Ginevra de' Benci*. c. 1474. Paint on wood. 38.8 × 36.7 (15¼ × 14½"). National Gallery of Art, Washington, D.C. Ailsa Mellon Bruce Fund.

3. **Interpret** Now it is time to express your own opinion. Add the facts you have collected to your own personal ideas and decide what theme or mood this painting communicates. Write a paragraph explaining your interpretation. Then write a new title for the work that sums up your interpretation.
4. **Judge** Now you are ready to make an aesthetic judgment. Do you think this is a successful work of art? Use one or more of the three aesthetic theories explained in Chapter 2 to defend your judgment.

COMPARING THE WORKS

Look at *Lady with a Bowl of Violets* (Figure 3.35) and *Ginevra de' Benci* (Figure 3.36) by Leonardo da Vinci. List the similarities and differences between the two works. How does each artist use the sitter's eyes to communicate an emotion to the viewer? How does each use color and light? Which of the two works would you prefer to hang in your room? Why? Note the year in which each work was completed. Do you find the styles in which one of the portraits was painted more appealing than the other? Why? Share your ideas in a class discussion.

MEET THE ARTIST

LILLA CABOT PERRY

American, 1848–1933

Lilla Cabot Perry was a late nineteenth-century artist who captured the atmosphere of the genteel world of turn-of-the-century Boston.

She was born in 1848 to the socially prominent Cabot family, the first of eight children. Encouraged by her parents, she was an exceptional student who was interested in literature, language, poetry, music, and especially visual art. At age twenty-six she married the noted scholar Thomas Perry.

Perry's husband was supportive of her desire to pursue a career in art, and they moved to Paris in 1887, where she attended classes at a French academy. As part of her training, she spent hours copying old masters at the Louvre. The turning point for Perry's art came in 1889 when she saw the work of Claude Monet (kload moh-**nay**). The family spent that summer, and many more, in Germany near Monet's famous home and gardens. The Perrys became close friends with the Monets, and Perry embraced the Impressionist style. Monet did not accept students on a formal basis, but he reviewed her work as a friend and offered suggestions to improve her painting techniques.

When the Perrys returned home, Lilla used her social influence to introduce and promote Impressionism in Boston. She painted portraits and landscapes, merging the lessons of Impressionism with her academic training.

Her career spanned half a century, and she was very successful. Near the end of her life she was able to turn down portrait commissions and devote herself to painting landscapes.

In her poem "Requiescat in Pace" (Rest in Peace), published in 1898, Perry summarized the many roles she had juggled throughout her career: "Artist and woman, daughter, mother, wife." Perry was painting on the day she died.

MORE PORTFOLIO IDEAS

I. Focusing on the eyes and how they communicate different moods, cut out and arrange faces of different sizes into an interesting composition that displays a variety of expressions. Use acrylic paints to fill in the background. You may modify the faces using paints, but do not cover the eyes.

II. Give the women in Perry's and da Vinci's paintings each a name. Choose a theme such as love or child care, and write a dialogue between these women. Let each woman's statements reflect the mood in her eyes.

CHAPTER 3 REVIEW

Building Vocabulary

On a separate sheet of paper, write the term that best matches each definition given below.

1. The artist's personal way of using the elements of art and principles of design to express feelings and ideas.
2. A period of time during which a single family provided a succession of rulers.
3. A style of art that used rich color and flat, stiff figures and blended Greek, Roman, and Asian styles.
4. A style of architecture in which churches soared upward, used pointed arches, and had stained-glass windows.
5. The name given to the period of rebirth, or awakening, at the end of the Middle Ages.
6. A graphic system that creates the illusion of depth and volume on a flat surface.
7. A seventeenth-century art style that emphasized movement, contrast, and variety.
8. An art style that captured everyday subjects and emphasized the momentary effects of sunlight by using broken brushstrokes.
9. An art style that stressed personal feelings rather than composition.
10. A style of art in which dreams, fantasy, and the subconscious served as inspiration.

Reviewing Art Facts

Answer the following questions using complete sentences.

1. Name the four steps used by art historians to gain information about a work of art. List them in the order in which they must be followed.
2. In which step would you examine the style of the work and decide if it fit into an art movement?
3. Select a painting shown in this chapter and list three characteristics of the artist's style.
4. Describe the rules that Egyptian artists were required to follow when painting or sculpting a relief figure.
5. How did the ancient Greek belief in a logical, harmonious world affect the art that was produced?
6. What effect did the Renaissance rebirth of interest in the classical art of Greece and Rome have on the art of that period?
7. Describe the difference between the art forms used in an Islamic mosque and in Islamic book illustration.
8. Name one similarity and one difference between the artworks created by the Realists and the Impressionists.
9. Describe the subject matter chosen by the Mexican Muralists.

Thinking Critically About Art

1. **Explain.** In Chapter 2 you learned how to use the four steps of art criticism. In this chapter you have learned the four steps of art history. Both of these systems are useful in learning about a work of art. Explain the difference between the two systems.
2. **Compare and contrast.** You can look at visual images from the past to learn what the people who lived before us were like. Compare two of the self-portraits in this chapter, Figure 3.1 on page 40 and Figure 3.20 on page 54, and explain how these two artists are similar and how they are different.

Making Art Connections

1. **Music.** Listen to a piece of music by a Baroque composer. In what way is the style of the music related to Baroque art?
2. **Science.** We know the cave paintings were created between 15,000 and 10,000 B.C. and that the bricks of Harappa were made in 2500 B.C. Scientists use a system known as carbon 14 dating that proves how old certain materials are. Go to the library and research carbon dating. Find out why it is possible and how it is done.

FIGURE 4.1 For forty-seven years Rockwell captured the look of America in his paintings that appeared on the covers of *The Saturday Evening Post*. He worked seven days a week to create the covers, advertisements, and many private commissions.

Norman Rockwell. *Triple Self-Portrait*. 1960. Oil on canvas. 113 × 87.2 cm (44½ × 34⅜″). The Norman Rockwell Museum, Stockbridge, Massachusetts. Norman Rockwell Family Trust.

CHAPTER 4

Careers in Art

Now is an exciting time to consider a career in the visual arts. There are many possibilities from which to choose. Every year more challenging and rewarding positions are becoming available in art-related careers. People who can perform art and design jobs are needed in schools, museums, galleries, small businesses, and large corporations.

In the distant past, a young person who wanted to be an artist would pay a master artist for permission to work as an *apprentice* in the master's studio. These apprentices learned as they observed and assisted the masters. Today students can develop their skills by taking courses in high school and postsecondary schools. Vocational schools and professional art schools provide the education for some art careers. Other careers may require four- or five-year college degrees.

In this chapter you will learn how to find out whether or not you might be suited for a career in art. You will also get a taste of the many different types of art careers from which you can choose. If you have been thinking that you might enjoy a career in art, this chapter should help you move closer to a career decision. If you have never considered an art career, this chapter may open the door to some exciting career possibilities.

First Impressions

Norman Rockwell had a very successful career as an illustrator. Look at his painting *Triple Self-Portrait* (Figure 4.1). Does the picture on the white canvas match the image in the mirror? Do you know anything about the small pictures taped to the right corner of the canvas? They do not look like Rockwell. Why are they there? What has Rockwell done to the background to help you concentrate on all the objects that make up the subject of the work?

Objectives

After completing this chapter, you will be able to:

- Name many fields in which an art career is possible.
- Name some of the skills artists need for various jobs.
- Make a meaningful decision about your own interest in a career in art.

Words to Know

animation
architect
industrial designer
interior designer
landscape architect
layout
logos
photojournalist
storyboards

FIGURE 4.2 Graphic designer working at a computer.

ART-RELATED CAREERS

You are probably beginning to consider ideas about your own future. If you have talent and art is something you enjoy, this chapter will open your mind to some exciting career possibilities. In addition to the major categories mentioned here, there are many careers within each field. As you read, think about each career and keep those that interest you in mind. You will be surprised at how many different opportunities exist.

BUSINESS AND INDUSTRY

Today the business world needs the skills of an art specialist in many areas. Company reports, publications, and advertising are all designed by someone with training in the visual arts. Some of this design work is done by company staff. Other, more complex projects are given to outside design or advertising firms with many different kinds of artists on staff. Following are descriptions of some of the areas in which artists work.

Graphic Design

The early Christian monks who illustrated religious writings were artists. After the invention of the printing press in the fifteenth century, the craftspeople who arranged type and illustrations were what we now call *graphic artists.* They had to plan the **layout,** *the way items were arranged on the page,* before a page could be printed. It was slow work because it all had to be done by hand. Today graphic designers use computers, laser scanners, and many other machines that work at speeds never before thought possible.

Computer Graphics. Using a computer, designers create images that can be moved, changed, erased, duplicated, shrunk or enlarged, colored, and textured. The designer works with tools such as electric-light pens on electronic tablets, as shown in Figure 4.2. With these tools, designers may draw and color images.

Software programs also exist that enable the user to design a page layout and insert artwork. Electronic equipment merely speeds up this design process. Some systems let the artist see the finished work in a variety of color and size arrangements. Computers can also be used to send images along telephone lines to customers all over the world.

There are also computer programs being developed that are interactive. These programs give the user many different ways of exploring a large database of information. Some interactive programs are very simple. Others combine information in written form; graphic images including animation and motion pictures; and sound, including music and sound effects. The viewer can use the mouse control to switch back and forth between the various kinds of information, following his or her own path to in-depth learning. Each segment of these complex interactive programs must be planned. One person may develop the overall concept, another may create the images, still others may integrate the various parts of the program.

Advertising Art. Graphic artists may be employed by corporations to design promotional material, by outdoor-advertising agencies to create billboards, and by advertising agencies to work on ad campaigns (Figure 4.3). Advertising agencies employ artists of many kinds. These artists work together as a team, and their work is coordinated by the art director. Graphic designers also create **logos**, or *identifying symbols*, such as the CBS eye or McDonald's golden arches.

Publishing Design and Illustration. Newspaper, magazine, and book publishers employ graphic designers. A designer created the look of this book. The size of the type, the length of the lines, the layout of the text and artwork, and the length of the columns were all carefully planned. Computers were used to type the manuscript, and the information was stored on a disk and given to the typesetting company. The typesetter then followed the design provided by the book designer.

In addition to the type and the paintings you see in this book, there are drawings by commercial illustrators, such as the viewing frame on page 351 of the Handbook. Some illustrators specialize in one area, such as fashion, medical, or technical illustration. Others accept assignments in many areas.

Cartoonists submit their work for publication in magazines and newspapers. They may choose to draw individual cartoons or comic strips. Editorial cartoonists must be interested in politics. They present complex ideas in a simple drawing that usually makes a humorous point. Editorial cartoonists try to make people think about current issues. They also try to influence public opinion.

Film and Video Graphics. Artists who work in film and video graphics design such things as stage sets, the graphic symbols and pictures that introduce sports programs, and the animated graphics in commercials. Video manufacturers use graphic artists to design the box covers for their tapes, set up photo shoots, and help produce the advertising campaigns that introduce the new product.

Industrial Design

Industrial designers *design the products of industry.* They plan everything from tools, home appliances, furniture, and toys to automobiles. They must be familiar with production processes as well as the characteristics of the different materials used

FIGURE 4.3 A poster advertising a marathon.

FIGURE 4.4 Look closely at this Avanti. Like many of today's aerodynamic cars, it has no grill. How do you think this design might affect the car's performance?

Raymond Loewy. *Avanti.* 1963.

in those processes. Industrial designers plan a product based on three requirements. First, it must do the job for which it was designed. Second, it must look like it can do the job. Third, it must be visually pleasing.

Package designers produce boxes, tubes, bottles, shopping bags, and other kinds of containers. They use shape and color to make every package unique and appealing. Package designers must also consider package function. For example, when pill bottles first came on the market, the caps were so easy to remove that children were able to open them. Designers had to come up with a cap that was childproof but could be opened by an adult.

Industrial designers usually specialize in one industry or product, such as machinery, furniture, medical equipment, or cars. The design of an automobile is a team effort. Special designers plan the outer form or body. Then other specialists who work with fabrics and plastics create new interiors to go with the body. Computers help ensure that all the parts fit together correctly.

Raymond Loewy is credited with making many advances in industrial design. He is best known for his automotive designs. The 1953 Starlight Coupe was chosen for exhibition at The Museum of Modern Art in New York because of its unique design quality. The Avanti (Figure 4.4) is a luxury sports car that was made between June 1962 and December 1963. It has such an unusual design that it was produced and sold until 1992. The Smithsonian Institution has the car on display as an outstanding example of industrial design.

Analyzing Design

1. Applying Your Skills. Compare the 1963 Avanti in Figure 4.4 with one of your favorite sports cars sold today. List any similarities or differences you find.

2. Further Challenge. Design a logo for your school, your favorite club, or your community.

3. Computer Option. Use any tools or options available on your computer software and design a logo for yourself, your family, or your school.

Fashion Design

Fashion designers plan and create clothing, hats, handbags, shoes, jewelry, and sportswear. They must know the appropriate materials to use for the articles being designed. High-fashion designers create one-of-a-kind originals that are very expensive (Figure 4.5). Fashion designers also work for manufacturers who make clothes everyone can afford. All clothing designers are supported by a team of patternmakers, cutters, tailors, and people who work in the factories that produce the clothes.

Photography

Figure 1.11 on page 15 in this book was created by Dorothea Lange. She captured the despair of a migrant mother and her children during the Great Depression.

Photojournalists are *visual reporters*. They work for newspapers and magazines and tell their stories through their photographs. Photojournalists understand design, know how to develop and print their own work, and have an eye for what is interesting to look at (Figure 4.6). Other photographers may be able to work in the comfort of a studio, but photojournalists must go where the news events are occurring.

Other careers in the field of photography include fashion, product and food photography, architectural photography, fine-art photography, and moving-picture photography for television, videos, and film.

FIGURE 4.5 Fashion designers must come up with fresh, new ideas every season. Anyone considering a career in this area must be able to work under intense pressure to meet deadlines.

FIGURE 4.6 Photojournalists covering a game.

ENVIRONMENTAL PLANNING AND DEVELOPMENT

The first environmental designers were the prehistoric cave dwellers who eventually moved out of their caves and into the countryside. They learned to build huts for protection and became the first architects. Today there are many kinds of designers who plan environmental space. Their jobs involve making homes, work space, and the surrounding landscape attractive and functional.

Architecture

An **architect** must *design buildings that are well constructed, aesthetically pleasing, and functional.*

To function properly a building must do what it was planned to do. Private houses and apartments must serve as comfortable homes for people. Office buildings, schools, and factories must also be comfortable, safe, efficient, and aesthetically pleasing. The aesthetic effect of a building is extremely important. The structure must fit the surrounding environment and improve the community. Because modern technology is so complex, architects

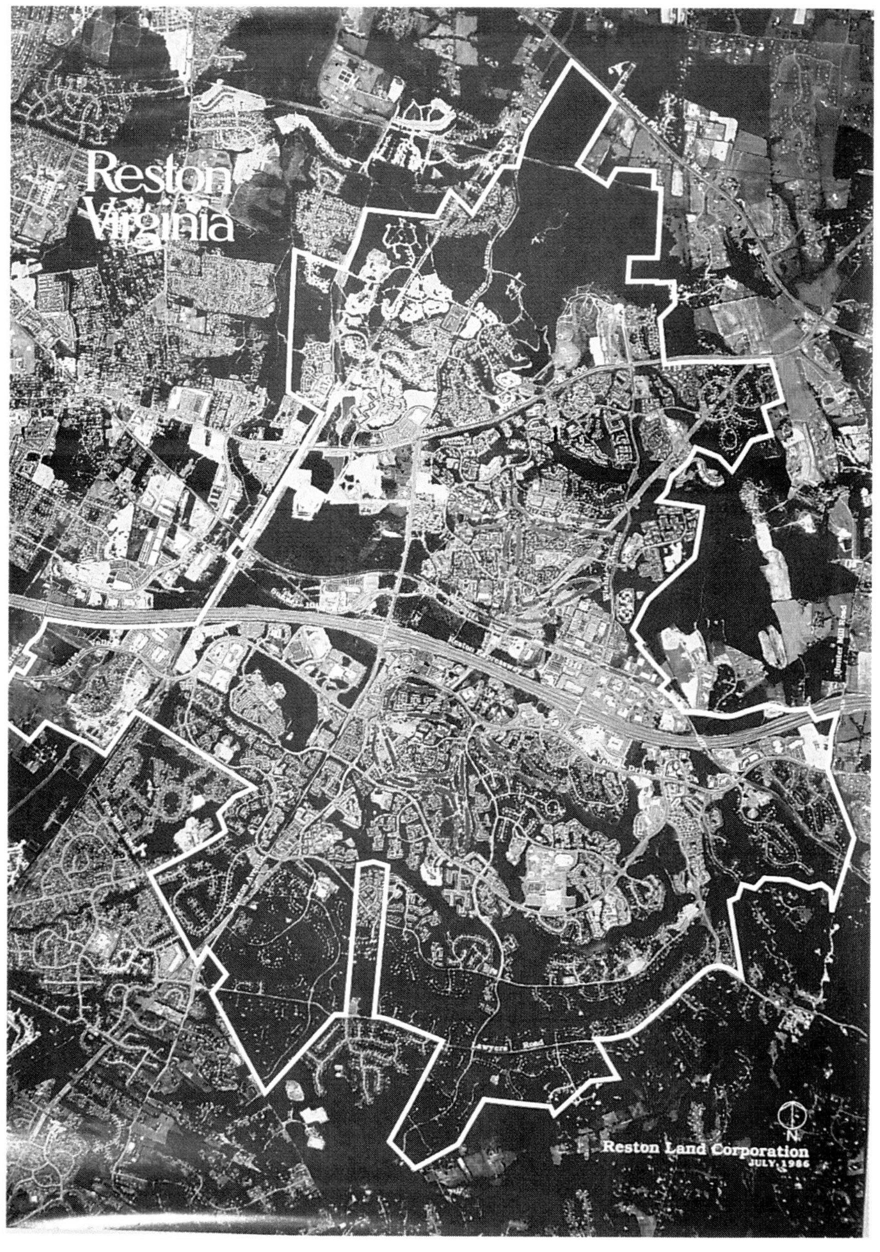

FIGURE 4.7 Reston is a planned community founded in 1962, with completion expected in the mid-1990s. About 40 percent of the total area has been planned for open space and public use. People can work, shop, attend school, and participate in a variety of leisure activities without leaving the community.

Aerial view of Reston, Virginia, a planned city. Courtesy of the Reston Land Corporation, Reston, Virginia.

FIGURE 4.8 Frederick Law Olmsted designed New York City's Central Park in 1858. He was the first person to call himself a landscape architect. He tried to create a calm, natural place in the center of America's largest city.

Courtesy of the Central Park Conservancy.

usually specialize in a particular type of building such as skyscrapers, shopping malls, or homes.

An architect must be knowledgeable about such things as building materials, ventilation, heating and cooling systems, plumbing, stairways, and elevators. In addition, an architect must be creative, be able to make accurate mechanical drawings, have a strong background in mathematics and drafting, and be able to deal with customers.

City Planning

City planners are trained as architects, but they are mainly concerned with the care and improvement of city environments. Every major American city has a city planner. This person helps control the growth and development of the city. Some of the responsibilities of the city planner are land use, urban renewal, and the development of harbors, city parks, and shopping malls. Reston, Virginia, shown in Figure 4.7, is a planned community.

Landscape Architecture

Landscape architects *design playgrounds, parks, and outdoor areas around buildings and along highways.* They work closely with architects and other planners to use and improve the natural setting so that it is easy to maintain and beautiful to look at. They create designs using flowers, plants, trees, shrubs, rivers, ponds, lakes, walks, benches, and signs, as shown in Figure 4.8.

Landscape artists work with architectural firms, government agencies, individual home owners, and facilities such as golf courses.

Interior Design

An **interior designer** *plans the design and decoration of the interior spaces in homes and offices.* Successful designers use styles and materials that blend with the architecture and that please the client.

Interior designers must understand decorating styles and materials. They must be able to look at an empty room and visualize the finished area. They must know the latest trends and developments in wallcoverings, carpets, furniture, appliances, and lamps.

Since interior designers spend as much time with clients as they do at the drawing board, they must have patience and the ability to make a client feel comfortable. Some designers work for individual home owners, while others plan and coordinate the interiors of department stores, offices, and large hotels.

Exhibit and Display Design

Exhibit designers work for trade shows, department stores, showrooms, galleries, and museums. They plan presentations of collections, temporary exhibits, and traveling shows of all types. They decide which things should be grouped together and how they should be lit.

Displays attract customers and help persuade them to buy. The display designer is an important member of the sales team. The way the designer makes the merchandise look in a store window helps draw customers into the store.

ACTIVITY Using Design for Display

1. Applying Your Skills. Think of one room in your school that looks as if it needs an interior designer. List some of the things you would like to change. Then describe how you would change them. Think in terms of color, traffic flow, furniture, and so on.

2. Further Challenge. Create a display of art objects for a display window in your school, or one of flat artwork for a bulletin board. Invent a title for your display, letter it neatly, and include it in the arrangement.

ENTERTAINMENT

The entertainment industry provides opportunities for artists with a wide range of skills. Motion pictures, TV shows, stage plays, and dance performances all use designers and artists to create the magic we see.

Animation

Animation, *the art of moving cartoons,* was invented for film, but it is used on television as well. Animation needs more visual artists than any other art-career area.

When artists create an animated film, they first select a story. They decide what styles of architecture and dress fit the story. Then they develop the story by drawing **storyboards,** *a series of still drawings that show the story's progress* (Figure 4.9). They draw approximately sixty sketches for each board. A short film needs three storyboards, and a full-length film needs more than twenty-five. The storyboards look like comic strips. They provide the outline for the development of the film.

Layout artists are responsible for the overall look of the film. Background artists paint the settings from the layout artist's sketches. To create action, animators draw the major poses of each character, then other artists fill in the many drawings required to complete each movement. Every second of film requires twenty-four drawings to make the movement look smooth.

Special Effects Design

Training for the field of special effects artist may require that you attend a school that has an art department as well as take courses in film production and technology. Many people who create the magic illusions we love in film and television have come up through the ranks. Today, however, there are

FIGURE 4.9 Artist working with storyboard.

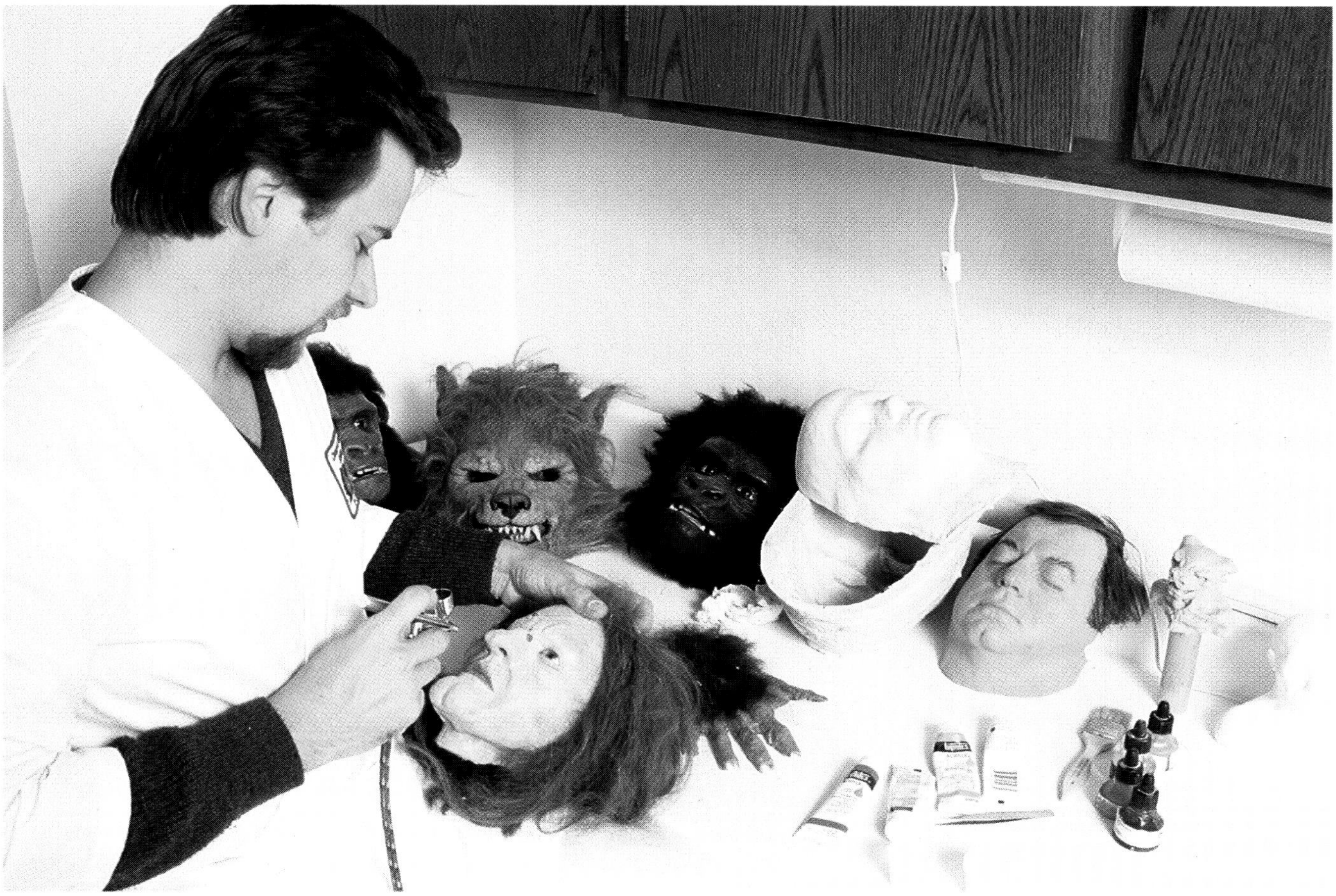

FIGURE 4.10 Special effects artist.

large universities with cinema departments that offer courses in many aspects of film production.

Special effects artists require the skills of a painter, sculptor, and engineer. They have the ability to imagine and create fantasy scenes or imaginary creatures that look real (Figure 4.10). They can make you believe you are watching a dinosaur driving a car or a battle scene in a galaxy light-years away. In their work they use papier-mâché, plaster, plastic molds, paint, makeup, trick photography, and computers.

Art Direction for the Performing Arts

In the theater the *art director* works with stage, costume, and lighting designers, as well as makeup artists and hairstylists, to bring all elements of the show together (Figure 4.11 on page 80). Art directors know art history as well as the special techniques of their craft. If a play is set in the past, the setting, furniture, costumes, and hairstyles must correctly reflect that period of history.

Art directors also coordinate all the visual elements involved in the production of a movie or a TV program. They work with set and costume designers, graphic artists, property designers, and location planners.

Critiquing Animation

1. Applying Your Skills. Watch several animated programs on television. Notice the differences in quality. Then list the programs you watched in order, from best to worst. How did the backgrounds compare? Describe the quality of the movement. Did the programs with the best movement have the best backgrounds?

2. Further Challenge. Create a character for a new animated film. Draw your character and list the specific qualities of this animated personality. Make at least three sketches showing the character in action.

FIGURE 4.11 Art directors must make backgrounds, costumes, and other visual elements work together. They coordinate the tasks of all the creative people who work in the theater.

EDUCATION AND CULTURAL ENRICHMENT

There are careers that combine an interest in art and in education. Teachers, art therapists, and people who work in museums all use their training in different ways.

Art Education

People who like to share their knowledge and skills and have a strong interest in art may choose to teach. Teachers work in elementary, middle, or high schools as well as colleges (Figure 4.12). They help students learn to make aesthetic judgments and to develop their artistic skills and talents.

Art therapists, who are also teachers, use art to help people with emotional and physical problems. They help patients change their behavior in a positive manner. They work in psychiatric hospitals, community centers, drug and alcohol treatment centers, and prisons.

Museums house collections of paintings, sculpture, crafts, costumes, books, jewelry, and artifacts from ancient cultures. People with training in art history organize, assemble, and display these collections. Others lead groups through the displays, providing information to the viewers. Some museums publish books that contain pictures of the objects in their collections. Many museums have stores that sell books and reproductions. Visiting a museum will open your eyes to art forms you may never have seen before.

Fine Arts and Crafts

Some people choose to work on their own as painters, sculptors, printmakers, weavers, jewelers, and so on. They are committed to making art. Many of these artists need a second job to help pay their living expenses. In the visual arts, as in the performing arts, the opportunities for stardom and large incomes are rare. Some artists work in the commercial art fields to supplement their income. Many teach in schools and colleges. Leo Twiggs (Figure 2.5, page 29, and Figure 5.1, page 88) is the head of the Art Department at Orangeberg State College in South Carolina. Larry Smith (Figure 6.44, page 144) teaches in a middle school in Georgia. Some, like Jacob Lawrence (Figure 5.39, page 114, and Figure 9.27, page 238), continue teaching even after they have become financially comfortable, because they feel that the ongoing interaction with art students enhances their creative thinking.

If you are driven to paint, sculpt, make prints, weave, or create other art forms and want to make a commitment to the arts, you must realize that you may have to consider taking a second job.

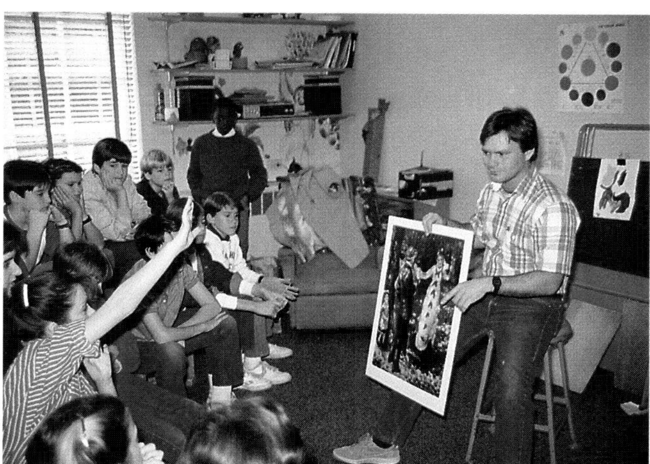

FIGURE 4.12 In addition to enjoying art, teachers must enjoy working with people and sharing their knowledge.

THINKING ABOUT AN ART CAREER

Are you suited for a career in the art world? It may be too soon for you to make a final decision about your future. However, if you have talent and art is something you enjoy, then an art career may be right for you.

Ask yourself the following questions. The more "yes" answers you give, the better your chances of being happy in the art field.

- Do you find yourself noticing things that your friends may miss, such as the colors of autumn leaves or the shapes of clouds?
- Are you curious?
- Do you like to solve problems?
- Do you keep an open mind about new and unusual forms of art?
- Do you like to draw or make things with your hands?
- Do you like to experiment with new materials and techniques?
- Do you get "lost" in an art project and lose track of time?
- When a work of art turns out wrong, are you willing to throw it out and start again?
- Do you keep at a project until it is finished?
- Can you meet deadlines?

If you decide you want a career in art, you should begin working toward that goal in high school. In the meantime, practice your skills on your own. Study the great artists. Ask teachers for advice. If you really want a career in art, it will be there for you!

Thinking About Careers

1. Applying Your Skills. Select a question from the list that is difficult for you to do. Write your own list of at least five ways in which to improve your performance in that area.

2. Further Challenge. From the visual art careers listed in this chapter, choose one that interests you. Through personal interviews or library research, write a brief biography of one person (famous or not so famous) who has had experience in this career.

ART CRITICISM IN ACTION

FIGURE 4.13 Leo and Diane Dillon. Book cover illustration for *A Wrinkle in Time*. 1979. Watercolor and pastel on paper. 48.4 × 33 cm (19 1/16 × 13″). Private collection.

FIGURE 4.14 Francisco Goya. *The Third of May, 1808.* Oil on canvas. Approximately 2.64 × 3.43 m (8′8″ × 11′2″). The Prado, Madrid, Spain.

CRITIQUING THE WORK

1. **Describe** Look at the dust jacket for *A Wrinkle in Time* in Figure 4.13. Read the credit line. List the size and media of the work. What is the purpose of this graphic design? Now look at the work and list and describe all the people, objects, and shapes you see.
2. **Analyze** What kinds of colors do you find in this cover? How many geometric shapes can you locate? Describe them. Identify the decorative patterns that you find and explain where they are located.
3. **Interpret** Can you tell into what category the book *A Wrinkle in Time* fits? What kind of idea or mood does this book cover express? Does the cover design make you curious about the story?
4. **Judge** Do you think this graphic design makes a successful book cover? Which of the three aesthetic theories would you use to judge this work?

COMPARING THE WORKS

Look at the book cover for *A Wrinkle in Time* (Figure 4.13) and the painting *The Third of May, 1808* (Figure 4.14) by Francisco Goya. Both the Dillons and Goya earned their living as artists. The Dillons work for publishers, ad agencies, and different companies that hire them to do a specific job. Goya painted portraits of nobles and others who paid him for his work.

The Dillons were paid to create this book cover. Do you think someone paid Goya to paint *The Third of May, 1808*? Why or why not?

Identify the similarities and differences you find in the two works. Look at the elements of art as well as the subject matter in your comparison. Notice the difference between the people in the Dillons' cover and the people in the Goya painting. Both works show strong contrast between black and white. How is the use of white light different? What are the themes of the two works? What, if anything, do the two works have in common?

MEET THE ARTIST

LEO AND DIANE DILLON

American, both b. 1933

Many long-married couples finish each other's sentences, but Diane and Leo Dillon finish each other's drawings. Married more than thirty-six years, they have achieved an award-winning career in graphic arts.

Their combined talents produce what they call "the third artist," one who creates something neither would do alone. They feel that the collaboration, which they compare to jazz improvisation, keeps their work fresh. When one gets stuck, the other comes up with a solution. When one gets tired, the other takes over. They never divide up an assignment. They think of each other as equals.

Before beginning an illustration for a book cover, the Dillons read the book carefully. They often research information in the book and look for additional photographs or images to help them better understand the book. One picture book the Dillons illustrated, *Ashanti to Zulu: African Traditions*, took three months to research. The artwork took only one month to complete.

The Dillons have won many awards for their graphic design. They won the Caldecott Medal two years in a row for *Why Mosquitos Buzz in People's Ears: A West African Tale* by Verna Aardema, and *Ashanti to Zulu: African Traditions* by Margaret W. Musgrove. They have also received the Hamilton King Award and the Hugo Award.

The Dillons' dedication to craftsmanship has given them more control over the reproduction of their work than most graphic artists have. Some publishers have even allowed them to design the type and layout for their cover illustrations, which is rare. The Dillons prove that it is possible to work within the limits of commercial realities and still produce art that meets the highest aesthetic standards. Their body of work is varied and impressive.

MORE PORTFOLIO IDEAS

I. Read *A Wrinkle in Time* by Madeleine L'Engle. Identify and explain the symbolic meaning of each of the people, creatures, and shapes on this book cover. Can you guess why there is a large area of black at the top of the design?

II. Select a story you have read recently. Design a book cover for the story.

CHAPTER 4 REVIEW

Building Vocabulary

On a separate sheet of paper, write the term that best matches the definition given below.

1. The way items are arranged on a page.
2. Identifying symbols.
3. One who designs the products of industry.
4. A photographer who is a visual reporter.
5. Designer of buildings that are well constructed, aesthetically pleasing, and functional.
6. Designer of playgrounds, parks, and outdoor areas around buildings, and along highways.
7. One who plans the design and decoration and design of the interior spaces in homes and offices.
8. The art of moving cartoons.
9. Series of still drawings that show a story's progress.

Reviewing Art Facts

Answer the following questions using complete sentences.

1. How did young people who wanted to be artists receive their training before there were art schools?
2. When did the field of graphic design begin? What invention made it possible?
3. List four ways in which the use of a computer can speed up the design process for a graphic artist.
4. Select a logo of a well-known product and describe how the artist has symbolized the product.
5. Name three characteristics of an editorial cartoon.
6. What elements of art do package designers use to make every package unique and visually appealing? What else must they consider?
7. What is the subject of Figure 1.11 on page 15? What do you think is the theme or message of this photograph?

Thinking Critically About Art

1. **Analyze.** Norman Rockwell earned his living as an illustrator and graphic artist. He is most famous for his magazine covers for *The Saturday Evening Post*. His work is so famous that today the term *Rockwell* is synonymous with nostalgia, as in "a Rockwell Christmas." Organize a debate in your class to discuss whether the work of Norman Rockwell is as important as the work of Andrew Wyeth and other artists from the same time period.
2. **Extend.** The Surrealist painter René Magritte has had a strong influence on commercial art. The CBS eye and a certain TV commercial are based on two of his famous works. Look for a book about his work in the library and search for the paintings that inspired the commercial. Write a paragraph taking a position that commercial artists should or should not use the works of other artists.
3. **Extend.** Contact someone who works in a career area mentioned in this chapter. Find out what kind of schooling and/or training this person needed to prepare for his or her career. Bring your findings to class.

Making Art Connections

1. **Photography.** Try out photography as a career. Decide whether you want to be a fine-art photographer such as Ansel Adams, a commercial photographer, or a photojournalist. Take a series of photos that qualify as fine art or as photojournalism. Select your best photo and mount or mat it.
2. **Literary and Art Awards.** Do some research on the Caldecott Medal, the Newbery Medal, the Hugo Award, and the Hamilton King Award. Write a report telling what each award is given for and what specific criteria are used in the judging for each award.

Claude Monet. *Poplars.* (Detail.) 1891. Oil on canvas. 81.9 × 81.6 cm (32¼ × 32⅛″). The Metropolitan Museum of Art, New York, New York. Bequest of Mrs. H. O. Havemeyer, 1929. The H. O. Havemeyer Collection.

UNIT 2

THE ELEMENTS OF ART

The next four chapters are devoted to the elements of art. These elements are *line, value, shape, form, space, color,* and *texture.*

In each chapter you will learn to recognize, identify, and describe the elements. You will also learn to use the elements to express ideas and feelings in your own works of art.

You will start by examining the elements as concrete, familiar things in your environment and then become acquainted with the more abstract, expressive qualities of the elements. After finishing a chapter, you will be able to use the element you have studied to uncover the mystery of the meaning in a work of art created by a master artist.

You will learn to recognize and use the elements one at a time. After completing Unit 2, however, you will have a full understanding of all the elements. You will have made a giant step toward learning the language of art and how to communicate your ideas.

FIGURE 5.1 This work is painted with the materials of batik, hot wax and dye, in a very untraditional manner. Twiggs must think backwards like a printmaker. First he blocks in the white lines and areas. Then he brushes on the lightest dyes. When the dye dries, he blocks in areas that must stay light and adds more dye with a brush. This process is repeated more than ten times before the work is finished.

Leo F. Twiggs. *East Wind Suite: Door*. Hugo Series. 1989. Batik: Dyes and wax resist on cotton. 61 × 51 cm (24 × 20″). Private collection.

CHAPTER 5

Line

Lines are everywhere. You write words, numbers, and symbols with the help of lines. You use lines to draw pictures. You read lines of printed words. The lines on a map help you find the best route from one place to another. Have you ever had to stand in line to get into the movies or to pay for merchandise in a store?

How many times a day do you see lines? What about the bare winter trees making lacy line patterns against the sky? Have you ever felt the lines of the grain in a piece of wood? Did you ever interrupt a line of ants parading from a piece of food to the anthill?

The photos in Figure 5.2 on the next page show just a few examples of lines in our environment. How many lines can you find in each picture? In this chapter, you will learn to use line in your artwork to create expressive qualities, to capture movement, and to control value change.

Objectives

After completing this chapter, you will be able to:

- Observe the lines in your environment more closely.
- Name the different kinds of lines.
- Tell the five ways lines can vary in appearance.
- Understand the expressive qualities or meanings of different lines in works of art.
- Use lines to make contour, gesture, and calligraphic drawings.
- Use lines to change values.

FIRST IMPRESSIONS

Look at *East Wind Suite: Door* from the Hugo Series by Leo Twiggs (Figure 5.1). Twiggs lives near the coast of South Carolina. To what event does he refer to when he calls a set of works the *Hugo Series?* Notice in the credit line that this work was painted in 1989. To what does the "East Wind" refer?

This particular work is called *Door.* Do you see a door or any part of a door? Look at the dark shape near the center of the painting. What kinds of lines outline the left side of the shape? What kind of line do you see on the right side of the shape? Why are they different? What kinds of lines define the shape of the door frame? What does that imply? What do the light horizontal lines and dark horizontal streaks suggest? How does the artist's use of line affect the mood of this painting?

Words to Know

calligraphy
contour line
crosshatching
dimension
gesture
implied lines
line
outline
static
value

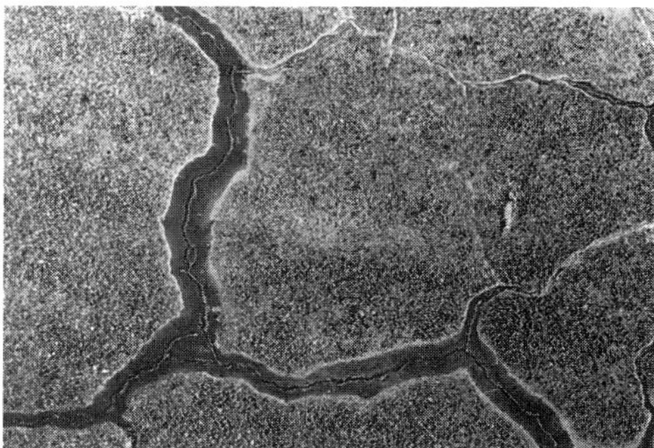

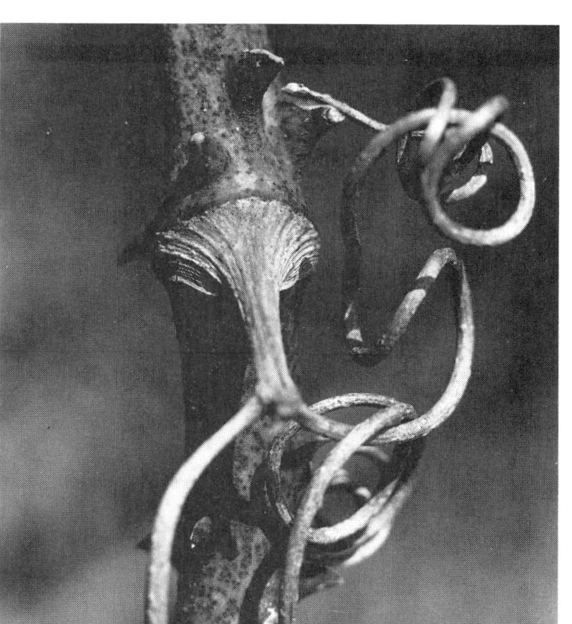

FIGURE 5.2 What lines do you see around you?

WHAT IS LINE?

In geometry, *line* is defined as an endless series of dots. In drawing, a **line** is *a mark drawn with a pointed, moving tool.* You can draw a line on paper with a pencil or scratch a line into wet clay with a stick.

Artists use lines to control your eye movement. Lines can lead your eyes into, around, and out of visual images, as in the painting in Figure 5.3.

A line has width as well as length, but the width of a line is always very small compared with its length. In fact, a line is thought of as being one-dimensional. Its one dimension is length. **Dimension** means *the amount of space an object takes up in*

LOOKING CLOSELY

FIGURE 5.3 In this painting Grant Wood uses the artificially smooth road to pull you into and through this picture story. Notice the dots of light on the top of a hill in the upper right corner. Now notice where the road begins at the top of that hill. The dark road comes leaping into the painting, and as it crests each hill it seems to get lighter. Now stop at the first house. The windows are lit with a yellow glow and there are at least three figures dressed in white standing in the roadway. What are they doing? Notice how each house that has been passed by Revere is lit and has people outside. Where the lights stop you see our hero riding into the dark ahead. Notice the house in the lower left corner. There is someone leaning out the window but the lights have not been lit yet. The smooth line of the road has pulled you into, through, and out of this enchanted memory of an American legend.

Grant Wood. *Midnight Ride of Paul Revere.* 1931. Oil on masonite. 76.2 × 101.6 cm (30 × 40″). The Metropolitan Museum of Art, New York, New York. Arthur Hoppock Hearn Fund, 1950. © Estate of Grant Wood/VAGA, New York 1987.

one direction. You will learn more about dimensions in the next chapter when you study shapes, forms, and spaces.

As mentioned in Chapter 1, line is one of the elements of art. Artists like to think of a line as the path of a dot through space. This definition is a good one to remember, because it reminds you that it takes movement to make a line. When you see a line, your eyes usually follow the movement of the line.

FIGURE 5.4 What edges do you see?

FIGURE 5.5 Student work. How have the edges on this picture been created?

Of course, the world is full of lines that were not drawn with a tool. Some thin, solid objects look like lines. Examples are flower stems, yarn, spiderwebs, and wires. These items look like lines because length is their most important dimension.

Some lines that we think we see in nature really do not exist. For instance, when you look at the edges of shapes, you think of lines. In the photo of the dogwood blossom (Figure 5.4), notice that there are no black lines around the outside of each petal. However, in a drawing of that same blossom in Figure 5.5, lines are used to show the edges of each shape. *A line that shows or creates the outer edges of a shape* is an **outline.**

Look at Figure 5.6 on the next page. The series of white dots representing car headlights creates lines that pull your eyes up into the picture. At first the dots are widely spaced, but as you follow them, they get closer and closer together until the line is almost solid. These are called *implied* lines. **Implied lines** are *a series of points that the viewer's eyes automatically connect.* Implied lines are only suggested; they are not real. A dotted line, a line of machine stitches, or a trail of wet footprints can create an implied line. A group of shapes arranged in a row can also create an implied line.

Creating Lines

1 Applying Your Skills. Draw a rough plan of your school building with a pencil and ruler. Use a felt-tip pen to make a line that marks the path you follow from room to room on an average day. Invent symbols to mark the locations of the lunchroom, math class, main entrance, principal's office, and so on.

2. Further Challenge. If you have a camera that can make a time exposure, try this experiment. Mount your camera on a tripod and record the movement of car headlights that pass your house during the night. Try different effects with a variety of lens openings and exposure times.

3. Computer Option. Choose the round Pencil tool. Do not hold down the mouse button as you draw. Simply click on it frequently to create an implied line. Choose a different drawing tool and repeat. Create a design using only implied lines.

FIGURE 5.6 Can you identify two examples of implied line in this painting?

Yvonne Jacquette. *East River Drive.* 1976. Pastel on paper. 47.6 × 58.4 cm (18¾ × 23"). The Metropolitan Museum of Art, New York, New York. Purchase. Friends of the Department gifts and matching funds from the National Endowment for the Arts, 1978.

KINDS OF LINES

There are five basic kinds of lines: vertical, horizontal, diagonal, curved, and zigzag.

Vertical lines (Figure 5.7, page 94) move straight up and down—they do not lean at all. A vertical line drawn on a piece of paper is perpendicular to the bottom edge of the paper. It is also perpendicular to the horizon (the line where earth and sky seem to meet). When you stand up straight, your body forms a vertical line.

Horizontal lines (Figure 5.8, page 94) are parallel to the horizon. They do not slant. When you lie flat on the floor, your body forms a horizontal line.

Diagonal lines (Figure 5.9, page 94) slant. Diagonals are somewhere between a vertical and a horizontal line. Diagonals look as if they are either rising or falling. Imagine you are standing straight up; then, with your body stiff, you fall to the floor. At any point during your fall, your body forms a diagonal line.

Curved lines (Figure 5.10, page 94) change direction gradually. When you draw wiggly lines, you

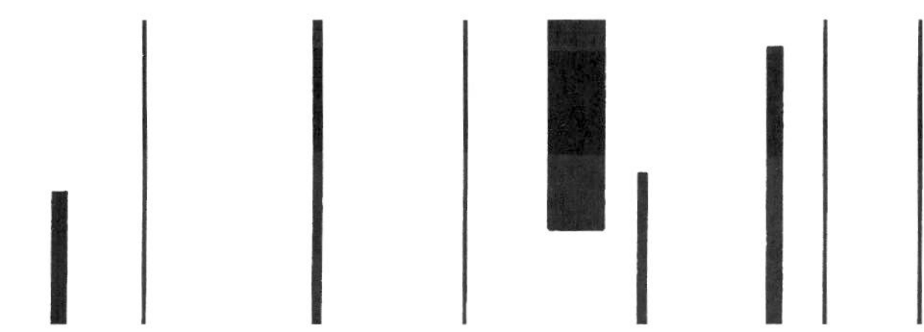

FIGURE 5.7 Vertical lines move straight up and down.

FIGURE 5.8 Horizontal lines lie parallel to the horizon.

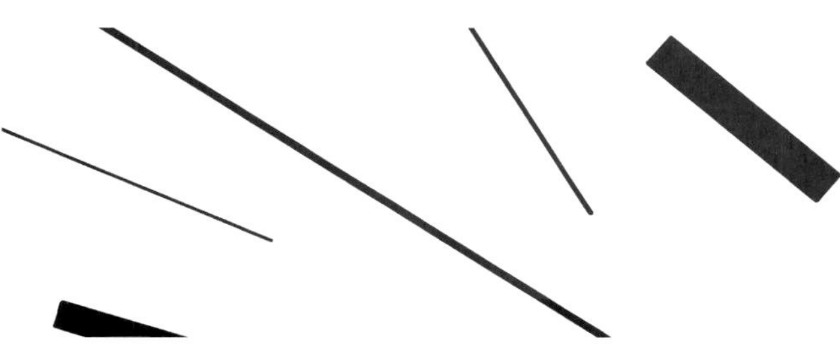

FIGURE 5.9 Diagonal lines slant.

FIGURE 5.10 Curved lines change direction gradually.

FIGURE 5.11 Zigzag lines are combinations of diagonals.

are putting together a series of curves. Other kinds of curved lines form spirals and circles.

Zigzag lines (Figure 5.11) are made from a combination of diagonal lines. The diagonals form angles and change direction suddenly.

ACTIVITY Identifying Lines

1. Applying Your Skills. Choose one of the following paintings from this chapter: Figure 5.1, 5.17, 5.22, 5.23, or 5.24. Diagram the lines of the painting. Use green for verticals, blue for horizontals, red for diagonals, and violet for curves. Place your diagram on display. Can your classmates identify the painting you represented by looking at the colors?

2. Further Challenge. Take a series of photographs to illustrate each of the five line types. Mount and label the photos with the type of line each illustrates.

3. Computer Option. Use the Line tool to create a series of drawings to illustrate each of the five line types. Vary the widths and lengths of your lines. You may also choose to vary patterns and colors. Label each drawing's line type.

LINE VARIATION

Lines vary in appearance in five major ways:

- *Length.* Lines can be long or short (Figure 5.12).
- *Width.* Lines can be wide or thin (Figure 5.13).
- *Texture.* Lines can be rough or smooth (Figure 5.14).
- *Direction.* Lines can move in any direction, such as vertical, horizontal, or diagonal (Figure 5.15).
- *Degree of curve.* Lines can curve gradually or not at all, become wavy, or form spirals (Figure 5.16).

These five variations can be combined in many, many ways. You can make long, wide lines; rough, short lines; and smooth, curved lines.

FIGURE 5.12 Lines can be long or short.

FIGURE 5.13 Lines can be wide or thin.

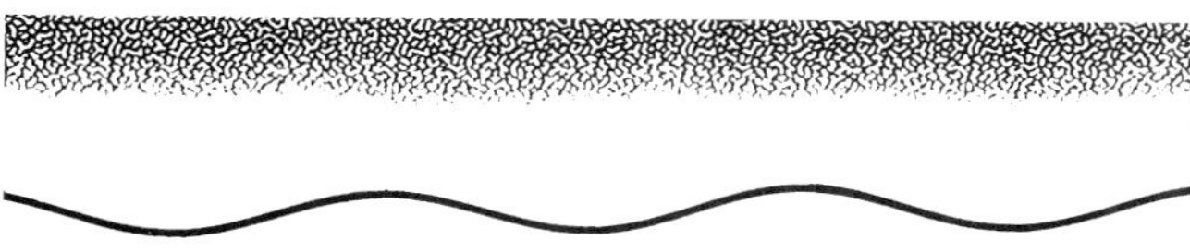

FIGURE 5.14 Lines can be rough or smooth.

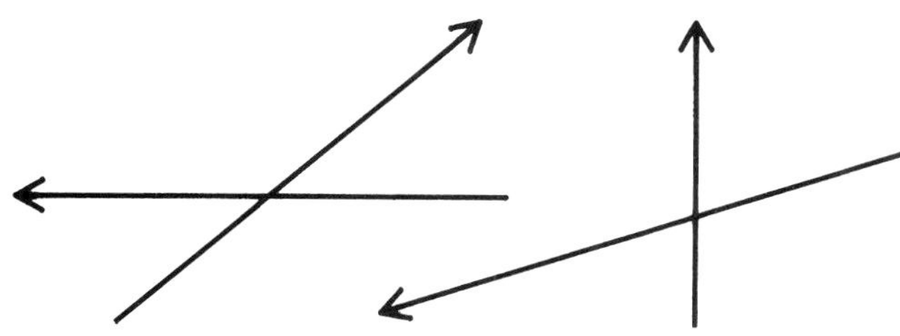

FIGURE 5.15 Lines can move in any direction.

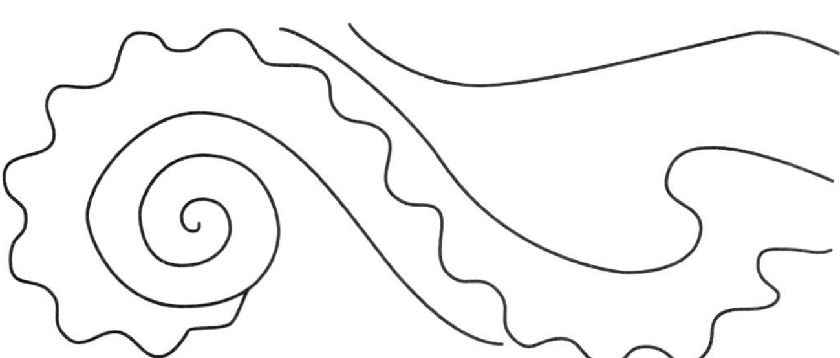

FIGURE 5.16 Lines can curve gradually, follow reverse curves, or turn inward to form spirals.

The media, tools, and surfaces used to make lines affect the way a line looks. As with the combination of various line types, a multitude of possible effects can be created.

Some common materials used by artists to make lines are graphite, chalk, crayon, ink, and paint. The material is applied by using a tool. Some tools used for making lines include pencils, markers, pens, brushes, and scissors. A line drawn with chalk on a chalkboard looks smoother than a line drawn with chalk on a sidewalk.

Artists use different tools and materials to create different types of lines. Some artists have discovered very unusual ways of using a line, as shown in Figures 5.17 and 5.18 on page 96.

Creating Varied Lines

1. Applying Your Skills. On a sheet of paper, do a close-up line drawing in pencil (Figure 5.19 on page 96) of one of the following:

- Bare twigs on the limb of a tree
- Pine needles on the end of a branch
- A patch of uncut weeds
- The cracks in one square of pavement
- The feathers of a bird
- The bark of a tree
- The bristles of a toothbrush

2. Further Challenge. Look carefully at a bicycle and think of it as an object made of thin and thick lines. Notice the difference between the thickness of the spokes and the thickness of the handlebars. On a large sheet of paper, make a pencil line drawing of the bicycle. Your drawing should use different line widths (Figure 5.20 on page 96) to show the different thicknesses of the parts.

3. Computer Option. Use the Line, Pencil, and Brush tools to create a wide variety of lines. Make line variations that are long, short, wide, thin, rough, smooth, vertical, horizontal, diagonal, and curved.

FIGURE 5.17 When Rouault was a boy he was apprenticed to a maker of stained glass. The thick black lines surrounding bright colors in his paintings remind the viewer of stained-glass windows.

Georges Rouault. *Christ and the Apostles.* 1937–38. Oil on canvas. 64.3 × 99.4 cm (25¼ × 39⅛″). The Metropolitan Museum of Art, New York, New York. The Jacques and Natasha Gelman Collection.

FIGURE 5.18 How many different line directions and line variations can you find in Curnoe's painting?

Greg Curnoe. *Mariposa 10 Speed.* 1973. Watercolor over graphite on paper. 101.1 × 181.4 cm (39⅜ × 71⅖″). National Gallery of Canada, Ottawa, Canada. © Estate of Greg Curnoe/VAGA, New York 1994.

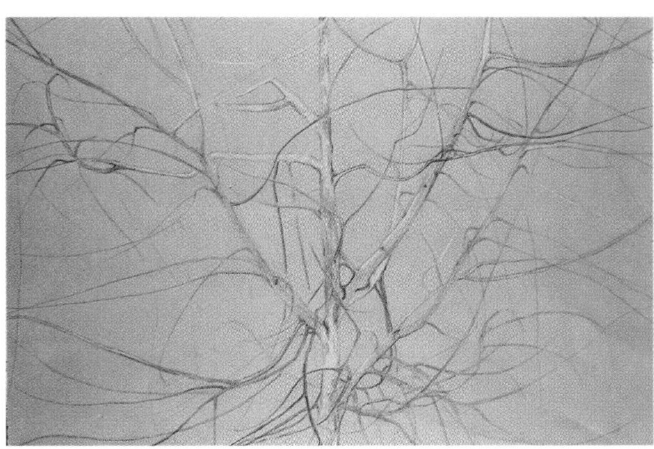

FIGURE 5.19 Student work. Close-up line drawing.

FIGURE 5.20 Student work. Using thin and thick lines.

WHAT DIFFERENT LINES EXPRESS

Depending on its direction, a line can communicate, or express, different ideas or feelings. This is why lines are an important part in the language of art. Vertical lines can make certain objects look taller. For example, vertical lines on wallpaper can make low ceilings seem higher. Clothing designers use vertical lines to make short people look taller and heavy people look thinner.

Vertical lines are **static**, or *inactive*. They appear to be at rest. For this reason, they express stability. Vertical lines can also give an impression of dignity, poise, stiffness, and formality, as shown in Figure 5.21.

Horizontal lines are also static. They express feelings of peace, rest, quiet, and stability, as in Figure 5.22, page 98. Horizontal lines make you feel content, relaxed, and calm. Modern, casual furniture uses horizontal lines to create a soft, comfortable look.

Unlike vertical and horizontal lines, diagonal and zigzag lines are *active* lines. They communicate action and movement because they seem to be pulled one way or the other. They are not at rest.

Diagonals express instability, tension, activity, and excitement, as shown in Figure 5.23, page 98. Since they can appear to be either falling or rising, they sometimes make a viewer feel uncomfortable. Artists use them to add tension or to create an exciting mood. However, when two diagonals meet and seem to support each other, as in the roof of a house, they appear more stable.

FIGURE 5.21 What do the lines tell you about the sound of the chant that this painting represents? Is it loud and wild, or quiet and dignified? How many different line directions can you find? What is the predominant line movement? How does that affect the mood of this work? How many line variations can you find? What do you think the different lines represent?

Dan Namingha. *Blessing Rain Chant*. 1992. Acrylic on canvas. 198 × 305 cm (78 × 120″). Niman Fine Art, Santa Fe, New Mexico.

FIGURE 5.22 Strong horizontal lines create a sense of calm on this empty street. As you look at this painting, you get the feeling that everyone is sleeping peacefully. How many real and how many implied horizontal lines can you find in this painting?

Edward Hopper. *Early Sunday Morning.* 1930. Oil on canvas. 89.2 × 152.4 cm (35 × 60″). Collection of Whitney Museum of American Art, New York, New York.

Zigzag lines create confusion. They are extremely active and evoke feelings of excitement and nervousness, as in Figure 5.24. The degree of intensity is indicated by the direction of the zigzag. Zigzags that move horizontally, such as those across the top of a picket fence, are less active than the irregular zigzags of a streak of lightning.

Because curved lines change direction, they too express some activity. How much activity they express depends on the type and direction of the curve. The less active the curve, the calmer the feeling. Whatever the amount of activity, all curved lines are graceful. Curved lines are often used in interior decoration to suggest a feeling of luxury, as in Figure 5.25, page 100. Spiral curves wind around a central point. They are hypnotic and draw the eye to their center.

FIGURE 5.23 In this print every line that should be static is diagonal. Look at the window, the lamp, the rug, the floor planks, and the fiddler's bench. The diagonal lines fill the work with a sense of excitement. Not only the people but also every corner of the room seems to be alive and dancing to the music of the fiddler.

Thomas Hart Benton. *I Got a Girl on Sourwood Mountain.* 1938. Lithograph. 31.7 × 23.4 cm (12½ × 9¼″). Courtesy of the Library of Congress, Washington, D.C. © T. H. Benton and R. P. Benton Testamentary Trusts/VAGA, New York 1994.

FIGURE 5.24 Sheeler uses diagonal lines to indicate the houses are sliding into the flood waters. Notice how the houses in the background are beginning to lean.

Charles Sheeler. *Catastrophe No. 2.* 1944. Tempera on panel. 43.2 × 35.5 cm (17 × 14″). Wichita Art Museum, Wichita, Kansas. The Roland P. Murdock Collection.

Using Lines Expressively

1. Applying Your Skills. Choose two words from the following list:

swimming	burning	praying
rocking	flowing	jumping
marching	running	growing
dancing	crawling	laughing
wagging	writing	flying

On separate sheets of paper, illustrate the words you have chosen by using line movement only (see Figure 5.26 on page 101). Do not draw objects. Choose the medium you think will work best. When you have finished, write the word on the back of each paper. Ask your friends to look at the lines and guess which words you have illustrated.

2. Further Challenge. Make two line drawings of crowded city buildings. Use static lines in one to express calm stability. Use active lines in the other to express the rush and confusion of a crowded city. Choose the medium you think is most effective for depicting each cityscape.(See Figure 5.27 on page 101.)

3. Computer Option. Make two drawings using lines, not objects. Let one drawing illustrate quiet, calm piano music, and let the other illustrate music produced by the loudest rock group you can imagine.

FIGURE 5.25 Many of the decorative elements in this luxurious bedroom seem to swirl with curves. How do you think you would feel living in a room like this? Would you be comfortable?

Italian, Venice. Bedroom from the Sagredo Palace. c. 1725–35. The Metropolitan Museum of Art. New York, New York. Rogers Fund, 1906.

CONTOUR DRAWING

A **contour line** *defines the edges and surface ridges of an object.* A contour line also creates a boundary separating one area from another. Contour drawing will add to your drawing skills as well as to your ability to observe and understand objects. See the examples in Figure 5.28 on page 101 and in 5.29 on page 102.

When you are drawing contours, do not lift the pencil from the paper. Let your eyes follow the contour of the object you are drawing, and move your pencil at the same speed as your eyes. The line should be continuous. Draw the line slowly and with care. Concentrate in order to draw accurately. See the Technique Tip on page 349 in the Handbook for help in making contour drawings.

Using Contour Lines

1. Applying Your Skills. Using a felt-tip or ballpoint pen, make a series of five contour drawings of your hand or bare foot on a single sheet of paper. You can indicate roundness by showing the curve of the wrinkles on your fingers or toes. Change the position of your hand or foot for each drawing. Then, on a second sheet of paper, do a contour drawing of your hand or foot from memory only.

2. Further Challenge. Use a water-based felt-tip or ballpoint pen and one sheet of paper to make a series of five contour drawings of a single object, such as a pair of scissors, a key, a shoe, or a hairbrush. Change the position of the object for each drawing. Then, on a new sheet of paper, draw the object from memory.

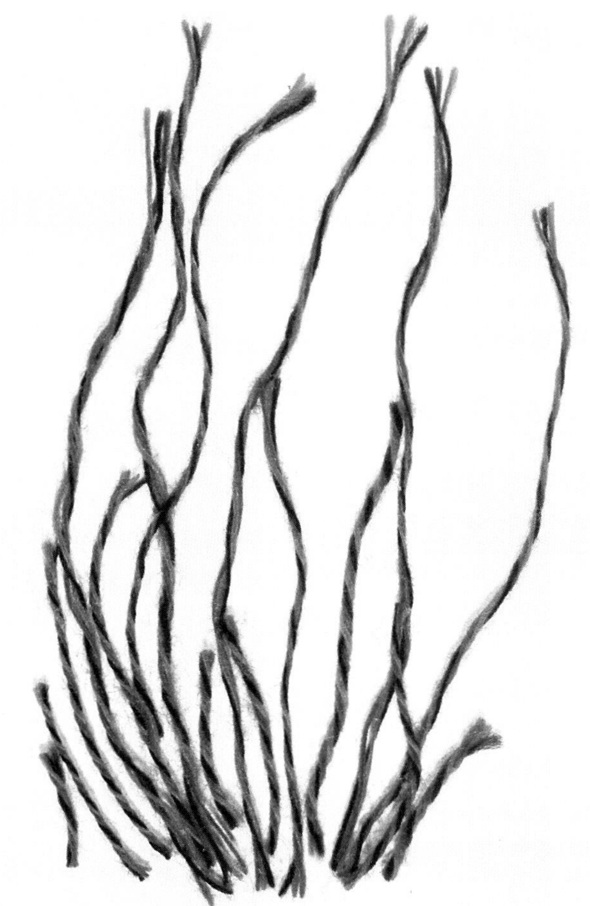

FIGURE 5.26 Student art. Which word fits this art?

FIGURE 5.28 Andrews indicates that this scholar is concentrating deeply by accenting the head with lines to indicate the wrinkles of thought. He leaves the rest of the scene, except for the book, very simple.

Benny Andrews. *The Scholar*. 1974. Pen and ink on paper. 30 × 23 cm (12 × 9″). Private collection.

FIGURE 5.27 Student art. What contrasting moods do these two scenes express?

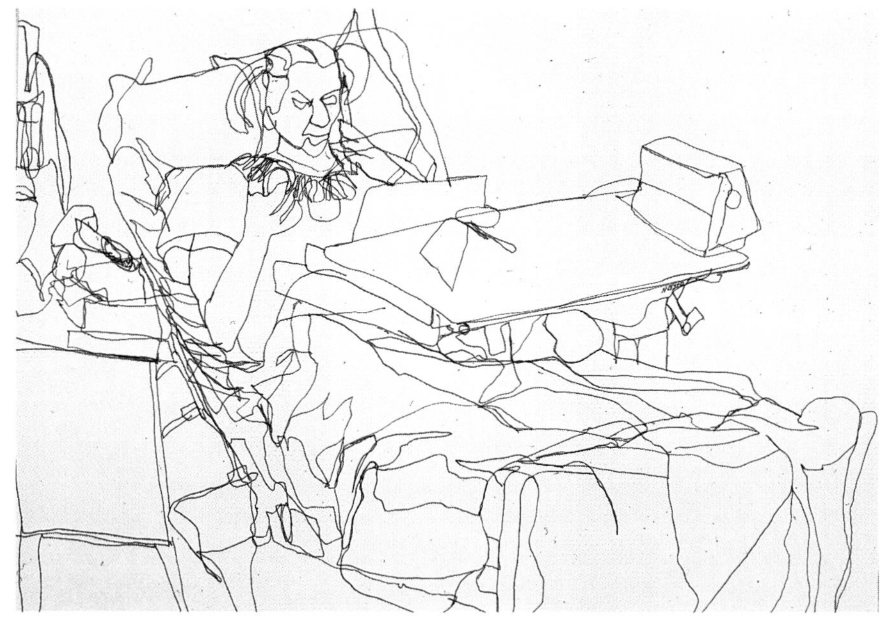

FIGURE 5.29 Student work. Notice how the line flows through this hospital scene. Look at the difference between the busy zigzag lines that describe the wrinkles in the sheet and the few lines that define the person's face.

GESTURE DRAWING

A **gesture** is *an expressive movement.* The purpose of drawing gestures is to capture the feeling of motion. A gesture drawing does not use a lot of detail (Figure 5.30).

Lines showing gestures are quickly drawn. They should be sketched freely and loosely, almost in a reckless manner in order to capture movement. Unlike contours, they represent the interior of an object. Your drawing of gestures may look like scribbles at first, but this is acceptable. Concentrate on showing position and movement.

Capturing Motion

1. Applying Your Skills. Make a series of gesture drawings. (See the Technique Tip on page 349 in the Handbook.) Classmates should take turns posing for

FIGURE 5.30 Tintoretto describes the gesture and bulk of this figure with just a few rough lines. You can sense the movement of the figure through the looseness of the quickly drawn lines.

Jacopo Tintoretto. *Standing Youth with His Arm Raised, Seen from Behind.* Black chalk on laid paper. 36.3 × 21.9 cm (14¼ × 8⅝"). National Gallery of Art, Washington, D.C. Ailsa Mellon Bruce Fund.

FIGURE 5.31 Student work. Gesture drawing.

one another. Start with thirty-second poses. Shorten the time by five seconds for each pose until you are down to ten seconds. Since the poses are so short, ask the model to be active. Have her or him twist, turn, bend, and kick, trying to avoid doing the same thing twice. (See Figure 5.31.)

2. Further Challenge. Play "musical gestures." You will need a record or tape player and a recording of your favorite music. Choose at least two people to be models and one to be a disc jockey. The DJ is in charge of starting and stopping the music and must face away from the models. When the music starts, the models dance; when it stops, the models freeze. As soon as the music stops, the artists draw the models in the positions in which they have frozen, using the same sheet of paper. The DJ may let a pose last from ten to thirty seconds. When the music starts again, the artists stop drawing, and the models resume dancing. This exercise can be repeated as many times as desired. Change crayon or pen color with each pose and feel free to overlap figures.

3. Computer Option. Choose a round, medium-size Brush or Pencil tool. Sit at the computer station, turn sideways, and look at other students who are modeling for gesture drawing. They will be changing positions every twenty or thirty seconds. Try to capture the feeling of motion, not detail. Change color each time the model changes positions. Some of your drawings will overlap.

CALLIGRAPHIC DRAWING

The word **calligraphy** means *beautiful handwriting.* Calligraphy is often thought of in connection with Oriental writing and art. In China and Japan, calligraphy is used to form *characters* that Oriental writers use in much the same way we use the alphabet. Chinese and Japanese characters are more like pictures, however. They can represent a complete idea, object, or verbal sound. They are more than just a letter. The Chinese and Japanese use the same types of calligraphic lines and brushstrokes in their paintings (Figure 5.32, page 104). In fact, in the Chinese language, the words *writing* and *painting* are represented by the same character.

Calligraphic lines are usually made with brushstrokes that change from thin to thick in one stroke. To make a very thin line, use the tip of the brush. As you press on the brush and more of it touches the paper, the line becomes wider. (See the Technique Tip 3 on page 349 in the Handbook.)

Thick-to-Thin Lines

1. Applying Your Skills. Practice making calligraphic lines with ink or watercolor paint. Use round, pointed brushes, both thin and thick. Also, try bamboo brushes.

LOOKING CLOSELY

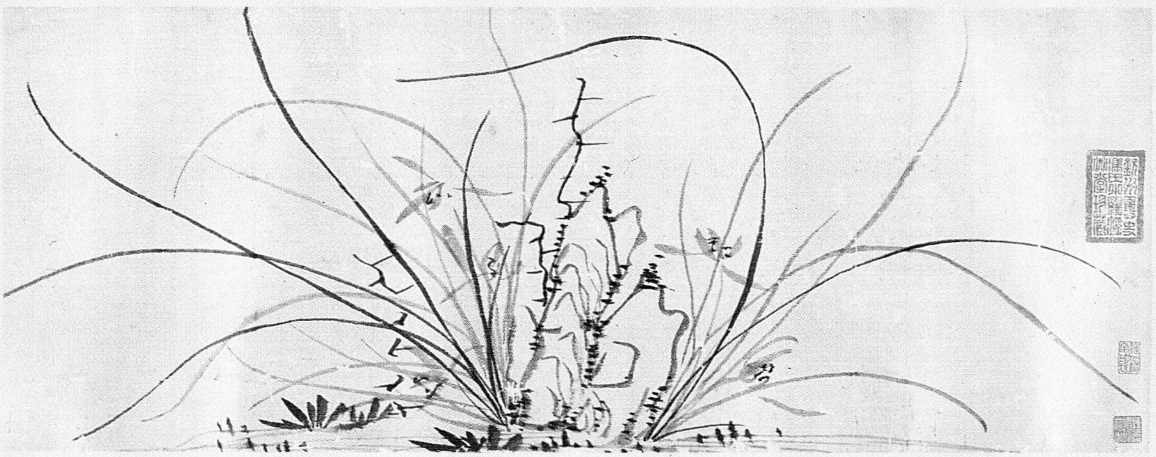

FIGURE 5.32 Gu Mei was a famous singer, poet, and painter of landscapes and ink orchids. She created this long handscroll containing three different sections depicting orchids and rocks. Notice how the long curving lines have been made with one brushstroke. Where else can you find lines that seem to have been painted with one brushstroke? Notice how the calligraphic Chinese writing is an integral part of the design.

Gu Mei. *Orchids and Rocks.* 1644. Ming dynasty. Detail of handscroll. Ink on paper. 27 × 170.8 cm (10⅝ × 67¼"). Arthur M. Sackler Gallery, Smithsonian Institution, Washington, D.C. Arthur M. Sackler Collection.

2. Further Challenge. Use a watercolor brush and ink or watercolor paint to make a series of five calligraphic studies of one natural object, such as a leaf or vegetable (Figure 5.33).

3. Computer Option. Research either Egyptian hieroglyphics or Southwestern pictographs to gain information about "picture writing." Create a picture writing by making up your own symbols. Use any computer tools and options available. Remember that the Cut and Paste options are helpful when you want to repeat a symbol without redrawing it.

FIGURE 5.33 Student work. A drawing made with calligraphic lines.

LINE AND VALUE

Value is *the art element that describes the darkness or lightness of an object.* Value depends on how much light a surface reflects. A surface has a dark value if it reflects little light. It has a light value if it reflects a lot of light. Because value is closely related to the way every element and principle of art works, it will be mentioned throughout *ArtTalk.*

Every time you make a pencil mark on a piece of white paper, you are creating a line with a certain value. The harder you press, the darker the value. A series of closely placed lines can create areas of dark value. The lines may be parallel or they may cross one another. **Crosshatching** is *the technique of using crossed lines for shading.* You will learn more about crosshatching in Chapter 6.

The values that line groups create depend on many things: the number of lines, the size of the spaces between the lines, the media, and the tools. A soft pencil (2B, 4B) makes a wide, dark line. A hard pencil (2H, 4H) makes a thin, gray line. A crayon stroked over a rough surface makes a broken line. A crayon stroked over smooth paper makes a solid line.

Look at the Dürer etching in Figure 6.23 on page 134. Use a magnifying glass to study the way Dürer has used a variety of line combinations to create dark and light values. What method did he use in the lightest areas? How did he create the darkest values? How many different kinds of line combinations can you find? How many different uses does Dürer make of line in this one work?

Using Line to Create Value

1. Applying Your Skills. Create a crosshatched value scale using a medium HB pencil on white paper. First, draw a long, thin rectangle using a ruler. Divide the rectangle into seven parts. Leave the section on the far left blank. The section on the far right should be as black as you can make it. Crosshatch the middle section so that it is a middle gray. Now crosshatch the other squares so the values move in gradual steps from white to black.

FIGURE 5.34 Student work. Using lines to create values.

2. Further Challenge. Fold a small sheet of white drawing paper into nine squares. In each square use a different combination of parallel or crosshatched lines to create a different value (Figure 5.34). Try a variety of pencils, from hard 2H to soft 4B lead. Try quill pens, ballpoint pens, and felt-tip pens. Think of some other tools and materials to use.

3. Computer Option. Use the Line tool to draw three diagonal lines from screen edge to screen edge. This will divide your screen into six or seven sections. Fill each section with lines. Vary the spacing of the lines by placing them close together in one section and farther apart in another. Lines can be crosshatched. You can choose the Patterns palette and fill the sections by using the Fill Bucket tool or create your own pattern. Use only black and white. Notice that the value of the area darkens as lines are placed close together and lightens when lines are farther apart.

STUDIO LESSON: YARN PAINTING

FIGURE 5.35 Artist unknown. Huichol Indian, Santa Caterina, Jalisco, Mexico. *Sacrifice to the Mother of the Eagles.* 1991. Braided yarn embedded in vegetable wax on wood. 40 × 49.5 cm (15¾ × 19½"). Private collection.

Supplies

- Pencil and sketchbook
- Heavy cardboard
- Scissors and white glue
- Yarns of various colors and textures
- Toothpicks or paper clips
- Damp sponge and towels

A Huichol Indian from Mexico created the yarn painting shown in Figure 5.35. Although the Huichol do not sign their artwork, other artists in the area can identify the creator of the work by examining the drawing style and the kinds of materials used by the artist. Notice the simple drawing style and how the braided yarn is laid in careful rows within the outlined figures. The colors of the yarn are bright and clear, and the picture tells a story. This work was created as an offering to please a goddess in the hope that she would send much-needed rain for the crops. The Mother of the Eagles in the center of the work can be identified by her wings. There are other symbols in the picture. Can you find them?

This work has been made with great care. Notice that the entire surface of the work was covered and that each figure was given a contrasting border to define the shape.

Select a theme for your yarn painting and decide on the symbol you will include. Design and create the painting using realistic or nonobjective shapes. After gluing yarn to the outlines of the shapes, fill in the shapes with strands of yarn. Use a variety of line directions, colors, and textures. Cover the entire surface so that no board shows.

FOCUSING

Study the Huichol yarn painting. Read the information about the work and discuss the meaning of the symbols in the painting. Notice that the outlines of the figures, flowers, candles, and rain lines were made first. Then study how the artist used lines of yarn to fill in the outlines.

CREATING

Decide whether you want to create a realistic or nonobjective design. Sketch several ideas for your yarn painting in your sketchbook. Keep the design simple, using just a few large shapes. Do not go into detail. Select your best design and draw it on the cardboard.

Plan the colors and types of yarn you will use. Collect all the materials you will need, including the yarn. Before you start gluing, cover your work space with newspaper and find a flat surface on which your work can be stored to dry.

Outline the major shapes on the cardboard by squeezing a thin line of glue over your pencil line and pressing one strand into the glue.

Spread the glue over the area inside the outline. Use the nozzle as a spreader. Then press the yarn firmly into the glue with toothpicks or unbent paper clips. Fill each area with sets of touching parallel strands. One shape may be filled with a vertical pattern. Other shapes may be filled with horizontal lines or with a spiral. Do not leave any spaces between the yarn lines. Be sure to cover the entire surface of the cardboard.

If your fingers or your pressing tools get sticky, use the damp sponge to clean off the glue. Between sessions, be sure to store the work on a flat surface, uncovered, so nothing sticks to the glue.

Mount or mat the finished work for display. (See Technique Tip 27 on page 363 in the Handbook.)

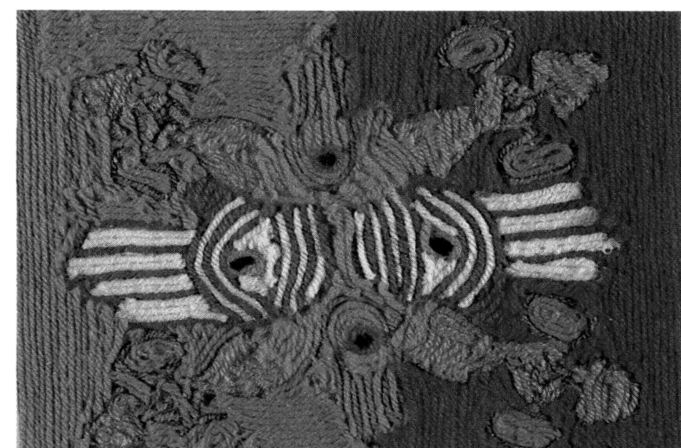

FIGURE 5.35A Student work.

CRITIQUING

Describe What kind of shapes did you choose for your design, realistic or nonobjective? Did the Huichol yarn painting influence your decision? How did you prepare your finished work for display?

Analyze Did you create outlines around the shapes? Describe the line directions you used to fill in the shapes and the spaces between them. Which yarn colors and textures did you use for the outlines, the shapes, and the background? Did you cover the entire surface of the board?

Interpret Did you select a realistic or a nonobjective theme? How do the line directions, the outlines, the colors, and the yarn textures affect the mood? Give your work a title.

Judge Is your work successful? Did the line directions, the outlines, the colors, and the yarn textures create the effect you planned? Is there anything you would change to make the work more successful? Which aesthetic theory fits your work?

STUDIO LESSON: CONTOUR WIRE SCULPTURE

FIGURE 5.36 Alexander Calder. *Varese.* 1931. Wire. 34.2 × 34.9 × 31.1 cm (13½ × 13¾ × 12¼"). Whitney Museum of American Art, New York, New York.

As a child, Alexander Calder made spiral-wire jewelry for his sister's dolls. Both his parents were artists, and Calder grew up in their studios. The path that led to his invention of the mobile sculpture and wire-line sculptures such as *Varese* (Figure 5.36) began in this family atmosphere of creativity.

While attending the Art Students' League in New York City, Calder and his fellow classmates would go out into the streets and rapidly sketch people as they passed by. He was well known for his skill in capturing a sense of movement with a single, unbroken line. In these simple contour drawings, he captured the essential characteristics of his subjects.

Eventually Calder began to experiment with wire sculptures. His new figures became three-dimensional forms drawn in space by wire lines. He made animals inspired by his childhood fascination with the circus, and he created portraits of people such as *Varese*. Many of his wire drawings were humorous, and each was interesting to look at from every angle.

Try your hand at wire sculpture and discover what kind of lively and interesting three-dimensional figure you can create.

Design and create a three-dimensional sculpture that defines space and shape through the movement of a wire line through space. Make this three-dimensional contour wire sculpture look interesting from every point of view. Base this sculpture on your own series of contour drawings of a single object. Prepare your finished work for display.

Supplies

- Sketchbook and pencil
- Needle-nose pliers
- Wire cutter
- Pliable wire

Optional:

- Small block of wood
- Staple gun or staple nail and hammer
- String

SAFETY NOTE

Wear safety glasses when working with long pieces of wire.

FIGURE 5.36A Student work.

FOCUSING

Brainstorm with classmates to identify objects for this project. Some possibilities are a houseplant, a bicycle, an animal, a person, or a head. Choose something that is interesting to you and that you can observe. Do not use a photograph. Study the photos of Calder's wire sculpture. Notice how the wire is used.

CREATING

Make a series of three or more contour studies of the object. Make each drawing from a different point of view.

Collect your materials and experiment with some scrap wire. Practice using the tools to bend, twist, loop, and cut the wire so that you understand the way the wire behaves.

Create your wire sculpture based on the drawings you have made. As you work, keep turning the sculpture so that every side looks interesting.

To prepare your work for display, you may staple or nail it to a small block of wood, hang it with string from a support, or invent your own method to show the finished piece.

CRITIQUING

Describe Name the object you chose as the subject of your wire sculpture. How many contour line drawings of the object did you make? List the contour line variations you used to create the outlines and ridges of your sculpture. How did you prepare your finished work for display?

Analyze Do the lines of your work follow the contours and ridges of the object you chose? Is the work interesting from every side and angle?

Interpret What kind of mood is created by the use of line in three-dimensional space? Describe the difference between the look of the two-dimensional contour line drawings and the three-dimensional wire sculpture. Give your work a title.

Judge Have you created a contour sculpture that is three-dimensional and interesting from all sides and angles? Is your work successful? Is there anything you would change to make the work more successful? Which aesthetic theory would be the best to judge your work?

STUDIO LESSON: IMAGINATION LANDSCAPE

FIGURE 5.37 Carolyn Clive. *Amplitude.* 1987. Oil paint used with stencil brush and torn paper stencil on paper, 61 × 46 cm (24 × 18″). Collection of the artist.

Supplies

- Sketchbook
- Oil pastels
- Large sheet of white paper
- Paper towels
- Newspaper for tearing into stencils
- Scissors (optional)

Look at *Amplitude* (Figure 5.37) and turn your imagination loose. What might this landscape be? Do you see misty mountains? Are there surging waves and an angry sky? What does the sphere in the rectangle represent, and how has the artist used line to create this landscape?

Carolyn Clive was driving through the Georgia countryside one bleak fall day. "The leaves had fallen and the crops were in. I looked out over the land and told myself, 'I don't know what I'm going to do, but I'm going to capture the spirit of this land.' "

Clive developed her own stenciling technique for working with oil paints and used line and value changes to create her abstract landscape. Notice how she has combined geometric shapes with flowing, overlapping waves of color. Observe how she has brought parts of the design outside the image area to provide added interest.

Experiment with Clive's stenciling technique to capture the spirit of the land and then create your own imaginary landscape.

Use torn paper stencils to form the edges of land masses. After you have made the land-mass edges, imagine what objects and living things belong in this landscape. Add these to your scene.

FOCUSING

Study the stencil painting by Carolyn Clive. Notice how the edges of the shapes are dark on one side and light on the other. This was done by holding a stencil in place and pulling oil color gently from the edge of the stencil into the shape with a stippling brush.

CREATING

First, practice the following technique in your sketchbook. Tear a 9 × 6 inch (23 × 15 cm) piece of newspaper to create a rough, curving edge that will be your stencil. Draw a heavy line of oil pastel along the rough edge of the stencil. With one hand, hold the stencil firmly on a page of your sketchbook. With the other hand, use a piece of paper towel to pull the color from the stencil onto paper. Experiment with different techniques until you feel comfortable. Try mixing colors. Compare your results with those of your classmates. Discuss the different effects you have created. For variety, try cutting the edge of your stencil with scissors.

Based on your findings from the experiments, make some rough plans in your sketchbook for the final work. Choose your best idea. Now you are ready to create your landscape.

Using newspaper or other scratch paper, tear or cut stencils for your finished work. Choose the colors you will use. In order to keep from smudging the pastel lines, work from the top of your page toward the bottom edge. Draw a very heavy line of oil pastel along the edge of your first stencil. Hold the stencil firmly in place and pull the oil pastel color from the stencil onto the large sheet of paper. Repeat this step until you have created the land masses you want.

FIGURE 5.37A Student work.

Study this work and imagine what objects and living creatures belong in your landscape. Add them using oil pastels. Give your work a title. Mount or mat your finished work for display.

CRITIQUING

Describe Tell what kind of a landscape you have created. What creatures and objects have you added to the land masses?

Analyze How did you create your stencils? What kinds of lines make up the edges of your land masses? How did the technique you used to pull the color from the stencil to the paper affect the look of your work?

Interpret Describe the mood of your imagination landscape. Did the stencil technique you used contribute to the mood?

Judge Which aesthetic theory would be best to judge your work? Do you think this work is successful? Is there anything you would change to make it more successful?

STUDIO LESSON: DRAWING EXPRESSING MOVEMENT

FIGURE 5.38 William H. Johnson. *Jitterbugs IV.* 1939–40. Gouache and pen and ink with pencil on paper, 32.7 × 26.9 cm ($12\frac{7}{8} \times 10\frac{9}{16}$″). National Museum of American Art, Smithsonian Institution, Washington, D.C. Gift of the Harmon Foundation.

Supplies

- Sketchbook, pencil, and eraser
- Large sheet of white paper
- Colored pencils or crayons
- Watercolor paints
- Variety of watercolor brushes

In *Jitterbugs IV* (Figure 5.38), William H. Johnson used diagonal lines to provide high-action, energetic movement. Although his dancers are abstract, simple figures, they *move.* For contrast he used vertical and horizontal lines to show stable, unmoving objects.

Johnson is considered a major African-American artist. He integrated the customs and cultures of New York, Europe, and North Africa into his African-American heritage, finally settling on the abstract forms and limited color palette you see here. In *Jitterbugs IV* Johnson used line and simple shapes to show the expressive movements of the jitterbug dance craze of the 1940s.

Create a drawing that expresses the linear movement of people involved in energetic action. Emphasize the lines that express movement. Base the figures on the gesture drawings you made while observing real people in action. If you wish, you may create contrast between the active figures and the background by using static lines for the background objects.

FOCUSING

Study the painting by William H. Johnson. Notice how he has represented two dancing people with a few geometric shapes and many diagonal lines. Can you find the floor, the drum, and the drumsticks? Observe how the lines of the floor under the dancers are diagonal, while the rest of the floor remains vertical and static.

CREATING

Think of an energetic activity you could represent using active lines. Ask a friend to act out the movement of the activity so that you can make several different gesture drawings in your sketchbook.

Study your sketches. Decide which line directions will best express the movement of the activity. Will you use diagonals and zigzags, or curved lines? Simplify the figures in your gesture drawings using the lines you have chosen.

Decide which objects you will use for the background. Remember that you may use static lines for these objects. Sketch your finished plan on white paper.

Go over the lines of your composition with colored pencils or crayons. Press hard to make the colors bright. Vary the lines. Emphasize the action lines by drawing them wide and using bold colors. Make the other lines thinner with softer colors.

Color the shapes between the lines and the spaces around the figures with watercolor paints. (See Technique Tip 12 on page 353 in the Handbook for using watercolors.) Mount or mat the finished work for display.

FIGURE 5.38A Student work.

CRITIQUING

Describe Which energetic action did you choose as the subject of your drawing? Did you make gesture drawings of a real person acting out that movement? How many gesture drawings did you make? How many figures did you put in your finished work? Did you use any objects for the background?

Analyze Which line directions did you choose to express the action? Which line directions did you choose for the background objects? Which lines did you emphasize and how did you emphasize them?

Interpret Does your work express the action you were trying to capture? Give your work an expressive title. Do not use the name of the action your figures are doing.

Judge Have you created a drawing that expresses the movement of people involved in energetic action? Is there anything you would change to make the work more successful? Which aesthetic theory would be best to judge this work?

ART CRITICISM IN ACTION

FIGURE 5.39 Jacob Lawrence. *Study for the Munich Olympic Games Poster.* 1971. Gouache on paper. 90.1 × 68.6 cm (35 ½ × 27″). Seattle Art Museum, Seattle, Washington. Purchased with funds from P.O.N.C.H.O.

FIGURE 5.40 Jacques Louis David. *Death of Socrates*. 1787. Oil on canvas. 129.5 × 196.2 cm (51 × 77¼″). The Metropolitan Museum of Art, New York, New York. Wolfe Fund, 1931. Catharine Lorillard Wolfe Collection.

CRITIQUING THE WORK

1. **Describe** Look at Jacob Lawrence's *Study for the Munich Olympic Games Poster.* Read the credit line for information about the work. Then list and describe everything you see in the work.
2. **Analyze** Do you see lines where the edge of one shape meets the edge of another? Do you see outlines? Can you find any contour lines? Can you find line variations? Are the lines active or static? Which kinds of lines seem to dominate the painting? Does Lawrence use value contrasts?
3. **Interpret** Remember that interpretation is more than telling a story about the subject matter. You must express your own opinion about the meaning or the mood of the work based on the facts you collected during the first two steps. Write a paragraph explaining your interpretation.
4. **Judge** Now it is time to make an aesthetic judgment. Do you think this is a successful work of art? Use one or more of the three aesthetic theories you studied in Chapter 2 to defend your judgment.

COMPARING THE WORKS

Look at *Study for the Munich Olympic Games Poster* by Jacob Lawrence (Figure 5.39) and the *Death of Socrates* by Jacques Louis David (Figure 5.40). Compare the way each artist uses line to create the expressive quality in each work. In which work are the line directions static? In which work are they active? Compare the way the two artists use value for expressive effect. Notice the facial expressions on the figures in each work. List all the other similarities and differences you find between the two works.

MEET THE ARTIST

JACOB LAWRENCE

American, b. 1917

The story of Jacob Lawrence's life is an American success story: he achieved success and fame before he was twenty-four. Lawrence was born in Atlantic City, New Jersey, in 1917. When he was twelve, his family moved to Harlem in New York City. The year was 1929, and it was the beginning of the Great Depression, which brought hard times upon all Americans.

Growing up in Harlem in the thirties was an important factor in Lawrence's development as an artist and in government support of the arts. The Harlem Renaissance of the twenties had attracted black intellectuals, artists, and musicians from all over the world, and many remained there during the thirties. The people of that community were Lawrence's role models.

Lawrence learned about art from many sources. He listened to the artists as they talked in their studios. The 135th Street Public Library, which he visited often, always had pieces of African sculpture on display. His many trips to The Metropolitan Museum of Art gave him a strong background in art history. He would walk sixty blocks to the museum and spend hours admiring all the works.

Lawrence became fascinated with black history and its heroic figures. His first subject was Toussaint L'Ouverture, the hero of Haiti, whose story was so interesting to Lawrence that he made a series of paintings to tell everything about L'Ouverture. For Lawrence could not always express all he wanted to say in just a single picture. He continued to make paintings in series. Some of his other subjects were Harriet Tubman and Frederick Douglass. Throughout his life he painted the everyday scenes of Harlem.

MORE PORTFOLIO IDEAS

I. Both Lawrence and David used line to create a specific feeling in their work. Select a magazine photograph of a scene in which static lines seem to predominate. Cut out the photo and paste it onto a page in your sketchbook. Redraw the scene, changing all the static lines to active lines. How does this change the mood of the scene?

II. Make a sketch of your home in your sketchbook. Copy that sketch, changing all the vertical and horizontal static lines to active diagonal lines. Compare the two sketches. How does changing the line directions affect the look of the house?

CHAPTER 5 REVIEW

Building Vocabulary

On a separate sheet of paper, write the term that best matches each definition given below.

1. A mark drawn with a pointed, moving tool. Line
2. The amount of space an object takes up in one direction. Dimension
3. A line that shows or creates the outer edges of a shape. Outline
4. A series of points that the viewer's eyes automatically connect. Implied line
5. The quality of being inactive. Static
6. A line that defines the edges and surface ridges of an object. contour drawing
7. An expressive movement. gesture
8. A term meaning beautiful handwriting. calligraphy
9. The art element that describes the darkness or lightness of an object. Value
10. The technique of using crossed lines for shading. crosshatching

Reviewing Art Facts

Answer the following questions using complete sentences.

1. Give an example of an implied line.
2. Name the five basic kinds of lines. Tell which three do not change direction, which kind changes direction gradually, and which kind changes direction suddenly.
3. Name five major ways in which lines can vary.
4. Tell which kind of line you would use to represent the surface of ridges in an object.
5. Name two kinds of lines that give the impression of stability.
6. Name the kind of line that conveys tension, instability, and action.
7. Tell what kind of drawing can be done quickly to capture movement.
8. What are the four factors that affect the value of a group of lines?

Thinking Critically About Art

1. **Analyze.** Study Figure 5.1 (page 88) by Twiggs, Figure 5.21 (page 97) by Namingha, Figure 5.24 (page 99) by Sheeler, and Figure 5.35 (page 106) by a Huichol Indian. What is the common thread that links the four works? The four works can be divided into two pairs, with each pair related to the other. How would you pair them, and what is the relationship in each set?
2. **Synthesize.** Explain why the four related works, Figures 5.1, 5.21, 5.24, and 5.35, belong in a chapter devoted to the concept of line.
3. **Compare and contrast.** In what way are Grant Wood's *Midnight Ride of Paul Revere* (Figure 5.3 on page 91) and Yvonne Jacquette's *East River Drive* (Figure 5.6 page 93) similar? In what ways are they different? Consider the element of line and the subject matter of each composition in your comparison.

Making Art Connections

1. **Music.** Investigate the importance of the element of line in music. Interview your school's music teacher or a friend who is studying music.
2. **Social Studies.** Jacob Lawrence arrived in Harlem near the end of the Harlem Renaissance. Find out when the Harlem Renaissance occurred, what caused it, and what was so important about that period in the history of American culture.
3. **History.** Neoclassicism was inspired by the discovery of Pompeii and Herculaneum. What and where were they? Why were they unknown before the mid-eighteenth century? Why was their discovery important? What did we learn from them? How did they affect the arts?

FIGURE 6.1 In the 1960s, Marisol was a star of the Pop art movement. She made assemblages that used humor to make viewers think about the materialistic attitude of the time. Today, her work uses the same media and has a similar purpose, but it is presented in a serious mood.

Marisol. *Poor Family I.* 1987. Wood, charcoal, stones, plastic doll. 198 × 396 × 213 cm (78 × 156 × 84″). Sidney Janis Gallery, New York, New York. © Marisol/VAGA, New York 1994.

CHAPTER 6

Shape, Form, and Space

You live in space, in a world full of objects. Each object—whether it be a car, an apple, this book, or you—has a shape or form. Often it is by their shapes or forms that you recognize objects. You identify a stop sign in the distance by its shape long before you can read the word *stop* on it. You identify a friend in the distance long before you see his or her face.

Shape, form, and space are all closely related to one another. They are elements of art, and artists use their knowledge of how these elements work together to speak the language of art. In this chapter you will learn how to "read" the meaning of these elements and how to use them to express your own ideas and feelings.

On the following pages you will begin to understand how artists create shapes, forms, and space in their artworks. You will learn how to use perspective to give depth to your drawings and paintings and how to use shapes, forms, and space to create a variety of expressive qualities. Your work will spring to life as you learn how to depict three dimensions on a two-dimensional surface.

Objectives

After reading this chapter, you will be able to:

- Explain the difference between shapes and forms.
- Create two- and three-dimensional works of art.
- Observe more carefully the shapes and forms in the space around you.
- Understand point of view and perspective.
- Use point of view and perspective to create drawings and paintings.
- Understand the expressive qualities, or meanings, of shapes, forms, and spaces in a work of art.

First Impressions

Look at *Poor Family I* (Figure 6.1). Notice how Marisol has used flat areas to create the illusion of depth in some areas of her assemblage, while she has carved some three-dimensional forms and attached them to the flat surfaces in other areas. Can you find the realistic three-dimensional forms? Can you find the flat surfaces that have been altered to look three-dimensional? What effect has the artist created by placing the figures so close together? Why has she left a wide space between the figures and the rocks? Why are the rocks included in this work?

Words to Know

chiaroscuro
form
free-form shapes
geometric shapes
highlights
holograms
perspective
shape
space

SHAPES

A **shape** is *a two-dimensional area that is defined in some way.* A shape may have an outline or a boundary around it, or you may recognize it by its area, such as the shadow in Figure 6.2. For instance, if you draw the outline of a square on a sheet of paper, you have created a shape. You could also create the same shape without an outline by painting the area of the square red.

You see many two-dimensional shapes every day. They are found in most designs, which in turn can be seen on many flat surfaces. Look for shapes on such things as floor coverings, fabrics, and wallpapers. Floors and walls are two-dimensional shapes; so are tabletops, book pages, posters, and billboards.

All shapes can be classified as either *geometric* or *free-form*. **Geometric shapes** are *precise shapes that can be described using mathematical formulas* (Figure 6.3). The basic geometric shapes are the circle, the square, and the triangle. All other geometric shapes are either variations or combinations of these basic shapes. Some of the variations include the oval, rectangle, parallelogram, trapezoid, pentagon, pentagram, hexagon, and octagon.

FIGURE 6.2 Shadow is the shape of darkness.

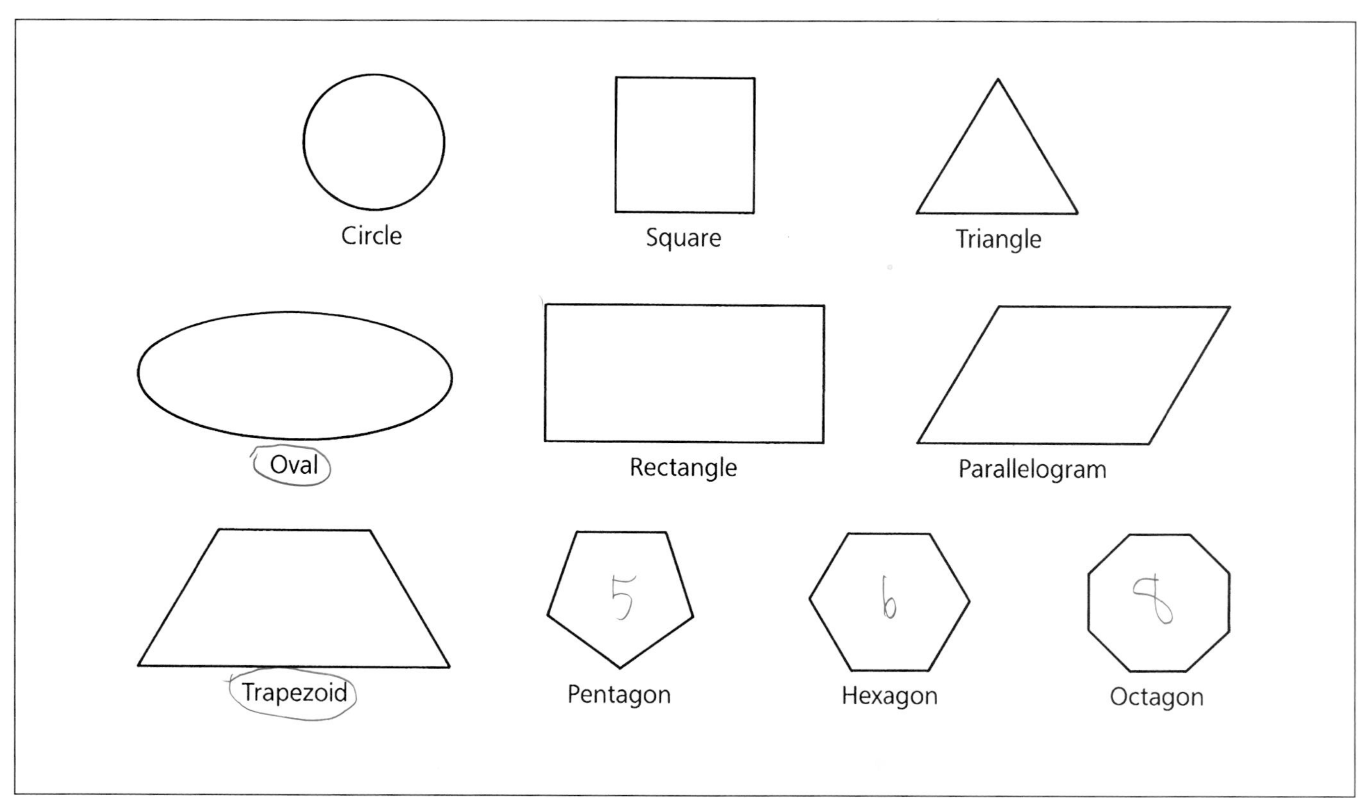

FIGURE 6.3 Geometric shapes.

Geometric shapes are used for decoration, uniformity, and organization. Road signs, for example, must be uniform. The same kind of sign must always have the same shape. Do you know the shape of a stop sign? Which shape is used for "Yield"? Which shape is used for TV screens? Why do you think ceiling tiles and window panes have geometric shapes?

Free-form shapes are *irregular and uneven shapes* (Figure 6.4). Their outlines may be curved, angular, or a combination of both. They often occur in nature. Free-form shapes may be silhouettes of living things, such as animals, people, or trees. Notice the decorative quality of the geometric shapes in the beadwork on the leggings shown in Figure 6.5. Geometric designs on white backgrounds were often used by the Blackfeet women. Now compare those designs to the free-form shapes on the leggings in Figure 6.6. These Chippewa formal leggings are an example of the refined floral style used by the Woodlands peoples. Which do you prefer?

FIGURE 6.5 The Native Americans produced formal clothing decorated with bead embroidery for social dances and formal events in the late nineteenth century.

Montata. *Blackfeet Man's Leggings.* Montana. 1880. Buckskin, glass beads, pigment. 101 × 49 cm (39¾ × 19¼"). Buffalo Bill Historical Center, Cody, Wyoming.

FIGURE 6.4 Free-form shapes.

FIGURE 6.6 The Chippewa women incorporated the free-form flower shapes they saw in the European decorative arts of the nineteenth century into their own designs.

Chippewa Man's Leggings. Minnesota. c. 1890. Cotton velveteen, polished cotton, glass beads, wool twill. 74.6 × 28 cm (29⅜ × 11"). Detroit Institute of Arts, Detroit, Michigan. Founders Society purchase.

Exploring Shapes

1. Applying Your Skills. Search your pockets or purse for objects small enough to fit on an overhead projector. Place the objects, one at a time, on the projector. Project the silhouette of the object on a screen or blank wall. Then draw only the outline of each object on a piece of white paper. After you have drawn several shapes, cut them out carefully. Arrange and glue them on a dark background.

2. Further Challenge. Using the printed areas of a newspaper, make two cut-paper designs. Make one design by measuring and cutting precise geometric shapes. Make the second design by tearing free-form shapes. Arrange the shapes and glue them on a sheet of black construction paper. Use a white crayon to print the words *free-form* and *geometric* on the appropriate design. Try to make the letters for *geometric* look geometric, and the letters for *free-form* look free-form.

3. Computer Option. Use the Shape tool to draw four different geometric shapes. Draw them spaced apart so you will be able to select them later. Make each of these shapes a solid color. Use the Select tool and the Copy and Paste options to repeat each of these shapes several times on your screen. When your screen is half filled with solid, geometric shapes, draw free-form shapes in between the geometric shapes. Use the Fill Bucket tool to fill the free-form shapes with a pattern. Do not overlap shapes.

FORMS

Although the words *shape* and *form* are often used interchangeably in everyday language, they have different meanings in the language of art. **Forms** are *objects having three dimensions.* Like shapes, they have both length and width, but forms also have depth. *You* are a three-dimensional form; so is a tree or a table.

Two-dimensional shapes and three-dimensional forms are related. The end of a cylinder is a circle. One side of a cube is a square (Figure 6.7). A triangle can "grow" into a cone or a pyramid.

Like shapes, forms may be either geometric (Figure 6.8) or free-form (Figure 6.9). Geometric forms are used in construction, for organization, and as parts in machines. Look around you. What forms were used to build your school, your church, your home? Look under the hood of a car. What forms were used to build the motor? Did you know that common table salt is made of a series of interlocking cubes? You can see these cubes when you look at salt through a microscope.

Free-form forms are irregular and uneven three-dimensional objects such as stones, puddles, and clouds. Your own body and the bodies of animals and plants are free-form forms.

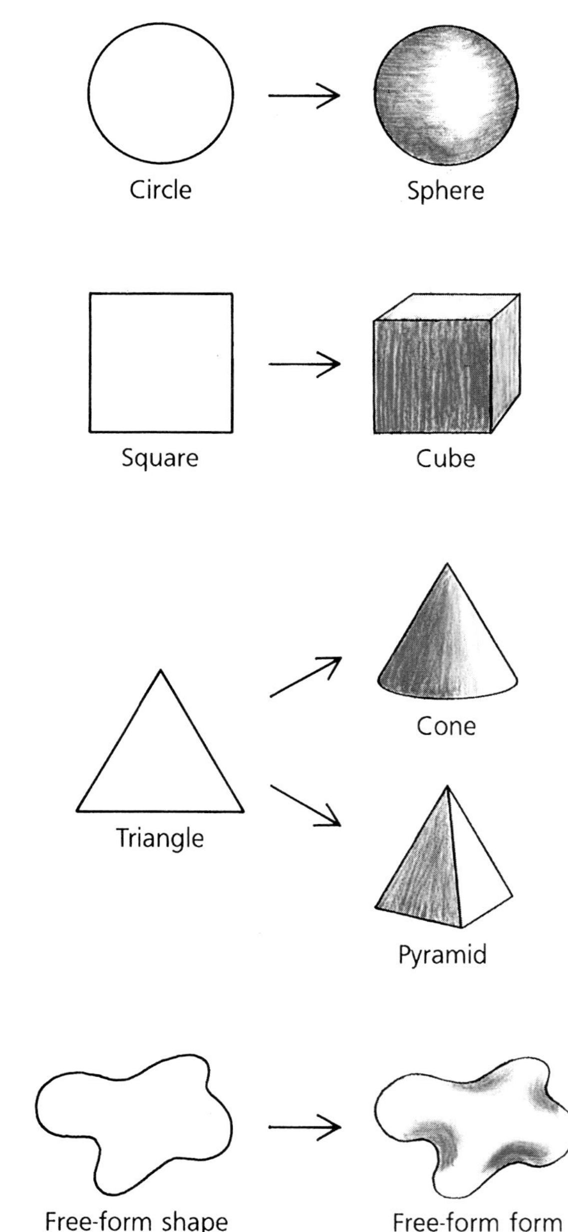

FIGURE 6.7 Do you see a relationship between two-dimensional shapes and three-dimensional forms?

FIGURE 6.8 This is one of Smith's earliest stainless steel geometric sculptures. It is made of steel plates joined to form rectangular solids. Smith insisted that his monumental sculptures were made to sit in nature, not in buildings. Because the smooth steel reflected light like chrome on a car, he burnished the surface to diffuse the light and so the surface would take on the colors of the natural environment.

David Smith. *Cubi IX.* 1961. Stainless steel. 268 × 149 × 111.4 cm (105¾ × 58⅝ × 43⅞"). Walker Art Center, Minneapolis, Minnesota. Gift of the T. B. Walker Foundation, 1966. © Estate of David Smith/VAGA, New York 1994.

Creating Forms

1. Applying Your Skills. Find a geometric object that is three dimensional. Use a pencil and ruler to draw its contours. Next, find a three-dimensional free-form object. Using brush and ink, draw it with flowing, calligraphic contour lines.

2. Further Challenge. Make a flat sheet of construction paper into a three-dimensional paper sculpture by using cutting and scoring techniques. (See Technique Tip on page 356 in the Handbook.) Give your sculpture a minimum of five different surfaces. Do not cut the paper into separate pieces. Use only slots and tabs if you wish to join any parts. Experiment with scratch paper before you construct your final paper sculpture.

3. Computer Option. Use the Oval shape to draw an oval shape on the screen. Draw another oval and use the Fill Bucket tool to fill it with a gradient. This will make it appear rounded and represent a form. Repeat this procedure using additional geometric and free-form shapes. Some software programs have both Uniform Gradient Fill and Gradient Fill to Shape options.

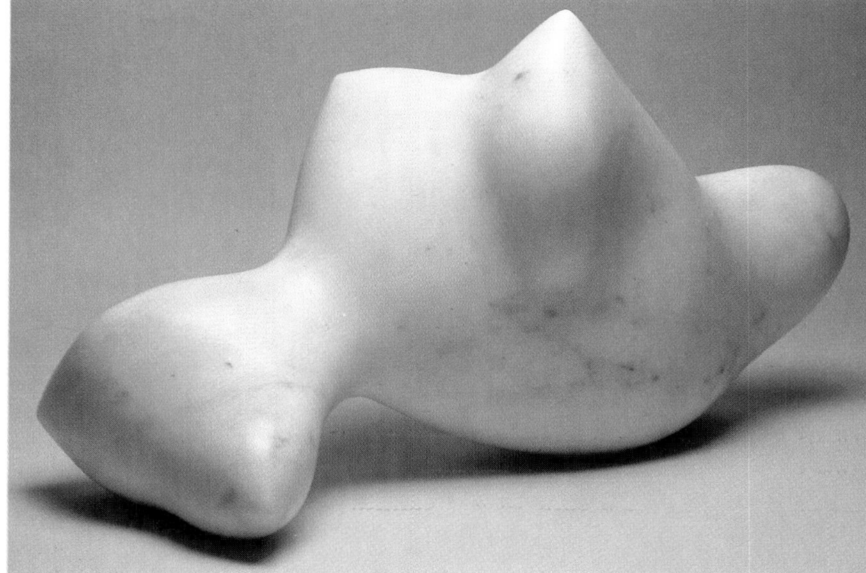

FIGURE 6.9 Arp always created sculpture that was free-form and organic looking. He never named his sculpture until it was finished. Can you see why he gave this form a title related to water?

Jean (Hans) Arp. *Aquatique.* 1953. Marble. 34 × 64.3 × 23.3 cm (13½ × 25⁵⁄₁₆ × 9³⁄₁₆"). Walker Art Center, Minneapolis, Minnesota. Gift of the T. B. Walker Foundation, 1955.

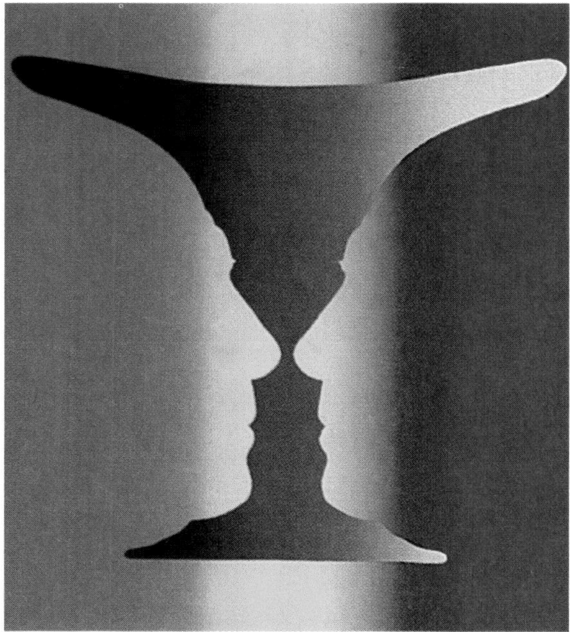

FIGURE 6.10 Do you see a vase or do you see two profiles of Picasso? Johns has deliberately organized this lithograph as a visual puzzle to confuse the viewer. One minute the faces are very clear and they seem to be the figure while the space between the profiles is the ground. The next moment the vase between the profiles becomes the figure and the space around the vase becomes the ground.

Jasper Johns. *Cups 4 Picasso.* 1972. Lithograph. 57 × 82 cm (22½ × 32¼"). The Museum of Modern Art, New York, New York. Gift of Celeste Bartos. © Jasper Johns/VAGA, New York 1994.

SPACE AND ITS RELATIONSHIP TO SHAPE AND FORM

Shapes and forms exist in **space**, which is *the element of art that refers to the emptiness or area between, around, above, below, or within objects.* All objects take up space. You, for example, are a living, breathing form moving through space.

Shapes and forms are defined by the space around and within them. They depend on space for their existence. This is why it is important to understand the relationship of space to shapes and forms.

Positive and Negative Spaces

In both two- and three-dimensional art, the shapes or forms are called the *positive space* or the *figure*. The empty spaces between the shapes or forms are called *negative spaces* or *ground*. Look at Figure 6.10 and read the caption for an example of figure and ground. In a portrait, the image of the person is the positive space; the negative space is the area surrounding the person (Figure 6.11).

The shape and size of negative spaces affect the way you interpret positive spaces. Large negative spaces around positive spaces may express loneliness or freedom. When the positive spaces are crowded together, you may feel tension or togetherness (Figure 6.12, page 126). The full meaning of a work depends on the interaction between the positive and negative spaces.

It is not always easy to tell which are the positive spaces and which are the negative spaces in two-dimensional art. Sometimes it is hard to find any negative space. This is because some artists give equal emphasis to both the figure and the ground.

Some artists even try to confuse the viewer. They create positive and negative spaces that reverse themselves while you are looking at them. These visual puzzles fascinate some viewers (Figure 6.13, page 127).

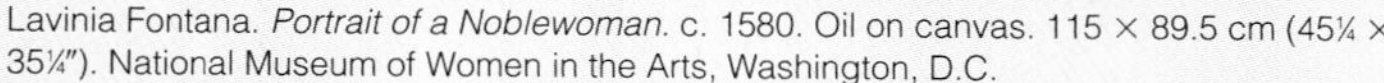
Lavinia Fontana. *Portrait of a Noblewoman.* c. 1580. Oil on canvas. 115 × 89.5 cm (45¼ × 35¼″). National Museum of Women in the Arts, Washington, D.C.

LOOKING CLOSELY

FIGURE 6.11 Notice how the negative space affects the look of the subject. There is more negative space on the woman's right than on her left, and both spaces have different shapes. The spaces between her arms and her dress are very different. Fontana's style of painting the background flat black forces the viewer to pay attention to the details in the positive space.

The light color of the sleeves pulls your eyes down to her hands. You can easily see what she is petting with her right hand. Do you know what she is holding in her left hand? Notice that it has a jeweled head and is attached to her waist with a chain.

Experimenting with Space

1. Applying Your Skills. Cut a large geometric shape from a sheet of black paper. Then cut the shape into nine or more separate pieces. Re-form the pieces into the original shape on a large sheet of white paper. Expand the shape by gradually sliding the pieces apart. Experiment by creating different amounts of space between the pieces, then glue down the best arrangement. You may not add or subtract any pieces from the original number, and the original shape must be recognizable. Shapes may touch the edges.

2. Further Challenge. Select a group of objects to draw. Make an arrangement with a variety of negative spaces between the shapes. Draw the arrangement lightly with pencil or chalk. Finish the work by (a) coloring only the negative spaces with crayons or paint, or (b) filling the negative spaces with closely drawn sets of parallel lines. Leave the positive spaces empty. What shapes did the negative spaces take?

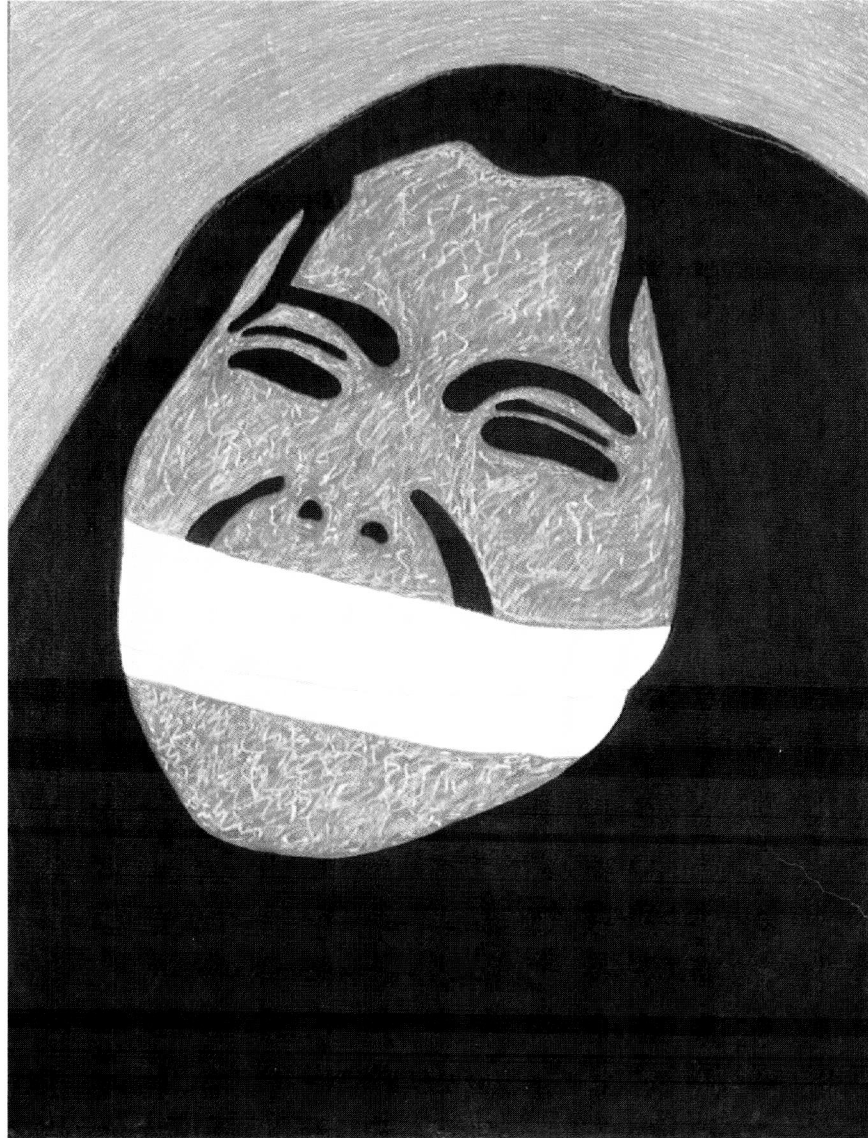

FIGURE 6.12 Garcia has created the feeling of a prisoner confined in a small space by eliminating almost all the negative space and filling the picture with the head of the woman. You can feel her sense of confinement because she is crushed by the edges of the picture.

Rupert Garcia. *Political Prisoner.* 1976. Pastel on paper. 122 × 91.5 cm (48 × 36″). National Museum of American Art, Smithsonian Institution, Washington, D.C.

3. Computer Option. Use the rectangle shape tool to draw a 2 x 3-inch (5 x 7.6-cm) solid rectangle in the middle of the screen. Use the Selection tool to select and then move part of the rectangle away from the original. Repeat until the rectangle has been broken into many smaller parts with varying spaces in between. Continue selecting and moving until you have created an interesting composition by the addition of space within the form.

Space in Three-Dimensional Art

Over, *under*, *through*, *behind*, and *around* are words that describe three-dimensional space. Architecture, sculpture, weaving, ceramics, and jewelry are three-dimensional art forms. They all take up real space. You can walk around, look through, look behind, peer over, and reach into three-dimensional art.

Architects shape space. They design structures that enclose a variety of spaces for people. They

M. C. Escher. *Other World.* 1947. Wood engraving in three colors. 31.8 × 26 cm (12½ × 10¼"). National Gallery of Art, Washington, D.C.

LOOKING CLOSELY

FIGURE 6.13 Escher uses two forms, the bird and an architectural structure, and presents them in an unusual distortion of reality. Look at the lower third of the picture. Where is the viewer in relation to the bird? Now look at the bird in the middle of the picture. Where is the viewer now? Then study the top third of the picture. Now what happened to the position of the viewer with relation to the bird? Can you figure out how Escher made this visual puzzle look logical?

create large spaces for group activities, such as the one you see in Figure 6.14 on page 128. They also create small spaces for privacy. Landscape architects and city planners are also involved in planning spaces for people to use.

Negative areas in three-dimensional art are very real. Most three-dimensional works are meant to be *freestanding,* which means they are surrounded by negative space (Figure 6.15, page 128). The viewer must move through this negative space to see all of the different views of a three-dimensional work.

Relief sculpture is not intended to be freestanding. It projects out from a flat surface into negative space. You can find relief sculpture on ceramic pots and plaster ceilings. When the positive areas project slightly from the flat surface, the work is called *bas relief*, or *low relief* (Figure 6.16, page 129). When the positive areas project farther out, the work is called *high relief* (Figure 6.17, page 129).

Most jewelry is planned as relief sculpture to decorate human surfaces. The inside of a ring or the back of a pendant is smooth. It is not meant to be seen; it simply rests on the person's surface.

Today many artists are experimenting and changing traditional art forms. Printmakers are creating relief prints. Some printmakers are molding relief designs in handmade paper. Painters are adding a third dimension to the painted surface. Some painters are cutting or tearing real negative spaces in two-dimensional surfaces.

FIGURE 6.14 The architect designed this auditorium to seat representatives from every country in the world. It was designed to look as if it could hold all of the world's people. Notice the ways in which line and implied line have been used to emphasize the feeling of space in this auditorium.

Wallace Kirkman Harrison. United Nations Buildings. Assembly Building, Main Auditorium. New York, New York. 1949. Photo by Sendak, Inc.

Weaving also has gone in new directions. It started as a practical craft, with weavers making two-dimensional fabrics for clothing, and has evolved into an art form. Today hand weavers are creating relief hangings and three-dimensional woven sculptures.

Photographers are creating **holograms,** *images in three dimensions created with a laser beam.* Sculptors are making *kinetic,* or moving, sculpture.

Using Three Dimensions

1. Applying Your Skills. Make a freestanding, three-dimensional design that projects into negative space on all sides. Using pieces of cardboard tubing and small boxes, join the design pieces with glue and tape. Paint the finished work in one color to emphasize its form.

2. Further Challenge. Set up a spotlight on one side of your freestanding sculpture from the above activity. In your sketchbook draw the contours of the sculpture and the shape of the shadow it casts. Move the spotlight to another angle. Draw the sculpture and its shadow. Notice how the changing light changes the shape of the shadow.

3. Computer Option. Draw a cube so that the top, side, and front are visible. Fill each surface with a different color or texture. Use the Select tool and the Copy and Paste options on the cube. Begin pasting the cube high on the page. Continue by pasting it repeatedly in the middle and lower portion of the screen. Notice that the cubes pasted low and last appear closer. Resize the cube that you are pasting or draw a smaller cube. Use the Copy and Paste options to add smaller cubes to the design. You will create an illusion of three-dimensional space. Imagine a small animal walking through the spaces and climbing over the cubes.

FIGURE 6.15 The negative shapes that pierce the shell of this form are as important to the structure as the solid bronze. They create the feeling of a person.

Barbara Hepworth. *Figure for Landscape.* 1960. Bronze. 269.2 × 128.3 × 67.3 cm (106 × 50½ × 26½"). Hirshhorn Museum and Sculpture Garden, Smithsonian Institution, Washington, D.C. Gift of Joseph H. Hirshhorn, 1966.

FIGURE 6.16 Student work. An example of low relief.

FIGURE 6.17 Notice how far out the animals and the decorative columns protrude from the surface of this building. There is a strong shadow behind the salamander over the arch that indicates how far it is raised from the surface. How many other examples of high relief can you find on the façade of this building?

Berenice Abbot. *Façade, Alwyn Court, 174–182 West 58th Street.* August 10, 1938. Museum of the City New York, New York. The Berenice Abbott Collection, #283-A. Federal Arts Project "Changing New York."

HOW WE PERCEIVE SHAPE, FORM, AND SPACE

Look up from this book to an object across the room to see if you can feel the movement of your eye muscles. If you didn't feel anything, try again until you become aware that your eyes are working to refocus.

You have just taken a trip through visual space. Your brain measured the amount of space between you and the object and sent a message to your eye muscles to adjust. The muscles then refocused your eyes so that you could clearly see the object.

Perceiving Depth

Your eyes and brain work together to enable you to see in three dimensions—*length*, *width*, and *depth*. Each eye sees an object from a slightly different angle. The brain merges these two separate and slightly different views into one, creating a three-dimensional image.

To see how this works try the following experiment. Close your right eye. Point to a specific spot in the room. Without moving your pointing finger, open your right eye and close your left eye. It will appear you have moved your finger, even though you know you have not.

Point of View

The shapes and forms you see depend on your *point of view*. Your point of view is the angle from which you see an object. Another person at another location will see the same shape or form differently. For example, a person looking down on a circle drawn on the sidewalk sees a round shape. If that person lies on the ground beside the circle and looks at it, the circle will appear to have an oblong shape. A person looking at the front end of a car will see a form different from the one seen by a person looking at the side of that same car. Figure 6.18 on page 130 shows three different views of a sculpture.

You can learn about points of view by doing the following experiments. Place your hand flat on the desk and spread your fingers apart. The shape and form you see are the shape and form you would probably draw. They are part of the mental image you have of the object "hand." Now lift your hand

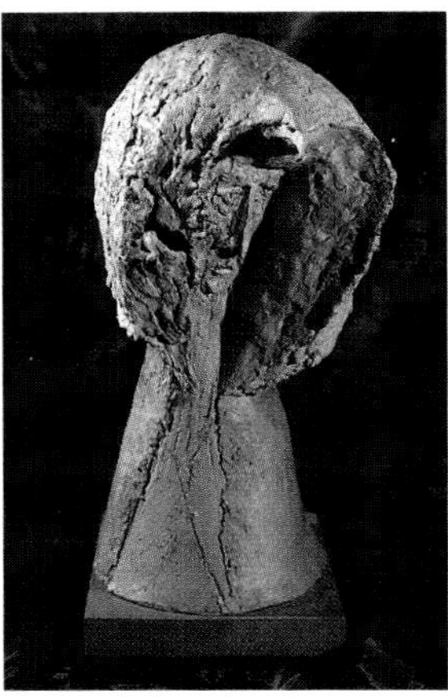

FIGURE 6.18 Notice how the feeling expressed by this ceramic sculpture changes as your point of view changes. You must view sculpture from all angles to truly understand it. Can you find the warrior's face and the bird's head?

Bob Owens. *Warrior with Carnivorous Helmet.* 1986. Ceramic. 53.3 cm (21″). Private collection.

FIGURE 6.19 In this painting the viewer can see all the tabletops easily. All the serving dishes and the food in them are clearly visible. Can you tell what kind of a party this is? Why was this point of view a good one for this painting?

William Kurelek. *Manitoba Party.* 1964. Oil on Masonite. 121.9 x 152.6 cm (48 × 60″). National Gallery of Canada, Ottawa, Canada.

and let your fingers relax. Notice how the shape and form of your hand change. Turn your hand and watch what happens. Your hand is still the same hand. Only its shape and form are different.

Next, look at a rectangular table. What shape does the top have when you are sitting at the table? Look at the top through a rectangular viewing frame. Are the edges of the table parallel to the edges of the frame? You know the top is a rectangle, but does it really look rectangular now? What shape does the top seem to take if you are sitting across the room from it? What would the shape look like if you viewed it from the top of a tall ladder? Do you think the shape you see will change if you lie on the floor directly under the table?

When you looked at your hand, your eyes stayed in the same place, but your hand moved. When you studied the table, it remained in one place, but you moved. In both cases, what you saw changed because your relationship to the object changed. Your point of view depends on where you are and where the object is. Look at Figure 6.19. Where is the artist's point of view in relation to the tables in that picture?

Shape and Point of View

1. Applying Your Skills. Look through magazines for three or more different views of one type of object. Look for TV sets, sofas, spoons, toasters, cars, or shoes. Cut out the objects and mount each one on a sheet of white paper. Emphasize the changes in shape by drawing around each outline with a crayon or marker.

2. Further Challenge. Study the three photographs of a baseball glove in Figure 6.20. Each picture looks different because the relationship between the camera and the glove changes. Using a pencil, make a contour drawing of each view of the glove. Go over the outline of each drawing of the glove with a crayon or watercolor marker to emphasize shape changes.

3. Computer Option. Use the Line tool to draw three cubes, each from a different point of view. Use the Fill Bucket tool to fill each front with one color or texture. Fill the sides with a second color or texture. Use a third color or texture for each top and a fourth for each bottom.

FIGURE 6.20 How does your perception of the glove change in each view?

HOW ARTISTS CREATE SHAPES AND FORMS IN SPACE

Shapes and forms can be classified as *natural* or *manufactured*. Natural shapes and forms are made by the forces of nature. For instance, animals, plants, and stones are natural forms. Manufactured forms are those created by people, whether mass-produced by the thousands in factories or made by hand.

Artists use many materials and techniques to make shapes. They concentrate on both outline and area. Some artists outline shapes in drawings and paintings. Others may paint shapes by placing brushstrokes together without using even a beginning outline. They cut shapes and print shapes as well (Figure 6.21).

Like shapes, forms can be made in many ways. Artists model clay forms, mold metal forms, and carve forms from wood or stone. They use glass, plastics, bricks, and cement to make forms as well as shapes.

The Illusion of Form

Artists can create the illusion of three-dimensional form on a two-dimensional surface. They can give the impression of depth and solidity by using changes in value. Figure 6.22 is an example of this illusion.

The *arrangement of light and shadow* is called **chiaroscuro** (**kyah**-roh-**skoo**-roh). In Italian *chiaro* means "bright," and *oscuro* means "dark." Chiaroscuro was introduced by Italian artists during the Renaissance. Figure 3.36, page 67, is an example. Later it was used for dramatic lighting effects by Baroque artists (Figure 12.5, page 317). Through careful observation, artists have learned how light is reflected off of three-dimensional forms. They have learned how to represent shadows realistically. Today, chiaroscuro is often called modeling or shading.

Look, for instance, at an object with angular surfaces, such as a cube. You will see a large jump in value from one surface of the cube to the next. One surface may be very light in value and the next very dark. Now look at an object such as a baseball. The curved surfaces of spheres and cylinders show gradual changes in value.

FIGURE 6.21 Matisse cut the shapes for this work directly from sheets of paper that he had colored with paint. He did not use anything to draw the shapes before he cut. Some of the shapes to look for in this work are fish, sea animals, sea plants, and coral.

Henri Matisse. *Beasts of the Sea.* 1950. Paper on canvas. 295.5 × 154 cm (116⅜ × 60⅝"). National Gallery of Art, Washington, D.C. Ailsa Mellon Bruce Fund.

The area of a curved surface that reflects the most light is, of course, the lightest in a drawing. **Highlights** are *small areas of white used to show the very brightest spots.* Starting at the highlights, the value changes gradually from light values of gray to dark values of gray. The darkest values are used to show areas that receive the least light. An area that is turned completely away from a light source is almost black. Look at Figure 6.23 on page 134 to see the ways an artist has created the illusion of form.

FIGURE 6.22 Giotto was the first artist to break away from the flat look of Byzantine painting. He studied the human form and used gestures and expressions that showed human qualities. Giotto's figures are so solid that they seem to be carved from rock.

Giotto. *Madonna and Child.* 1320–30. Paint on wood. 85.5 × 62 cm (33⅝ × 24⅜"). National Gallery of Art, Washington, D.C. Samuel H. Kress Collection.

Using Shading

1. Applying Your Skills. Set up an arrangement of geometric forms. Use boxes, books, balls, and cylindrical containers. Study the way light reflects off the surfaces of the objects. Draw the arrangement. Give the shapes in your drawing the illusion of three dimensions by using the medium and shading technique of your choice. Use values that range from black to white, and employ many value steps in between.

2. Further Challenge. Using yourself as the model, make a shaded drawing of a face (Figure 6.24, page 135). Sit facing a mirror. Set up a lamp to light your face from one side. Study the lights and shadows that fall on your face. Notice that there appears to be no edge to the side of your nose. It is a form with a rounded surface. Then, using the medium and shading technique that you prefer, model shadows and highlights. Avoid drawing contour lines. This drawing does not have to look like you.

3. Computer Option. Several computer tools can be used for shading objects. Experiment with the Pencil, Brush, Line, Gradient Fill, and Air Brush tools. Some software programs have a Smudge tool that also can be used for shading. Small Pencil and Brush tools can be used with shading techniques like those used when working with pen and ink.

FIGURE 6.23 Notice how Dürer has created the illusion of form using hatching and cross-hatching. Which side of the robe is getting more light, and which side is darker? How can you tell?

Albrecht Dürer. *An Oriental Ruler Seated on His Throne.* c. 1495. Pen and black ink. 30.6 × 19.7 cm (12 × 7¾″). National Gallery of Art, Washington, D.C. Ailsa Mellon Bruce Fund.

FIGURE 6.24 Student work. A self-portrait.

The Illusion of Depth

In their paintings artists often create the illusion of depth. When you look at these paintings, you see objects and shapes, some of which seem closer to you than others. You seem to be looking through a window into a real place (Figure 6.25). This idea—that a painting should be like a window to the real world—has dominated traditional Western art since the early Renaissance.

There are several terms that will help you as you talk about and create depth in a painting or drawing. The surface of a painting or drawing is sometimes called the *picture plane*. The part of the picture plane that appears nearest to you is the *foreground*. The part that appears farthest away is the *background*. The area in between is called the *middle ground*.

FIGURE 6.25 Everything is carefully placed within the frame of this scene. In the foreground, figures dressed in bright robes kneel before the Christ Child. Beyond the human activity there is a background of calm, rolling, green hills. Notice how the artist tries to focus your attention on the Child. After reading about perspective, see if you can find examples of each of the six devices used for creating perspective in this painting.

Sandro Botticelli. *The Adoration of the Magi.* c. 1481–82. Tempera on wood. 70.1 × 104.1 cm (27⅜ × 41″). National Gallery of Art, Washington, D.C. Andrew W. Mellon Collection, 1937.

Perspective is *a graphic system that creates the illusion of depth and volume on a two-dimensional surface.* In the following pages are techniques artists use to give their paintings and drawings perspective.

Overlapping. When one object covers part of a second object, the first seems to be closer to the viewer, as in Figure 6.26.

Size. Large objects appear to be closer to the viewer than small objects, as in Figure 6.27. The farther an object is from you, the smaller it appears. Cars far down the road seem to be much smaller than the ones close to you. If you stand at the end of a long hallway and raise your hand, you can block your view of a whole crowd of people. You know that each is about your size, but at a distance the crowd appears to be smaller than your hand.

Placement. Objects placed low on the picture plane seem to be closer to the viewer than objects placed near eye level. The most distant shapes seem to be exactly at eye level (Figure 6.28).

Detail. Objects with clear, sharp edges and visible details seem to be close to you (Figure 6.29). Objects that lack detail and have hazy outlines seem to be farther away. Look closely at your own hand. You can see very tiny lines clearly. Now look at someone's hand from across the room. You have trouble seeing the lines between the fingers. All the details seem to melt together because of the distance between you and what you are seeing.

Color. Brightly colored objects seem closer to you, and objects with dull, light colors seem to be farther away (Figure 6.30). This is called *atmospheric* perspective. The air around us is not empty. It is full of moisture and dust that create a haze. The more air there is between you and an object, the more the object seems to fade. Have you ever noticed that trees close to you seem to be a much brighter green than trees farther down the road? You have probably been coloring mountains blue-gray since first grade, but of course they really aren't blue-gray.

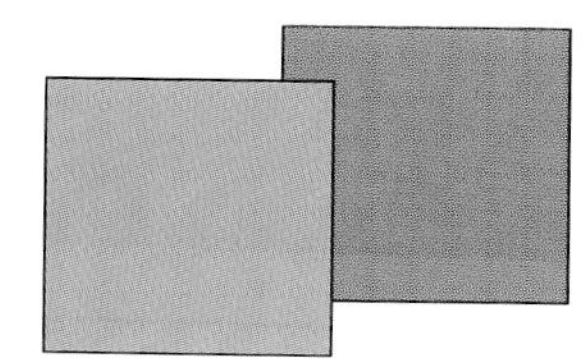

FIGURE 6.26 Overlapping.

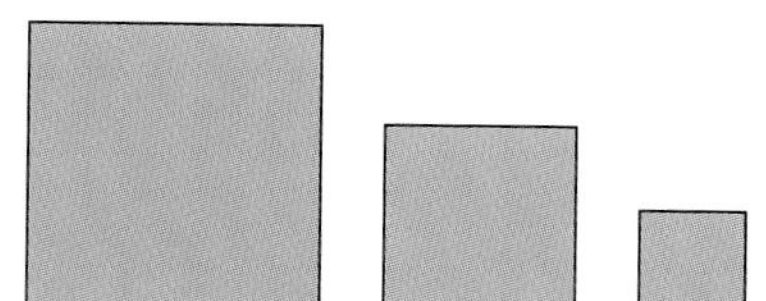

FIGURE 6.27 Size.

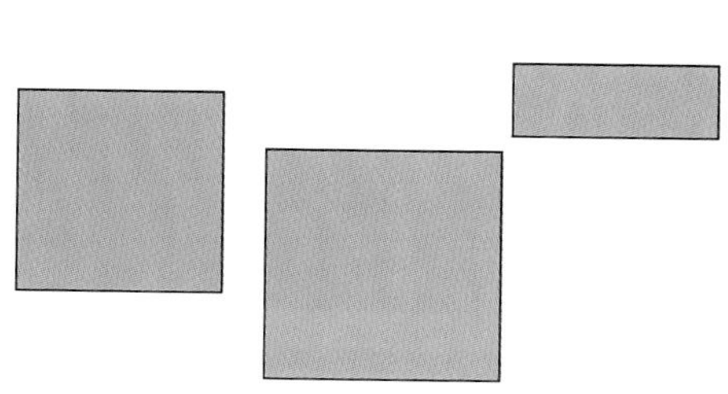

FIGURE 6.28 Placement.

FIGURE 6.29 Detail.

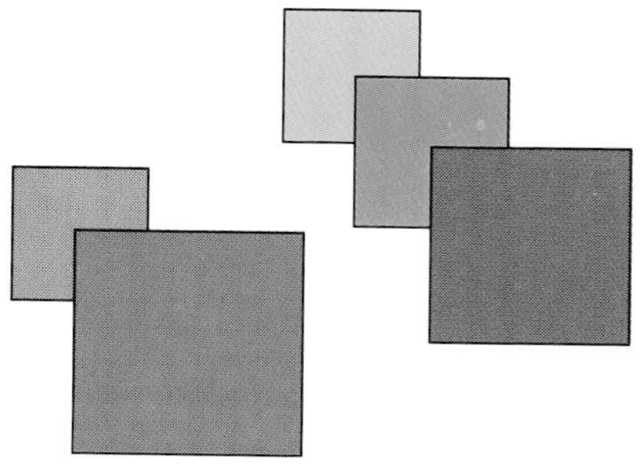

FIGURE 6.30 Color.

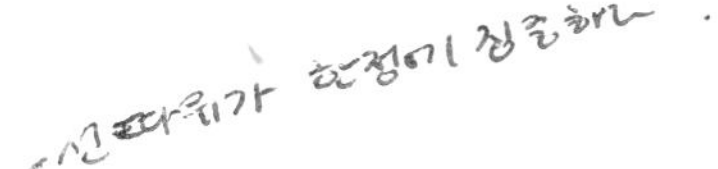

Converging Lines. *Linear* perspective is one way of using lines to show distance and depth. As parallel lines move away from you, they seem to move closer together toward the horizon line (Figure 6.31). When you look at the highway ahead of you, the sides of the road appear to move closer together. You don't worry, though, because you know this is an illusion. You know that the sides of the road ahead of you actually are just as far apart as they are in your present position.

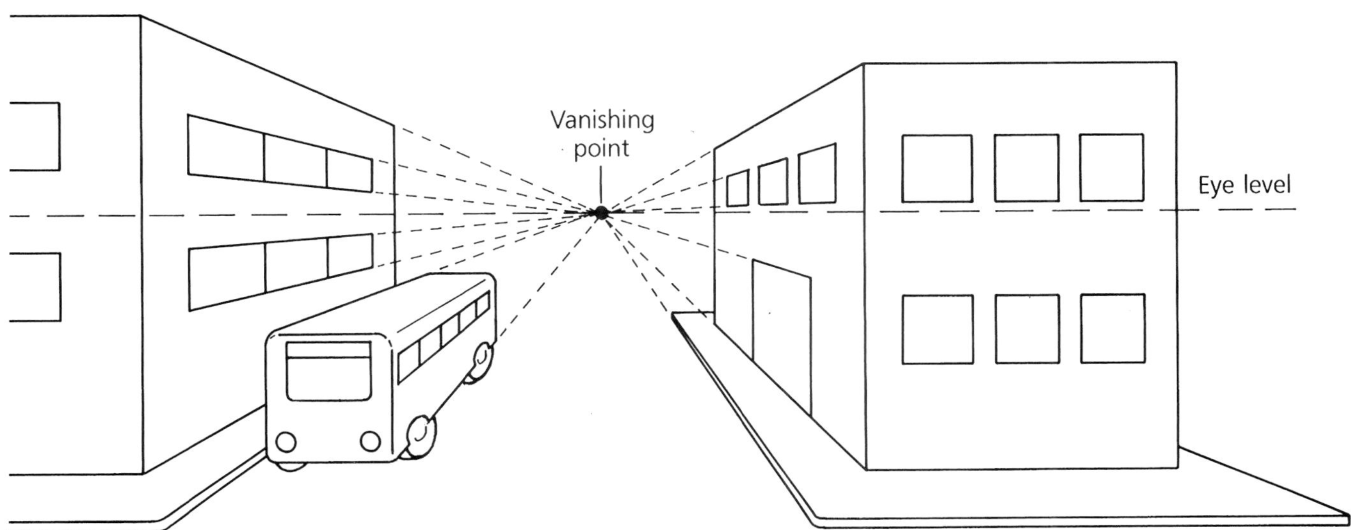

FIGURE 6.31 In this drawing the lines gradually come together and meet at one point in the distance. This is one-point linear perspective.

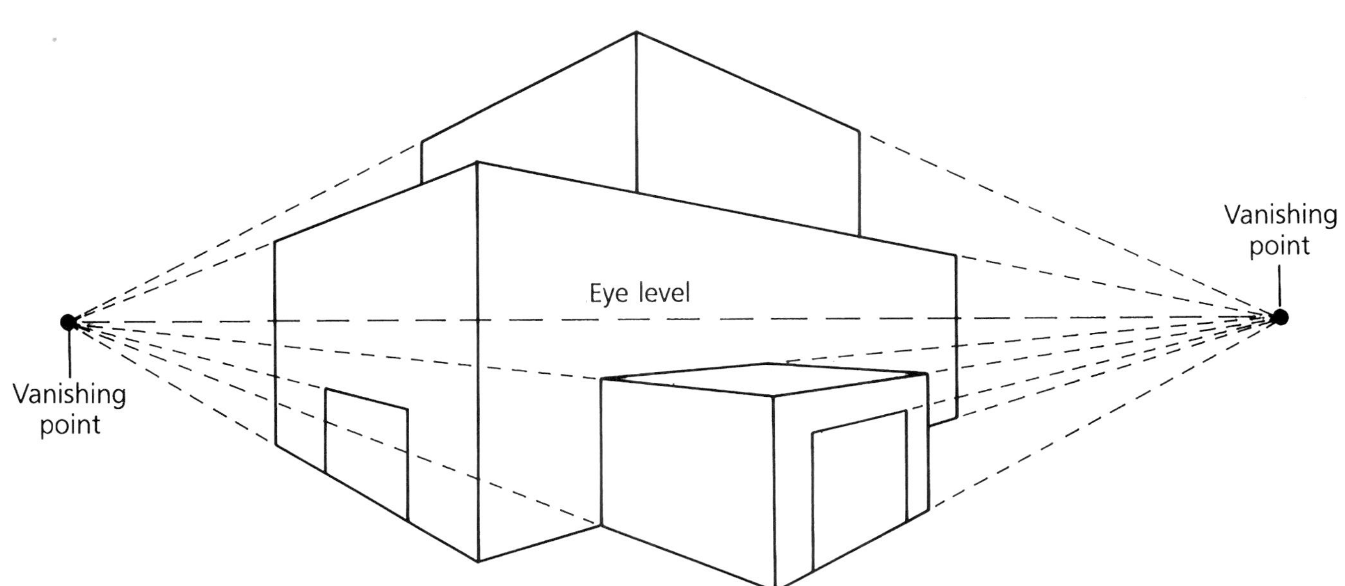

FIGURE 6.32 In this drawing the lines come together and meet at two points. This is two-point linear perspective.

Sometimes lines appear to meet at a point on the horizon line called the *vanishing point*. In one-point linear perspective, all receding lines meet at a single vanishing point. In two-point linear perspective, different sets of parallel lines meet at different vanishing points (Figure 6.32, page 137). Because two-point perspective creates more diagonal lines in a painting, it seems more active. Renaissance artists used strict mathematical formulas to calculate perspective. Most of today's artists rely on visual perception rather than mathematical formulas. Notice the ways in which Doris Lee has used perspective to show depth in her busy kitchen scene (Figure 6.33).

Creating Depth

1. Applying Your Skills. Create three different designs on three separate sheets of paper. Each design should contain five shapes. Use the same five shapes in each design as follows:

- Draw all of the items as close to the foreground as possible.
- Draw one item close to the foreground and make the others look as if they are slightly farther back.
- Draw one item close to the foreground, one far in the background, and the other three in the middle ground.

FIGURE 6.33 Can you find the six perspective techniques in this scene?

Doris Lee. *Thanksgiving*. 1935. Oil on canvas. 71.4 × 101.6 cm (28 × 40″). The Art Institute of Chicago, Chicago, Illinois. Mr. and Mrs. Frank G. Logan Prize Fund, 1935.

2. Further Challenge. Do the same exercise using three-dimensional forms instead of shapes.

3. Computer Option. Use the Brush or Pencil tool and the Fill Bucket tool to create a simple landscape. Divide the land into the background, middle ground, and foreground. Draw one or two small trees in the middle ground. Draw at least one large tree in the foreground. It can overlap those in the middle ground if you wish. Add other details. Keep in mind the methods for creating the illusion of depth that were discussed in this section.

WHAT DIFFERENT SPACES, SHAPES, AND FORMS EXPRESS

Shapes, forms, and spaces in art communicate certain feelings. This is possible because you associate them with similar shapes, forms, and spaces in real life. When you see a certain shape or form in a work of art, you may think of an object from real life. Any feelings you have about that object will affect your feelings about the artistic work. Artists use this relationship between art and your environment to communicate with you.

Outline and Surface

The outline of a shape and the surface of a form carry messages. Artists often use free-form shapes and forms to symbolize living things. When they want to please and soothe viewers, they use shapes and forms with smooth, curved outlines and surfaces (Figure 6.34). Forms that remind us of well-worn river rocks or curled-up kittens tempt us to touch them. These forms are comfortable. They appeal to us through our memories of pleasant touching experiences.

Angular shapes with zigzag outlines and forms with pointed projections remind us of sharp, jagged things (Figure 6.35, on page 140). We remember the pain caused by broken glass and sharp knives. We would never carelessly grab a pointed, angular form. If we were to touch it at all, we would do so very carefully.

Geometric shapes suggest mechanical perfection. It is impossible to draw a perfect circle freehand. The special appeal of geometric shapes and forms has been felt throughout the ages. Their lines, contours, and surfaces are clean and crisp. This appeals to people's sense of order.

As used by modern artists, geometric shapes and forms express less feeling than other types. They are unemotional; in fact, they may express a total lack of feeling. Geometric forms in artworks appeal to viewers' minds rather than to their emotions (Figure 6.36, page 140).

FIGURE 6.34 "William," this round, roly-poly hippo, has such an appealing shape that he has become the unofficial mascot of The Metropolitan Museum of Art in New York City.

Egyptian. *Figure of Hippopotamus.* XII dynasty (1991–1786 B.C.). Ceramics-Faience. Meir, Tomb of Senbi. 11 × 20 cm (4⅜ × 7⅞"). The Metropolitan Museum of Art, New York, New York. Gift of Edward S. Harkness, 1917.

FIGURE 6.35 This painting shows contrast between the static, solid form of the man and the active movement of the stems and thorns. This is a moment of tension. The viewer can imagine the pain that will occur when the blind botanist moves his hands to study the plant.

Ben Shahn. *The Blind Botanist.* 1954. Tempera on Masonite. 132 × 78.8 cm (52 × 31″). Wichita Museum of Art, Wichita, Kansas. The Roland P. Murdock Collection. © Estate of Ben Shahn/VAGA, New York 1994.

FIGURE 6.36 The artist has transformed the free-form, soft human torso into a metallic, dense, geometric abstraction.

Constantin Brancusi. *Torso of a Young Man.* 1924. Polished bronze on stone and wood base. 45.7 × 27.9 × 17.8 cm (18 × 11 × 7″). Hirshhorn Museum and Sculpture Garden, Smithsonian Institution, Washington, D.C. Gift of Joseph H. Hirshhorn, 1966.

Density

The *density* of an object refers to how compact it is. Dense materials are solid and heavy. Granite and lead, for example, are very dense. They are so solid and firm that you cannot make a dent on their surfaces when you press on them. Dense forms seem unyielding. They resist impact. For this reason, you may associate them with the idea of protection. In two-dimensional art, you can depict dense objects by using shading techniques and hard-edge contours.

Soft, fluffy forms are less dense. When you press on them, you can make a dent. These forms have air inside them, and they look more comfortable than denser forms. In two-dimensional art, you can depict soft forms by using shading techniques and curved contours.

Openness

An open shape or form appears inviting. It seems to say, "Come in." You can see into or through it. An armchair is an open form that invites you to sit. An open door invites you to enter. An empty cup invites you to fill it. Transparent objects, such as a glass wall, invite you to look inside (Figure 6.37). When you extend your hand to invite someone to join you, the form of your outstretched hand is an open form.

Open spaces in sculpture invite your eyes to wander through the work. Weavers leave openings in fabrics and hangings to let you see through them. If you remove an oak table from a room and replace it with a glass table, the room will seem less crowded. Architects use glass walls to open small spaces. Windows open up a building and bring in the outdoors.

Closed shapes and forms look solid and self-contained. Windowless buildings look forbidding. Closed doors keep people out; closed drapes and shades keep light out. When you make a tight fist, your hand is a closed form that seems to say, "Keep away." Folding your arms tightly to your body closes you off from others. Open arms invite people to come closer to you. The woman shown in Figure 6.38 has wrapped her robes around herself, creating a closed form to repel any contact. She tells you that she wants to be alone without saying a word. Her body language says it all.

FIGURE 6.37 The openness of the transparent glass walls of this house invites you to look inside, but when you are inside, the transparent walls invite you to look out at the beauty of the natural surroundings.

Phillip Johnson. *Johnson House.* 1949. New Canaan, Connecticut. View: exterior of glass house.

FIGURE 6.38 Notice how the artist has indicated the extreme feeling of isolation one experiences at the loss of a loved one. She has created this effect by using a closed form to represent the grieving person.

Marie Apel. *Grief.* 1940. Bronze. 51 × 17.8 × 15.2 cm (20 × 7 × 6″). National Museum of Women in the Arts, Washington, D.C. Gift of the artist's daughter.

Activity and Stability

You have already learned about active and static lines. Shapes and forms, also, can look as if they are about to move or as if they are fixed in one place.

Active shapes and forms seem to defy gravity. They slant diagonally, as if they are falling or running. In Figure 6.39 notice how the back of the wave and all the horse forms are arranged in diagonal, active positions.

Static shapes and forms are motionless, or stable. Their direction is usually horizontal (Figure 6.40). However, if two diagonal shapes or forms are balanced against each other, a static shape results. For instance, if an equilateral triangle rests on a horizontal base, the two diagonal edges balance each other.

Because static shapes and forms are firmly fixed in position, they evoke quiet and calm feelings. For instance, in landscape paintings the land forms are horizontal and the trees are vertical. They look very peaceful. This is probably why so many landscape paintings are chosen for people's homes.

FIGURE 6.39 The diagonal push of the back of the wave creates an unstable, active feeling. The wave is caught at the moment before it will collapse.

Anna Hyatt Huntington. *Riders to the Sea.* c. 1912. Bronze. 47 × 61 × 53 cm (18½ × 24 × 21″). Collection of the Newark Museum, Newark, New Jersey. Gift of the estate of Mrs. Florence P. Eagleton, 1954.

FIGURE 6.40 This figure expresses a stable feeling because of the long horizontal base and the vertical position of the mother's torso.

Henry Moore. *Reclining Mother and Child.* 1974–76. Plaster. 132 × 216 × 105 cm (51$\frac{15}{16}$ × 85⅛ × 41¼″). Dallas Museum of Art, Dallas, Texas. Lent by the Henry Moore Foundation.

Active and Static Shapes

1. Applying Your Skills. Cut out pictures of free-form objects from magazines. Arrange them to create a living fantasy creature (Figure 6.41). Use parts of people if you wish, but include other shapes as well. Glue your creature on a large sheet of paper. Draw or paint an environment full of free-form shapes for this fantasy creature.

2. Further Challenge. Make a simple design with geometric shapes. Lightly draw it with pencil on a small sheet of watercolor paper. Repeat the same design on another sheet of watercolor paper of the same size. Next, paint the first design precisely. Use a pointed brush to make sure that all of the edges are clearly defined (Figure 6.42). Wet the second sheet of paper by sponging it with water. Using exactly the same colors, paint the second design while the paper is wet so that the edges of the shapes run and look soft (Figure 6.43). Mount the two designs, side by side, on a sheet of black paper. Label the first "hard-edged" and the second "soft-edged."

FIGURE 6.41 Student work. A living fantasy creature.

3. Computer Option. Use the Rectangle shape tool to draw several solid black rectangles. Arrange them on the screen to create a static feeling. Use the Line tool to add static black lines to the design. On a new screen, draw several solid black triangles of various sizes to create an active feeling. Use the Line tool to add active black lines to the design. Label the designs either "stable" or "active." The Line tool can be constrained to draw a straight horizontal, vertical, or diagonal line in many software programs by holding down the shift key while drawing with the mouse.

FIGURE 6.42 Student work. Hard edges.

FIGURE 6.43 Student work. Soft edges.

STUDIO LESSON: DRAWING AN OUTDOOR SCENE

FIGURE 6.44 Larry Smith. *North Georgia Waterfall.* 1993. Pen and ink on paper. 66 x 61 cm (26 × 24″). Collection of the artist.

Supplies

- Sketchbook
- Large sheet of white drawing paper
- Drawing board and tape
- Pencils and erasers
- Viewing frame

Larry Smith is an artist in love with the land. Born and raised in Georgia, he has committed his professional life to capturing its majestic scenery on paper. In this view of Tallula Falls (Figure 6.44), he shares his impression of water cascading down the rocks and collecting in the lake below.

Smith uses a realistic style to create his artwork. Regionalists such as Winslow Homer (Figures 1.7 and 1.8, page 12) and Edward Hopper (Figure 5.22, page 98) inspired him to preserve the historical significance of a building, a landscape, or an environmental treasure. Smith likes to use pencil, colored pencils, or pen and ink to draw the scenes that represent his local environment. He is concerned with capturing light, and in this landscape he has used stippling for the shadows and has left the white of the paper to represent the white froth of the foaming falls.

Observe the different ways in which Larry Smith has created three-dimensional forms and depth in his landscape. Watch how your drawing springs to life when you use shading to create three-dimensional forms and perspective techniques to show deep space.

Make a drawing of an outdoor scene that is interesting to you. This scene should have a foreground, middle ground, and background. Create the illusion of three-dimensional forms in the scene by using a variety of shading techniques. Use values that range from black to various grays to white. Create the illusion of deep, three-dimensional space by using one or more perspective techniques. Mount or mat the finished work for display.

FOCUSING

Larry Smith chooses scenes from his local environment to record for others to enjoy. Find an outdoor scene that is important to you and that you think is important enough to record for the future. Think of the view from your window, a country or park scene, or a view of boats in a harbor. Do not use a photograph or another drawing.

CREATING

Make a viewing frame and use it to help select the exact view you wish to draw. (See Technique Tip on page 351 in the Handbook.) Be sure to include a large shape in the foreground. All parts of the large shape do not have to fit in the picture. Take time to study the relationship of each shape and form to the frame. Each shape and form will have the same relationship to the edges of the paper as it does to the edges of the frame. Make some rough sketches of the scene in your sketchbook.

Now look through the frame at the objects in the scene and write notes in your sketchbook about how they are arranged. Pay attention to overlapping, placement, size differences, details, values, and receding parallel lines.

Tape your paper to the drawing board and lightly draw in the shapes, paying careful attention to the placement of the major objects on the page. Shade the shapes using a value scale that includes black, white, and all the grays in between. Use a variety of shading techniques to create the illusion of flat and rounded three-dimensional forms.

Give your work a title that expresses the mood or meaning of the work. Mount or mat your work for display.

FIGURE 6.44A Student work.

CRITIQUING

Describe What scene did you choose as the subject of your drawing? Tell why you selected this scene. How did the use of the viewing frame affect your work? How did you prepare the work for display?

Analyze Which shading techniques did you use to create three-dimensional forms? Which perspective techniques did you use to create the illusion of depth?

Interpret What kind of a feeling does this drawing express? Does the title you chose express the mood or meaning of the work?

Judge Which aesthetic theory would you use to judge your work? Do you think the work was successful? What would you change to improve it?

STUDIO LESSON: CLAY PLAQUE WITH HIGH RELIEF

FIGURE 6.45 *Warrior Chief, Warriors, and Attendants.* Plaque. Nigeria, Edo. Court of Benin. Sixteenth to seventeenth centuries. Brass. Height 48 cm (18⅞″). The Metropolitan Museum of Art, New York, New York. Gift of Mr. and Mrs. Klaus G. Perls, 1990.

Supplies

- Sketchbook and pencil
- Clay
- Clay tools and equipment
- Newspaper and scissors
- Slip and brush
- Large plastic bag
- Kiln
- Glaze or acrylic paints and brushes (optional)

The brass plaque shown in Figure 6.45 was one of many that decorated the walls of the palace of the Oba, the divine ruler of the Benin kingdom (now the capital of Nigeria's Bendel state). *Warrior Chief, Warriors, and Attendants* depicts ceremonies and rituals that were carried out in the court. In fact, because the plaques so accurately documented the costumes, ornaments, hairstyles, weapons, and musical instruments employed in these ceremonies, they were often used in later centuries to answer questions about court procedures.

The technique of high and low relief, shown here, indicates a person's rank. Notice how the most important figure, located in the center of the plaque, is larger and in higher relief than the others. People of less importance are placed to the side and are shown smaller and in low relief. Many detailed objects are added to the surfaces and are used to fill the spaces in between.

Create a clay plaque depicting an event from current events or history that you find interesting. Using high and low relief, include three or more people and the necessary objects to illustrate the scene. In the style of the Benin plaque, the most important person should be the largest and in the highest relief.

FOCUSING

Study the Benin plaque. What can you learn about the people by observing their relative sizes and the degrees of relief? Brainstorm ideas for your plaque with your classmates. Once you have selected a topic, do some visual research.

CREATING

Do research sketching. Draw examples in your sketchbook of clothing, the setting, and the objects related to the event. Make detail sketches of the most important items. These do not have to be complete drawings. Think of them as visual note taking.

If you have not worked with clay, take time to become familiar with clay and the proper clay-joining techniques. (See Technique Tips on page 354 in the Handbook.)

Make a complete plan for your plaque in your sketchbook. First, sketch the figures using the Benin style of making the most important figure the largest. Then add objects and a natural setting, if necessary. Finally, plan the shape of the plaque.

Draw a pattern for the shape of the plaque on a sheet of newspaper and cut it out. Roll out a slab of clay approximately ½ inch (1.3 cm) thick. Trace the shape of the plaque pattern onto the slab and cut the slab into the shape of the pattern.

Model the figures and objects you have designed for the plaque. Add the figures and the objects to the plaque using scoring and slip. Notice how the Benin plaque has details added to the main figures as well as details that are carved and stippled into the work. Use clay tools to add details to your plaque.

Punch holes into the slab for hanging the plaque. Make sure they are more than ½ inch (1.3 cm) from every edge of the slab.

FIGURE 6.45A Student work.

When the clay is bone dry, fire it in the kiln following your teacher's instructions.

CRITIQUING

Describe What is the subject matter of your plaque? Describe the event and identify the people you have included. Did you use proper clay-modeling procedures? Did the clay stay joined, and did it come through the firing process successfully? Which option did you choose to finish the work?

Analyze Did you follow the style of the Benin relief by making the most important figure larger and in higher relief than the others? What kind of a shape did you make the background slab? Did you fill the negative space with patterns?

Interpret Can the viewer recognize the event by just looking at your work? What is the mood you were trying to convey? Have you caught the mood of the occasion?

Judge Were the viewers able to understand the event you were illustrating? Which aesthetic theory would you use to judge this work?

STUDIO LESSON: LANDSCAPE USING SURREAL SPACE

FIGURE 6.46 René Magritte. *The Blank Signature.* 1965. Oil on canvas. 81 × 65 cm (32 × 25½″). National Gallery of Art, Washington, D.C. Collection of Mr. and Mrs. Paul Mellon, 1985.

Supplies

- Sketchbook and pencil
- Sheet of tracing paper
- Two large sheets of white paper
- Yellow chalk and soap eraser
- Oil pastels

René Magritte was a Belgian Surrealist who loved to create visual puzzles. He began his career as a graphic artist, and by the time he was forty, he was able to give up commercial art and work full time as a painter.

While French Surrealists were exploring fantasy, psychology, and the subconscious mind to find subjects for their art, Magritte worked with ordinary images from the real world. His painting style was very realistic, and his ideas were powerful because the images he used were familiar and lifelike.

In the painting *The Blank Signature* (Figure 6.46), Magritte was trying to find a way to express the visible and the invisible. He said, "Visible things can be invisible. When someone rides a horse in the forest, first you see her, then you don't, but you know that she is there . . . the rider hides the trees and the trees hide her."

Look at Magritte's painting to see how he created his surreal landscape. See if you can turn your painting into a visual puzzle.

Using oil pastels on white paper, create a surreal seascape, landscape, or cityscape in which the positive shapes and negative spaces are interwoven into a reversal of the visible and invisible, as in Magritte's painting *The Blank Signature* (Figure 6.46).

FOCUSING

Brainstorm with your classmates about ways that you can create Magritte's visible/invisible effect. Trees, a network of branches, or haystacks might divide the positive and negative in a landscape. Signposts, lampposts, or buildings with big windows can divide the space in a cityscape.

Design the realistic scene as a whole first. What makes Magritte's work so successful is that every object looks realistic. To make your scene work, choose a subject with which you are familiar. First, make rough sketches in your sketchbook and then organize them into a good composition on a sheet of white paper. Plan to use colors in the realistic scene that are different from and contrast with the color of the dividing scene, as Magritte used greens and blues for his scenery and purple and brown for the woman and her horse.

Place a sheet of tracing paper over the realistic composition. On the tracing paper, sketch the second drawing into which you will weave your first scene.

Using yellow chalk, lightly copy your realistic scene onto the other large sheet of white paper. Then sketch the dividing drawing over the first using another light chalk color. Now decide which scene will be visible in each area. Use the soap eraser to remove the chalk lines that will be invisible.

Apply color lightly until you have all the positive and negative areas worked out. Then apply the oil pastel color heavily, blending colors when necessary to build up layers of color.

Give your work a title that helps viewers to understand your work. Mount or mat your work for display.

FIGURE 6.46A Student work.

CRITIQUING

Describe Explain how you have created a surreal scene by telling what realistic scene you chose for the subject matter. Then, explain what device you have used to divide the scene so that the visible and invisible are reversed.

Analyze Explain how you managed to create a reversal of visible and invisible through your arrangement of positive and negative space. Describe how you used contrasting colors to help the viewer see the two different scenes.

Interpret Describe the emotional effect you have achieved in your work. Does the title you gave your piece help the viewer understand your work?

Judge Was your attempt to create a surreal space successful? Which aesthetic theory would you use to evaluate this work?

ART CRITICISM IN ACTION

FIGURE 6.47 Michael Naranjo. *Spirits Soaring.* 1985. Bronze. Height 51 cm (20″). Private collection.

CRITIQUING THE WORK

1. **Describe** Notice the photographs of *Spirits Soaring* in Figure 6.47. Each is a different view of the same work. If you were looking at the real sculpture, you would be able to walk around it and look at it from every point of view. Since it is in a book, we have given you more than one point of view to study. Read the credit information. What material did the sculptor use to create this work? How tall is it? Study the three views of the work. Describe what you see.
2. **Analyze** Is *Spirits Soaring* a shape or a form? Is it geometric or free-form? Does it look dense or soft? Does it look heavy or light? How has the artist used space? Is it real or an illusion? As you look at the three views, do they look open or closed? Does the work seem to be active or static? Explain by describing the parts that make it look active or static. Do you see many intricate details, or are the details simplified? What color is the work?
3. **Interpret** What kind of mood is the artist creating with this sculpture? Review the clues you have collected during the Analysis step. Now let your own feelings combine with the facts. Write a paragraph explaining your personal interpretation of the work. Then write a new title for the work that sums up your interpretation.
4. **Judge** Do you think this is a successful work? Use one or more of the aesthetic theories of art to defend your judgment.

FIGURE 6.48 *Nike of Samothrace.* c. 190 B.C. Marble. Approx. 2.4 m (8′). The Louvre, Paris, France.

COMPARING THE WORKS

Look at *Spirits Soaring* (Figure 6.47) and *Nike of Samothrace* (Figure 6.48). In what way are the two works similar? In what ways are they different? Notice the amount of detail, the posture of each figure, the costumes, and the interaction between positive and negative space. What is the difference in the relationship between wing and body in each work? Nike is the Greek goddess of victory. The nickname for this work is "Winged Victory." Based on the rest of the work, what do you think her head and arms would look like? Would they be similar to or different from those in *Spirits Soaring?* What would she be doing with her arms and hands? What position would her head hold? In what way does each work accentuate the difference between the philosophies of the cultures from which they come?

MEET THE ARTIST

MICHAEL NARANJO

Native American, b. 1944

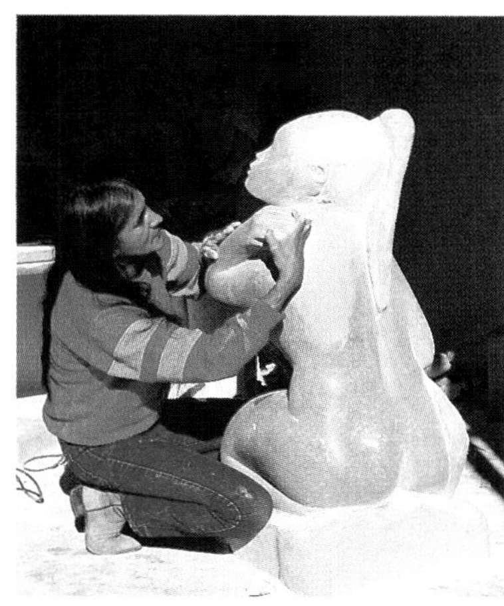

Just like every other sculptor, Michael Naranjo feels the need to study the works of other artists. When he looks, however, he sees with his hands. In 1968, while serving in the army, he was blinded by a grenade in Vietnam.

Naranjo has always been interested in art. He was born near Santa Fe, New Mexico, a Tewa Indian of the Santa Clara Pueblo. His mother was a potter, and he has pleasant memories of helping her mix the white clay with the brown by stepping on it. Mixing clay was like a dance, a rhythmic stepping.

Michael was drafted in 1967 and was sent to Vietnam for active duty. While there, he was caught on his hands and knees in an ambush. A grenade exploded, lifting him up in the air. When he awoke in a hospital, he found his right arm damaged and his sight gone. In a hospital bed in Japan he began modeling a piece of clay. In a hospital in Denver he made an Indian whipping a horse across the plain.

He gets ideas from the things he saw in the past. He has to visualize the image in his mind. That takes a long time. Then he models his idea in wax or carves it from stone. Wax carving is easier, because he can correct mistakes. He has to keep the whole of the image in his mind so he knows how much he has taken away. Because Naranjo works in a three-dimensional art form with challenging media, he only produces a few sculptures a year.

MORE PORTFOLIO IDEAS

I. Tape a piece of white paper to the table. Put on a blindfold. Think about an object you know very well—something you use every day. Visualize it in your mind. Using a pencil, make a contour drawing of the object with the blindfold in place. Remove the blindfold. Can you see what your mind was telling your eyes to draw?

II. Using the blindfold again, visualize your own face and head in your mind. Think about what you have seen in the mirror. Model your face and head in clay using only your fingers and nails as tools. You may touch your own face and head as you work to check proportions and details. Keep a damp sponge nearby to clean your fingers before you touch your face.

CHAPTER 6 REVIEW

Building Vocabulary

On a separate sheet of paper, write the term that best matches each definition given below.

1. A two-dimensional area that is defined in some way.
2. Precise shapes that can be described using mathematical formulas.
3. Irregular and uneven shapes.
4. Objects having three dimensions.
5. The element of art that refers to the area between, around, above, below, or within objects.
6. Images in three dimensions created with a laser beam.
7. The arrangement of light and shadow.
8. Small areas of white used to show the very brightest spots.
9. A graphic system that creates the illusion of depth and volume on a two-dimensional surface.

Reviewing Art Facts

Answer the following questions using complete sentences.

1. Name the two basic types of shapes and tell which is more often used for decorative purposes.
2. What is the difference between shapes and forms?
3. By what are shapes and forms defined?
4. Name the two kinds of space found in art.
5. Using a portrait as an example, name the kind of space the subject occupies.
6. Explain how the eyes and brain enable us to see in three dimensions.
7. Explain how an artist is able to create the illusion of three-dimensional form on a two-dimensional surface.
8. Name the six devices for creating perspective in drawing.
9. Name two kinds of perspective.
10. Give an example of an active shape and tell what makes it look active.
11. Give an example of a static shape and tell what makes it look motionless, or stable.

Thinking Critically About Art

1. **Explain.** Matisse started his artistic career as a painter. He made important contributions to the field of painting. Do some research on Matisse at the library. Find out what his contributions were. Then find out why he created *Beasts of the Sea* (Figure 6.21, page 132) by cutting shapes with scissors. Write a brief paper explaining your findings.
2. **Compare and contrast.** Look at *Johnson House* by Philip Johnson (Figure 6.37, page 141) and *Falling Water* by Frank Lloyd Wright (Figure 12.21, page 330). Evaluate the architects' use of forms and space. In what ways are these two houses similar? In what ways are they different? Explain.
3. **Analyze.** Look at *Other World* by M.C. Escher (Figure 6.13, page 127) and *The Blank Signature* by René Magritte (Figure 6.46, page 148). Both artists used optical illusions. Look for information about each artist in the library. Are they both from the same art movement? Do they have the same philosophy? Explain your findings in a brief paragraph.

Making Art Connections

1. **Science.** Research the theory of Gestalt psychology. Explain the Figure/Ground theory in gestalt psychology to your classmates. Make a poster or chart to help explain your findings.
2. **Social Studies.** Choose a manufactured object such as a telephone, coffee pot, ship, airplane, TV set, sewing machine, shoe, radio, or something else that interests you personally. Research the history of its form and function. Use the library, an encyclopedia, or interview a grandparent. Make a chart showing how, when, and why the form changed. Was it changed because of improved technology, for the convenience of the user, or for some other reason? Explain your findings to your class.

FIGURE 7.1 Gauguin gave up a successful career as a stockbroker to devote his time to art. He traveled around the world to find freedom from traditions. In Tahiti he produced art that was simplified and full of brilliant colors.

Paul Gauguin. *Faaturuma (The Dreamer).* c. 1891. Oil on canvas. 95 × 68.6 cm (37½ × 27"). Nelson-Atkins Museum of Art, Kansas City, Missouri. Museum purchase, 1938.

CHAPTER 7

Color

Color is exciting! We are so sensitive to color that it appeals directly to our emotions. Color is the most expressive element of art and most of us have a favorite color, but it is also the most difficult element to talk about. Try to imagine how to describe the difference between red and orange to a blind person. It is almost impossible to describe color without also talking about other colors.

Colors stand for ideas and feelings. You use color symbolically when you say, "I feel blue," "She's green with envy," or "He's a yellow coward."

You may remember a time when you mixed some beautiful, bright colors into a muddy, dull gray mess. Color can be very frustrating. Sometimes it acts like a wild thing, but it *can* be tamed. In this chapter you will learn how to speak with color in the language of art.

Objectives

After completing this chapter, you will be able to:

- Understand how your eyes see color.
- Name the properties of color and the colors of the spectrum.
- Identify different color schemes.
- Mix your own paints using different pigments and vehicles.
- Use color as the expressive element in creating two- and three-dimensional artworks.
- Recognize the expressive qualities of color that artists use to create meaning.

FIRST IMPRESSIONS

Look at the bright colors in this painting (Figure 7.1). This Tahitian woman has golden skin but in the four areas where you can see her skin you see four different colors. What is the difference between the colors used for her face, her right hand, her left hand, and the exposed foot? She is wearing a red robe, yet look at the varieties of red with which Gauguin has painted that robe. What color did he use in the shadows? How many different blues can you find in the wall? What colors has he used on the foot? How many greens are there inside the picture frame? How many colors can you find on the wooden rocking chair? Notice how he has even used color to enhance the white handkerchief.

Words to Know

analogous colors
binder
color
color spectrum
color wheel
complementary colors
dyes
hue
intensity
monochromatic
pigments
shade
solvent
tint

How we see color

Color is *an element of art that is derived from reflected light* (Figure 7.2). You see color because light waves are reflected from objects to your eyes (Figure 7.3). White light from the sun is actually a combination of all colors.

When light passes through a wedge-shaped glass, called a prism, the beam of white light is bent and separated into bands of color, called the **color spectrum.** The colors of the spectrum always appear in the same order: red, orange, yellow, green, blue, and violet.

A rainbow is a natural example of a spectrum. Rainbows occur when sunlight is bent by water, oil, or a glass prism. You can find rainbows in the sky, in the spray from a garden hose, or in a puddle of oil in a parking lot.

Objects absorb some waves of light and reflect others. A red apple looks red because it reflects red waves and absorbs the rest of the colors (Figure 7.4). Special color receptors in your eyes detect these red light waves, and your mind then reads the light as being a certain color. The light enters your eye and travels to a membrane of nerve tissue, called the retina, at the back of your eyeball. There, two types of cells react to the light. One type receives impressions of lightness and darkness. The other type receives color.

FIGURE 7.2 Can you imagine how dull and drab our world would be without color?

FIGURE 7.3 These colors glow as daylight shines through the stained-glass window.

Bronislaw M. Bak. *Holocaust.* 1969. Stained-glass windows (detail). Whole window: 3 × 9.1 m (10 × 30′). Temple Emanu-El, Chicago, Illinois.

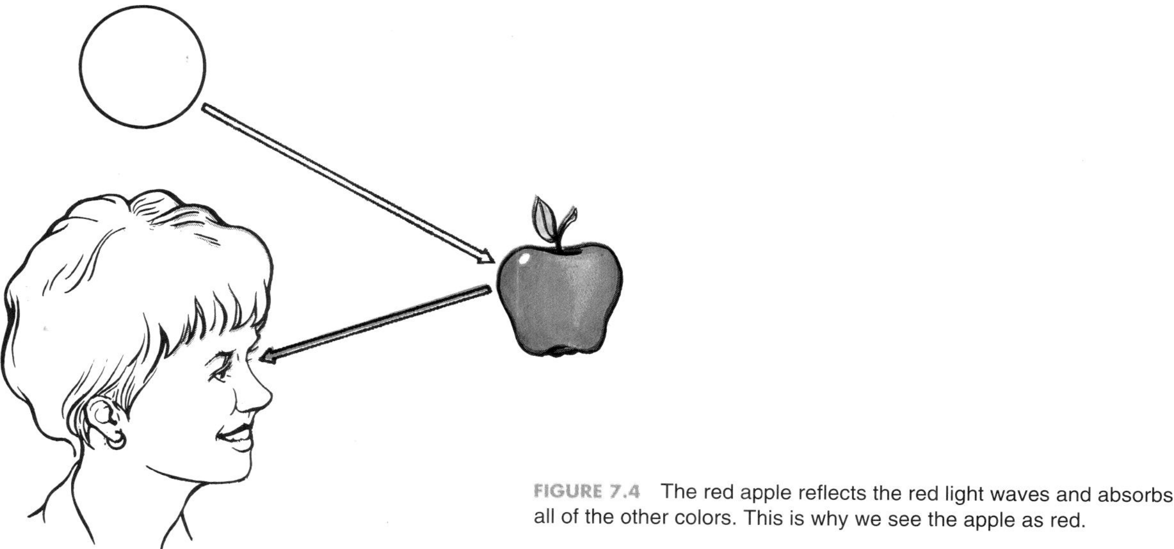

FIGURE 7.4 The red apple reflects the red light waves and absorbs all of the other colors. This is why we see the apple as red.

FIGURE 7.5 What color do you see when you shift your gaze from the red to the white area? Your eyes can fool you about color.

Colors really don't change, but your ability to distinguish between them does. That is why your eyes have trouble seeing colors in dim light, whether the light is from the sun or a lamp.

Some people are color-blind. There are many different types of color blindness. Some people cannot tell the difference between red and green, and others see only black, white, and gray. Many animals have limited color vision. Others—birds and bees, for example—see light waves that are invisible to humans.

When you are looking at colors, your eyes can sometimes fool you. For instance, stare at the bright red shape in Figure 7.5 for thirty seconds; then quickly shift your gaze to the white area next to it. Did you see a green shape on the white surface? This is called an *afterimage*. It occurs because the receptors in your eyes retain the visual stimulation even after it has ceased.

The afterimage of a color is the opposite of that color. Green is the opposite of red. The afterimage of black is white, and the afterimage of blue is orange. Don't expect an afterimage to be a strong color—it is only the ghost of a color. Your brain creates the afterimage as a reaction to the color you stared at originally. Some artists make use of the

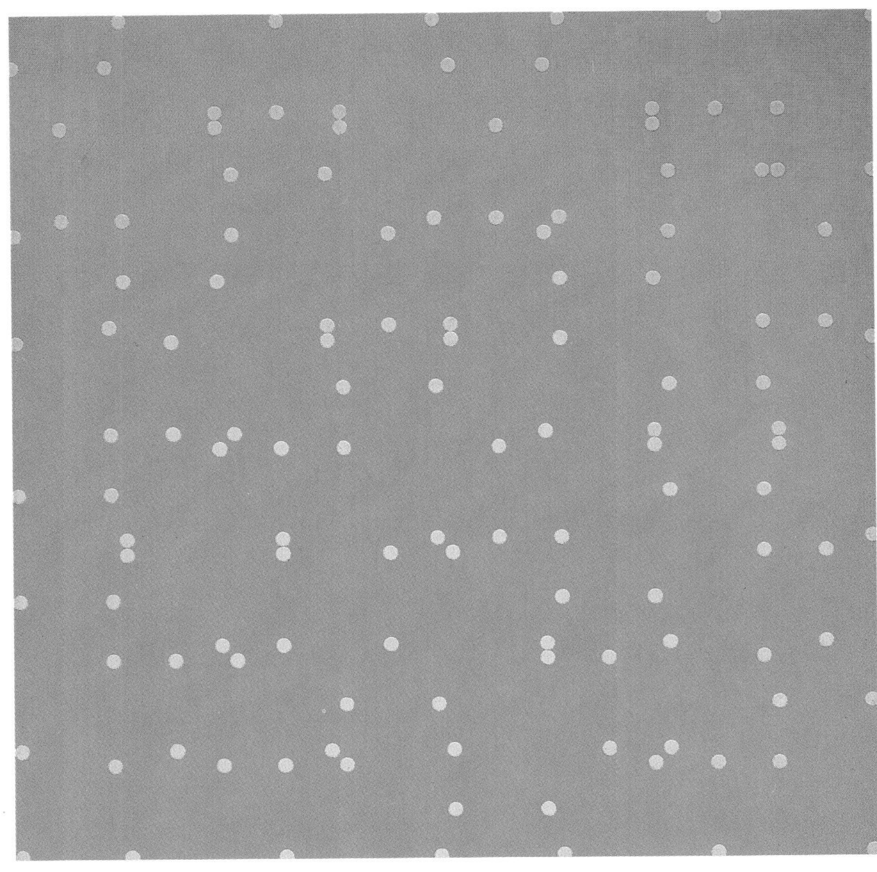

FIGURE 7.6 This painting is named for the soft drink that has an unnatural, man-made color similar to the orange of this painting. The blue-green dots seem to have no order, but they were carefully planned. The dots are meant to suggest musical notes. As you stare at this work, the afterimage of the dots creates the feeling of dancelike movements. Try to make the dots remain still!

Larry Poons. *Orange Crush.* 1963. Acrylic on canvas. 203.2 × 203.2 cm (80 × 80″). Albright-Knox Art Gallery, Buffalo, New York. Gift of Seymour H. Knox, 1964. © Larry Poons/VAGA, New York 1994.

way your eyes work when they create optical illusions of color and movement (Figure 7.6).

Understanding the three properties of color will help you work with color. The properties are *hue, value,* and *intensity.*

Hue

Hue is *the name of a spectral color,* such as red, blue, or yellow. Red, yellow, and blue are the *primary* hues. You cannot make primary hues by mixing other hues together. By combining only the three primary colors and black and white, however, you can produce almost every other color.

The *secondary hues* are made by mixing two primary colors (Figure 7.7). Red and yellow make orange; red and blue make violet; and blue and yellow make green. Orange, violet, and green are the secondary hues.

The six *intermediate* colors are made by mixing a primary color with its secondary color. For example, red and orange make red-orange, red and violet make red-violet, blue and violet make

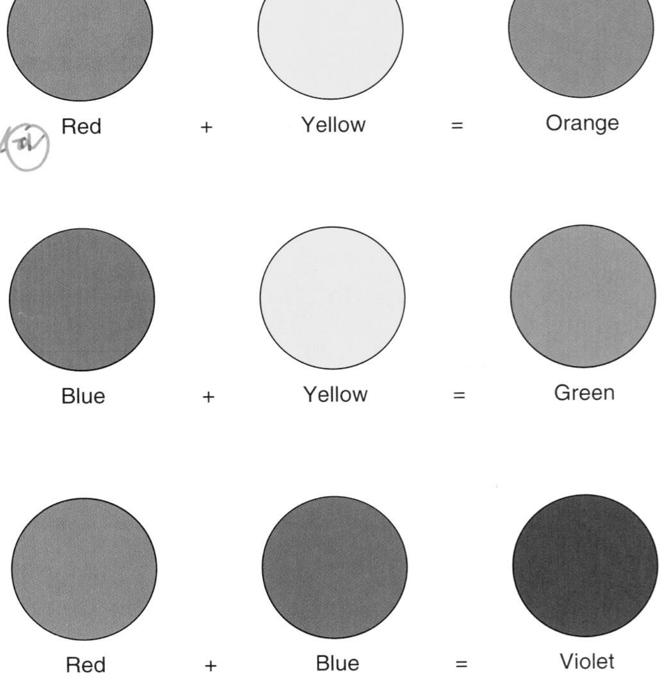

FIGURE 7.7 Primary and secondary hues.

When artists want to show a bright, sunny day, they use tints (Figure 7.12). Paintings having many tints are referred to as *high-key* paintings. Monet's *Ice Floes* is an example of a high-key painting. *Low-key* paintings have shades, or dark values, which are used when the artist wants to represent dark, gloomy days, nighttime, and dusk (Figure 7.13). Dark values can add a feeling of mystery to a work. They can also be used to create a sense of foreboding or danger.

If the change in value is gradual, the design produces a calm feeling. If the values take large leaps up and down the scale, from almost white to almost black, the artwork has an active, even nervous effect.

FIGURE 7.12 The tints of blue used in this painting gives the impression of a cold, icy day.

Claude Monet. *Ice Floes.* 1893. Oil on canvas. 66 × 100 cm (26 × 39½″). The Metropolitan Museum of Art, New York, New York. Bequest of Mrs. H. O. Havemeyer, 1929. The H. O. Havemeyer Collection.

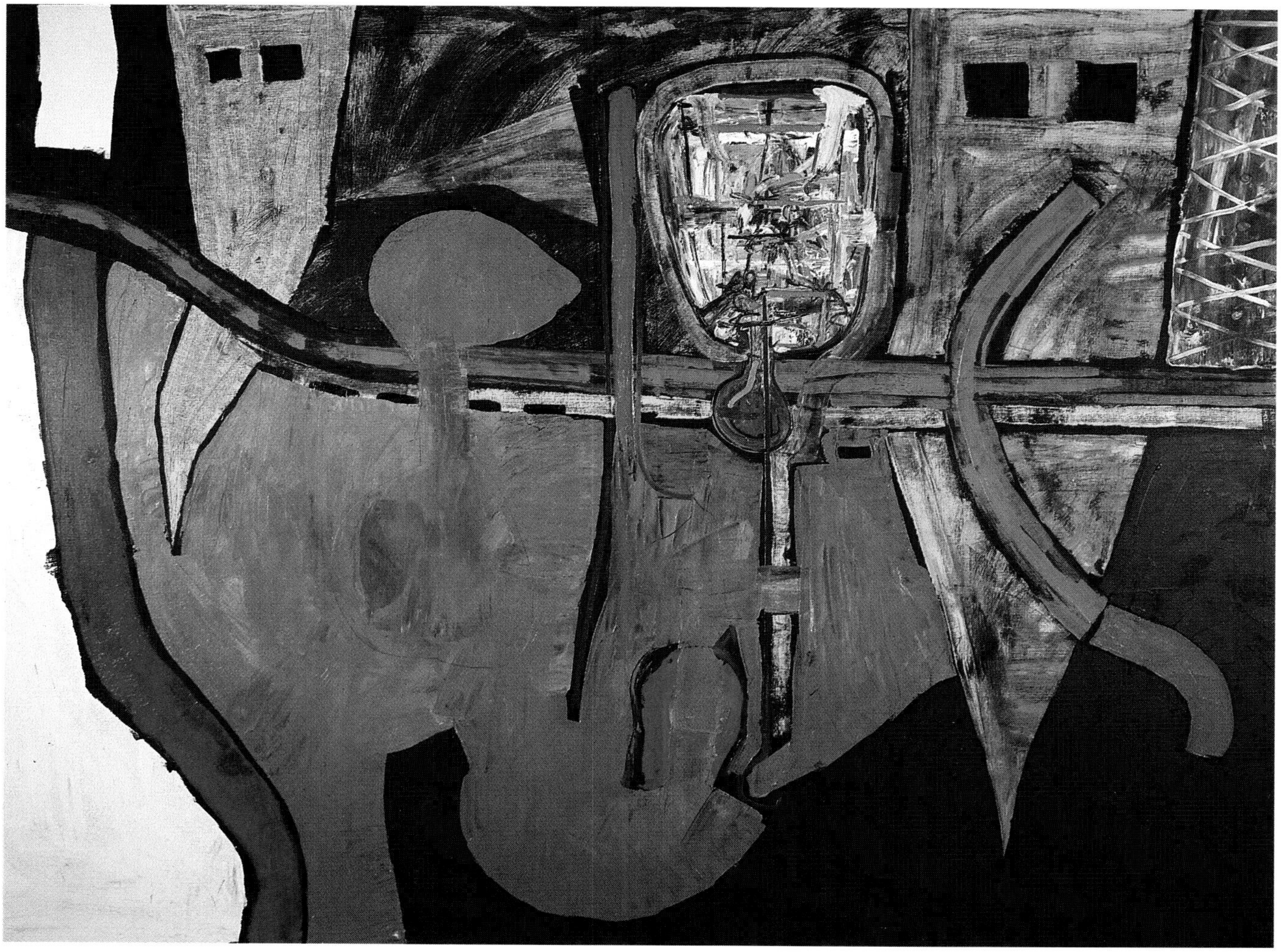

FIGURE 7.13 The dark color values in this painting add to the threatening mood of the work. Do you see any shapes that add to this mood?

Harold Town. *Night Riders.* 1960. Oil and lucite on canvas. 204 × 274.5 cm (80½ × 108″). Collection of the Art Gallery of Nova Scotia, Halifax, Nova Scotia, Canada. Gift of the Barling Company, Toronto, Ontario, Canada, 1987.

Creating Values

1. Applying Your Skills. Select a hue. Draw a row of three equal shapes. If you are using an opaque paint, such as tempera, add only a small amount of the hue to white. Fill the first shape with the light value. Paint the pure hue in the second shape. Add a small amount of black to the hue to create a dark value, and paint this in the third shape.

If you are using transparent watercolor paint, make a light value by thinning the paint with water to let more white paper show through. Make a hue darker by adding a small amount of black. Fill the three shapes as in the above directions.

2. Further Challenge. Make a seven-step value scale for one hue (see Figure 7.11, page 160). Select a hue, then draw a row of seven equal shapes, one for each step. Make the first step almost white; make the fourth step the pure hue; and make the seventh step almost black. The second step should be a very light tint of the hue, and the third step should be a little darker. The fifth step needs a small amount of black; the sixth, a little more.

Safety Note. When paints are called for, use watercolors, liquid tempera, or acrylics if possible. If you must use powdered tempera, wear a dust mask and work away from other class members.

Remember to check the safety labels on your paints. All materials used in the classroom should be properly labeled. You should know the following safety codes:

AP—Approved Product
CP—Certified Product
HL—Health Label

AP and **CP** labels assure you that the product contains no materials in sufficient amounts to be dangerous or toxic. The **CP** label further assures you that the art materials meet certain quality standards. An **HL** label can indicate that the art materials contain toxic ingredients.

FIGURE 7.14 Intensity scale. This scale shows how the intensity of one hue changes as you add its complement to it. The first box is pure, high-intensity green. Each time you add more red, the green becomes duller. Eventually the even mix of green and red creates an interesting, low-intensity gray.

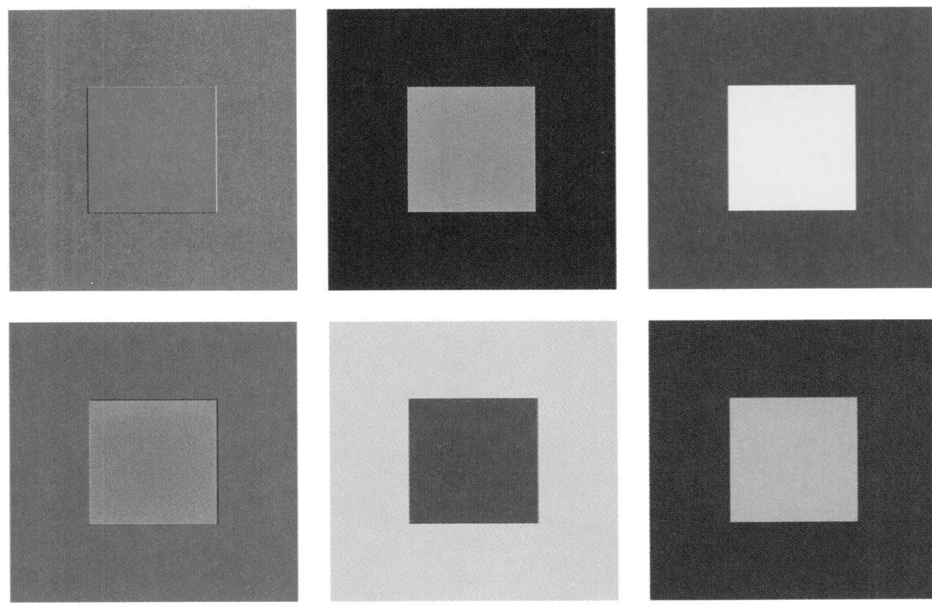

FIGURE 7.15 Sets of complements.

COLOR SCHEMES

Single colors are like musical instruments. Each instrument has its own special sound. When you hear an instrument in an orchestra, the sound you hear is affected by the sounds of the other instruments. When the musicians tune up before a performance, you hear confusing noises. When they play together in an organized way, they can make beautiful sounds. Unplanned colors can be as confusing to your eyes as unplanned sound is to your ears. Color without organization can look like a visual argument.

When two colors come into direct contact, their differences increase. A yellow-green surrounded by a green looks yellower. A yellow-green surrounded by yellow seems greener. Grayish green will brighten when it is placed against a gray background (Figure 7.17).

"Dogtown." To capture
limited his colors to a

8½ × 24"). High Museum of

Analogous Colors

Analogous colors are *colors that sit side by side on the color wheel and have a common hue* (Figure 7.19). Violet, red-violet, red, red-orange, and orange all have red in common. A more narrowly related scheme would be limited to only three hues, such as violet, red-violet, and red.

Analogous colors can be blended to create a design that ties one shape to the next through a common color (Figure 7.20, page 166). Because of their common hue, these colors are easy to organize.

Complementary Colors

The strongest contrast of a hue is produced by complementary colors. When a pair of high-

FIGURE 7.20 Rothko limited the colors in this painting to an analogous scheme of yellow and orange. He uses soft edges and colors that blend so that the painting seems to have no borders or edges. The yellow and orange float against a ground that glows mysteriously. Standing in front of this work, which is almost 8 feet (2.4 m) high, the viewer can have an intense visual experience.

Mark Rothko. *Orange and Yellow.* 1956. Oil on canvas. 231.1 × 180.3 cm (91 × 71″). Albright-Knox Art Gallery, Buffalo, New York. Gift of Seymour H. Knox, 1956.

intensity complements are placed side by side, they seem to vibrate. It is difficult to focus on the edge where the complements touch. Some artists use this visual vibration to create special effects. They make designs that sparkle, snap, and sizzle as if charged with electricity. (See Figure 7.21.)

Complementary color schemes are exciting. They are loud, and they demand to be noticed. They are frequently used to catch the viewer's attention. How many ways do people use the red-and-green color scheme? Where else have you seen complementary color schemes used to grab attention?

Not all color schemes based on complements are loud and demanding. If the hues are of low intensity, the contrast is not so harsh. Changing the values of the hues will also soften the effect of the design.

Color Triads

A color triad is composed of three colors spaced an equal distance apart on the color wheel. The contrast between triad colors is not as strong as that between complements. The primary triad is composed of red, yellow, and blue. The secondary triad contains orange, green, and violet (Figure 7.22 on page 168).

A high-intensity primary triad is very difficult to work with. The contrast between the three hues is so strong that they might make people uncomfortable. A triad can be made more comfortable to the

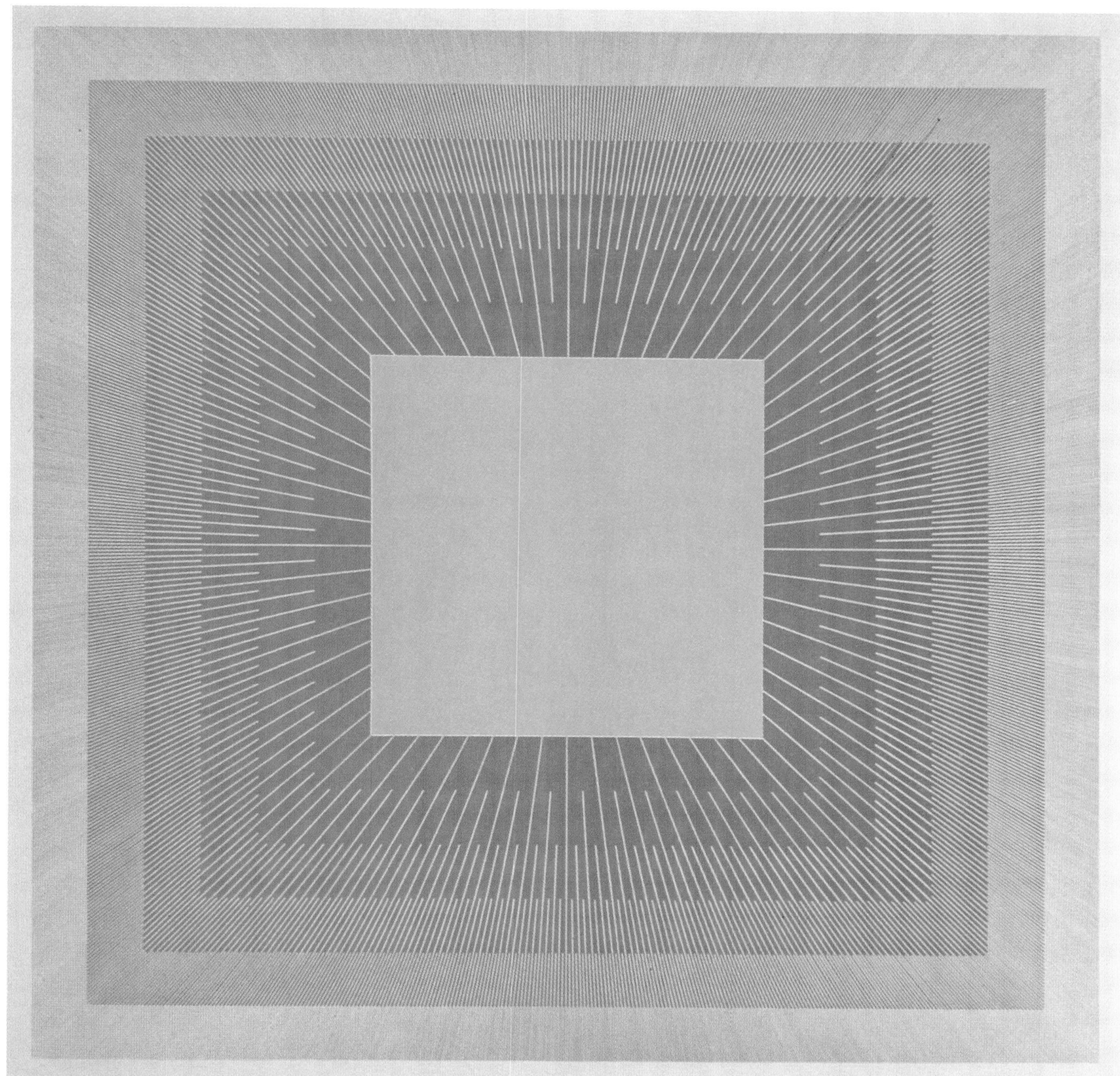

FIGURE 7.21 This painting is an experiment with the effects of high-intensity, complementary colors. The well-defined squares have been created by precise lines, evenly placed. Notice how the red ground changes color according to the density of the alternating blue and green lines. Stare at this painting. Do the afterimages affect your perception?

Richard Anuszkiewicz. *Iridescence.* 1965. Acrylic on canvas. 152.4 × 152.4 cm (60 × 60″). Albright-Knox Art Gallery, Buffalo, New York. Gift of Seymour H. Knox, 1966.

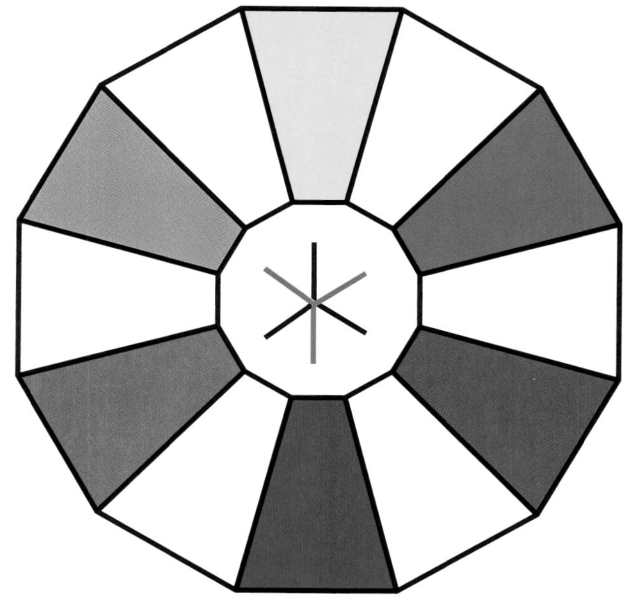

FIGURE 7.22 Color triads.

FIGURE 7.23 Even though this painting is based on the primary triad, it is very comfortable to view. What has the artist done with the colors to make this painting easy to look at?

Fritz Glarner. *Relational Painting #93.* 1962. Oil on canvas. 169.9 × 111.8 cm (66⅞ × 44″). Albright-Knox Art Gallery, Buffalo, New York. Gift of the Seymour H. Knox Foundation, Inc., 1966.

viewer by changing the intensity or values (Figure 7.23). A triad of secondary colors is less disturbing.

Split Complements

A *split complement* is the combination of one hue plus the hues on each side of its complement (Figure 7.24). This is easier to work with than a straight complementary scheme because it offers more variety. For example, start with red-orange. Check the color wheel to find its complement, blue-green. The two hues next to blue-green are blue and green. Red-orange, blue, and green form a split-complementary color scheme.

Warm and Cool Colors

Sometimes the colors are divided into two groups, called *warm* and *cool* (Figure 7.25). Warm colors are red, orange, and yellow. They are usually associated with warm things, such as sunshine or fire (Figure 7.26). Cool colors are blue, green, and violet. They are usually associated with cool things, such as ice, snow, water, or grass (Figure 7.27, page 170). Warm colors seem to move toward the viewer and cool colors seem to recede, or move away.

The amount of warmth or coolness is relative. Violet on a red background appears much cooler than violet alone. However, the same violet on a blue background seems much warmer than the violet alone.

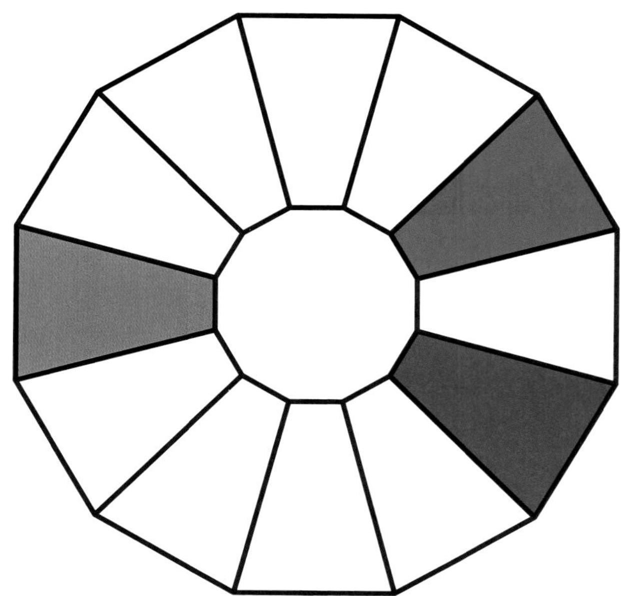

FIGURE 7.24 Split complement.

Using Color Schemes

1. Applying Your Skills. Make a chart to demonstrate the effects of colors on one another. Select a sheet of construction paper of a primary hue. Cut the paper into sixteen equal rectangles. Mount each small rectangle on a different-colored background. Use a variety of materials for the backgrounds. Try colored photos, painted areas, fabric samples, construction paper, and tissue paper. Group the color pairs according to color scheme or degree of contrast. Can you think of other ways to group them?

2. Further Challenge. In your sketchbook, write your initials or the letters of your name. Draw several squares and arrange the letters in a design in one of the squares. The letters must touch the four edges of the square. Do several different designs using the remaining squares. Play with the letters—turn them upside down, twist them out of shape, make them fat, or overlap them. Consider the letters as shapes. They do not have to be readable.

When you find a design you like, reproduce it on four squares of white paper. Now paint each design using one of the following color schemes: monochromatic, analogous, complementary, triad, split-complementary, warm, and cool. How do the color arrangements affect the design? (See Figures 7.28 and 7.29, page 171.)

3. Computer Option. Draw the initials or letters of your name into a design on the computer screen. The letters must touch the four edges of the screen. Play with the letters—turn them upside down or twist them out of shape. Try making them fat or overlapping them. Use only solid color areas and solid lines, since you will

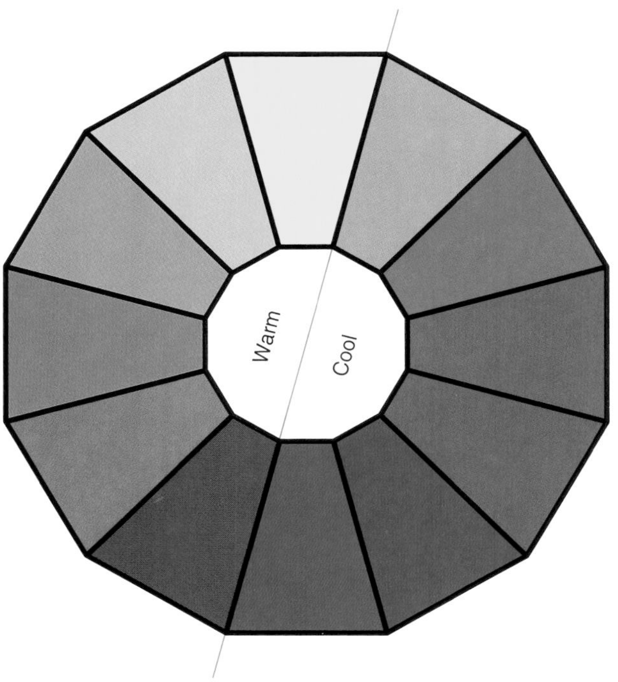

FIGURE 7.25 Warm and cool colors.

FIGURE 7.26 The warm colors in this painting tell us the mood the artist is trying to create.

Rufino Tamayo. *Toast to the Sun.* 1956. Oil on canvas. 80 × 99 cm (31½ × 39"). Wichita Art Museum, Wichita, Kansas. The Roland P. Murdock Collection.

Emily Carr. *Above the Trees.* c. 1939. Oil on paper. 91.2 × 61 cm (36 × 24″). Vancouver Art Gallery, Vancouver, British Columbia, Canada.

LOOKING CLOSELY

FIGURE 7.27 Notice how Carr has used cool colors to represent the moisture-laden atmosphere of the forests of Victoria. The foliage of the trees has been portrayed as solid forms. What forms do they look like? The curves in the sky seem to echo the forms of the trees. Look at the light values in the sky near the top of the painting. What light hue has Carr used in addition to blue? Why do you think she used that color? What color has she used to represent the darker sky in the bottom right corner?

Besides blue and green, what other hues can you find? Which neutral colors have been used?

Why do you think Carr has painted the forms of the foliage as if they are solid?

need to fill them with new colors as you progress through the assignment. Consider the letters as shapes. They do not have to be readable. You may use any tools or options available on your computer software. Resize and Distort options would be useful.

When you find a design you like, label it "Basic Design" and save it. Use the Fill Bucket and other tools to fill in all the shapes, lines, and spaces with each of the following color schemes: monochromatic, analogous, complementary, triad, split-complementary, warm, and cool.

Label and save each color scheme as you finish it. When you finish all the color schemes, evaluate their effect on the basic design. Also evaluate your personal preferences in the use of color schemes.

FIGURE 7.28 Student work. Designing the letters of a name.

FIGURE 7.29 Student work. Designing the letters of a name.

COLOR IN PIGMENTS

Artists' **pigments** are *finely ground, colored powders that form paint when mixed with a liquid.* Pigment colors cannot match the purity and intensity of the colors of light.

Artists' paints are sometimes named according to the mineral from which the pigment powder is made. For example, cadmium yellow is made with the mineral cadmium sulfide. Sometimes the pigment gets its name from the place where it was discovered. Burnt sienna, for instance, is made with clay found in the soil in Siena, Italy.

Before you buy paint, look at the manufacturer's color chart to find out what the color looks like. You will see that ultramarine blue, cobalt blue, cerulean blue, and thalo blue all look different.

Paint

All paints used in art are made up of three basic ingredients: pigment, binder, and solvent. The **binder** is *a liquid that holds together the grains of pigment* in a form that can be spread over some surface. Linseed oil is the binder for oil paints. Wax is the binder for encaustic paint. Gum arabic is the binder for watercolor paints. Acrylic polymer is the binder for acrylic paints. A chemical emulsion is used to make school tempera paint. Many professional artists mix pure pigments with egg yolk for a translucent tempera paint. The **solvent** is *the liquid that controls the thickness or the thinness of the paint.* The solvent for oil paints is turpentine. Water is the solvent for watercolors and tempera. Acrylics can be thinned with water or acrylic medium while wet, but once acrylic paint dries, it is waterproof.

Paint pigments do not dissolve—they remain suspended in the medium. When applied to a surface, the pigments stay on top of the surface and they dry there. *Pigments that dissolve in liquid* are called **dyes.** Dyes do not remain on the surfaces as paints do. Dyes sink into the fabric to which they are applied and color the fabric by staining it.

The pigment, the binder, the solvent, and the surface to which the paint is applied all affect the color you see. Wet colors look brighter and darker than dry ones. Tempera and watercolor paints always look lighter and duller after they dry. Oil paints glow even when dry because of their oil vehicle. If diluted with turpentine, oil paints dry to a dull finish.

The density and color of the surface receiving the paint affects the way the light waves will be reflected back to your eyes. Have you ever applied wax crayon to colored paper? The crayon lets light through to the paper, and the colored paper absorbs some of these light waves and reflects the rest. Only white paper allows the true color of the crayon to show, because it reflects all the light.

Have you ever tried to match colors that are on two different surfaces? A fuzzy brown sweater can

FIGURE 7.30 This Soninke woman is applying a paste of ground natural pigment and water to the mud wall. All the paints are made from materials found in the local environment. The scratch lines on the unpainted wall are the outlines for the paints that will be applied.

Photo from *African Canvas* by Margaret Courtney-Clarke. Rizzoli, 1990.

never truly match a brown leather bag. A shiny green polyester shirt looks brighter than green knit pants even though the same dye is used. Shiny, dense surfaces always look brighter because they reflect more light.

Sources of Pigment

In the past, pigments came from animals, vegetables, and minerals. A kind of beetle and the root of a certain plant were both sources for red. Another plant produced a deep, transparent blue. Ultramarine blue was made by grinding a semiprecious stone. The color ocher is natural clay colored by iron rust. Prehistoric people made paint from natural minerals. They ground different-colored pieces of earth and combined them with animal fat to make paint.

Today synthetic (artificially made) pigments have been developed by scientists. The synthetics are brighter and more permanent than natural pigments, but some artists still prefer to use natural colors (Figure 7.30). Many weavers color their yarns with natural dyes. Andrew Wyeth is a modern artist who uses only natural earth pigments.

Mixing Colors

1. Applying Your Skills. Collect and grind three of your own earth pigments (see Technique Tip 11 on page 353 in the Handbook). Mix them with a binder and solvent and experiment with them. Try using a variety of brushes and surfaces. Finally, paint a design that shows all the colors you can obtain from the pigments. (See Figure 7.31.)

2. Further Challenge. Experiment by applying a variety of paint media to many different surfaces. Collect as many paints and surfaces as possible and cut the surfaces into regular, matching shapes. Try every paint on every surface. What conclusions can you make about paints and surfaces?

3. Computer Option. Mixing colors with light on a computer is very different from mixing colors with pigment. If your computer software has the capabilities, practice making secondary and intermediate colors. Also mix tints, shades, and intensity changes. Fill a variety of geometric shapes with all the new colors you have made, and show off your work by filling your screen with repeated shapes.

FIGURE 7.31 Student work. Earth pigments were used to create this painting. What would be the result if the student painted the same scene with synthetic paints?

How Artists Use Color

You have studied the facts of color. Now you need to look at how artists use color in the language of art. There are many ways to communicate with color, and realistic representation is only one of them.

Optical Color

Sometimes artists reproduce colors as they see them. Until the late nineteenth century, this was the way all Western artists painted. For example, in an automobile dealer's showroom, the color of a blue car is affected by light and other factors surrounding it. The car may sparkle as it reflects the showroom lights. Shadows on the car may look dark blue or blue-violet. The red from the car next to it may cause a red-violet reflection on the blue surface.

A painter who is trying to show the car in its setting will use all the colors involved. He or she will make use of *optical color,* the color that results when a true color is affected by the atmosphere or unusual lighting. Optical color is the color that people actually perceive. Compare the two paintings by Claude Monet shown in Figures 7.32 and 7.33 to see how the time of day affects color.

The Impressionists were deeply involved with optical color. They tried to express the sensation of light and atmosphere with their unique style of painting. They applied dots and dabs of spectral colors and did not mix black with any colors. They made gray, low-intensity colors by putting complements together instead of mixing just black and white. These low-intensity grays, such as dull blue and dull green, are much richer and look more natural in landscapes than do grays made by mixing black and white.

FIGURE 7.32 Monet was one of the first artists to take his paints and canvases outdoors. He realized that the colors of the scene changed as the time of day changed, so he carried several canvases. As the light changed, he moved on to another painting.

Claude Monet. *Poplars.* 1891. Oil on canvas. 100 × 65.2 cm (39½ × 25¹¹⁄₁₆"). Philadelphia Museum of Art, Philadelphia, Pennsylvania. Bequest of Anne Thomson as a memorial to her father Frank Thomson and her mother Mary Elizabeth Clarke Thomson.

Arbitrary Color

When artists use color to express feelings, they usually ignore the optical colors of objects. They choose the colors *arbitrarily*, which means they make their choices on the basis of personal preference. They choose arbitrary colors rather than optical colors because they want to use color to express meaning (Figure 7.34, page 175). In abstract art, color is teamed with the other elements to become the subject as well as the meaning of the work (Figure 7.21, page 167, and Figure 7.35, page 176).

Bright colors are loud. Light, bright colors can create happy, upbeat moods. Cool, dark colors can express mysterious or depressing themes. Warm, low-intensity earth tones are very comfortable and friendly and are often used to decorate rooms in which people gather. A unique light value of red-orange has been used to calm people and has even been successful in calming violent prisoners. Bright yellow is stimulating; blue soothes; and red excites.

FIGURE 7.33 This painting shows the cool shadows of late afternoon.

Claude Monet. *Poplars.* 1891. Oil on canvas. 81.9 × 81.6 cm (32¼ × 32⅛″). The Metropolitan Museum of Art, New York, New York. Bequest of Mrs. H. O. Havemeyer, 1929. The H. O. Havemeyer Collection.

Artists today have put their knowledge of color psychology to work to develop unusual methods for using color. Many of their choices are personal—they make color say what they wish to express.

Space

The placement of warm and cool colors can create illusions of depth. Warm colors advance toward the viewer, and cool colors seem to recede and pull away. The French artist Paul Cézanne was the first to use warm and cool colors to create depth. He painted a cool, blue outline around the shape of a warm, round orange. The fruit seemed to be pushed forward by the surrounding blue.

FIGURE 7.34 Marc developed his own personal scheme for the symbolic meaning of color. To him, blue represented the spiritual. Red represented matter, and in this work he used it to represent the land. Yellow represented comfort, and green served to set off red. The combination of the abstract, curved forms of the horses and the blue spiritual color reveal Marc's philosophy that animals have a purer relationship with the earth than human beings do.

Franz Marc. *The Large Blue Horses.* 1911. Oil on canvas. 106 x 181 cm (41⅝ × 71¼″). Walker Art Center, Minneapolis, Minnesota. Gift of the T. B. Walker Foundation, Gilbert M. Walker Fund, 1942.

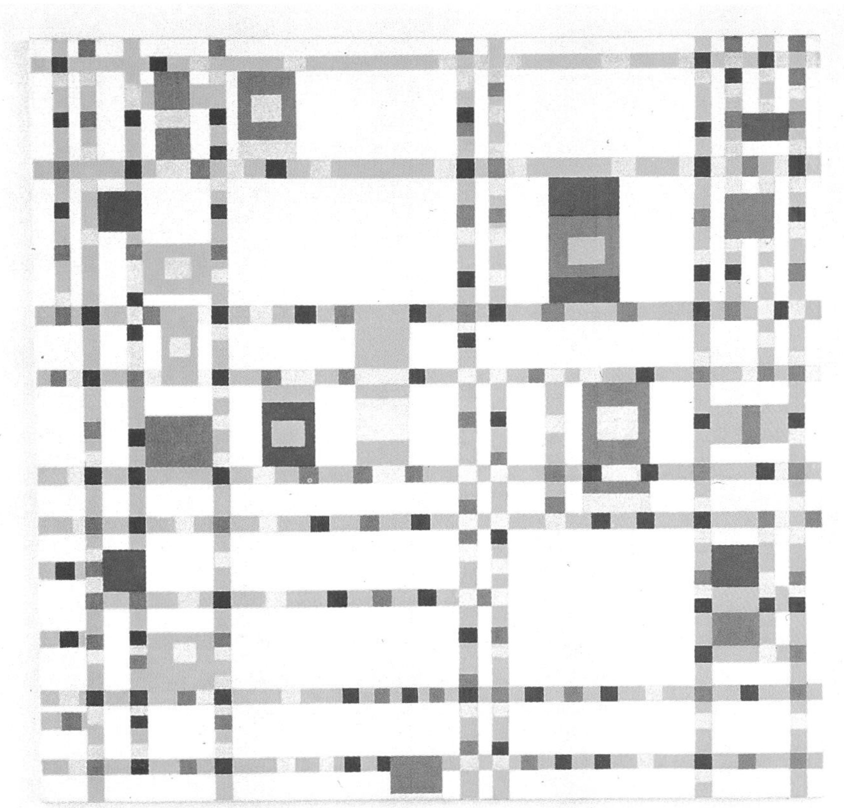

FIGURE 7.35 In this painting you feel the syncopated beat of the Boogie Woogie as your eyes bounce along the paths created by the squares and rectangles of yellow, red, blue, and gray. All of this is painted against a white background. The jumps in value from very light grays and light yellows to darker blues and reds create a sense of movement similar to the beat of the dance.

Piet Mondrian. *Broadway Boogie Woogie.* 1942–43. Oil on canvas. 127 × 127 cm (50 × 50″). Collection, The Museum of Modern Art, New York, New York.

Movement

Color can create a sense of movement. When the values in a work jump quickly from very high key to very low key, a feeling of excitement and movement is created (Figure 7.35). When all the values are close together, the work seems much calmer. Today's artists use color to create movement and depth in abstract art.

When you work with color to create movement, remember to use values of pure hues as well as those of tints and shades. You will need to remember, for instance, that the pure hue yellow is much lighter than red or blue.

Tonality

Sometimes an artist lets one color, such as blue, dominate the work. In such a case, the work is said to have a blue *tonality*. (See Figure 7.36.) The painting does not have to be monochrome—there may be other colors present. The overall effect of the work, however, is an impression of blueness. Tonality has a unifying effect.

Using Color for Effect

1. Applying Your Skills. Create three small sketches of trees with leaves. Use a simple color medium such as crayon. Color each sketch to illustrate one of the following: true color; arbitrary color; or tonality.

2. Further Challenge. Make three drawings of trees with leaves. Use a simple color medium such as crayon or oil pastel. Color each sketch to illustrate one of the following: optical color; depth through the use of warm and cool colors; or movement through value.

3. Computer Option. Using the tools of your choice, draw and label six sketches of trees with leaves. Let each sketch illustrate one of the following: true color; optical color; color that expresses personal feelings; depth through the use of warm and cool colors; movement through value; or tonality.

Evaluate the results of your work. Develop your favorite into a finished drawing.

LOOKING CLOSELY

FIGURE 7.36 The blue tonality of this work conveys the cool impression of water. The jellyfish are in the inlet and swimming close to the rocks. They are spots of contrast in the blue water.

This is not a monochrome. Hassam has used other hues. What are they? Where do you see the brightest blue? Where do you find the darkest area of blue? Can you find light gray-blue, gray-blue, and dark gray-blue? Where are they?

There is no sky. What point of view has the artist taken? How has he divided the composition?

Childe Hassam. *Jelly Fish.* 1912. Oil on canvas. 51.4 × 61.6 cm (20¼ × 24¼″). Wichita Art Museum, Wichita, Kansas. The John W. and Mildred L. Graves Collection.

STUDIO LESSON: PHOTO COLLAGE AND MIXED MEDIA

FIGURE 7.37 Romare Bearden. *Prevalence of Ritual: Baptism.* 1964. Photomechanical reproduction, synthetic polymer, and pencil on board. 23.2 x 30.5 cm (9⅛ × 12″). Hirshhorn Museum and Sculpture Garden, Smithsonian Institution, Washington, D.C. Gift of Joseph H. Hirshhorn, 1966.

Supplies

- Sketchbook and pencils
- Magazines and newspapers
- Envelope and scissors
- 6 x 9″ (15 x 23 cm) white paper
- White glue, damp sponge, paper towels
- Photocopy machine
- Crayons
- Oil pastels
- Colored pencils
- Acrylic paints, gloss medium, and brushes
- Felt-tip fine-line marker

Romare Bearden's collage looks deceptively simple. If you look closely, however, you will see an unusual mixture of media and color. Bearden's art was influenced by his experience as an African-American, but his goal was to create a universal art. He said, "I am trying to explore, in terms of the particulars of life I know best, those things common to all cultures."

Figure 7.37 is one of Bearden's many collages. In this example, he combined many different pieces to complete the picture. To compose the figures and background, he used photographs of textiles, water, cloth, wood, leaves, grass, metal, and people. He made his faces by cutting details from pictures of African masks, marbles, animal eyes, and mossy vegetation. For this work he had his small, original works enlarged photographically. Finally, he added paint to complete the colorful collage you see here.

For Bearden, any meaningful art had to have a subject. He once said, "All painting is a kind of talking about life."

Choose a theme that interests you. Cut out objects and shapes from black-and-white magazine and newspaper photographs. On a small background approximately 6 x 9 inches (15 x 23 cm), arrange the shapes and recut them as necessary to create a composition in the manner of Bearden's work. Using a photocopy machine, enlarge your work as much as possible. Paint your enlarged work with a color scheme that best expresses the theme of your work. Use any combination of the following: crayons, oil pastels, colored pencils, and school acrylics.

FOCUSING

Study Bearden's collage. Notice how the faces take on a masklike quality because they are made of parts that do not necessarily match. Notice how the entire space is filled. Select a theme related to people to use in your work.

FIGURE 7.37A Student work.

CREATING

Collect magazines and newspapers. Cut small pieces from the photos that you might use. Remember that the first step of the finished product will be small, so keep your pieces small. Put the cut pieces into the envelope for storage. You may combine color with black and white, since the photocopy machine will produce a black-and-white product. You must consider how the values of the colors will reproduce in the photocopy.

Arrange and rearrange the cut pieces until you are pleased with your composition. Do not leave any negative space. Every area must be filled. When you are satisfied with your composition, glue it down.

When your work is dry, enlarge it using the photocopy machine. Make more than one copy so you can experiment with one or more and use the final one as the finished product.

Choose a color scheme that is appropriate for your theme. Use crayons, oil pastels, colored pencils, school acrylics with gloss medium, and brushes, or any combination of the mentioned color media.

CRITIQUING

Describe Tell the theme you chose and explain how you carried it out. Did you have to create most of the shapes you needed or were you able to find them in photographs?

Analyze Did the shapes you arranged carry out the effect of your theme? What color scheme did you choose?

Interpret Did your work express the mood of the theme you selected? Does your title enhance the expressive effect?

Judge Is your work successful? Does it have the look of the Bearden collage style? Which aesthetic theory would be best to judge this work?

STUDIO LESSON: PHOTO ENLARGEMENT

FIGURE 7.38 Pat Steir. *The Brueghel Series (A Vanitas of Style).* 1982–84. Oil on canvas. Sixty-four panels, each 72.4 × 57 cm (28 ½ × 22½″); total dimensions approximately 5.8 × 4.6 m (19 × 15′). Courtesy of Robert Miller Gallery, New York, New York.

Supplies

- Reproduction of a masterpiece
- Ruler, pencil, soft eraser, and scissors
- Large rectangles of white paper
- Sketchbook
- Acrylic paints, brushes

Pat Steir was looking for a unique way to express her vision of the history of painting.

Pat Steir had studied art history, and as a painter she had practiced the styles of the masters. She explored the colors and brushwork of Rembrandt, Bosch, Rubens, and the Brueghels. To practice, she used what she called *appropriation:* the themes and styles of the masters. The subject for her painting-about-painting was a reproduction of a sixteenth-century still life by Jan Brueghel (**broi**-gul) the Elder called *Flower Piece in Blue Vase.*

After laying grids over the reproduction to divide it evenly into rectangles, Steir painted each panel as an homage to one of the great artists of history.

Study a work of art by *appropriating* it in the manner of Pat Steir. Working in a group, divide a reproduction of a master work into rectangles using a grid. Distribute the pieces among the group members. Enlarge your individual rectangle using a grid. (See Technique Tip 8 on page 352 in the Handbook for instructions on how to enlarge a work using a grid.) Paint your individual rectangle using colors that are the complements of the original colors.

FOCUSING

Study Steir's *Brueghel Series (A Vanitas of Style)*. Notice how each rectangle is painted in a different style.

CREATING

Using a ruler and pencil, divide the back of the reproduction evenly into rectangles. Number them in order and then cut them apart.

Follow directions on page 352 to draw a grid on the face of your rectangle and a matching grid on your large sheet of white paper. Using the grid as a guide, enlarge your section of the reproduction onto the white paper. You do not have to erase the grid lines. They are part of your work.

Paint your enlarged composition using complements of the original colors. For example, if one shape was red-orange in the reproduction, you will paint it blue-green. Keep the values the same. If the shape was a light red-orange, paint it a light blue-green.

Join all the finished works back together using the numbers as a guide.

FIGURE 7.38A Student work.

CRITIQUING

Describe What is the name of the artwork your group appropriated? Describe the look of your individual rectangle. Is it realistic or nonobjective? When you join your work with that of the rest of your group, can you recognize the original subject?

Analyze Describe the lines, shapes, and colors in your individual panel. When you join the group's panels together, do they fit? Do the shapes and lines match? Have you all interpreted the color complements the same way? Do the colors match?

Interpret Has changing the colors to their complements affected the expressive quality of the whole work? Do the individual styles affect the look of the work?

Judge Which aesthetic theory would you use to judge your individual panel? Would you use the same theory to judge the whole group's work?

STUDIO LESSON: USING COLOR TO CREATE AN EXPRESSIVE STATEMENT

FIGURE 7.39 Jaune Quick-To-See Smith. *Spotted Owl.* 1990. Oil and beeswax on canvas, wood panels, and axes. 203 x 294.6 cm (80 × 116″). Courtesy of the Steinbaum-Krauss Gallery, New York, New York. Collection of the artist.

Supplies

- Sketchbook and pencil
- Large sheet of white paper
- Crayons and chalk
- Acrylic paints and assorted brushes
- Scissors and nontoxic rubber cement
- Large sheets of colored poster board

Jaune Quick-To-See Smith was born in St. Ignatius, a small town on the Flathead reservation of the Confederated Salish and Kootenai tribes of southwestern Montana. Her Shoshone grandmother gave her her name: *Jaune*, French for "yellow," relates to her French-Cree ancestors; Quick-To-See was an insightful prediction of her life's work.

Drawing came easily to Smith, who wanted to be an artist from childhood. Her hunger for learning took her on a long journey out of the Flathead valley, but the things she learned there are still a part of everything she does. In 1980 she received a master's degree, and in her work she combines her university training with her tribal heritage. She draws deeply from her own life experiences as well as from mainstream modern art to communicate her concern for the vanishing West.

In *Spotted Owl* (Figure 7.39), Smith focuses on the new West. This work symbolizes the current concern over endangered species, and she uses neutral color and visual symbols to convey her message that all living things must coexist. Her paintings are a plea to each of us to save the earth.

Jaune Quick-to-See Smith expresses her concerns in her paintings. Choose an issue that is personally important to you. Create a shaped painting, without words, that expresses your concern. Use visual symbols and color contrast to emphasize your point.

FOCUSING

Select an issue. Discuss your concerns with your classmates. This may help you think of ways to express your ideas visually. Your subject may be as personal as your relationships with friends or family. It may be about school issues such as rules or teacher-student relationships. Your subject could be a world issue such as politics or the environment.

Write about your issue in your sketchbook. List words and concepts. Make several small sketches for your painting. Use crayons to plan your color scheme. The shape of your finished work does not have to be rectangular. You may choose a circle, a free-form shape, or the shape of an object that is part of your idea. Things may protrude from the edges of the shape for emphasis.

Discuss your sketches with a small group of classmates and share composition ideas. For example, you might want to make the people larger, or make the negative spaces larger than the positive shape to emphasize loneliness. Try painting everything in warm colors except a calm area. Express the calmness with a cool color.

CREATING

Draw your final idea on a large sheet of white paper with beige or yellow chalk. Paint with acrylics before you cut out the final outline. Remember to use color contrast for emphasis.

Cut out your finished piece. Test your work on several different colors of poster board before you choose the final background color. Certain colors could change the message of your painting while others may enhance it. Mount your painting on the poster board. Make up a title for your work that incorporates a reference to the issue.

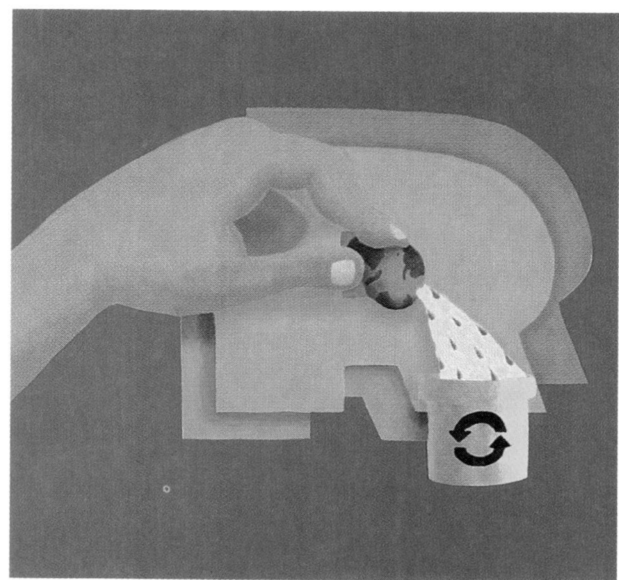

FIGURE 7.39A Student work.

CRITIQUING

Describe Name the issue that is the subject of your painting. Tell which visual symbols you selected to illustrate your idea and explain why you chose them.

Analyze How did you use color contrast to make your point? Which other elements did you emphasize to express your ideas? Explain.

Interpret Did your work convey your message without words? Were your classmates able to understand your visual symbols?

Judge Which aesthetic theory would you use to judge this work? Was it successful? If you were to do it over, what would you change?

STUDIO LESSON: CREATING A RAINBOW CREATURE

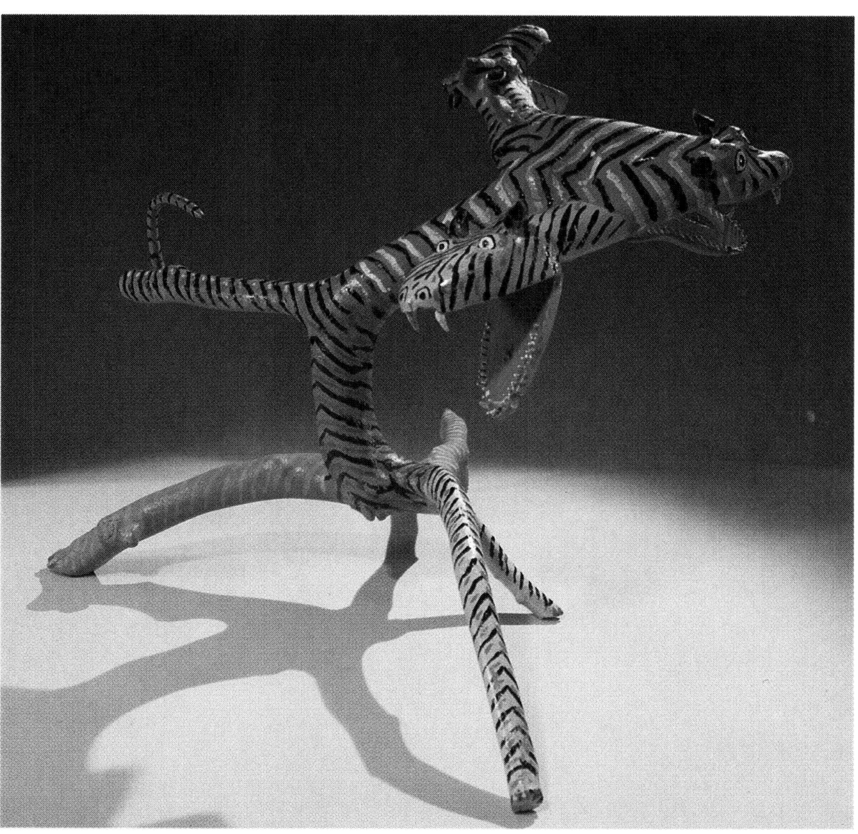

FIGURE 7.40 Miles Burkholder Carpenter. *Root Monster.* 1968. Carved and painted tree roots, rubber, metal, and string. 57.5 × 72.7 × 71.7 cm (22⅝ × 28⅝ × 28¼″). The National Museum of American Art, Washington, D.C. Gift of Herbert Waide Hemphill, Jr. and Museum purchase made possible by Ralph Cross Johnson.

Supplies

- Sketchbook, pencil, and crayons
- One large found object that will be the main body of your creature
- White glue, nontoxic rubber cement, and masking tape
- String, rubber bands, straight pins, and other joining materials
- Small found objects
- Acrylic paints, brushes

Miles Burkholder Carpenter is a folk artist; he just started carving without any training. He says, "There's something in there under the surface of every piece of wood."

Carpenter was also an experienced lumberman. He collected fallen branches and exposed roots, and he cut trees into thick planks for his carvings. The wood of poplar trees, which grew near his home in Waverly, Virginia, was his favorite because it was soft but solid and almost grainless.

When he found the piece of root shown in Figure 7.40, his imagination quickly began working. He saw legs and the hint of a tail, so he made rubber ears and carved separate jaws and teeth for the three heads of his "root monster." Then he attached strings and rubber hands so the teeth could clack when someone pulled the string.

Look at *Root Monster* for ideas. Then search for a found object that can serve as the basis for your rainbow creature.

Bring a natural or manufactured found object to class. Transform the object into a rainbow creature by adding to or subtracting from the original form. Paint your creature using the hues of the rainbow. The hues on the main body of the creature must be arranged in spectral order.

FOCUSING

Study Carpenter's *Root Monster*. Notice the humor he has added to his work by attaching the rubber ears and the clacking jaws. Brainstorm with your classmates for ideas about what kind of found objects to look for. Some natural things you might find outdoors are branches, roots, rocks, pebbles, twigs, pine needles, pinecones, feathers, and dried leaves. In addition to the buttons and plastic forks, manufactured objects might include pieces of broken furniture, bottle caps, crushed cans, beads, broken costume jewelry, broken toys, empty pill bottles, cardboard tubes, pencil stubs, hangers, and boxes of all sizes. Remember that you need one large object to serve as the body of your creature.

CREATING

Identify the found object that will serve as the main body of your rainbow creature. Study it. Make rough sketches of it in your sketchbook. Draw it from different points of view. Then make some drawings showing what you will add or carve away. Don't forget that you are working with three dimensions and you must keep turning your object as you organize your ideas. Design your arrangement of colors in your sketchbook using crayons. Try to devise a way to give your creature humor and movement. Give it a name.

Join all the parts. If you are gluing a piece that is hanging down, you can keep it from falling off by using tape to hold it in place until the glue sets. You may have to paint over the tape, so add it neatly. If you are adding parts that will move, plan them carefully so that the paint won't get in the way of the movement.

Paint your creature. Make sure that you have the colors in correct spectral order. Add yarns, silk flowers, or articles of clothing if they are appropriate.

Prepare the creature for display. Include a name card in the display.

FIGURE 7.40A Student work.

CRITIQUING

Describe Explain how you made the creature. Tell what found objects you used, and how you joined them together. Are there any moving parts? Explain what they do. How did you prepare your creature for display?

Analyze Describe what you have added to or subtracted from the original form to change it. Can you recognize the original form? Describe the colors you added. How many spectral colors did you use? Did you repeat them?

Interpret What mood does your finished creature convey? Did the final display improve the mood or take away from it?

Judge Which aesthetic theory would you use to judge this work? Do you think this project was successful? If you wanted to improve it, what would you change?

ART CRITICISM IN ACTION

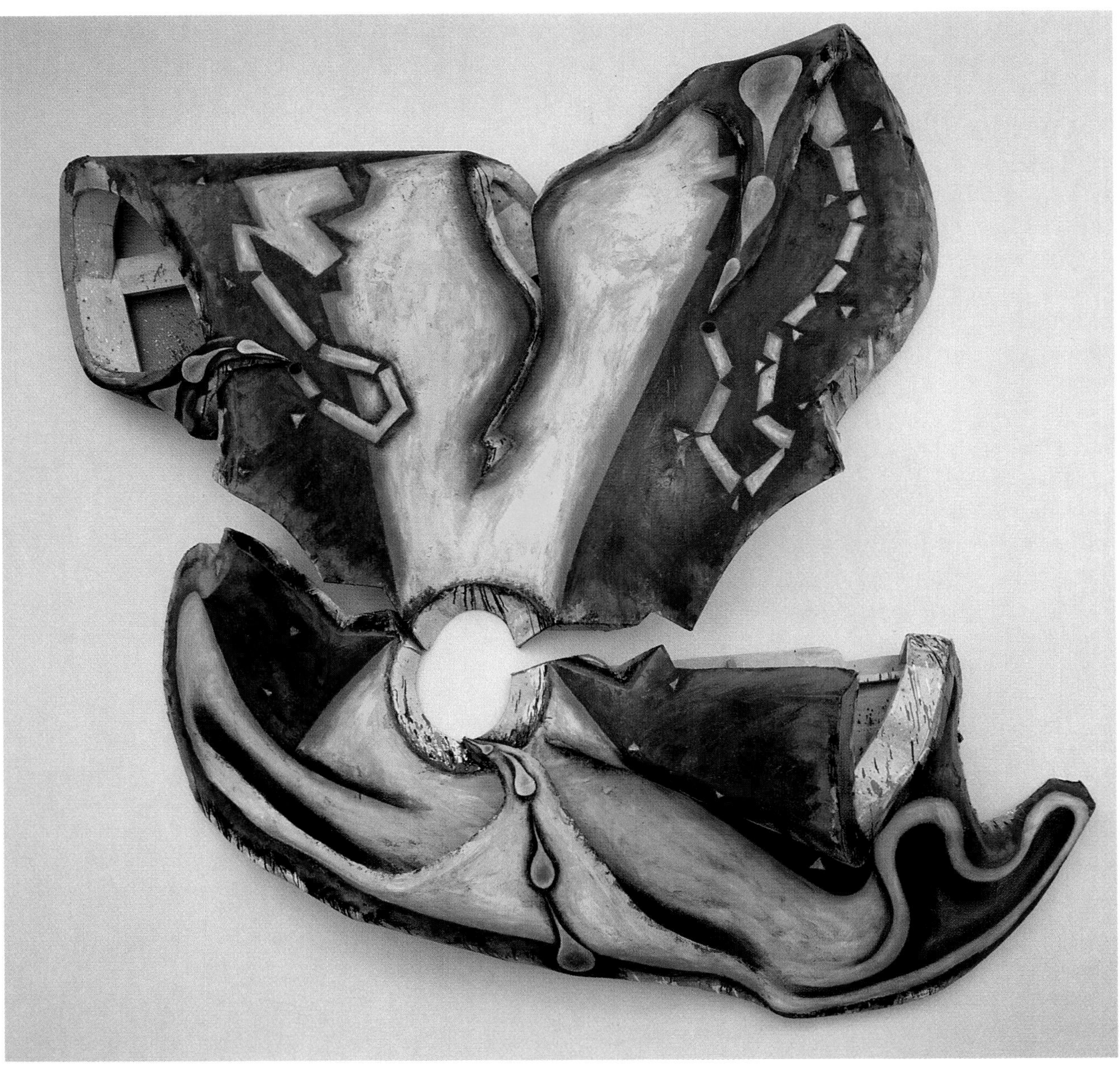

FIGURE 7.41 Elizabeth Murray. *Things to Come*. 1988. Oil on canvas. 292 × 287 × 71 cm (115 × 113 × 27″). Paula Cooper Gallery, New York, New York. Private Collection, San Francisco. California.

FIGURE 7.42 Jan van Eyck. *The Annunciation.* 1434–36. Oil on wood transferred to canvas. 90.2 × 34.1 cm (35⅜ × 13⅞″). National Gallery of Art, Washington, D.C. Andrew W. Mellon Collection.

CRITIQUING THE WORK

1. **Describe** Read the credit line under Figure 7.41. Notice the dimensions. How high is the painting? How wide? How far does it protrude from the wall? This is not a typical rectangle or oval shape. This is an abstract work in which the shape represents something. Describe what you see.
2. **Analyze** What hues do you see? Where do you find light values? Where are the dark values? Do you see any neutral colors? Are the colors predominantly of high or low intensity? Is all of the work that is visible to the viewer covered carefully with paint?

   How does the artist use space in this work? Is it easy to tell the difference between the three-dimensional areas and the dimensions? Are the shapes geometric or free-form?
3. **Interpret** Based on the clues you collected and your own personal ideas, what communication do you receive from this work? What is the mood of the work? Write a paragraph explaining your interpretation.
4. **Judge** Do you think this is a successful work? Use one or more of the aesthetic theories of art explained in Chapter 2 to defend your judgment.

COMPARING THE WORKS

Look at *Things to Come* by Elizabeth Murray (Figure 7.41) and *The Annunciation* by Jan van Eyck (Figure 7.42). At first glance, you might think there is no possible way these two works could be related. In what style is the van Eyck painted and what style did Murray use? How does van Eyck use space in his work? How does Murray use space in her work? Are there symbols in the van Eyck? Has Murray used symbols? What color scheme does each painter use? In what way does each work represent the culture of its time?

MEET THE ARTIST

ELIZABETH MURRAY

American, b. 1940

Elizabeth Murray is an American artist who was born in Chicago in 1940 and grew up in small towns in Michigan and Illinois.

She always loved to draw, and her parents encouraged her dream of becoming an artist when she grew up. As far back as elementary school she sold drawings of elephants, cowboys, and stagecoaches to her classmates for twenty-five cents a piece. She was lucky to have a high school teacher who recognized her talent and created a scholarship for Murray at the Art Institute of Chicago. Murray blossomed in Chicago. For the first time in her life she found students her own age who liked the same things she did. She took classes in figure drawing, landscape painting, and traditional techniques. To get to her classes she had to walk through the exhibit halls of the museum of the Art Institute. The masterpieces she saw every day changed her life; they gave her the drive to become a painter.

When she was told in the 1960s that painting was dead, she refused to listen and kept painting. She developed a style that combines painting and sculpture and is now considered a master of the shaped canvas.

She says that she loves and respects traditional painting, but she is fascinated with relief—with the possibilities of two dimensions becoming three. She is always trying to devise a new way of painting and redefining the structure of things. Her work is famous because of her creative compositions and her daring adventures into unknown territory.

MORE PORTFOLIO IDEAS

1. Change a flat, two-dimensional shape of paper into a three-dimensional form. Use the paper sculpture techniques explained in Technique Tip 20 on page 356 in the Handbook. You may cut into the paper, but do not cut it into two pieces. Use markers to emphasize the edges of the forms where they overlap and to decorate some of the surfaces with line patterns.

2. Create a three-dimensional form from a sheet of paper following the directions given above. This time paint the surfaces before the final gluing. Try to create optical illusions as Murray does in her work. Shade some flat areas so they look rounded and paint some joined areas in one color so that they look flat.

CHAPTER 7 REVIEW

Building Vocabulary

On a separate sheet of paper, write the term that best matches each definition given below.

1. An element of art that is derived from reflected light.
2. Bands of color produced when white light passes through a prism and is broken into separate wavelengths.
3. The name of a spectral color.
4. The spectrum bent into a circle.
5. A light value of a hue.
6. A dark value of a hue.
7. The brightness or dullness of a hue.
8. The colors opposite each other on the color wheel.
9. A scheme that uses only one hue and the values, tints, and shades of that hue.
10. Colors that sit side by side on the color wheel.
11. Finely ground, colored powders that form paint when mixed with a liquid.
12. The liquid that holds together the grains of pigment.
13. The liquid that controls the thickness or thinness of the paint.
14. Pigments that dissolve in liquid.

Reviewing Art Facts

Answer the following questions using complete sentences.

1. Explain how the eye sees color.
2. What is an afterimage? Why is it always a weak color?
3. Name the three properties of color.
4. What are the colors of the spectrum? Name them in the correct order.
5. What is color value?
6. Tell how to dull, or lower the intensity of, a hue.
7. Name the seven different kinds of color schemes.
8. What are complementary colors? How do complementary colors affect each other?
9. What is arbitrary color?

Thinking Critically About Art

1. **Synthesize.** Tamayo's *Toast to the Sun* (Figure 7.26, page 169) and Carr's *Above the Trees* (Figure 7.27, page 170) use very different color schemes. Compare the two works. List the similarities and differences in their style and use of color. Look up each artist in Artists and Their Works on pages 366–370. Then explain why each work appropriately represents the climate of the country in which the artists worked.
2. **Interpret.** Look at Town's *Night Riders* (Figure 7.13, page 161). The artist has used a color scheme of dark values to create a specific mood. Study the lines and shapes in this work. Note the positive and negative spaces. Do the shapes suggest some images you can recognize? Does the title add to the mood? Based on the clues you have collected, write a brief interpretation of this painting.

Making Art Connections

1. **Social Studies.** Paul Gauguin left his family and his work in France to live on a tropical island. It was in Tahiti that he found the freedom to create great masterpieces. Research the lifestyle of a stockbroker in France in the late nineteenth century and the lifestyle of the people of Tahiti during the same time period. Why might the first lifestyle inhibit an artist, and why might the second inspire him? Report your conclusions to the class.
2. **Science.** Consult the science teacher or do some research in the library to find out the difference between mixing color with pigments and mixing the colors of light. If you have a theater department at your school, ask the teacher in charge to help you set up a demonstration of mixing light colors.

FIGURE 8.1 This feather bonnet was created for a ceremonial dance. All of the materials used to create the bonnet, except one, came from the immediate environment, the Northwestern Plains. Do you know which one was not native to the area?

Northwestern Plains Indian. *Feather Bonnet.* c. 1890. Rooster hackles, wood rods, porcupine hair, ermine skins, horsehair, buckskin, glass beads. 84 × 68.6 cm (33 × 27″). Buffalo Bill Historical Center, Cody, Wyoming. Chandler-Pohrt Collection.

CHAPTER 8

Texture

Every surface has a texture. **Texture** is *the element of art that refers to how things feel, or look as if they might feel if touched.* No one needs to teach you about texture—you know what is rough and what is smooth. There are certain textures you enjoy touching, and there are certain surfaces you avoid because you do not like the way they feel.

Textures play an active part in many of the decisions you make about the clothes you wear. Think how often fabric textures have influenced your choices. Would you buy skintight pants made from rough burlap? Clothing manufacturers consider textures when they decide what fabrics to use. Why do you think they put silky linings inside winter coats and jackets? Which are more comfortable—prewashed jeans or stiff, scratchy new jeans?

The textures of foods influence what you eat. Think about the smoothness of ice cream, and consider how different it is from the angular roughness of potato chips. Would grilled steak taste the same if it were ground up in a blender?

Objectives

After completing this chapter, you will be able to:

- Understand how texture is perceived through the senses.
- Describe various textures.
- Reproduce textures by changing values.
- Use texture as the expressive element in creating two- and three-dimensional works of art.
- Understand how artists communicate by means of textures.

Words to Know

appliqué
collage
decalcomania
frottage
grattage
matte surface
texture
visual texture

First Impressions

Look at the headdress in Figure 8.1 on the opposite page. This feather bonnet was made to be worn during special dance ceremonies. Try to determine your reaction to the overall design before looking closely at the details. What is your evaluation of the artist's selection of textures? Look at the media listed in the credits and try to identify the materials with the roughest and the smoothest textures.

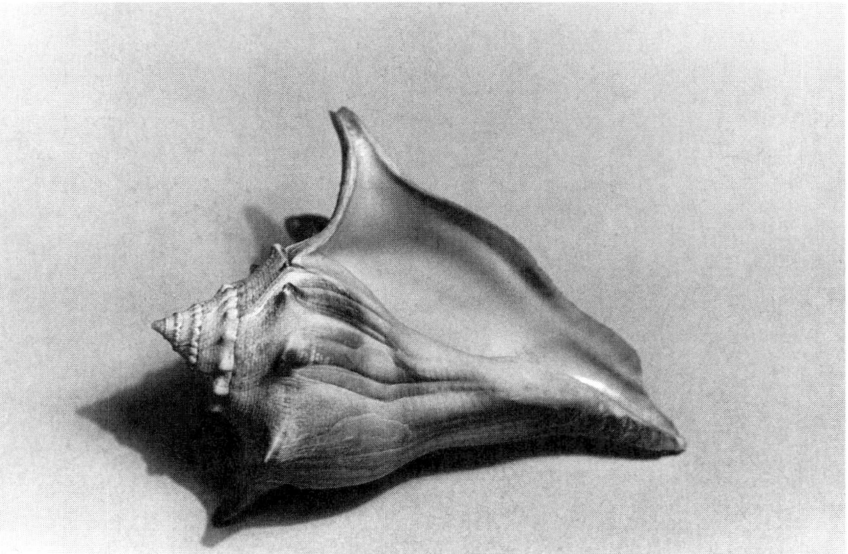

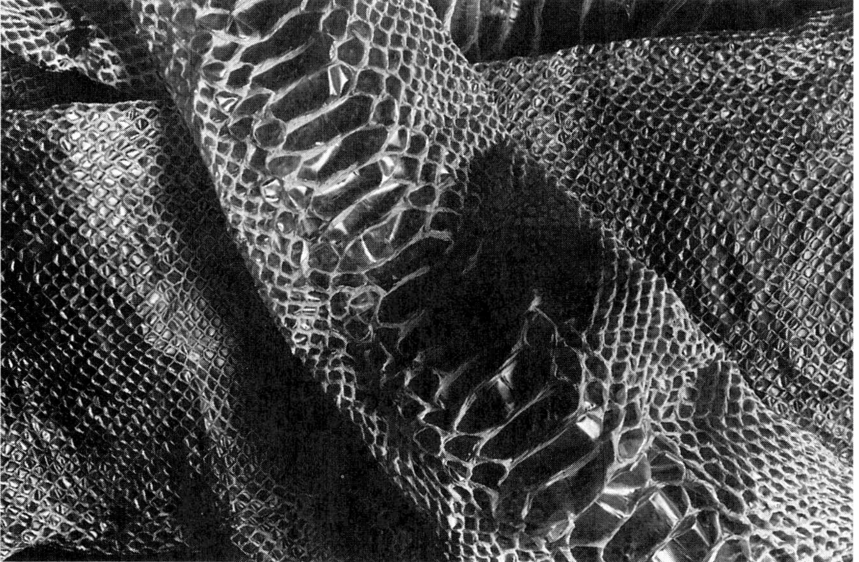

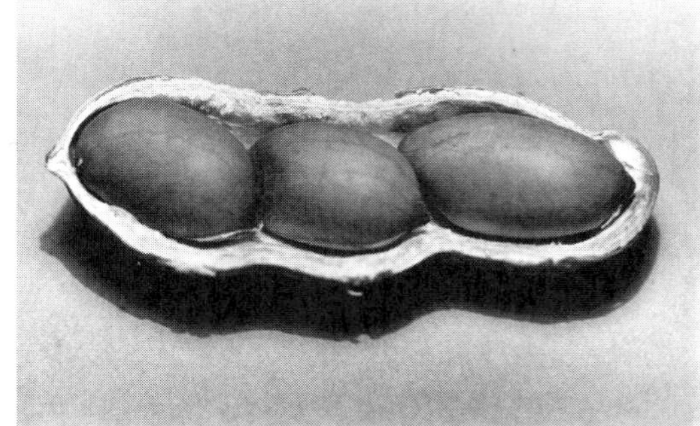

FIGURE 8.2 What textures are represented in these photographs?

HOW YOU PERCEIVE TEXTURE

You perceive texture with two of your senses: touch and vision. Infants learn about things by touching them and by putting them into their mouths. Toddlers, who cannot keep their hands off anything, are visually attracted to all objects within their reach. In a way you still use your sense of touch when you look at surfaces. Your eyes tell you what something would feel like if you were to touch it. (See Figure 8.2.)

When you actually touch something to determine its texture, you experience real texture. When you look at a photograph of velvet, leather, concrete, or ice, you see surface patterns of light and dark that bring back memories of how those objects actually feel. When this happens, you are experiencing **visual texture**, *the illusion of a three-dimensional surface*. If you touch visual textures, you do not feel what your eyes told you to expect.

There are two kinds of visual texture: *simulated* and *invented*. Simulated textures imitate real textures. Plastic tabletops can be made to look like wood. Some vinyl flooring is made to look like ceramic tile or stone. Manufactured fabrics imitate natural leather and fur. Figure 8.3 is an example of simulated texture in a painting.

Invented textures are two-dimensional patterns created by the repetition of lines or shapes. These textures do not represent any real surface qualities, but the patterns of light and dark stimulate your

FIGURE 8.3 Vigée-Lebrun was one of the most highly paid portrait painters of her time. She always showed her subject at his or her best. She was able to manipulate the paint to show off the rich fabrics and fine jewels of her sitter. How many different kinds of textured surfaces can you identify in this painting?

Élisabeth Vigée-Lebrun. *Self-Portrait.* c. 1781. Oil on canvas. 65 × 54 cm (25½ × 21¼"). Kimbell Art Museum, Fort Worth, Texas.

FIGURE 8.4 In this print the artist has invented textures by attaching textured materials to the printing plate. Looking closely, you can see areas that appear to be wrinkled fabrics and paper. If you look at the work as a whole, the textures remind you of rocks and layers of earth.

Hedi Bak. *Grand Canyon #2.* 1980. Collograph print. 49.5 × 75 cm (19½ × 29½″). Private collection.

memories of actual textures. The purpose of invented texture is to create decorated surfaces that evoke memories of unusual textures (Figure 8.4).

Creating Textures

1. Applying Your Skills. Make a collection of texture rubbings. To make a rubbing, place a sheet of thin paper against a rough surface. Hold the paper in place with one hand. Use the flat side of an unwrapped crayon or the side of a pencil lead to rub over the paper (Figure 8.5). Always rub away from the hand holding the paper. Never rub back and forth because the paper or object may slip. Examine the rubbings closely, paying special attention to the lines, dots, shapes, and values (Figure 8.6).

2. Further Challenge. Make a small dream landscape by cutting shapes of visual textures out of magazines and arranging them on a background sheet of paper. Try to get a variety of textures from different objects. Turn your imagination loose. Concentrate more on the textures than on the shapes. Look at a large photograph of a piece of chocolate cake. Consider the visual texture of a picture of dog food. What can you do with the texture of hair? Of a rug or of tree foliage (Figure 8.7)?

3. Computer Option. Use a Pencil tool, or Brush tool, or Shape tool to create several unfilled objects. Fill each object with a different preprogrammed texture from the pattern menu and, if the application you are using permits, blend the objects. Identify which objects and blends look rough to the touch and which do not (Figure 8.8).

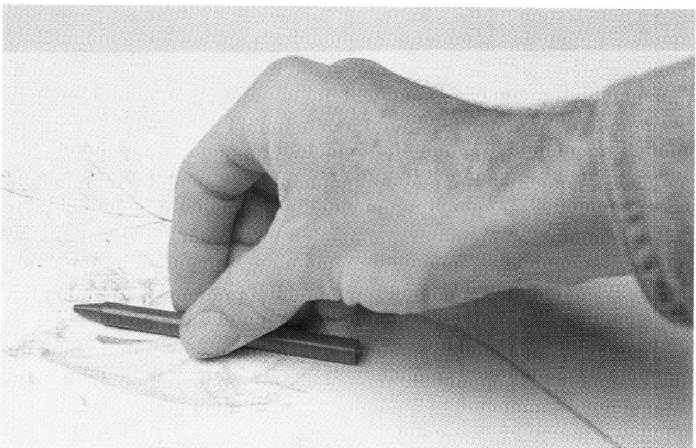

FIGURE 8.5 Rub the surface with the flat side of the crayon.

FIGURE 8.6 Student work. A page full of texture rubbings.

FIGURE 8.7 Student work.

FIGURE 8.8 Student work. Textures done on a computer.

FIGURE 8.9 Even though you can't touch the real texture, your eyes recognize the irregular patterns of light and dark. As a result, you can guess what this surface would feel like.

TEXTURE AND VALUE

The look of a surface depends on the manner in which it reflects light. Every surface is an arrangement of light and dark values.

Rough and Smooth Textures

The roughness or smoothness of a texture can be determined by looking at the shadows. A rough surface reflects light unevenly (Figure 8.9). Rough textures show irregular patterns of light and shadow. Look at a shag rug, an orange, tree bark, or a patch of bare ground. Notice how the high places catch the light, creating shadows of different sizes and shapes.

A smooth texture reflects light evenly (Figure 8.10). Look at a sheet of paper, an apple, or a new,

FIGURE 8.10 These apples reflect light evenly. The shadows you see are caused by the spherical forms.

FIGURE 8.11 The soft, white, downy fiber of the cotton plant has been lit with bright light, but you see no highlights. Even though the fibers are not smoothly arranged, they reflect light evenly. The cotton has a matte surface.

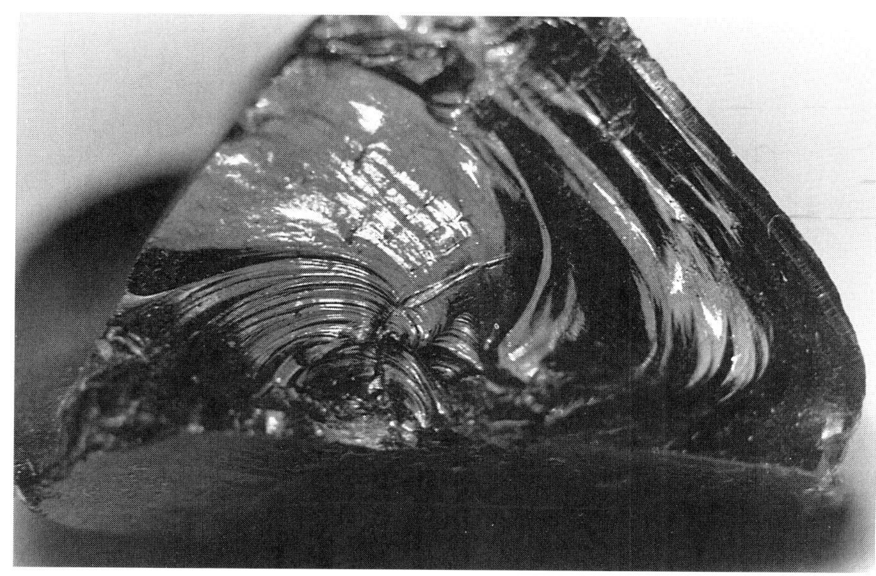

FIGURE 8.12 The irregular pattern of dark and light tells you that this rock is far from smooth, but the streaks, or white highlights, tell you that this surface is also shiny.

unmarked desktop. Your eyes glide across these objects, uninterrupted by shadows, just as your fingers would glide across them, uninterrupted by bumps and dents.

Matte and Shiny Textures

A **matte surface** is *a surface that reflects a soft, dull light*. It absorbs some light and reflects the rest. Matte surfaces, such as paper, denim, unfinished wood, and your skin, have a soft, dull look (Figure 8.11).

A shiny surface is the opposite of a matte surface. A shiny surface reflects so much bright light that it seems to glow (Figure 8.12). Shiny surfaces also have highlights. Some surfaces reflect bright sunlight with such intensity that you have to squint your eyes. Window glass is shiny; so is a new car, a polished brass candlestick, and the surface of a calm pool of water.

Matte and shiny surfaces can be rough or smooth. Sandpaper is matte rough, and a freshly ironed pillowcase is matte smooth. Aluminum foil is shiny and smooth until it gets crumpled up; then it becomes shiny and rough.

Creating Contrasting Textures

1. Applying Your Skills. Make a series of small drawings and paintings of objects that have different textures. Try to reproduce both smooth and rough textures (See Figure 8.13, page 198). You may use a different medium for each drawing. Study the lights and shadows on each object before you choose the medium. For example, you might examine a hairbrush, an old work shoe, weathered wood, a wig, a fuzzy slipper, or a satin slip, then select a medium for each texture.

2. Further Challenge. Make a texture collage on a small piece of heavy paper or cardboard by pasting various two-dimensional materials onto the surface. Place contrasting textures next to each other to make an interesting design (Figure 8.14 on page 198).

3. Computer Option. Draw the texture collage from the preceding activity using the Pencil or Brush tool on the computer. First, sketch your shapes; then copy the texture of each shape using dots, lines, and value blending. Concentrate on the shadows, lights, and highlights of each different texture.

FIGURE 8.13 This artist likes to be referred to as a perceptual realist. Notice how she captures the image of light reflecting from various surfaces. What is the difference between the way she paints the light on Jonathan's arm and the light on the red vase? Study the way she has used paint to make the yellow platter, the red vase, the green pitcher, and the transparent red bowl all look different.

Janet Fish. *Jonathan and Lorraine.* 1988. Oil on canvas. 163 × 185 cm (64 × 72¾″). Grace Borgenicht Gallery, New York, New York.

FIGURE 8.14 Student work. A texture collage.

How Artists Use Texture

The texture of surfaces is important to every form of visual art. Our minds are full of texture memories. Artists use both visual and real textures to make you remember those texture experiences.

The artist Pierre Auguste Renoir (ren-**wahr**) painted young people with healthy, glowing complexions (Figure 8.15). Another artist, Ivan Albright, was concerned with the wrinkles of old age (Figure 8.16, page 200). In their works, both of these artists have imitated human skin. In one the skin is appealing; in the other it is repulsive because of the excessive attention to detail. Both artists try to control your reactions to the people in the paintings through the use of visual texture.

In the past many painters reproduced the color and value patterns of textures. Look, for instance, at the paintings by Judith Leyster (Figure 3.20, page 54) or Rembrandt van Rijn (ryne) (Figure 12.5, page 317). These artists were experts at suggesting textures such as soft velvet, shiny satin, delicate lace, and fluffy feathers. When you look closely at their paintings, you discover that these artists do not paint every texture in photographic detail. They use a few brushstrokes to suggest the texture from a certain distance.

FIGURE 8.15 Renoir started his career as an artist in a porcelain factory. His job was to copy famous portraits of beautiful women onto the porcelain plates. Renoir spent the rest of his life painting beautiful people. Notice how he uses his brushstrokes to create texture.

Pierre Auguste Renoir. *Madame Henriot.* 1876. Oil on canvas. 66 × 50 cm (26 × 19⅝″). National Gallery of Art, Washington, D.C. Gift of Adele R. Levy Fund, Inc.

LOOKING CLOSELY

FIGURE 8.16 Ivan Albright's painting contains many textured surfaces—too many to take in with a casual glance. Find an object or small area that intrigues you. Look closely at the surface pattern you see. Try to determine how the artist gave that area its unique texture. Analyze the technique he used to produce the visual quality you see and experiment with that technique in your sketchbook.

Ivan Albright. *The Farmer's Kitchen.* 1933–34. Oil on canvas. 91.5 × 76.5 cm (36 × 30″). National Museum of American Art, Smithsonian Institution, Washington, D.C.

FIGURE 8.17 At times van Gogh became so impatient with the progress of his work that he squeezed the paint directly from the tube onto the canvas. Then he used anything that was handy, including his fingers, to move and swirl the globs of paint around.

Vincent van Gogh. *Landscape at Saint-Rémy (Enclosed Field with Peasant).* 1889. Oil on canvas. 73.6 × 92 cm (29 × 36¼″). © 1993, Indianapolis Museum of Art, Indianapolis, Indiana. Gift of Mrs. James W. Fesler in memory of Daniel W. and Elizabeth C. Marmon.

FIGURE 8.18 Schapiro invented the word *Femmage* to describe her collages. Rather than scraps of discarded paper, she used pieces of embroidered, appliquéd, and crocheted fabrics, that were created by women, to add real textures to her work. In this way she connected her work to the traditional women's arts of the past.

Miriam Schapiro. *Yard Sale.* 1993. Acrylic and fabric on canvas. 208 × 228 cm (82 × 90″). Courtesy of the Steinbaum Krauss Gallery, New York, New York.

The *trompe-l'oeil* (French for "fool the eye") painters were masters of visual texture. See Figure 6.13 on page 127. All of the objects were depicted in sharp focus with great care. Every color and value pattern of every surface was copied exactly. In these works the appearance of the objects is so realistic that, for a moment, you think you can touch what you see.

Many painters add real textures to their paintings. Vincent van Gogh (goh) used such thick paint on his canvas that his swirling brushstrokes created a rough surface (Figure 8.17). The surface ridges of the thick paint actually make the paint look brighter. The ridges catch more light and reflect brighter colors to the viewer.

Some painters add real textures to their work by attaching various materials to the work's surface. Some artists add sand and other materials to the paint. In some cases, artists create what is called a **collage** (kul-**lahzh**), in which *bits and pieces of textured paper and fabric have been pasted onto a painting.* Folk artists have used this technique for centuries. Miriam Schapiro added bits of fabric, lace, and thread to her paintings to enrich the surfaces (Figure 8.18).

Architects use a variety of materials to create interesting surfaces in buildings. You can find stucco, brick, wood, stone, concrete, metal, and glass in modern buildings (Figure 8.19). Interior designers select textures for rugs, drapes, furniture, pottery, and sculpture that complement different wall textures (Figure 8.20 on page 202).

FIGURE 8.19 The colors, forms, and textures of this building were planned so that Taliesin West would blend into the colors, forms, and textures of its desert setting. Wright believed that a building should be in harmony with its environment.

Frank Lloyd Wright. *Taliesin West.* Near Phoenix, Arizona.

John Hoover. *Loon Song.* 1990. Cedar and natural pigments. 152 × 61 cm (60 × 24″). Glenn Green Galleries, Scottsdale, Arizona.

LOOKING CLOSELY

FIGURE 8.20 John Hoover is an Aleut sculptor. He uses the folklore of his people as subject matter, but he has developed a style that is not traditional. Notice how he lets the texture of the cedar wood show through the paint. He uses only natural pigments. Can you identify the colors? What kinds of lines and forms did he use to give texture to the work? How does he use the elements of art to link the human heads and the loons? Do you see the hinges? This work can be closed like a box. If it were closed, you would see a symbolic design on the back.

Sculptors must be aware of texture as they work because the texture of each surface must fit the whole. Some sculptors imitate the real texture of skin, hair, and cloth, while others create new textures to fit new forms (Figure 8.21).

Weavers control texture through the use of fibers and weaving techniques (Figure 8.22). Potters change textures by pressing different objects into wet clay. They can also change surfaces by applying glazes. Some glazes are shiny, and others have matte finishes (Figure 8.23). Feathers, river

FIGURE 8.22 Which materials in this wall hanging would never be used by a traditional weaver who was creating cloth to be made into clothing?

Olga de Amaral. *Alquimia XIII*. 1984. Woven hanging. Cotton, linen, rice paper, gesso, paint, and gold leaf. 180 × 75 cm (71 × 29½"). The Metropolitan Museum of Art, New York, New York. Gift of Olga and Jim Amaral, 1987.

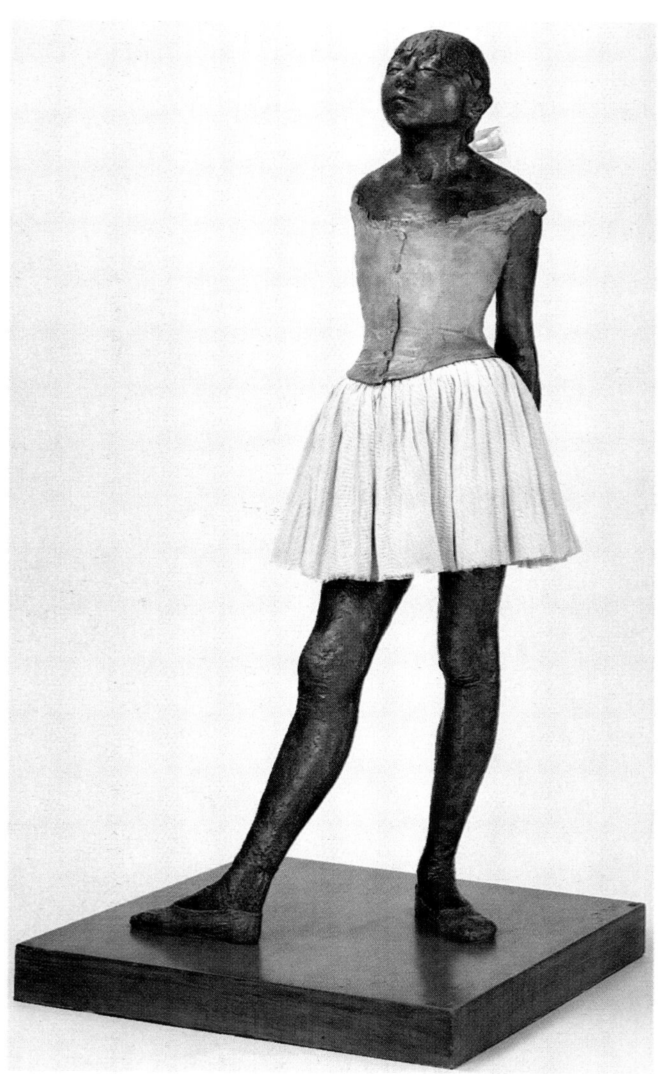

FIGURE 8.21 What an unusual combination of textures! The figure of the young dancer is cast in bronze. Even the vest and the ballet shoes she wears are bronze. To that Degas added a skirt made of gauzelike fabric and a satin hair ribbon. Why do you think he added real textures to the metal figure?

Edgar Degas. *Little Fourteen-Year-Old Dancer*. 1880, cast 1922. Bronze, cotton skirt, satin ribbon. 104.5 cm (41½") high. The Metropolitan Museum of Art, New York, New York. Havemeyer Collection, bequest of Mrs. H. O. Havemeyer, 1929.

FIGURE 8.23 To create the shiny surface, Tafoya rubs his clay with a smooth river rock before it is fired. After he has planned his design, he gently carves away the areas where he wants a matte surface. The turquoise is added after the work is fired.

Juan Tafoya of San Ildefonso Pueblo. *Seed Pot*. 1992. Black-on-black pottery with turquoise. 8.9 x 7 x 7 cm (3½ × 2¾ × 2¾"). Private collection.

rocks, seashells, seeds, bones, and teeth have been used to make jewelry and hair ornaments (Figure 8.24).

Today, the true textures of paint, stone, and fibers are more important to some artists. They feel that the media contribute textural qualities that enhance the work. Some painters brush on paint and do not try to smooth out the brushstrokes (Figure 8.25).

Painters and printmakers invent textures to enrich their works. Max Ernst used three unusual techniques—*frottage*, *grattage*, and *decalcomania*—to create his fantasies. In **frottage** (froh-**tahzh**), Ernst placed *freshly painted canvas right-side-up over a raised texture and scraped across the surface of the paint*. The paint that remained created a pattern that was an image of the texture below. The texture rubbings you made earlier in this chapter are another form of frottage. To create **grattage** (grah-**tahzh**) effects, Ernst *scratched into wet paint with a variety of tools, such as forks, razors, and combs*. Finally, Ernst squeezed wet blobs of paint between two canvas surfaces and then pulled the canvases apart (Figure 8.26). In this technique, called **decalcomania**, *paint is forced into random textured patterns*. Using the random patterns as a basis, Ernst elaborated on the design. The patterns inspired him to create fantasy landscapes (Figure 8.27, page 206). The textures created with these techniques contributed to the surface interest and created varied patterns and values to the work.

Inventing Textures

1. Applying Your Skills. On a small piece of white paper, draw nine shapes of different sizes with a pencil or felt-tip pen. Have some shapes touch the edges of the paper. Fill each shape with sketches of a different texture. The textures should be invented. For instance, you could put lines of writing close together in one shape, or you could try repeating small shapes in another. Try line patterns, stippling, or smooth shadow.

2. Further Challenge. Experiment with decalcomania by using two different surfaces: white drawing paper and small squares of acetate. Place large lumps of thick, creamy paint on the white paper. Then place the transparent acetate over the paint. Work with a partner to pull the two pieces apart. One person pulls the top surface while the other holds down the bottom surface so the paint textures are not damaged. Then both people lift the work, holding all four corners, and place it on a heavy piece of paper or thick stack of newspapers to dry.

3. Computer Option. Use the Pencil or Brush tool to create three shapes. Select a preprogrammed texture from the pattern menu to fill the first shape. Repeat with the second shape, selecting a different texture. Invent a texture for the third shape, giving it a three-dimensional look.

FIGURE 8.24 The forest Indians of Ecuador use brilliant, tropical bird feathers to create ornaments. These ornaments were created to decorate ears and hair.

South American Indian. *Featherwork Ornaments*. Collected in 1938 by E. Erskine. National Museum of the American Indian, Smithsonian Institution, Heye Foundation, New York, New York.

FIGURE 8.25 Joan Mitchell remained an Abstract Expressionist throughout her entire painting career. This work refers to the snow and cold of her Chicago childhood. Notice how she uses the brushstrokes to show the excitement and tension of a snowy day in the city. What kinds of lines do you find in the brushstrokes?

Joan Mitchell. *Dirty Snow.* 1980. Oil on canvas. 220 × 180 cm (86¼ × 70⅞"). National Museum of Women in the Arts, Washington, D.C. Gift of Wallace and Wilhelmina Holladay.

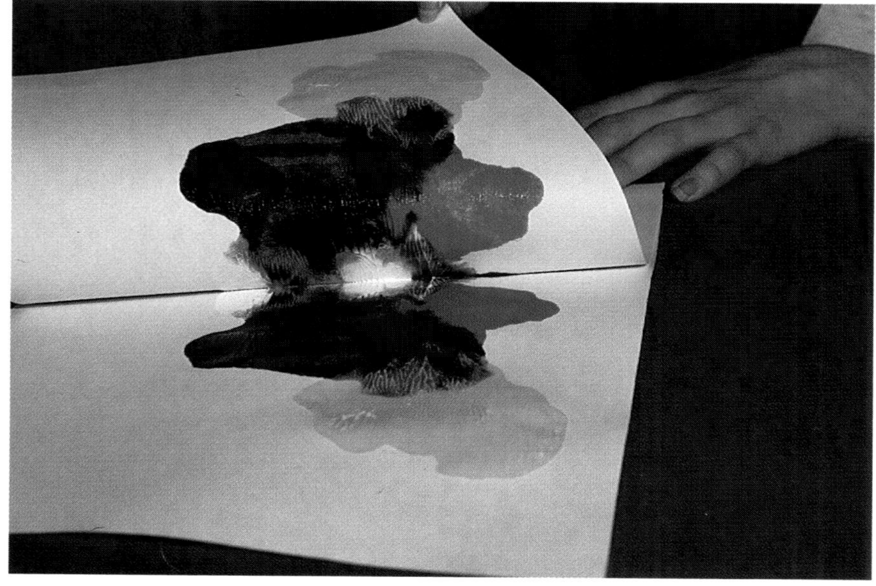

FIGURE 8.26 Decalcomania technique.

STUDIO LESSON: FANTASY LANDSCAPE

FIGURE 8.27 Max Ernst. *The Eye of Silence.* 1943–44. Oil on canvas. 108 × 141 cm (42½ × 55½″). Washington University Gallery of Art, St. Louis, Missouri.

Supplies

- Acrylic paints and assorted brushes
- One sheet of heavy paper or canvas
- Scratch paper for practice
- Wax paper
- Scratching and rubbing tools such as combs or rulers
- Magazine clippings
- Scissors and white glue

Max Ernst was among the artists, philosophers, and writers who formed the Surrealist movement in the mid-1920s. Surrealists searched for a new reality—one that rejected the long-established rules of composition and logic. They believed that this reality could be found in the subconscious mind, and they created paintings that took on the look of dreams or nightmares. Salvador Dali (Figure 3.28, page 60) and René Magritte (Figure 6.46, page 148) were members of this movement.

Ernst used three unusual techniques—*frottage, grattage,* and *decalcomania*—to bring his fantasies to life. Ernst then elaborated on the design. Sometimes he cut the textured pieces into forms with which he created collages. Sometimes he painted over areas such as the sky in *The Eye of Silence* (Figure 8.27).

Create a fantasy painting using Max Ernst's techniques to produce textured areas. You may cut and rearrange the textured area to make new shapes. Add details and contrasting shapes using paint, oil pastels, markers, and collage. The work should be unified. One object must blend into the next without empty spaces separating them. When you are finished, the work must look like a Surrealist's dream.

FOCUSING

Study Ernst's painting (Figure 8.27). Notice that the woman's face has been cut from another picture and pasted on. Notice also how the realistic sky has been painted up to the edges of the textured areas. Can you guess which shapes have been cut and attached to the surface of the canvas? Can you tell where he has brushed on paint and where he has used decalcomania, frottage, or grattage?

CREATING

Using scratch paper, experiment with Ernst's three techniques. For decalcomania, try placing translucent wax paper over the blobs of paint so that you can see the way the paint moves as you gently push the colors around. With a little practice you can control the shapes and the blending of colors. Don't let the paint dry before you separate the sheets of paper. You will need a partner to hold the bottom paper down while you quickly pull the top paper off the surface.

Apply blobs of color to your large sheet of paper. Place the second painting surface over the first and use gentle pressure to push the paints around. Then pull the surfaces apart quickly. Rub or scratch the wet surfaces if you wish. Let the paint dry. Save both surfaces.

Study the textured shapes you have made and let them give you ideas for your fantasy picture. Do you see land or animal forms among the shapes and textures? Do you want to cut up one of the surfaces and glue it on the other? Do you need to paint out some parts?

Release your imagination. Add details using paint, oil pastels, markers, and collage. If you glue on shapes cut from magazine pictures, you may need to paint over the edges of the added shapes with a color that unifies them with the background.

Mount or mat your finished copy for display.

FIGURE 8.27A Student work.

CRITIQUING

Describe Identify the subjects of the fantasy scene you created. List and explain the techniques you used to create visual textures in your fantasy scene.

Analyze How did the visual textures affect the look of your work? Did you attach any textured shapes or magazine cutouts? What color scheme did you use? How did it affect the work? Are the shapes predominantly geometric or free-form? How does that affect the look of the work?

Interpret What kind of mood does your work express? Give it a title that sums up your feelings about the meaning of this work.

Judge Which aesthetic theories would be the most important in judging this work? Do you think your work is successful? If you were to do it over, is there anything you would change to improve it?

STUDIO LESSON: ASSEMBLAGE

FIGURE 8.28 James Hampton. *The Throne of the Third Heaven of the Nations' Millennium General Assembly.* c. 1950–64. Aluminum and gold foil over wood furniture, plastic, paper, and glass. 3.2 × 8.2 × 4.2 m (10½ × 27 × 14′). National Museum of American Art, Washington, D.C.

Supplies

- Sketchbook and pencils
- Materials that will serve as a base for the throne
- Found objects such as boxes, tubes, lightbulbs, and small spice jars
- White glue, nontoxic rubber cement, masking tape, duct tape
- String, rope, wire
- Scissors and utility knife
- Aluminum foil, foil wrapping paper, sequins

Vases, lightbulbs, jelly glasses, and used furniture may seem like unusual art media to you, but not to James Hampton. These are a few of the objects he used to create his unique assemblage (Figure 8.28).

Hampton, a soft-spoken African-American, was born in 1909 in a small South Carolina community. Around 1950 he rented an unheated, poorly lit garage near the boarding house where he lived. By November 4, 1964, the day he died, Hampton had built in that garage *The Throne of the Third Heaven of the Nations' Millennium General Assembly,* a collection of 180 glittering objects.

Hampton believed that God and his angels regularly visited him in the garage to direct him in creating *The Throne*. Each night, upon returning from his janitorial job around midnight, Hampton would work on the project for five or six hours. Although Hampton never studied art, he had a natural sense of design. Notice how the throne at the center of the rear line of objects serves as the heart of the assemblage. Bordering both sides of the throne are matching pairs of objects. He used old furniture and discarded objects, such as cardboard tubes and insulation board, to construct the major pieces. He joined the pieces with strips of cardboard or metal cut from coffee cans. Glass vases, lightbulbs, and jelly glasses completed the tops and corners of objects. Upholstery tacks, small nails, and straight pins held everything together. Finally, all of the objects were covered with recycled foil of various colors. Some of his foil came from store displays, some from gift wrap, and some was ordinary aluminum foil.

After Hampton's death, the massive construction was moved to the National Museum of American Art in Washington, D.C.

SAFETY NOTE

When cutting with a sharp blade, always cut away from your body. Never hold the object being cut so that your hand is in the path of the cutting tool.

Design and create a small throne with a theme by assembling and joining found materials. Working individually or in small groups, symmetrically join the found materials to make a chairlike structure. Then, as James Hampton did, alter the look of the work by changing the surface texture: cover the entire structure with foil and foil wrapping paper.

FOCUSING

Brainstorm with classmates for themes for your throne. Think of school subjects such as math, science, or history. Think of activities you do after school and create a skating throne, movie throne, auto throne, food throne, or music throne. Let your imaginations loose and come up with outer-space themes, underwater themes, or time-period themes. How about a throne for your favorite hero? Decide on a theme for your group.

CREATING

Working in a small group, design a chair-shaped object that will serve as the base for your throne. Collect small discarded objects and pieces of heavy cardboard that can be used to construct and decorate the throne.

Each person should look at the objects collected and make sketches of his or her ideas for the throne structure and the decorations that will go on it. Then, as a group, study all the sketches and select the best ideas. Each member of the group should make one final drawing of the combined ideas.

Join your found objects, organizing them symmetrically. If necessary, cut shapes out of heavy cardboard. Before you cover the finished work with foil, decorate the surfaces with rope and wire, buttons, and layers of cardboard to create raised surfaces and various textures. Be sure everything is joined securely. You may even add words or phrases with raised block letters or rope that imitates cursive writing.

Change the surface by covering everything with shiny foil. You may glue paper-backed foil to smooth surfaces, or press aluminum foil tightly to irregular surfaces. Some aluminum foil may be left smooth, and some may be crumpled up. Sequins and other shiny objects can be attached with pins or glue. Give your throne a poetic title.

FIGURE 8.28A Student work.

CRITIQUING

Describe Describe the way you constructed the basic form of the throne. Name the theme. Identify the objects and shapes you attached to the main form and explain how they represented the theme.

Analyze What kinds of materials did you use to create your throne? Did you use symmetry to organize your decorative objects? How did the addition of shiny foil change the surface quality of the structure?

Interpret Can your classmates recognize the theme? Did your group find a poetic title that reflects the theme?

Judge Which aesthetic theories would you use to judge this work? Do you think your throne is successful? If you were going to do it over, what would you change?

STUDIO LESSON: PAPER SCULPTURE CREATURE

FIGURE 8.29 Artist unknown. Mexico. *Bird.* 1988. Tin and gold paint. 28 × 22 × 17.8 cm (11 × 8½ × 7″). Private collection.

Supplies

- Sketchbook and pencil
- Colored construction paper
- Variety of other papers to decorate the surface, such as wallpaper samples, shiny wrapping papers, and paper ribbons
- Scissors, ruler, and sharp knife
- Pointed tool for piercing, such as compass point
- Transparent tape, white glue, straight pins
- Cardboard tubes and containers for internal support

Visit Mexico and you can see beautiful traditional tinwork pieces such as frames, lanterns, sconces, candleholders, chandeliers, crosses, and trinket boxes. Using flat sheets of tin, craftspeople cut, score, and pierce the tin to form three-dimensional works of art that are used to decorate their homes and churches.

This bird was made by a craftsperson in Mexico just a few years ago. However, the techniques used by the artist are the same as the tinwork processes that have been used in Mexico for more than two hundred years. The decorative processes used by the tinsmiths are part of a long tradition of surface decoration practices developed in Spain and brought to Mexico by the Spaniards.

These surface decorations, which produce highly textured real and visual effects, are made by using processes of cutting, piercing, stamping, scoring, and soldering. Another method of joining, tab-and-slot construction, is also used.

As you study the tin bird in Figure 8.29, you can see how the artist used these processes to create a three-dimensional form. Many of these same processes are used to create forms with paper sculpture.

The back has been scored and is bent into a curve. The textural effects of the feathers have been created by layers of fringe that have been curled. Notice the contrast obtained by using fringes of different lengths. The fringes on the head and around the eyes are short. The wing areas have short and long fringes. The longest fringes are cut from a long strip and shaped into a spiral to create the round tail. The breast of the bird is decorated with oval shapes that have been applied to the form in a repeated, overlapping pattern.

Try to use many forms of decoration to give your paper sculpture varied textures. Design a creature that is interesting from every point of view.

After studying the photo of the Mexican bird and practicing paper sculpture techniques, design and create a three-dimensional, freestanding, imaginary paper creature using a variety of strong papers. Cover the surface with a variety of interesting textures using fringing, cutting, curling, and scoring. This sculpture should look interesting from every point of view.

FOCUSING

Study the paper sculpture techniques on page 356 in the Handbook. Practice them all using construction paper. Study the tin bird to see what techniques you think were used to construct that sculpture.

CREATING

Make several sketches in your sketchbook to plan the sculpture you will make. Select your best design. Make some sketches showing different views of the sculpture. List the materials and techniques you will use to construct your three-dimensional creature and those you will use to create surface textures.

Collect the materials you will need. Construct your sculpture based on the drawings you have made. You may change your plan as you go along. If your creature is too heavy and does not stand up, support it on the inside with cardboard tubes and containers.

Place the finished sculpture on a firm base for display. Glue or pin it to the base.

FIGURE 8.29A Student work.

CRITIQUING

Describe List the materials and paper-sculpture techniques you used to create your sculpture. Did the practice session with paper-sculpture techniques help you in planning your final project? How did you prepare it for display?

Analyze What form did you create for your sculpture? Describe the different textures you created. Is the work interesting from every point of view?

Interpret What kind of mood or idea does your finished sculpture express? Give your work a title that expresses the mood.

Judge Have you created a freestanding, three-dimensional, fantasy creature? Is your work successful? Is there anything you would change to make the work more successful? Which aesthetic view would be best to judge this work?

STUDIO LESSON: STITCHERY AND APPLIQUÉ

FIGURE 8.30 Ayako Miyawaki. *The Red Crab.* 1981. Fabric and thread. 29.5 × 57.5 cm (11⅝ × 22⅝"). The future Toyota Municipal Museum of Art, Aichi, Japan.

Supplies

- Sketchbook and pencil
- One large piece of fabric for the background
- Variety of scraps for appliqué
- Embroidery threads, yarns, and other fibers
- Pins, needles, tapestry needles, and a pincushion
- Sharp fabric scissors
- Envelope for storing cut pieces
- Dowel or other straight rod for hanging

SAFETY NOTE

Use a pincushion or a container to hold your pins as you remove them from the work. Never put them in your mouth.

Many Japanese kimonos and banners are decorated using appliqué. **Appliqué** is *an art form in which cutout decorations are fastened to a larger surface to create a new design.* This technique enables the artist to use an assortment of fabrics with varying textures to create contrast and emphasis in the design.

Ayako Miyawaki is a Japanese artist who uses appliqué. She began her work after World War II. Having no formal art training, she created her own designs and modeled them after objects she observed in her everyday life—objects such as fish, fruit, vegetables, and flowers (Figure 8.30).

Miyawaki has a unique style, cutting her fabrics freely without patterns and applying them boldly, creating the effect of bright splashes of pigment on canvas. She collects brightly colored fabrics and those decorated with Japanese designs. Sometimes she stitches the fabrics to the background as she has done in this work, and sometimes she uses glue to hold her pieces in place. She also uses fibers and threads as lines in her compositions.

Design and create an appliqué work selecting an ordinary object from your daily life as subject matter. Starting with a large piece of fabric for the background, cut and apply a variety of contrasting fabrics, using different fibers and stitches. Emphasize the elements of color and texture for contrast.

FOCUSING

Study Miyawaki's appliqué *The Red Crab*. Notice the contrasts of the complementary red and green colors. Observe the contrast between the smoother weave of the crab fabric and the rougher weave in the background. Can you find where the artist created line using only thread?

CREATING

Collect and bring to class fabric scraps that have a variety of textures and colors and fibers such as sewing threads, yarns, dried grasses, and pieces of thin rope.

Study the fabrics using your imagination. What ordinary, everyday objects do the fabrics and the patterns on the fabrics suggest to you? Discuss your ideas with classmates. Give each other suggestions.

Select the fabrics you will use to make the objects. Then select a large piece for the background that will provide a contrast in color and texture.

Plan your composition before you start cutting. Make notes and sketches in your sketchbook. Cut a sample of each fabric you will use and tape it to the page, noting how it will be used. If your background shape is some variation of a rectangle, your work will be easy to hang, but you may choose another shape.

Cut all the pieces you will need before you do any stitching. Keep all your cut fabrics in an envelope so they won't get lost before you begin sewing. Arrange and rearrange the cut pieces on the background until the composition looks right to you. Pin your final composition to the background.

Study the embroidery stitches in the Handbook on page 357. Practice on extra scraps if necessary. Use a variety of stitches to appliqué your fabrics to the background. Stitch your signature or initials on your finished work.

Turn the edges of your background fabric under at least 1/4 inch (6 mm) and sew them down using a running stitch or a hemstitch.

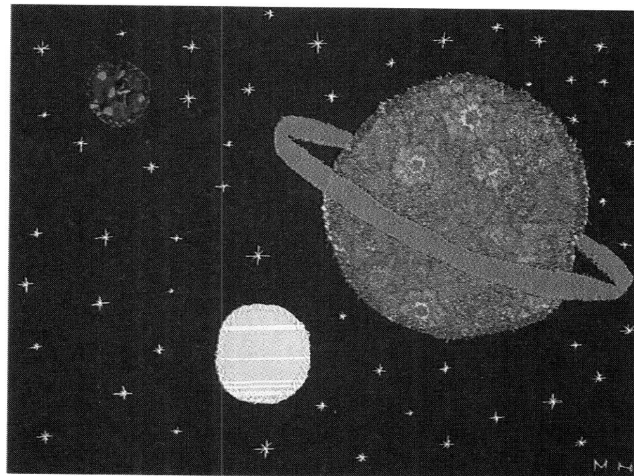

FIGURE 8.30A Student work.

Add loops to the top of your fabric so that it can be hung on a dowel rod, or invent some other way to display your work. Give your work a creative title.

CRITIQUING

Describe Tell what subject matter you selected for your appliqué and explain why. Did you tape fabric swatches in your sketchbook and make notes explaining how they were to be used? What kinds of stitches did you use to attach your fabrics? Did you use fibers as an addition to your design or were they just used to attach fabrics?

Analyze Describe the contrasting colors and textures you used in the work. Did the printed designs on your fabric help you think of objects to make?

Interpret Is your subject matter obvious or is it hard to recognize? What is the mood of your work? Does the title you gave your appliqué enhance the feeling of the work?

Judge Which aesthetic theories would you use to judge this work? Are you satisfied with your finished product? If you were going to redo it, what would you change?

ART CRITICISM IN ACTION

FIGURE 8.31 Sandy Skoglund. *The Green House.* 1990. Cibachrome photograph. 127 × 178 cm (50 × 70″). Skoglund Art Gallery, New York, New York.

CRITIQUING THE WORK

1. **Describe** Study the photograph *The Green House* by Sandy Skoglund (Figure 8.31). Describe exactly what you see in this work.
2. **Analyze** What kind of color scheme was used by the artist? Notice the color of the people. How did she use texture? Did she use real or visual textures? Did Skoglund reproduce textures as she saw them or did she invent her own? Locate and describe rough, smooth, matte textured surfaces. Do you see different degrees of texture?
3. **Interpret** When the artist created *The Green House,* she selected various elements and positioned them in unusual ways. Does the photograph convey a mood, feeling, or idea to you? How did Skoglund use texture to enhance her work? How does the color of the people affect your interpretation of the work? Write a paragraph explaining your interpretation. Then write a new title for the work. Your title should sum up your interpretation.

FIGURE 8.32 Peter Paul Rubens. *Daniel in the Lions' Den.* c. 1615. Oil on linen. 224.3 × 330.4 cm (88¼ × 130⅛"). National Gallery of Art, Washington, D.C. Ailsa Mellon Bruce Fund.

4. **Judge** Do you think this is a successful work of art? Use one of the theories of art explained in Chapter 2 to defend your answer.

COMPARING THE WORKS

Look at *The Green House* (Figure 8.31) and *Daniel in the Lions' Den* by Peter Paul Rubens (Figure 8.32). Identify the similarities and differences between the two works. What idea is communicated in *The Green House?* Is a similar idea conveyed by the painting *Daniel in the Lions' Den?* How does each artist use animals in communicating the idea or message to the viewer? How does each use texture? Decide which artwork you find more interesting and share your reaction in a class discussion.

FYI This painting by Rubens hung for many years in the boardroom of an English business firm. People assumed it was only a copy of a work by the master. When it was finally purchased by an art lover who had admired it for years, the painting was authenticated as being a lost original by Rubens himself.

MEET THE ARTIST

SANDY SKOGLUND

American, b. 1946

Sandy Skoglund is a contemporary American artist who works in an unusual mix of media. She builds installations, working with found materials and strangely colored animal sculptures. Her installations often are intricate reproductions of everyday environments, like a lawn or a living room, being overrun by nature in the form of brightly colored animals. She does the photography of these works herself, and the prints she produces are considered as much a part of the work as the installation itself.

Each installation Skoglund creates takes an average of six months to complete. She constructs the environment using found materials, and she hand sculpts the animals that appear in her work. Each is like a movie set that is then painted in a single color and filled with objects to create a fantastic and absurd scenario. Each conveys a symbolic message. The title of *The Green House* provides a clue to the message of this work. Just as the man and woman in the photograph seem unaware that they are literally living in a green house and are surrounded by blue and green dogs, many people are unaware of their own relationship to nature. The title also suggests the dangers that man can create for nature. The "greenhouse effect" is a global warming created by pollution. The artist may be pointing out that the modern technologies that cause pollution are out of control, and many people, like those in the picture, do not notice or care.

MORE PORTFOLIO IDEAS

Create a tabletop model of a staged environment that juxtaposes unexpected objects. Plan a theme and title for the scene. Using a large carton open at the front, bring found objects in to fill the "room" and carry out the theme. Select a compatible color scheme and photograph the finished project.

Write a poem or story from the point of view of the dog on the mantle in Skoglund's photograph.

Create a still life or landscape using variations from an all-blue palette to create depth and interest. To begin, draw several objects with closed paths, including a large rectangle to serve as a backdrop. Move and resize the foreground objects to create a visually pleasing design.

CHAPTER 8 REVIEW

Building Vocabulary

On a separate sheet of paper, write the term that best matches each definition given below.

1. The element of art that refers to how things feel, or look as if they might feel if touched.
2. The illusion of a three-dimensional surface.
3. A surface that reflects a soft, dull light.
4. An artwork onto which bits and pieces of textured paper and fabric have been pasted.
5. A method of producing textures by rubbing crayon over paper placed over a rough-textured surface, or scraping across a freshly painted canvas that has been placed over a similar surface.
6. The technique of scratching into wet paint with a variety of tools to create texture.
7. A technique of creating random texture patterns by applying thick paint to two surfaces, pressing them together, and then pulling them apart.

Reviewing Art Facts

Answer the following questions using complete sentences.

1. With what senses is texture perceived?
2. What is the difference between real and visual texture?
3. What is the difference between simulated and invented texture?
4. Name the four types of textures.
5. What determines how a surface looks?
6. How can the roughness or smoothness of a texture be determined?
7. What kind of a surface reflects light unevenly?
8. What kind of texture reflects light evenly?

Thinking Critically About Art

1. **Describe.** Look at the photographs in Figure 8.2 on page 192. Describe three of these photographs without naming any of the objects in them. Describe only the lines, shapes, spaces, values, and textures in the photographs. From your description have classmates guess the photograph you are describing.
2. **Analyze.** Which kinds of visual textures are shown in Figure 8.4 on page 194? Which surfaces in this print appear to be rough? Which appear to be smooth?
3. **Analyze.** How would you describe the different surface textures in Figure 8.17 on page 200? How were the different effects created?
4. **Compare and contrast.** Compare the ways Vigée-Lebrun (Figure 8.3, page 193), Renoir (Figure 8.15, page 199), and Albright (Figure 8.16, page 200) have used texture in the representation of women's clothes.
5. **Compare.** Compare the texture in Figure 3.32 (page 64) and Figure 8.17 (page 200). What purpose does it serve in each?

Making Art Connections

1. **Music.** Hedi Bak created many textures in *Grand Canyon #2* (Figure 8.4, page 194) that resemble the walls of the gorge in northern Arizona. Listen to a recording of Ferde Grofé's *Grand Canyon Suite*. Does the music convey the magnitude of the Grand Canyon? Can you detect any *audible* color or texture?
2. **Literature.** Rubens's painting *Daniel in the Lions' Den* (Figure 8.32, page 215) illustrates a biblical story. Read this story for a deeper understanding of the relationship shown between Daniel and the lions. Write your own version of this story.
3. **Technology.** At about the same time Edgar Degas was completing *Little Fourteen-Year-Old Dancer* (Figure 8.21, page 203), three developments in electricity were taking place. Research the incandescent lightbulb, steam power for generating electricity, or electric streetcars and share your findings with the class.

Miriam Schapiro. *Master of Ceremonies.* (Detail.) 1985. Acrylic and fabric on canvas. 228.6 × 365.7 cm (90 × 144″). Courtesy Steinbaum Krauss Gallery, New York, New York.

UNIT 3

THE PRINCIPLES OF DESIGN

Putting art together is the purpose for learning the principles of design. In this unit of *ArtTalk* you will learn about the principles of design. They are *rhythm, balance, proportion, variety, emphasis, harmony,* and *unity.*

Understanding the principles of design will help you understand how art objects are organized. It will also help you create successful works of your own. You will learn to recognize each principle in your natural environment and in works of art. You will then see how artists use a principle to express their feelings and ideas. At the same time, you will work to develop a skillful use of that principle in your own art.

As you did with the elements in Unit 2, you will learn one principle at a time. At the end of each chapter you will add this new principle to your accumulated knowledge of elements and principles. After completing Chapter 12, you will have all the "words" and "grammar" you need to speak the language of art. You will be able to communicate your own artistic ideas in creative and exciting ways.

FIGURE 9.1 The woman who made this story cloth currently lives in Providence, Rhode Island. Her people fought beside the Americans during the Vietnam conflict. This picture tells the story of her flight from Laos, across the Mekong River, to an American refugee camp in Thailand. The story starts in the upper right corner. Can you follow her as she moves toward safety?

Chaing Xiong. *Hmong Story Cloth.* 1987. Pieced and embroidered polyester, cotton blend. 140.3 × 145.4 cm (55¼ × 57¼"). Wadsworth Atheneum, Hartford, Connecticut. Florence Paull Berger Fund.

CHAPTER 9

Rhythm and Movement

Rhythm is a hand-clapping, toe-tapping musical beat. Rhythm is the throb of bass notes booming out of stereo speakers. It is the steady strumming on a guitar.

Rhythm is the synchronization of a marching band and a drill team making snappy moves.

Rhythm is the flashing lights and wailing sounds of fire engines.

Rhythm is the coming and going of the moon.

Rhythm is the steady beating of a heart.

Rhythm is tempo.

Rhythm is beat.

Life is full of rhythmic events. People crave the dependable rhythms of life. Rhythms are comforting. There is a rhythmic cycle to the seasons. Spring always follows winter, and when it comes, people feel like celebrating. When you go to bed at night, you expect the next day. You are sure the earth will turn, the sun will rise, and day will follow night. The rhythmic routines of daily living give your life a sense of stability and security.

FIRST IMPRESSIONS

Look at Figure 9.1 and read the caption. To tell this story the artist uses many different kinds of rhythmic repetition. Can you find the steady beat of a regular rhythm? Can you find objects that are repeated in a random manner? Can you find a flowing rhythm that moves your eye through the picture? Can you find the repetitions of the family, starting from when they fled the village until they crossed the river and reached the Americans? What other repetitions can you find?

Objectives

After completing this chapter, you will be able to:

- Identify rhythms occurring in the world around you.
- Understand how rhythm adds a sense of movement to a work of art.
- Identify and explain motif and pattern.
- Name and identify the types of rhythm.
- Use the principle of rhythm to create your own works.

Words to Know

kinetic
module
motif
movement
pattern
rhythm
visual rhythm

HOW WE PERCEIVE VISUAL RHYTHM

Rhythm is *the principle of design that indicates movement by the repetition of elements.* The principle of rhythm is used in every art form.

In music, rhythm is created by the measure of time between musical sounds. There is a beat followed by a rest. **Visual rhythm** is *rhythm you receive through your eyes rather than through your ears* (Figure 9.2). Visual rhythm is created by repeated positive shapes separated by negative spaces. The positive areas are the "beats." Each beat is separated by negative spaces, which are the "rests." Look at Figure 9.3 for an example of visual beats and rests.

FIGURE 9.2 Visual rhythms can be both natural and manufactured.

FIGURE 9.3 This artist saw the meaning of existence in the changes of weather and seasons. He uses rhythms to express the living force in the natural environment. The elements in this painting seem to dance the dance of life.

Charles Burchfield. *October Wind and Sunlight in the Woods.* c. 1962–63. Watercolor on paper. 101.6 × 137.2 cm (40 × 54″). Georgia Museum of Art, University of Georgia, Athens, Georgia. University purchase.

Everywhere you look you can see visual rhythms. Sometimes, without even thinking, you note the beats and the spaces between the beats. The books in a bookcase and the cars in a parking lot show visual rhythms. A line of people in the cafeteria has visual rhythm. Each person is a positive beat, and the space between each person is the negative area.

A beat may be one element or a combination of elements. Look at the photograph of the lily pads in Figure 9.2. The strongest beats are the round shapes that vary in size. Each round shape has one split from its center to its edge. Each split is turned in a slightly different direction. Since this is a black-and-white photograph, you cannot see the colors of the round shapes, but you can see the value changes. Some leaves are very light—almost white. Most have a middle-gray value, and some are almost as dark as the negative spaces. Look closely and you will see a second, less noticeable beat: the thin curving and diagonal lines of the stems linking the lily pads.

The negative space between the beats varies greatly. Some shapes touch or overlap, and in other areas the space between the shapes is wide. The value of the negative space varies from dark gray to black. The lightest areas of negative space are on the left side and at the bottom of the photograph.

Visual rhythms create a sensation of movement as the viewer's eyes follow the visual beats through a work of art. Visual movement is different from real action, which involves a physical change in position. For example, a ball bouncing across a room is real action. Round shapes separated by negative spaces in a picture can create the same visual sensation as the movement of the ball because your eyes bounce from one round shape to the next. Artists use this type of visual movement to control the way the viewer looks at a work of art (Figure 9.4 on page 224).

Using Visual Beats

1. Applying Your Skills. Look through newspapers and magazines for two advertisements that use rhythm to create visual movement. Circle the positive beats with a crayon or a marker.

2. Further Challenge. Bonheur creates a sense of movement through her work by repeating the horses in Figure 9.4 on page 224. The horses are the major beat in the rhythm, and the men are the secondary beat in her composition. Create a composition of your own in which trees in a forest are the major beat that leads the viewer's eyes through the work. Then add a secondary

LOOKING CLOSELY

FIGURE 9.4 What are the beats of the rhythm that move your eyes through this painting? Are the beats all the same? Can you see any negative spaces between the beats as in the photograph of the lily pads? Where does the movement start? Which way has the artist pulled you through the work? How has she accomplished this? Are there any other objects in this painting that make up a counterpoint of beats? Can you find a steady beat that moves along in the same direction as the more active beats? How do they help create the rhythmic movement?

Rosa Bonheur. *The Horse Fair.* 1853–55. Oil on canvas. 244.5 x 506.7 cm (96¼ × 199½″). The Metropolitan Museum of Art, New York, New York. Gift of Cornelius Vanderbilt, 1887.

beat that enhances the sense of movement. Be creative in what you decide to use for the secondary beat.

3. Computer Option. Choose the Line tool of your computer program and draw one straight, wide line. Make several exact copies of this line by using the Select, Copy, and Paste options. Choose the Circle tool and draw one circle using a *cool color* with *no pattern*. Make several exact copies of this circle by using the Select, Copy, and Paste options. You will create rhythm as you place each line and circle. Additional smaller circles may be added. If your monitor is monochrome, make your lines solid and put patterns in the circles. Remember that you can add, rearrange, or remove elements easily when drawing with the computer.

REPETITION

Rhythm results from repetition. *Motif* and *pattern* are often used to talk about repetition in art.

A **motif** is *a unit that is repeated in visual rhythm*. Sometimes every motif is an exact duplicate of the first unit, and sometimes the repetitions vary from the original (Figure 9.5).

Look around and you will find examples of motif and repetition. In a marching band, one band member is a motif, even though each band member carries a different instrument. On a grocery store shelf full of canned goods, one can is a motif. In a herd of cattle, one cow is a motif.

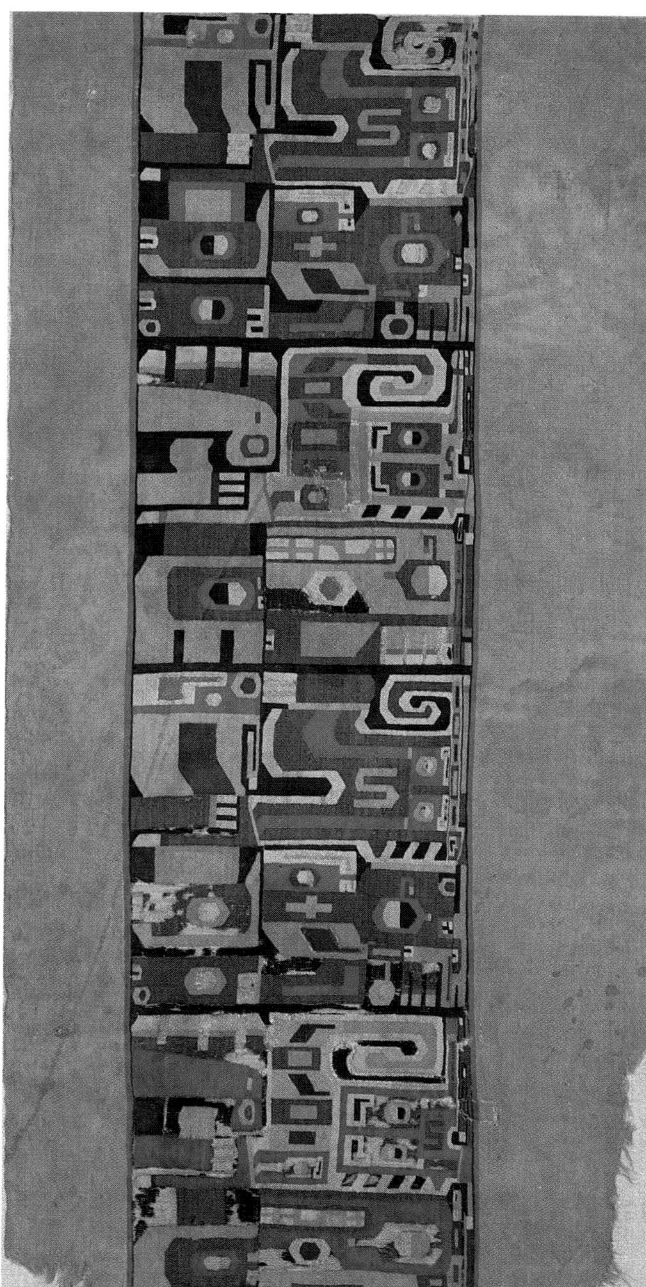

FIGURE 9.5 See if you can identify one or more motifs in this design.

Mantle. Coastal Huari (Tiahuanaco), Peru. 600–1000. Cotton and wool. 103.5 × 50.5 cm (40¾ × 19⅞"). The Metropolitan Museum of Art, New York, New York. The Michael C. Rockefeller Memorial Collection, bequest of Nelson A. Rockefeller, 1979.

FIGURE 9.6 This elevator grill is a delicate pattern of lines and round forms. It was once part of a large bank of elevators in the 1893 Chicago Stock Exchange. The building was torn down in 1972, but parts of it, such as this grill, have been saved and housed in various museums.

Louis Sullivan. *Elevator Grille.* 1893–94. Bronze-plated cast iron. 185.4 × 78.7 cm (73 × 31"). High Museum of Art, Atlanta, Georgia. Carroll Crawford Collection, 1982.

In sculpture and architecture *a three-dimensional motif* is sometimes called a **module**. Modular furniture is composed of standard matching units.

Pattern is a word used to describe a decorative surface design. **Pattern** is *a two-dimensional decorative visual repetition.*

You have seen a pattern of lines decorating fabric or a pattern used in construction (Figure 9.6).

Some of these patterns are functional; others are used only as decoration. They tend to be stiff and rather dull. If you remember that rhythm is a repetition intended to create the feeling of movement, and that pattern is intended to be flat and decorative, you will have no trouble telling the difference between the two.

Motifs and Patterns

1. Applying Your Skills. Make a collection of decorative patterns. You may use photographs, clippings from magazines, scraps of fabric, and so on. Identify the motif in each pattern by drawing a circle around one. Organize your pattern collection into a poster, a bulletin board, a booklet, or some other kind of presentation.

2. Further Challenge. Find a house in your neighborhood that has interesting visual rhythms. Make a pencil drawing of it, emphasizing the rhythmic areas. For example, you might draw the outer shape with a light line and then darken any rectangular shapes. Or, starting with a light line drawing, you might use a colored marker to accent vertical repetitions.

3. Computer Option. Start with a rectangle and design a simple motif. Use three colors or three original textures in black and white. Create a variety of patterns with that motif. Print your patterns. If your printer is black and white, you can add color with other media such as colored pencil after the design is printed out.

FIGURE 9.7 The potter who created this bowl made an aesthetic decision to splash the ware with vegetable juices to create a random pattern of round shapes and lines.

Bowl. Sundi group, Kongo peoples. Congo, Zaire, and Angola. Before 1910. Fired clay and natural pigment. 11.3 × 15.6 cm (4½ × 6¼"). National Museum of African Art, Smithsonian Institution, Washington, D.C. Purchased with funds provided by the Smithsonian Collections Acquisition Program, 89–13–31.

TYPES OF RHYTHM

Different visual rhythms are created with different arrangements of motif and space. There are many ways to combine motifs and space. Each way gives a different character to the rhythm depicted.

Random

A motif repeated in no apparent order, with no regular spaces in between, creates a *random* rhythm. One example is autumn leaves that cover the ground. Cracks in mud and splashes of paint are two more examples of random rhythm.

Crowds often create random rhythms—think of holiday shoppers, rush-hour commuters, and students in the halls between classes. A large group of people pushing into a subway train is full of rhythm. The motif is one person. Every person is different, and every space is slightly different.

The Sundi woman who created the bowl shown in Figure 9.7 deliberately splashed the bowl with vegetable juices immediately after pulling it from the fire to create the random pattern of round shapes that decorate the surface. If she had dipped it into the liquid, the bowl would have had an even brown hue. The vegetable liquid applied while the clay is still hot makes it able to resist the heat of the cooking fire. The bowl can be used over an open fire without shattering. In some parts of Africa, the marks left by the vegetable juices are interpreted as proof of the thermal strength of the vessel.

Using Random Rhythm

1. Applying Your Skills. Make a stamp motif and print it in a random rhythm (Figure 9.8).

2. Further Challenge. Choose one letter of the alphabet. Look through newspapers and magazines for large examples of that letter. Neatly cut out twenty or more. Arrange them on a piece of colored paper in a random pattern (Figure 9.9). If you have trouble finding large letters, you can add some neatly drawn letters of your own to your design.

3. Computer Option. Depending on your computer program capabilities: (1) design a motif, (2) choose a stamp, (3) edit a stamp, or (4) edit a brush. Use the resulting motif in a random manner. You can use Flip, Rotate, Size Change, and Color options if your program has them.

FIGURE 9.8 Student work.

Regular

Regular rhythm has identical motifs and equal amounts of space between them (Figure 9.10). Regular rhythm has a steady beat.

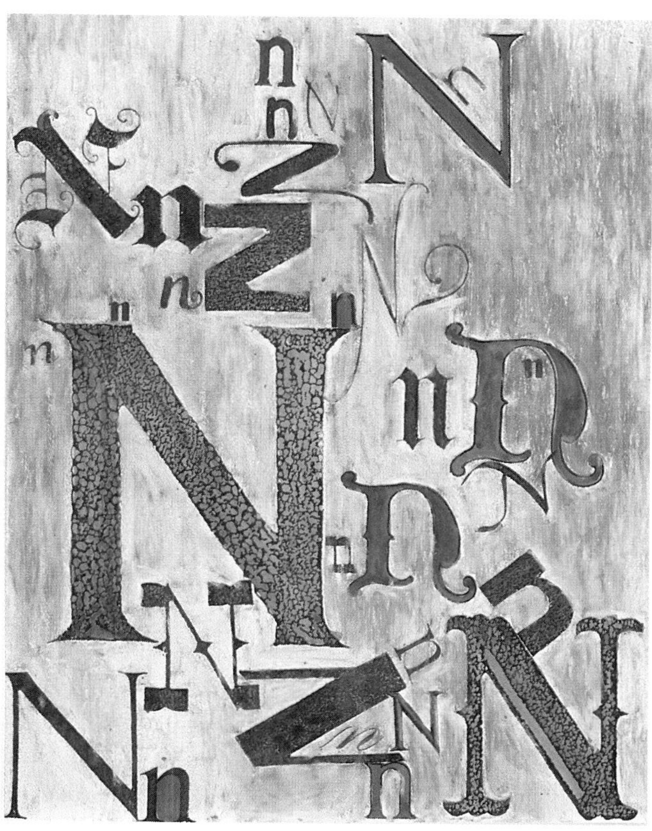

FIGURE 9.9 Student work. Random arrangement of letters.

FIGURE 9.10 This fern shows the regular rhythm found in nature.

Regular repetitions are used to organize things. Parking spaces and office mailboxes are laid out with regular rhythm. Stores organize merchandise into regular stacks and rows. This makes it easier for you to find things, and it also makes the displays more attractive than if items were arranged in a random fashion.

A grid is based on regular rhythm. It is a regular arrangement of parallel lines. A football field is laid out in a grid, as is a checkerboard. Windows form a grid pattern on the side of a skyscraper. The artist who created the cloth in Figure 9.11 had a grid pattern in his mind as he wove the long, narrow strips of cloth. Later he cut and sewed the strips together to make the wide cloth you see. Notice the regular repetition of the various motifs.

Regular rhythm can be boring if it is overdone. One note played on a piano over and over again is an example. Pop artist Andy Warhol used regular rhythm to make a social-protest statement (Figure 9.12). How would you describe the effect of this regular rhythm? What do you suppose Warhol intended to convey with this repeated motif?

Alternating

Alternating rhythm can occur in several ways. One way is to introduce a second motif. Another way is to make a change in the placement or content of the original motif. A third way is to change the spaces between the motifs. Sometimes alternation is created simply by changing the position of the motif. For example, the motif may be turned upside down. The Japanese artist who painted the wave design on the bowl shown in Figure 9.13 created the feeling of movement by alternating the placement of the wave shapes. The Native American who embroidered the shoulder bag in Figure 9.14 on page 230 made the design interesting by changing the sets of motifs several times.

Bricks are often laid in an alternating pattern. As a child, did you ever play with interlocking blocks? You had to use an alternating pattern to join the blocks.

An alternating rhythm using two motifs can still be very repetitive. Your eyes keep returning to the first motif even after the second motif joins the design, but the alternation does create interest and relieve monotony.

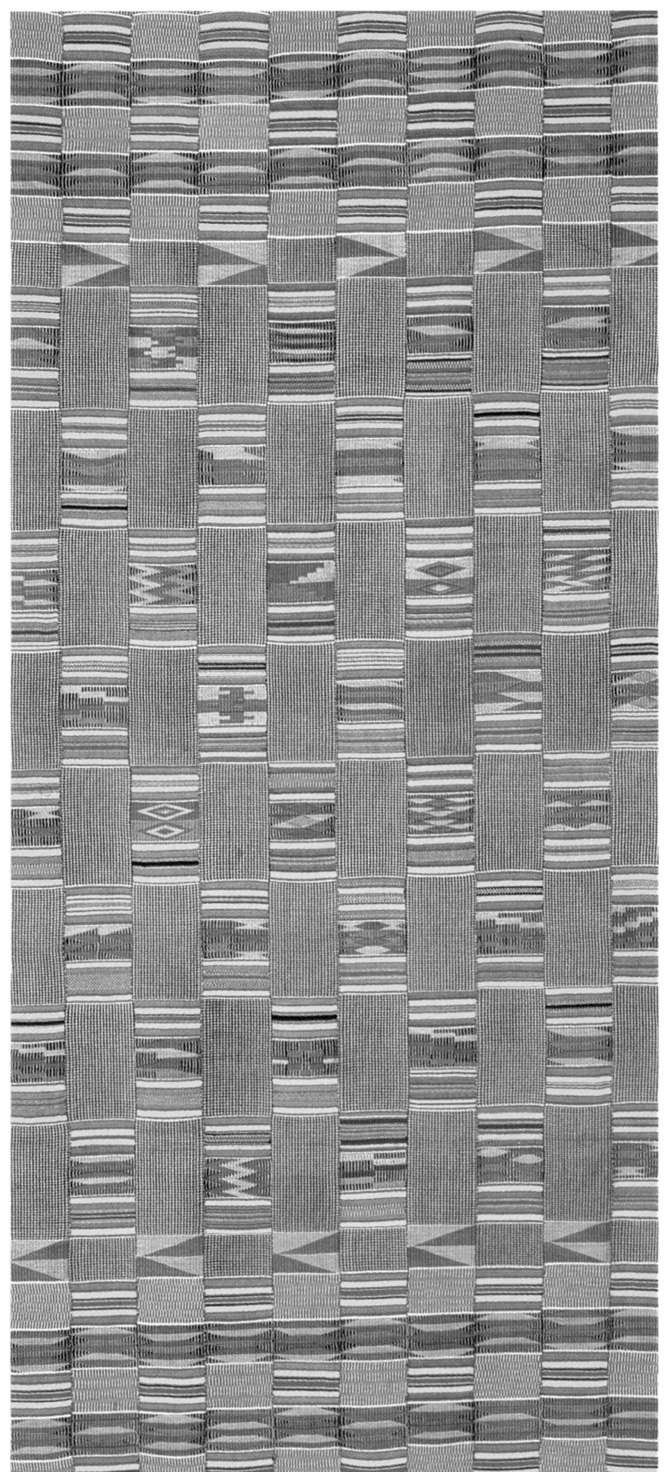

FIGURE 9.11 The elaborate grid pattern fits together perfectly because the weaver has memorized the whole plan through many years of practice.

Wrapper. Asante peoples, Ghana. Date unknown. Cotton and rayon plain weave with supplementary rayon weft. 190 × 83 cm (74⅞ × 32¾″). National Museum of African Art and National Museum of Natural History, Washington, D.C. Purchased with funds provided by the Smithsonian Institution. Collection Acquisition Program, 1983–85.

FIGURE 9.12 One pair of lips on the face of Marilyn Monroe would be beautiful and appealing. What has Andy Warhol done to them by repeating them in a regular rhythm?

Andy Warhol. *Marilyn Monroe's Lips.* 1962. Diptych. Synthetic polymer, enamel, and pencil on canvas. Left: 210.7 × 204.9 cm (82¾ × 80¾″). Right: 210.7 × 209.7 cm (82¾ × 82⅜″). Hirshhorn Museum and Sculpture Garden, Smithsonian Institution, Washington, D.C. Gift of Joseph H. Hirshhorn, 1972.

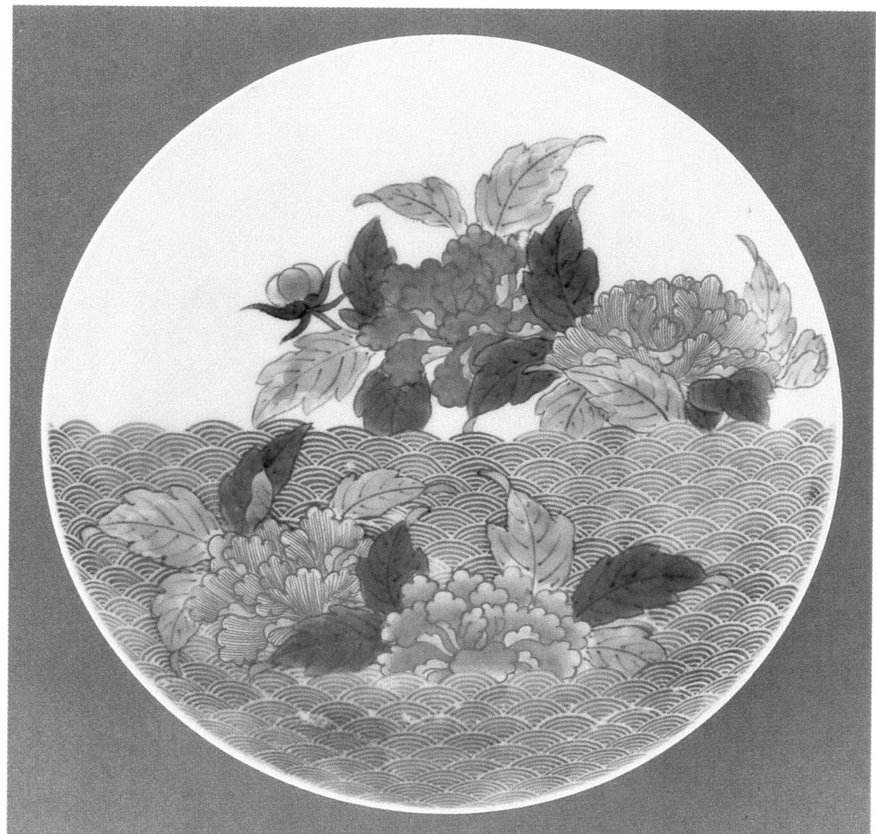

FIGURE 9.13 The artist who painted this dish used an alternating pattern of sets of blue curved lines to symbolize waves of water.

Footed Dish. Japanese, Nabeshima ware. 1700–50. Porcelain with underglaze blue and overglaze polychrome enamel decoration. 5.4 × 20 cm (2⅛ × 7⅞″). Nelson-Atkins Museum of Art, Kansas City, Missouri. Purchase: Nelson Trust.

FIGURE 9.14 How many sets of motifs can you find embroidered on this Creek shoulder bag? How many different ways has the artist alternated the motifs?

Shoulder Bag. Creek. Georgia or Alabama. 1810–30. Wool fabric, cotton fabric and thread, silk ribbon, glass beads. Strap: 135 × 18.7 cm (53¼ × 7⅜"). Bag: 19.4 × 10 cm (7⅝ × 4"). The Detroit Institute of Arts, Detroit, Michigan. Founders Society Purchase with funds from Flint Ink Corporation.

Alternating Rhythm

1. Applying Your Skills. Draw a checkerboard grid and create an alternating rhythm using one motif. Turn the motif upside down in every other box (See Figure 9.15).

2. Further Challenge. Draw a checkerboard grid and create an alternating rhythm using two motifs (Figure 9.16).

3. Computer Option. Design two motifs using the tools of your choice. Use the Select tool and the Copy and Paste options to create an alternating rhythm using both motifs. On a new screen, create an alternating

FIGURE 9.15 Student work. Alternating rhythm with one motif.

FIGURE 9.16 Student work. Alternating rhythm with two motifs.

rhythm using only one motif. In this design, you can change the placement of the motif; for example, turn it upside down or change the spaces between the motifs. Label and save both designs.

Flowing

Flowing rhythm is created by repeating wavy lines. Curved shapes, such as rolling hills or ocean waves, create flowing rhythms (Figure 9.17 on page 232). Your eyes glide along a curving path that changes direction gradually (Figure 9.18 on page 232). There are no sudden breaks in the movement of a flowing line.

Flowing rhythm is all upward swells and downward slides. You might think of the upward moves as the beats and the downward moves as the rests. Allan Houser has used flowing rhythms symbolically in his sculpture *Coming of Age* (Figure 9.19

FIGURE 9.17 The natural curves in this tree bark create a flowing rhythm.

FIGURE 9.18 Student work. Relief design with flowing rhythm.

FIGURE 9.19 This sculpture, with its upturned head and flowing hair, was created to celebrate feminine youth and beauty. The upturned head symbolizes the girl's desire to run to the four directions of the earth. The small shape above her forehead represents an abalone shell, a fertility symbol. The feather worn in her hair signifies a long life.

Allan Houser. *Coming of Age.* 1977. Bronze, edition of 12. 19 × 39.4 × 17.8 cm (7½ × 15½ × 7"). Denver Art Museum, Denver, Colorado.

above). The work expresses the symbolic union of nature and feminity. The thick, rhythmically flowing strands of her hair suggest motion and the act of running. They also suggest the movement of the wind, of water, or even the blazing motion of flames.

Using Flowing Rhythm

1. Applying Your Skills. Look through magazines and newspapers for pictures that feature flowing rhythms. Be sure to look at all the advertisements as you search for the flowing rhythms. Mount and label the best examples that you find.

2. Further Challenge. Create a relief design showing flowing rhythm. Cut strips of construction paper 1/2 inch (1.3 cm) wide. Glue them on edge to a small piece of poster board. Use analogous colors for the strips and a complement of one of the colors for the background. Curl the strips so that they will hold their curve after you have glued them. Arrange the strips in sets of almost parallel ridges.

3. Computer Option. Draw a modified S shape using the Pencil or Brush tool. Use the Select tool and Copy and Paste options to repeat this curved shape, covering most of the screen. Have shapes touch or overlap. Pay attention to the negative shapes created as you paste positive shapes. Save your work. Experiment by pouring colors into the shapes. Make all the connected shapes one color and one original shape a different color. Pour a gradient or a rainbow of colors into the connected shapes. Save the experiments you like. The designs you have created use flowing rhythm. Create another flowing rhythm design without cutting and pasting.

Progressive

In *progressive* rhythm there is a change in the motif each time the motif is repeated. It is like the number series *x plus 1, x plus 2, x plus 3.*

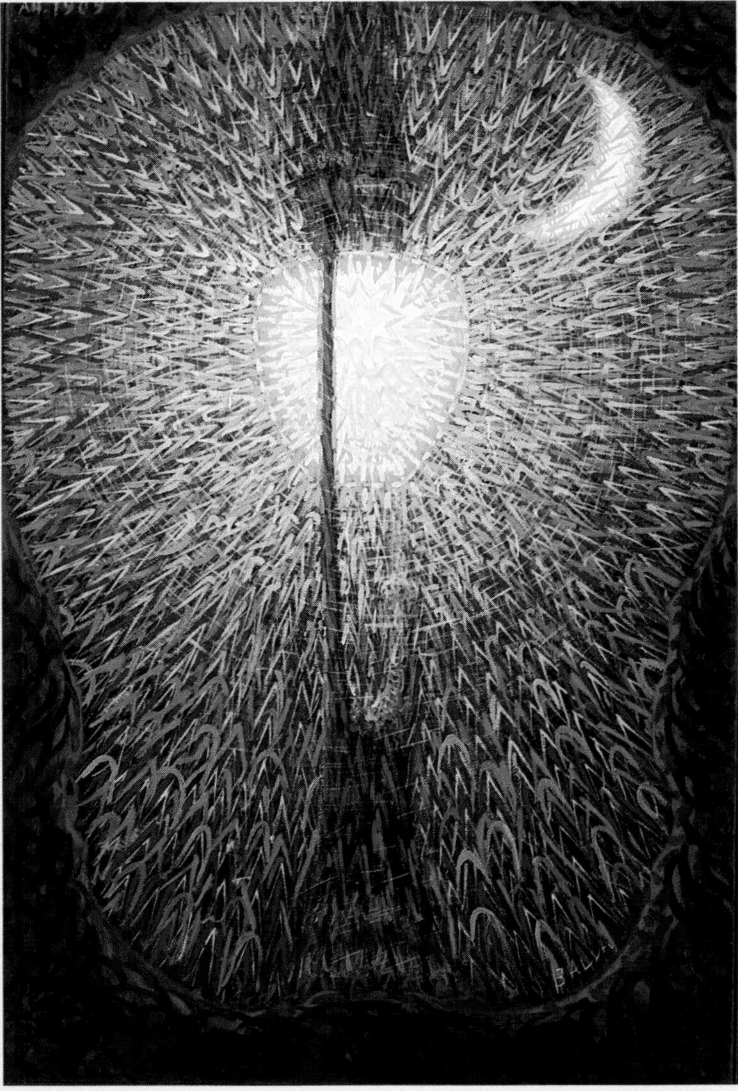

Giacomo Balla. *Street Light.* 1909. Oil on canvas. 174.7 × 114.7 cm (68¾ × 45¼″). Collection, The Museum of Modern Art, New York, New York. Hillman Periodicals Fund.

LOOKING CLOSELY

FIGURE 9.20 The light glowing from the street lamp is represented by a progressive rhythm of both line and color. Notice how the light close to the lamp is white and yellow in color and is created with thin, small V-shaped lines. The light that is farther from the source gradually changes into mostly reds and lavenders, and the V-shaped lines are wider and larger. Why do you think the artist has used the V lines to represent the movement of light from the lamp out into the darkness?

FIGURE 9.21 Student work. Progressive rhythm.

FIGURE 9.22 Student work. Progressive rhythm.

A progressive rhythm may start with a square as its motif. The size of the square may be changed by making it slightly smaller each time it is repeated, or each square may be made a different color of the spectrum or a different step on the value scale each time it is repeated. Shapes can be progressively changed. The sides of a square can be gradually rounded until the square becomes a circle. (See Figure 9.20.)

Progressive Rhythm

1. Applying Your Skills. Starting with a simple geometric shape such as a square for your motif, create a progressive rhythm by gradually changing the square into a free-form shape (Figure 9.21).

2. Further Challenge. Begin by drawing a picture using simple shapes. Change the shapes gradually, using progressive rhythm, to tell a visual story. (See Figure 9.22.)

3. Computer Option. Use the tools of your choice to create a simple motif such as a circle or a free-form shape. Gradually change this motif in six or seven steps to create a progressive rhythm. You may change the size, the value, or the color of the motif to create progression. Tip: After finishing each step, make a copy of it and place it next to the one you just finished. You will have the starting point for the next step of your progression.

How Artists Use Rhythm to Create Movement

In Figure 9.23 on page 236, a photograph of the Golden Gate bridge in San Francisco, nothing is really moving. Everything is frozen in time, but your eye is pulled to the right side of the photograph by the repetition of diagonal lines. **Movement** is *the principle of art used to create the look and feeling of action and to guide the viewer's eyes throughout the work of art.* Notice how the upper lines of the bridge structure slant downward to the right. Even though the supports are vertical, the active sweep of the diagonal lines carry the eyes into the distance. The photographer who took this picture decided to photograph it from an angle that emphasizes the sweeping lines.

What memories does the picture of this bridge arouse for you? A trip to a large city? Fresh air and summer vacations? The rhythm of the diagonal lines creates the excitement here.

Artists use rhythm in a work of art just as they use the elements and other principles of art—to communicate feelings and ideas. As your eyes follow the visual beats through a work of art, you experience the sensation of movement. Is the movement slow and easy, or quick and excited? Does it soothe you or make you nervous? An artist uses rhythm to create these feelings.

One group of artists tried to do more than control the way in which viewers looked at works of

FIGURE 9.23 Your eye is drawn through this photograph by the repeated diagonal lines.

FIGURE 9.24 The many repetitions of the legs, feet, tail, and chain in this work give it the appearance of actual movement.

Giacomo Balla. *Dynamism of a Dog on a Leash*. 1912. Oil on canvas. 89.9 × 109.9 cm (35⅜ × 43¼″). Albright-Knox Art Gallery, Buffalo, New York. Bequest of A. Conger Goodyear and gift of George F. Goodyear, 1964.

FIGURE 9.25 McKelvey's repetition of lines and forms that swirl out from the neck of her pot create the illusion of movement. The intricate sandpainting design along the graceful curve of a vessel is the hallmark of a McKelvey pot.

Lucy Leuppe McKelvey. *Whirling Rainbow Goddesses.* Ceramic container. 18 × 30 cm (6¾ × 12″). Keams Canyon Arts and Crafts, Keams Canyon, Arizona.

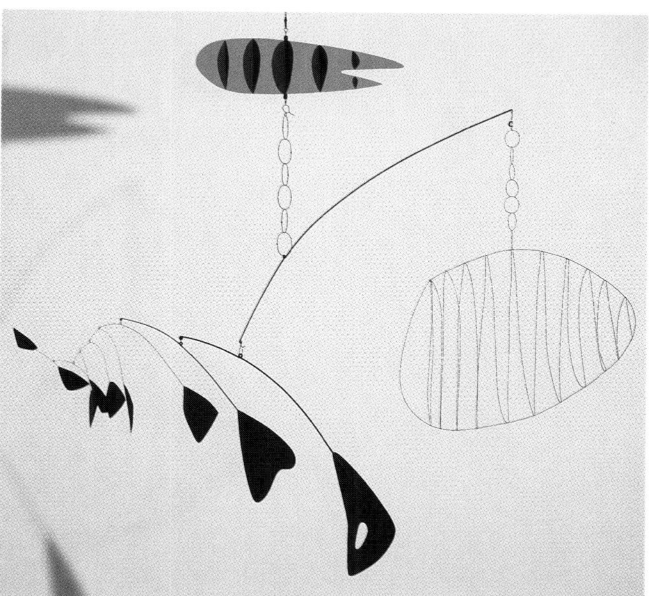

FIGURE 9.26 Look closely at the places where the rods are joined by a carefully planned set of loops. Calder's works are so carefully balanced that the slightest movement of air will set the sculpture in motion. Watching a Calder sculpture is like watching a graceful dancer.

Alexander Calder. *Lobster Trap and Fish Tail.* 1939. Hanging mobile. Painted steel wire and sheet aluminum. About 2.6 × 2.9 m (8′ 6″ × 9′ 6″). Collection, The Museum of Modern Art, New York, New York. Commissioned by the Advisory Committee for the stairwell of the museum.

art. This group of artists, called the *Futurists* (Figure 9.24), used rhythm to capture the idea of movement itself. They used the word *dynamism* to refer to the forces of movement. They believed that nothing was solid or stable. They also believed that art should show such dynamism. They showed forms changing into energy by slanting and overlapping surfaces, which made the surfaces seem to move.

When you look at the modern Navajo pottery by Native American artist Lucy McKelvey, you will also find rhythmic repetitions of shapes and lines that seem to move across the surface. The designs are inspired by traditional Navajo sandpaintings. McKelvey says that her grandfather, who was a medicine man, told her she could use the designs as long as she did not reproduce one of the sacred sandpainting figures exactly as it was depicted in a ritual ceremony. She always changes the original and adds something different. (Figure 9.25.)

You can also see movement in the visual art of Alexander Calder (**call**-dur). He was a mechanical engineer, but his father was a sculptor. Calder believed in what the Futurists were doing. In his work he repeated abstract shapes and he put them into real motion. He did this using the real forces of air currents and gravity. Calder's creations were dubbed **kinetic** sculpture, because *they actually move in space.* (Figure 9.26.)

Artist Marcel Duchamp gave Calder's moving sculptures another name, *mobiles,* which you read about in Chapter 3. Moving sculptures of this kind have been called mobiles ever since.

STUDIO LESSON: PAINTING WITH A RHYTHMIC ACTIVITY

FIGURE 9.27 Jacob Lawrence. *Parade.* 1960. Egg tempera on fiberboard. 60.6 × 76.3 cm (23⅞ × 30⅛″). Hirshhorn Museum and Sculpture Garden, Smithsonian Institution, Washington, D.C. Gift of Joseph H. Hirshhorn, 1966.

Supplies

- Sketchbook and pencils
- Large white paper
- Yellow chalk
- Acrylic paints and a variety of brushes

When Jacob Lawrence arrived in Harlem as a young boy, he had never seen such crowded city streets. The shapes of the tall buildings, the windows full of excited people, and the fire escapes that zigzagged down the outside walls fascinated him. He loved the excitement that filled the neighborhood.

To tell a story, Lawrence painted series of pictures. In 1940–41 he painted sixty paintings in a series called *The Migration of the Negro,* which depicts the southern Negroes coming north to find work. This was familiar subject matter, because the people in his neighborhood were part of that migration. These paintings brought him fame and success, and in 1942–43 he painted thirty paintings about the neighborhood itself and called it, simply, *Harlem Series.*

However, that was not the end of his paintings about Harlem. He returned to the subject many times. The painting *Parade* in Figure 9.27 depicts the neighborhood during one of its happiest times. People are dressed in their best clothes, and everyone is having a good time. Observe the many ways Lawrence has used rhythm in his painting, and think of ways you can use it in your painting.

Create a painting expressing rhythmic movement. Show one or more groups of people involved in rhythmic activity. Base the figures in your work on your own sketches of people in action. As in Lawrence's *Parade*, use more than one motif. Strengthen the rhythmic quality of your work by using four of the five kinds of visual rhythm described in this chapter. Use repetition to accent the visual rhythms. Choose a color scheme that will help to express the mood of the rhythms in your work.

FOCUSING

Brainstorm with your classmates for ideas of rhythmic activities. Think of marching bands, sports, cheerleaders, dancers, joggers, or children on a playground.

Select the rhythmic activities you will use in your painting. Do visual research by making gesture sketches in your sketchbook of active people involved in the activities.

CREATING

Select your best gesture drawings. In your sketchbook, make rough plans of how to organize the figures into a composition emphasizing rhythmic movement that will pull the viewer's eye through the painting. As in Lawrence's *Parade*, you may create several different rhythms by using more than one motif. Be sure to use rhythmic repetition.

Choose your best rhythmic composition and sketch it on a large sheet of white paper using yellow chalk. Press lightly with the chalk so it will disappear when you paint over it. Chalk marks should not remain.

FIGURE 9.27A Student work.

Before you start painting, plan how you will repeat the elements of line, shape, space, and color to accent the visual rhythms in your painting. Also plan a color scheme that will express the mood of the rhythms in your work. Make notes with crayons or colored pencils in your sketchbook.

Paint your work, covering the entire surface of the paper.

Mount or mat your work for display.

CRITIQUING

Describe Tell which rhythmic activities you chose. Describe how you did your visual research. How many motifs did you use?

Analyze Explain how and where you repeated the elements of line, shape, space, and color. What color scheme did you choose? Which kinds of rhythm did you use? Explain how and where you used them.

Interpret What is the expressive mood of your work? Which elements helped to create that mood?

Judge Which aesthetic theories would you use to judge this work? Were you satisfied with the finished work? If you were to do it over, what, if anything, would you change to improve it?

STUDIO LESSON: A PATTERN COLLAGE

FIGURE 9.28 'Abd Allah Musawwir. *The Meeting of the Theologians.* c. 1540–49. Colors on paper. 28.4 × 19 cm (11⅛ × 7½″). Nelson-Atkins Museum of Art, Kansas City, Missouri. Purchase: Nelson Trust.

Supplies

- Sketchbook and pencils
- Ruler, scissors, and white glue
- One large sheet of paper or poster board
- A variety of patterned fabrics and papers
- Colored pencils, watercolors, or acrylics
- Assorted brushes
- Small pieces of white paper for figures

Persian miniature paintings such as the one shown in Figure 9.28 are book illustrations. The primary purpose of these illustrations is to tell stories about sacred religious events and depict the exploits of heroes who accomplished superhuman feats.

Persian painters used pattern, rhythmic designs, and brilliant colors enhanced with gold to create pages that looked like jewels. Artists created many of the pigments used in these paintings by grinding minerals such as gold, silver, lapis lazuli, and malachite. They filled every available space with a rhythmic pattern. Notice how each pattern is filled with intense colors. This emphasis on pattern compresses space. Everything seems to lie flat against the picture plane.

The style of Persian art is not like Western realism. More than one point of view appears in the composition, allowing the artist to portray several events in the same picture.

The Meeting of the Theologians (Figure 9.28) takes place in a religious school, where a young man is seated with a teacher and seven other bearded men. In the doorway a theologian approaches while two beggars hold out their hands begging for alms. This artwork was one page of an illustrated book. Look at it closely and see how the colors, patterns, and calligraphy have been merged to make the story easy to read and visually interesting.

Create a collage in the Persian style by presenting more than one point of view. In this way you can show different aspects of one event in the picture. Organize your work so every shape and space is filled with brightly colored patterns. Create the background shapes using patterned fabrics and papers. People and other objects can be made by drawing and painting them on white paper and cutting them out. The finished composition should not have any feeling of three-dimensional form or space.

FOCUSING

Brainstorm with classmates about complex events that would be appropriate subjects for this project. Think of an event that can be best explained by showing several scenes. For example, a play involves auditions, rehearsals, costume fittings, and performing.

After the group discussion, choose a situation from your personal experience to illustrate. Think it through by listing the different incidents of this event in your sketchbook. Make some rough sketches. Choose the scenes that you would like to illustrate.

CREATING

Now sketch a plan for dividing your composition into shapes of different sizes and decide where to place your figures. Using the ruler and pencil, lightly draw the dividing lines on a large sheet of paper.

Before you add figures, fill all the rectangles with patterns. Measure each shape and cut out patterned fabrics and papers to fit each shape. As you select each pattern for the background, consider how one will look next to another. Use contrasting patterns so you can see the distinction between each shape. If you wish, you may draw and color patterns in some of the spaces. Glue the fabrics and papers to the background.

On the small pieces of white paper, draw and paint figures and objects to place in different shapes. Consider the pattern you will place each figure against so that the figure will contrast. Cut out the drawn figures and objects and glue them onto the design.

Mount or mat your finished work for display.

FIGURE 9.28A Student work.

CRITIQUING

Describe Identify the event you chose to illustrate. Describe the different scenes. What kinds of patterned materials did you use for your background spaces?

Analyze How did you organize your background spaces? How did you arrange the figures? Did you fill the background with patterns? Is there contrast between patterns and between the figures and the background? Does everything look flat?

Interpret What mood does your finished product express? Give your work an expressive title.

Judge Which aesthetic theories would you use to judge this work? Is it successful? If you were going to do it over, what, if anything, would you change?

STUDIO LESSON: WEAVING WITH A PATTERN

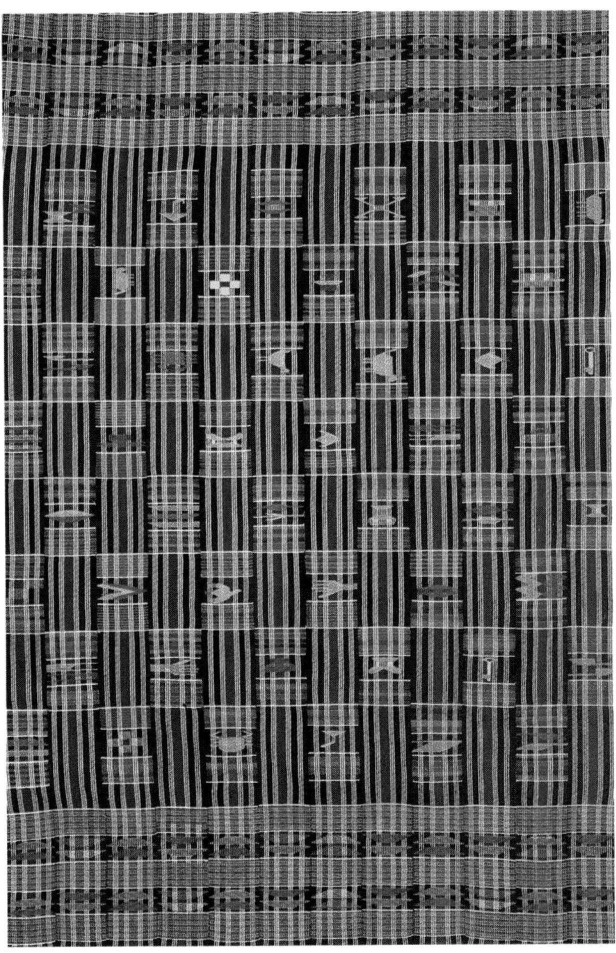

FIGURE 9.29 *Wrapper.* Ewe peoples, Volta region, Ghana. 1972. Cotton and rayon plain weave with cotton and rayon supplementary weft. 201 × 125 cm (79⅛ × 49″). National Museum of African Art, Smithsonian Institution, Washington, D.C.

Supplies

- Sketchbook and pencils
- Ruler, scissors, and tape
- Heavy cardboard, 6 x 20 inches (15 x 50.8 cm)
- Ball of strong, thin crochet thread
- Yarns and fibers that vary in color and texture
- Tapestry needle and comb
- Bag to hold materials

In the court at Kumasi, fine textiles were one of the symbols of leadership among the Asante people. The cloth identified the rank and purpose of the wearer. This cloth in Figure 9.29 is commonly known as *kente.*

It is woven on a portable, horizontal treadle loom in strips of cloth 2 to 6 inches (5 to 15 cm) wide. The treadles enable the men to weave elaborate patterns into the strips of cloth. The length of the strips may be a few yards or several hundred yards. When the single strip is finished, it is cut into pieces and sewn together, edge to edge, to make a wider cloth.

Weavers begin as apprentices to master weavers. By the time they become a master weaver, they have memorized the patterns they will weave and the length of each motif. They know what the finished product will look like before they begin. The simplest warp stripes are called *ahwepan.* The most complex, and therefore most costly, weft designs are called *adweneasa,* which means "my skill is exhausted."

Create a narrow strip of kente-type weaving, in the manner of the Asante weavers, using a cardboard loom as a frame. Work with a group of four or five classmates and coordinate your colors and designs. Create a repeat pattern by using one of five techniques. The strip should be 3–4 inches (7.6–10 cm) wide. You can control the length of the strip by the length of your loom. Sew the four or five strips together to make a piece of cloth.

FOCUSING

Confer with your weaving team. Keep visual and verbal notes from the conference in your sketchbook. Decide which of the following weaving techniques you will use to create repeating patterns: (1) Change weft colors to create rectangles; (2) insert weft threads that deflect the ground threads; (3) embroider shapes on the rectangles; (4) change weaving techniques to alter texture; (5) add supplementary weft threads; (6) appliqué shapes on the rectangles. Choose the color scheme, the length of the repeat in the pattern, and the length of the woven strip. See Technique Tip 23 on page 358 in the Handbook.

CREATING

To make your loom, hold the ruler along the top edge of your cardboard. With the pencil, mark off every 1/4 inch (6 mm). Using the scissors, make a cut about 1/2 inch (13 mm) deep at each mark. Do the same thing along the bottom of your cardboard.

Tape the end of your thread to the back of the cardboard. Bring the spool to the front, passing the thread through the top left notch. Pull the spool down to the bottom of the loom. Pass the thread through the bottom left notch to the back. Move one notch to the right. Pull the thread through and up the front of the loom. Keep working until you reach the last notch. Bring the spool to the back. Cut the thread and tape the end of it to the back.

Collect the yarns and fibers that your team selected. Keep all materials in a bag.

Thread one of your thinner yarns through the eye of the tapestry needle. Start to weave at the bottom of your loom. Move the weft thread across the warp, passing over one thread and under the next. When you reach the end of the warp, reverse direction. If you wove over the last thread you must weave under it when you start the second line of weft. Do not pull the weft tightly. Curve it slightly as you pull it through the warp. This is called *ballooning*, and it will prevent the strip from getting narrower as you weave.

After weaving a few rows, pack the weft threads tightly with the comb. The tighter the weft, the stronger the fabric will be. Tight weft will be easier to match with your team. Weave 1 inch (2.5 cm) of tabby before you start making designs.

Be sure to end with another inch of thin, tightly packed tabby weave. Join your strip with those of the other members of your team by sewing them together.

FIGURE 9.29A Student work.

Prepare your fabric for display. You may mount it on a flat board or hang it from a dowel.

CRITIQUING

Describe Explain the procedures your team used to make decisions about the kente-type cloth and list the decisions your team made. Which weaving techniques did you use? How did you display the finished product?

Analyze What kind of rhythmic pattern did you create in your own strip? What kind of a pattern did you create as a team? Describe the color scheme in your strip. Describe the color scheme of the team's cloth.

Interpret Considering the colors, textures, and patterns, what useful function could the team's cloth have if it were larger? What mood does it convey?

Judge What aesthetic theories would you use to judge this work? If you were to do the whole project over, what would you change to improve the finished product?

STUDIO LESSON: COIL BASKETS

FIGURE 9.30 Louisa Keyser (Dat So La Lee). *Basket.* c. 1917–18. Willow, redbud, braken fern. 30 × 41.2 cm (12 × 16¼"). Philbrook Art Center, Tulsa, Oklahoma. Clark Field Collection.

Supplies

- Core material for the warp
- Fibers for the weft: colored yarns, raffia, or natural fibers
- Tapestry needle
- Sharp scissors
- Masking tape
- Sketchbook, pencil, and crayons

The basket shown in Figure 9.30 was created by Louisa Keyser (Dat So La Lee). She belonged to a small Native American tribe known as the Washoe. They were hunters and gatherers who ranged through the territory around Lake Tahoe, California, following the seasons. The Washoe women made many types of baskets for carrying possessions as the tribe moved between the lakes, mountains, hills, and valley floors in their yearly gathering circuit. Washoe basketry is woven primarily from willow, which was found in the valleys. The Washoe used the coiling technique to make large storage baskets, watertight cooking baskets, and *degikups,* which were small spherical baskets for ceremonial use.

This basket is one of Keyser's variations of the *degikup* form. It rises gradually from a narrow base until it reaches a maximum width at three-quarters of its height. This design is called the scatter pattern. It consists of a series of stepped triangles arranged vertically. In this basket the artist has increased the size of the triangles to match the form of the basket. Then she has diminished the design as the form curves inward. She has used the progressive rhythm of the design to emphasize the form of the basket. She created an illusion of perspective in which the exaggerated curve of the design mirrors the form of the basket, unifying the basket with its design.

Study Louisa Keyser's basket to see how she used rhythm in her design and then plan your own coil basket.

To prepare for this lesson, practice the coil method of basket making until you have satisfactorily started and completed a simple flat coaster using the "lazy squaw" stitch in a regular rhythm. When you have mastered the technique, design and create a unique coil basket form that has either a functional or decorative purpose. Organize arrangement of the colors of the weft into a random, regular, alternating, or progressive rhythm.

FOCUSING

Study the directions for the coil method of basket making in Technique Tip 24 in the Handbook, page 360. Following those directions, use about 2 feet (61 cm) of core material to make a small coaster using the "lazy squaw" stitch. If the center of your coaster does not look right the first time, undo it and start over. This is the most difficult part of making the basket. Finish the coaster using the taper method.

CREATING

Draw several plans in your sketchbook and select your best plan. Choose your color scheme and note the materials and colors you will use to make the weft. Decide whether you will use regular, alternating, or progressive rhythm to organize your colors. Note your decision in the sketchbook and color the design to indicate how you will use the colors.

FIGURE 9.30A Student work.

Construct the basket form based on your design. You will control the position of the warp coils by holding them in position as you sew the stitches that connect the coils. You can position them to go up vertically or to slant in or out. Finish your basket using the taper method.

CRITIQUING

Describe Explain the procedures you followed to create your basket, including the practice coaster.

Analyze Describe the form of your basket. Tell what color scheme you used and explain which type of rhythm you used to organize your colors.

Interpret Did you create a functional or decorative basket? Explain. How did your use of color and pattern affect the feeling of your basket?

Judge Which aesthetic theories would you use to judge this work? If you were to make another basket, what, if anything, would you change? Explain.

ART CRITICISM IN ACTION

FIGURE 9.31 Chuck Close. *Janet.* 1989. Oil on canvas. 91.4 × 76.2 cm (36 × 30″). Photo by Bill Jacobson. Courtesy of the Pace Gallery, New York, New York.

CRITIQUING THE WORK

1. **Describe** Read the credit line for Figure 9.31 to find out the size of the work and the medium with which it was created. Now describe the subject of this painting. What do you see?
2. **Analyze** Before you study Close's use of rhythm, look at the way he has used the elements. Do you see any lines? Where? What kind? How has he used shape and space? Is there any illusion of three dimensions in the work? How has he used color? What kinds of color dominate the work? Has he imitated the texture of the subject or has he emphasized the texture of the paint itself?

   What kinds of visual rhythms do you see? Can you find any examples of random, regular, alternating, flowing, and progressive rhythm? How does Close's unusual use of rhythm affect the look of this work?
3. **Interpret** Based on the clues you collected and your own personal experience, write a brief paragraph explaining your interpretation of the painting *Janet.* What type of

FIGURE 9.32 Jan Vermeer. *The Girl with the Red Hat.* c. 1665. Oil on panel. 23.1 × 18.1 cm (9⅛ × 7⅛"). National Gallery of Art, Washington, D.C. Andrew W. Mellon Collection.

person do you think Janet is? How does she make you feel? Write a new title for this work that sums up your interpretation.

4. **Judge** Do you think this is a successful work of art? Why or why not? Use one or more of the aesthetic theories explained in Chapter 2 to defend your opinion.

COMPARING THE WORKS

Look at *Janet* by Chuck Close (Figure 9.31) and *The Girl with the Red Hat* by Jan Vermeer (Figure 9.32). At first you may think there are no similarities between the two works. Look, however, at the subject matter, the colors, the contrast of dark and light values, and the relationship of positive and negative space. What did you discover? In what ways are the two works different? You have analyzed Close's use of rhythm. How did Vermeer use rhythm in the organization of his work?

MEET THE ARTIST

CHUCK CLOSE

American, b. 1940

Chuck Close is not a portrait painter in the traditional sense. He does not paint portraits of people, he creates paintings based on photographs that he has taken of people. For twenty years he was known as a leading Photo-Realist. He painted black-and-white, exact imitations of photographs and he was very successful.

Then in the late 1980s he suffered an illness that left him partially paralyzed. During his recovery he was determined to get back to painting, although he could use only his arms—his hands didn't work.

Sitting in a wheelchair, Close paints using a device that straps around the middle of his forearm, his wrist, and his fingers and thumb. At first, he needed help getting the brush in and out of the brush holder. Gradually, he developed a technique for accomplishing this with his teeth. He also has a forklift that raises him to the top of his gigantic paintings.

Close feared that others would pity him as a disabled artist. When the Museum of Modern Art bought the first large painting he made after he was dismissed from the hospital, however, he was encouraged. He knew the Museum of Modern Art did not buy art just to make someone feel better.

His new work is no longer photo-realistic, but he still works with a grid from photographs. His new works, in color, have been widely praised by the critics for their abundance of color and light.

MORE PORTFOLIO IDEAS

I. Take a small school photograph of yourself and make a copy of it on a photocopier. The copy will be black and white. Make a grid and copy the photo on a piece of white paper. Shade the work to match the values in the photocopy.

II. Use an old, small, colored school photograph of yourself. Draw a grid on the photo and then draw a grid double the original size on a sheet of white paper. Working directly with paint and brush, use dabs and shapes of color in the style of Close's *Janet* to make a loose color copy of the photo.

CHAPTER 9 REVIEW

Building Vocabulary

On a separate sheet of paper, write the term that best matches each definition given below.

1. The principle of design that indicates movement by the repetition of elements.
2. Rhythm you receive through your eyes rather than through your ears.
3. A unit that is repeated in visual rhythm.
4. A three-dimensional motif.
5. A two-dimensional decorative visual repetition.
6. The principle of art used to create the look and feeling of action and to guide the viewer's eyes throughout the work of art.
7. A kind of sculpture that actually moves in space.

Reviewing Art Facts

Answer the following questions using complete sentences.

1. How is rhythm created in music?
2. In general, how is visual rhythm created?
3. How does rhythm add a sense of movement to a work of art?
4. What is the difference between rhythm and pattern?
5. In general, how are different rhythms created?
6. How is random rhythm created?
7. Tell how regular rhythm is created.
8. Describe how alternating rhythm is created.
9. How is flowing rhythm created?
10. Tell how progressive rhythm is created.

Thinking Critically About Art

1. **Compare and contrast.** Study the subject matter of the *Hmong Story Cloth* (Figure 9.1 on page 220) and *Parade* (Figure 9.27 on page 238). List the similarities and differences you find. Are the themes of the two works similar or different? Explain.
2. **Extend.** The *Elevator Grille* in Figure 9.6 on page 225 was designed by the architect Louis Sullivan for a building he designed. Find information about Louis Sullivan in the library. Discover what contributions he had made to the field of architecture in the late nineteenth and early twentieth centuries. Give a brief report to the class about the importance of Louis Sullivan in the history of American architecture.
3. **Synthesize.** Use a tape recorder to collect nonmusical rhythmic sounds. Try to find sounds that match the various types of visual rhythm: random, regular, alternating, progressive, and flowing. Bring your tape to class and share the sounds with your classmates.

Making Art Connections

1. **Language Arts.** Write a poem or paragraph to express the differences between the rhythms of today's technological world and the pace of horse-and-buggy days gone by. Use rhythm in your language.
2. **Science.** Make a chart illustrating the life cycle of a plant or animal. Emphasize the rhythmic quality of that cycle.
3. **Music.** Discuss the principle of rhythm with your music teacher. Find out if musicians use the same types of rhythms as visual artists do. Try to find a work of music to illustrate at least two of the visual rhythms or create a musical rhythm to match at least two of the visual rhythm types.
4. **Language Arts.** To tell her story in the *Hmong Story Cloth* (Figure 9.1, page 220), Chaing Xiong used repetition and movement to carry you through her story. Can you find an example in literature where the author used repetition to help create the mood of the story? Write a brief paragraph about the author's use of repetition and how you think it affected the mood or theme of the work.

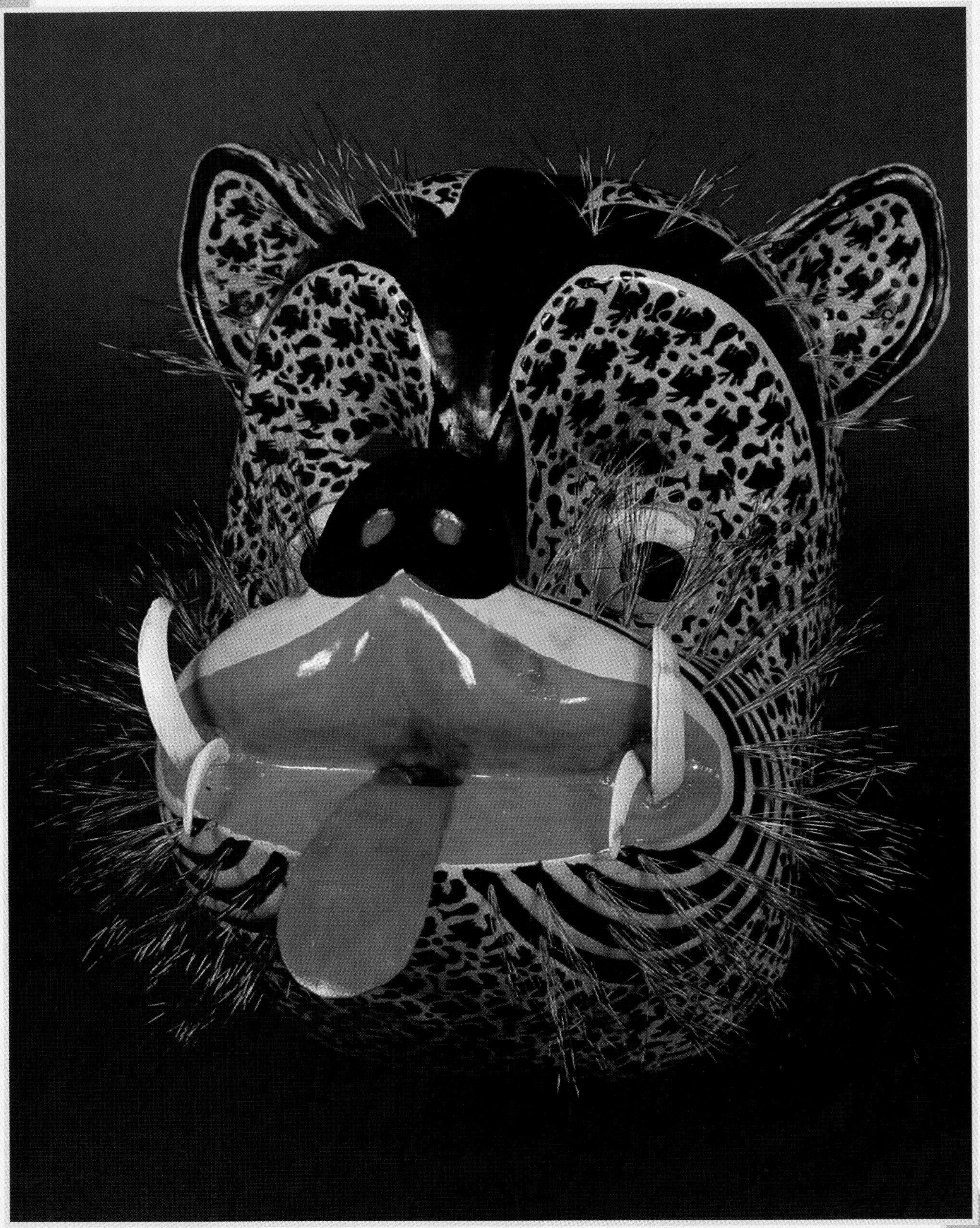

FIGURE 10.1 This mask was made to be worn during a ceremony called the Dance of the Jaguar. It was carved from wood and then painted.

Artist unknown. *Jaguar Mask.* Mexico. Papier-mâché, enamel paint, straw.

CHAPTER 10

Balance

Balance is a principle of life. Every animal must balance breathing in and breathing out. The earth stays in orbit because the pull of the sun is balanced by the earth's revolution around the sun. Without balance we feel uncomfortable. Artists use this feeling to communicate with us.

We all need to use balance to function from day to day. It is hard to keep your balance when you are standing up in a moving train or bus. It is also hard to balance a stack of books you are carrying to your locker. Because of your ability to balance, you can stand erect and walk on two limbs instead of four.

Have you ever watched a toddler wobble, fall, and struggle to get back up? The toddler learns to use leg muscles and shifts in weight to overcome the effects of gravity. He or she learns to balance the force of gravity with the force of muscle.

As you read this chapter, you will begin to understand how artists use the elements of art to create different kinds of balance in their works. You will learn why balance is important in both two-dimensional and three-dimensional art, and you will discover techniques for creating balance in your own artworks.

Objectives

After completing this chapter, you will be able to:

- Understand why balance is important in a work of art.
- Explain how visual weight is created and produce it in your own work.
- Describe the types of balance and use them in your own work.
- Tell what different types of balance can mean in a work of art.

Words to Know

balance
central axis
formal balance
informal balance
radial balance
symmetry

FIRST IMPRESSIONS

Do you know what kind of balance was used to organize the features of this mask shown in Figure 10.1? Notice that the black spots of the fur represent small creatures. Can you recognize the shapes? What other features do you notice that contribute to the impact of this jaguar mask?

FIGURE 10.2 This building is known throughout the world, not because of its beauty or because the architect is well known, but because it leans. The many diagonal lines tell the viewer that this building must either straighten up or fall down. Because it remains off balance, defying gravity, it is famous.

Bell Tower of the Cathedral at Pisa (The Leaning Tower of Pisa). Begun in 1174.

VISUAL BALANCE

A work of art must contain balance. **Balance** is *the principle of design concerned with equalizing visual forces, or elements, in a work of art.* Visual balance causes you to feel that the elements have been arranged just right.

A visual *imbalance* creates a feeling of uneasiness. It makes you feel that something isn't quite right. You feel a need to rearrange the elements, just like you might feel a need to straighten a picture on the wall (Figure 10.2).

In the real world a balance scale can be used to measure equal weights. In visual art balance must be *seen* rather than weighed. The art elements become the visual forces, or weights, in an art object. A **central axis** is *a dividing line that works like the point of balance in the balance scale.*

Many works of art have a central vertical axis (Figure 10.3) with equal visual weight on both sides. Artists also use a horizontal axis. In works with a horizontal axis, the weight is balanced between top and bottom (Figure 10.4).

There are basically two types of balance: formal and informal. They differ in how elements are arranged around the axis.

Formal Balance

Formal balance occurs *when equal, or very similar, elements are placed on opposite sides of a central axis.* The axis may be a real part of the design, or it

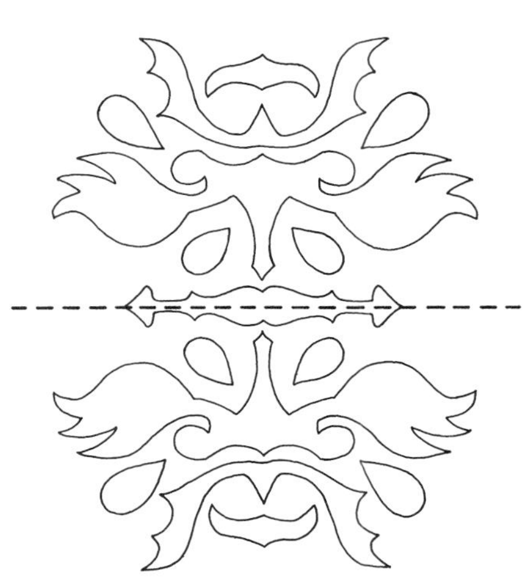

FIGURE 10.3 (at left) With a vertical axis, there is equal visual weight on both sides.

FIGURE 10.4 (at right) Artists also use a horizontal axis, arranging the balance between top and bottom.

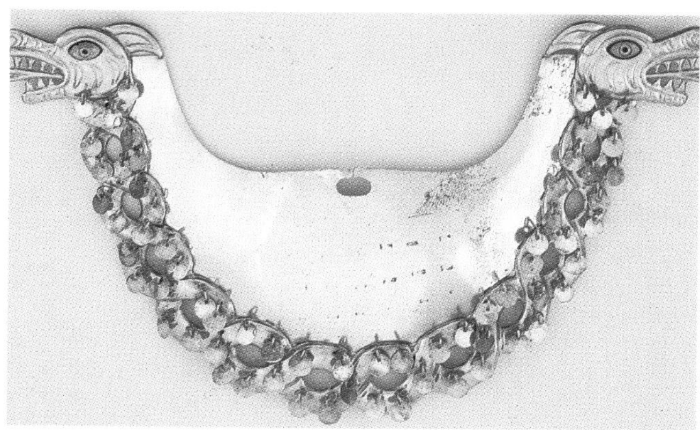

FIGURE 10.5 This unusually large nose ornament was designed using formal balance to fit the balance of the human face. It was fitted to the pierced septum by the clips at the middle of the top edge. The beast heads on either side rise up over the cheekbones.

Loma Negra, Peru. *Nose Ornament.* Moche period, first to third century. Silver, gold, inlays of shell. Width: 20.8 × 12.3 cm (8$\frac{3}{16}$ × 4$\frac{7}{8}$″). The Metropolitan Museum of Art, New York, New York. The Michael C. Rockefeller Memorial Collection. Bequest of Nelson A. Rockefeller, 1979.

may be an imaginary line, such as that in Figures 10.3 and 10.4.

Formal balance is the easiest type of balance to recognize and to create (Figure 10.5). After you find the axis, all you have to do is match objects on each side and place them equally distant from the center.

Symmetry. Symmetry is *a special type of formal balance in which two halves of a balanced composition are identical, mirror images of each other* (Figure 10.6). Another term for this is *bilateral* symmetry.

The strong appeal symmetry has for us may be related to the bilateral symmetry of the human body. Things closely associated with our bodies, such as clothing and furniture, are usually symmetrical. Most traditional architecture, especially public architecture, is symmetrical (Figure 10.7 on page 254).

Symmetry is very stiff. Artists use it to express dignity, endurance, and stability. Because formal balance is so predictable, however, it can be dull. Many artists avoid boring the viewer by using approximate symmetry, which is *almost* symmetrical.

Approximate symmetry has the stability of formal balance (Figure 10.8, page 254). Some small differences make it more interesting than perfect symmetry. If you look carefully in a mirror, you may discover that your face has approximate symmetry. The two sides do not match perfectly.

FIGURE 10.6 This body adornment is symmetrical to match the symmetry of the human body. The symmetry communicates dignity, which was the expressive intent of the artist who designed the adornment.

Leslie Mims Tichich. *Body Adornment.* c. 1970. Copper, brass, and leather with decorative ornaments applied. Private collection.

Using Symmetry

1. Applying Your Skills. Using shapes cut from construction paper, create a symmetrical design on a small sheet of paper. Organize both sides into accurate mirror images of each other before you glue them down on the sheet of paper.

2. Further Challenge. Arrange a symmetrical still life and make a pencil drawing of the arrangement on a small sheet of paper (Figure 10.9 on page 255). Then rearrange or change the objects slightly to create approximate symmetry (Figure 10.10, page 255). Make a drawing of the second arrangement. Mount the drawings side by side on a sheet of construction paper and label each drawing. Which one do you prefer? Survey your friends to find out their preferences.

FIGURE 10.7 This entrance to the Federal Reserve Building in Washington, D.C., is very important looking. The symmetrical arrangement of vertical and horizontal shapes gives the building a secure, stable look.

Cram, Goodhue, and Ferguson. Federal Reserve Building. 1935. Washington, D.C. Façade. Photography by Sandak, Inc., Stamford, Connecticut.

FIGURE 10.8 This painting has become a symbol of what people mean when they talk about, "the good old days." It represents a Midwestern farmer and his daughter. The models were the artist's sister and his dentist. By using formal balance, Wood gives the work a stiff, serious mood, but by switching to approximate symmetry rather than pure symmetry, he adds that nostalgic, "folksy" look.

Grant Wood. *American Gothic.* 1930. Oil on beaverboard. 76 × 63.3 cm (29⅞ × 24⅞"). Collection, Friends of American Art Collection. © 1987 The Art Institute of Chicago, Chicago, Illinois. 1930.

FIGURE 10.9 Student work. A symmetrical still life.

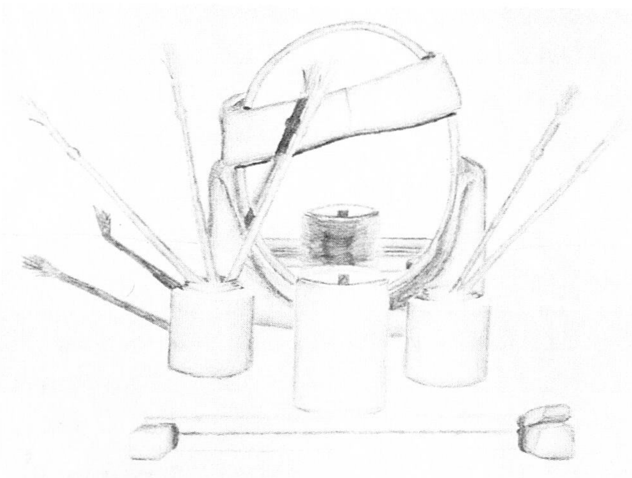

FIGURE 10.10 Student work. A still life arranged with approximate symmetry.

FIGURE 10.11 Radial balance.

3. Computer Option. Do a simple landscape drawing on the left half of the screen. Use the Select tool and the Copy, Paste, and Flip options to duplicate the drawing on the right half of the screen. This will create a symmetrical landscape. If your software does not have these options, you can simply draw a mirror image of the landscape you drew on the left half of the screen. Save the drawing. Use the Select tool to slightly rearrange the placement by moving certain objects in the landscape. Save the second drawing. Compare the two drawings. Which do you prefer? Why?

Radial Balance. Radial balance occurs *when the forces or elements of a design come out (radiate) from a central point.* The axis in a radial design is the center point. In almost all cases the elements are spaced evenly around the axis to form circular patterns (Figure 10.11).

Radial balance is really a complicated variation of symmetry. While symmetry means only two matching units, designs with radial balance may involve four or more matching units (Figure 10.12). The design seen in a kaleidoscope is a good

FIGURE 10.12 Notice how the radial design of this tray starts with four matching units at the center. As the design moves outward, the repetitions become more complicated and increase to eight around the rim of the tray.

Southeastern Song dynasty. *Carved Lacquer Circular Tray.* 1127–1279. Black, red, and yellow lacquer on wood. 5.2 × 34.9 cm (2⅙ × 13¾"). Arthur M. Sackler Gallery, Smithsonian Institution, Washington, D.C. Arthur M Sackler Collection.

LOOKING CLOSELY

FIGURE 10.13 Garrison designed this quilt for the 100th anniversary of the Statue of Liberty. She used the traditional radial design of the Star of Bethlehem pattern to represent the light of liberty but surrounded it with scenes that celebrate liberty throughout our country. What parts of American culture do you see represented? What shapes has the artist pieced together to create the radial design of the eight-pointed star? How did the artist use radial balance to gradually change the colors? What does this quilt tell you about the artist's attitude toward her country?

Elizabeth Garrison. *Long May Our Land Be Bright.* 1986. Quilt. Private collection.

example of radial balance. The continually changing shapes at the end of the tube radiate from a central axis. Elizabeth Garrison used the traditional radial design of the Star of Bethlehem quilting pattern to represent the light of liberty. She designed this quilt to celebrate the anniversary of the Statue of Liberty (Figure 10.13).

Radial balance occurs frequently in nature. Most flower petals are arranged around a central axis and radiate outward. Many plants follow radial patterns of growth. For instance, if you cut an apple in half horizontally, you will see a radial star design. Cut an orange the same way and notice the radial pattern of segments.

You can find many examples of radial balance in architecture. Domes are designed on the principle of radial balance. Manufactured items such as gears, wheels, tires, dials, and clocks are also radial in structure. Radial designs are used by many potters to decorate the surfaces of their work because they adapt well to the rounded forms of pottery (Figure 10.14).

Creating Radial Balance

1. Applying Your Skills. Collect magazine and newspaper photographs of at least six objects that have radial balance. Mount them for display.

2. Further Challenge. Make a series of drawings of five natural or manufactured objects that have a radial structure. Emphasize the radial quality of each object.

3. Computer Option. Use the Shape tool and the Copy and Paste options to produce a design consisting of five squares. One square should be in the center of the screen. The other four should be placed over, under, and on either side of the center square to form the shape of a plus sign (+). Use the Shape tool to draw another symmetrical shape. Copy and Paste this shape on the edge of the four outside squares that are farthest away from the center square. Continue adding shapes to create radial balance. You may add to the center square, but you must maintain radial balance within the square. Save your work. Try a more complex radial design. Use the Flip and Rotate options if your computer software has them.

Informal Balance

Informal balance gives the viewer the same comfortable feeling as does formal balance, but in a much more subtle way. **Informal balance** involves *a balance of unlike objects.* This is possible because two unlike objects can have equal *visual weight* (Figure 10.15).

FIGURE 10.14 Torivio is a Native American potter who has developed her own style for decorating her pots. She repeats the designs in radial patterns, and she plans the design carefully. The motif starts out small at the top rim and then expands to the widest part of the vessel.

Dorothy Torivio. *Vase.* c. 1984. Clay. Height about 20 cm (8″). Heard Museum Collection, Phoenix, Arizona.

FIGURE 10.15 The complex shapes of the wagon and the child are informally balanced by the potted plant and the foliage in this casual scene. Informal balance gives this composition the look of a snapshot.

Thomas Eakins. *Baby at Play.* 1876. Oil on canvas. 81.9 × 122.8 cm (32¼ × 48⅜″). National Gallery of Art, Washington, D.C. John Hay Whitney Collection.

FIGURE 10.16 The many small shapes in the lower right corner of this painting balance the large shape of the stage with its closed curtain.

Edward Hopper. *First Row Orchestra.* 1951. Oil on canvas. 79.3 × 102 cm (31¼ × 40⅛"). Hirshhorn Museum and Sculpture Garden, Smithsonian Institution, Washington, D.C. Gift of Joseph H. Hirshhorn Foundation, 1966.

Informal, or *asymmetrical,* balance creates a very casual effect. It seems less planned than formal balance; however, it is not. What appears to be an accidental arrangement of elements can be quite complicated. Symmetry merely requires that elements be repeated in a mirror image. Informal balance goes beyond that. Artists consider all the visual weight factors and put them together correctly.

Of course, gravity does not pull on an object in a two-dimensional work of art. The viewer does, however, perceive the objects in the work as if gravity were in effect. Many factors influence the visual weight, or the attraction, that elements in a work of art have for the viewer's eyes.

Size and Contour. A large shape or form appears to be heavier than a small shape. Several small shapes or forms can balance one large shape (Figure 10.16).

An object with a complicated contour is more interesting and appears to be heavier than one with a simple contour. A small, complex object can balance a large, simple object (Figure 10.17).

Color. A high-intensity color has more visual weight than a low-intensity color. The viewer's eyes are drawn to the area of bright color. What does this mean in terms of balance? It means that a small area of bright color is able to balance a larger area of a dull, more neutral color as seen in the stained-glass window shown in Figure 10.18.

FIGURE 10.17 In this wedding portrait of Frida Kahlo and Diego Rivera, Frida depicts herself in the ribbons, jewels, and native Mexican dress she often wore. Her small body, enveloped in all the ruffles and folds, balances Diego's solid, heavy form.

Frida (Frieda) Kahlo. *Frida and Diego Rivera*. 1931. Oil on canvas. 100 × 78.7 cm (39⅜ × 31″). San Francisco Museum of Modern Art, San Francisco, California. Albert M. Bender Collection. Gift of Albert M. Bender.

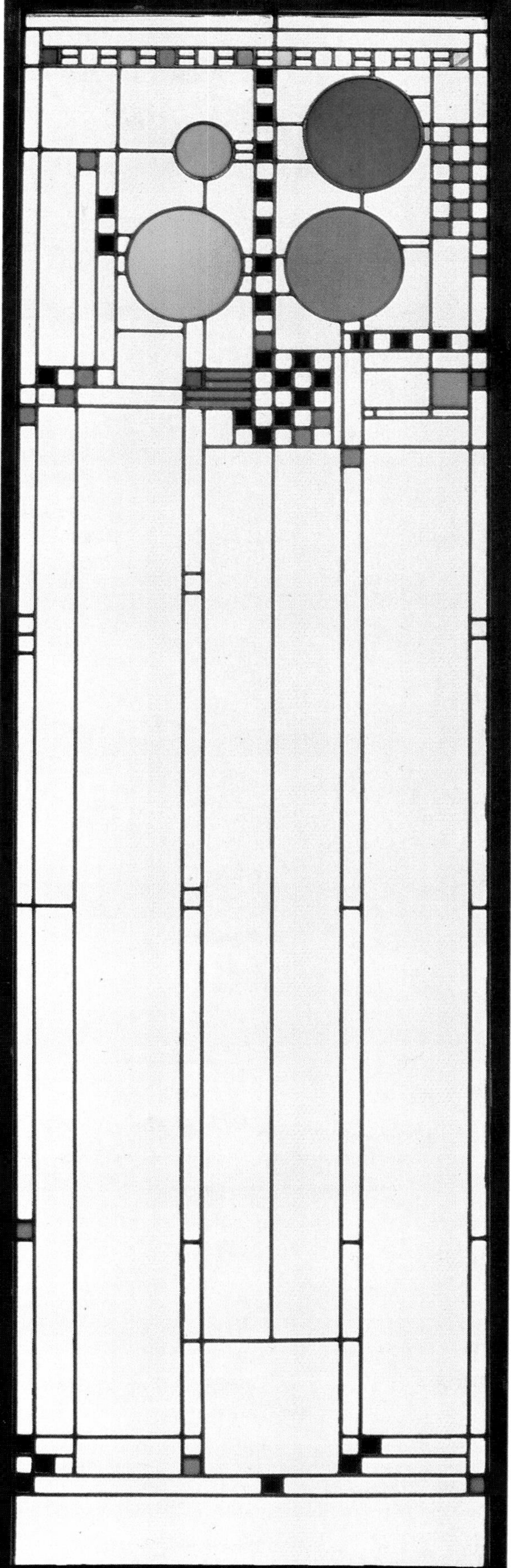

FIGURE 10.18 In the stained-glass window to the right, the bright colors of the geometric shapes balance the large area of clear glass.

Designed by Frank Lloyd Wright. American stained-glass window, one of a triptych. Twentieth century. Glass, lead, wood. 219 × 71 × 5 cm (86¼ × 28 × 2″). The Metropolitan Museum of Art, New York, New York. Purchase. Edward C. Moore, Jr., gift and Edgar J. Kaufmann Charitable Foundation gift, 1967.

FIGURE 10.19 In this Rococo painting, Fragonard balances all the cool, low-intensity colors with the warm, bright red on the dress in the foreground.

Jean-Honoré Fragonard. *A Game of Hot Cockles.* 1767–73. Oil on canvas. 115.5 × 91.4 cm (45½ × 36″). National Gallery of Art, Washington, D.C. Samuel H. Kress Collection.

Warm colors carry more visual weight than cool colors. Red appears heavier than blue, and orange appears heavier than green (Figure 10.19).

Value. The stronger the contrast in value between an object and the background, the more visual weight the object has (Figure 10.20). Black against white has more weight than gray against white. Dark values are heavier than light values. A dark red seems heavier than a light red.

Texture. As you know, a rough texture has an uneven pattern of light highlights and dark, irregular shadows. For this reason a rough surface attracts the viewer's eye more easily than a smooth, even surface. This means that a small, rough-textured area can balance a large, smooth surface. In a poster or advertisement, a block of printed words has the quality of rough texture because of the irregular pattern of light and dark. Poster designers must keep this in mind when balancing words and other visual elements.

Position. Children playing on a seesaw quickly discover that two friends of unequal weight can balance the seesaw by adjusting their positions. The heavier child moves toward the center; the lighter child slides toward the end. The board is then in balance (Figure 10.21, page 262).

In visual art, a large object close to the dominant area of the work can be balanced by a smaller object placed far from the dominant area (Figure 10.22, page 262). A large, positive shape and a small, negative space can be balanced against a small, positive shape and a large, negative space.

LOOKING CLOSELY

FIGURE 10.20 The face and head scarf of the Virgin are no lighter in value than the infant on his blanket or the shepherd's white skirt. Her face stands out so much more because it is placed against the dark value of the cave's interior, while the infant and the shepherd are placed against the midvalue tan of the ground.

Giorgione. *The Adoration of the Shepherds*. c. 1505–10. Oil on wood. 91 × 111 cm (35¾ × 43½"). National Gallery of Art, Washington, D.C. Samuel H. Kress Collection.

Using Informal Balance

1. Applying Your Skills. Find five magazine illustrations, designs, or drawings that illustrate informal balance. Mount each example. Label the works, indicating how the visual weight is arranged in the illustration. Explain how the balance is achieved.

2. Further Challenge. Create small designs using cut paper and/or fabric shapes to illustrate five weight arrangements that create informal balance (Figure 10.23, page 263). In each design keep all of the elements as alike as possible. Vary only the weight factors. For example, to illustrate differences in size, a large red circle could be balanced by several small red circles.

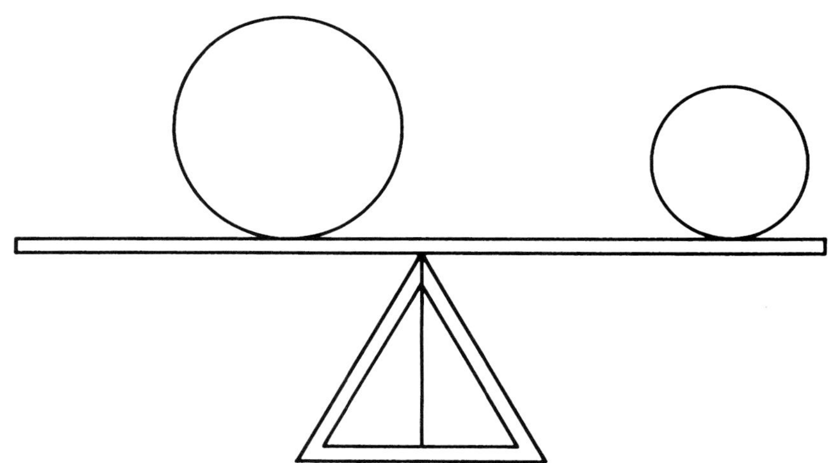

FIGURE 10.21 Does the seesaw look balanced?

LOOKING CLOSELY

FIGURE 10.22 Notice the large wave on the left. It is balanced informally by the small triangular shape of Mount Fuji in the distance. Notice the shape of the negative space of the yellow sky. How does it help to balance the positive shape of the wave? How do the three fishing boats affect the balance of the work? Why do the men sit so low in the boats? What does their position have to do with balance? How do the many small curved shapes in the white foam of the large wave affect the mood of the work?

Katsushika Hokusai. *The Great Wave off Kanagawa* (from the series The Thirty-Six Views of Fuji). c. 1823–29. Woodblock print. 25.7 × 38 cm (10⅛ × 14 15/16″). The Metropolitan Museum of Art, New York, New York. Bequest of Mrs. H. O. Havemeyer, 1929. The H. O. Havemeyer Collection

FIGURE 10.23 Student work. Informal balance.

3. Computer Option. Use the drawing tools of your choice to create a design using informal balance. Save your work. Use the Fill Bucket tool to experiment with changes in color, value, and texture. Save experiments that you consider successful. Draw another design that illustrates informal balance. Save your work and then experiment with the new design. Once again, save experiments you consider successful. Look through the files you saved. Choose the two that you think most successfully illustrate informal balance and print them.

FIGURE 10.24 In this work the formal balance takes away from the violent impact of these "terrorists." How do lines and colors affect the feeling expressed by this work?

Bob Clements. *Evening Up the Score.* 1986. Painted wood. 274.3 × 152.4 × 15.2 cm (108 × 60 × 6"). Private collection.

THE EXPRESSIVE QUALITIES OF BALANCE

The type of balance used by an artist to organize a design has a strong impact on the feeling expressed by that design. Following are some general explanations of how artists use balance to express emotion.

Formal balance is a calm arrangement (Figure 10.24). It has been used to present a person in a dignified portrait (Figure 10.25, page 264). Formal balance has also been used in some religious paintings. Paintings used as altarpieces in churches were designed to fit in with the formal balance of the church altar. Some modern works, such as Josef Albers's *Homage to the Square: Glow* (Figure 10.26 on page 265), are symmetrical. This use of symmetry reduces complexity and allows viewers to concentrate completely on the element of color.

Government buildings, hospitals, and office buildings are designed using formal balance. One purpose of this type of balance is to imply that the people working in these buildings are stable and dignified. In colonial times, homes were built with formal balance to make them appear dignified and calm. This style is still popular today because people want their homes to look like a place where

FIGURE 10.25 Kahlo has organized this self-portrait using formal balance to make herself look proud and imposing.

Frida Kahlo. *Self Portrait Dedicated to Leon Trotsky.* 1937. Oil on masonite. 76.2 × 61 cm (30 × 24″). National Museum of Women in the Arts, Washington, D.C. Gift of the Honorable Clare Boothe Luce.

they can go to escape the hustle and bustle of daily life (Figure 10.27).

With approximate symmetry, artists express the same sense of calm stability, but they avoid the rigid formality of pure symmetry (Figure 10.28, page 266).

Radial design is decorative. It appears in architecture, jewelry, pottery, weaving, and textile design. It is not often used by painters in its pure form. You can, however, find loose arrangements of radiating lines in many paintings (Figure 10.29, page 266). Artists use this technique to focus attention on an important part of the painting.

Informal balance has a more natural look. When you look around your natural environment, you seldom find objects arranged with formal balance. To keep the natural quality of the real world in their works, artists use informal balance in arranging landscapes or groups of people (Figure 10.30, page 267).

Architects are using informal balance in many modern structures (see the David Wright house Figure 3.30 on page 62). Single-family suburban homes have become the symbol of casual living. These houses are designed with informal balance.

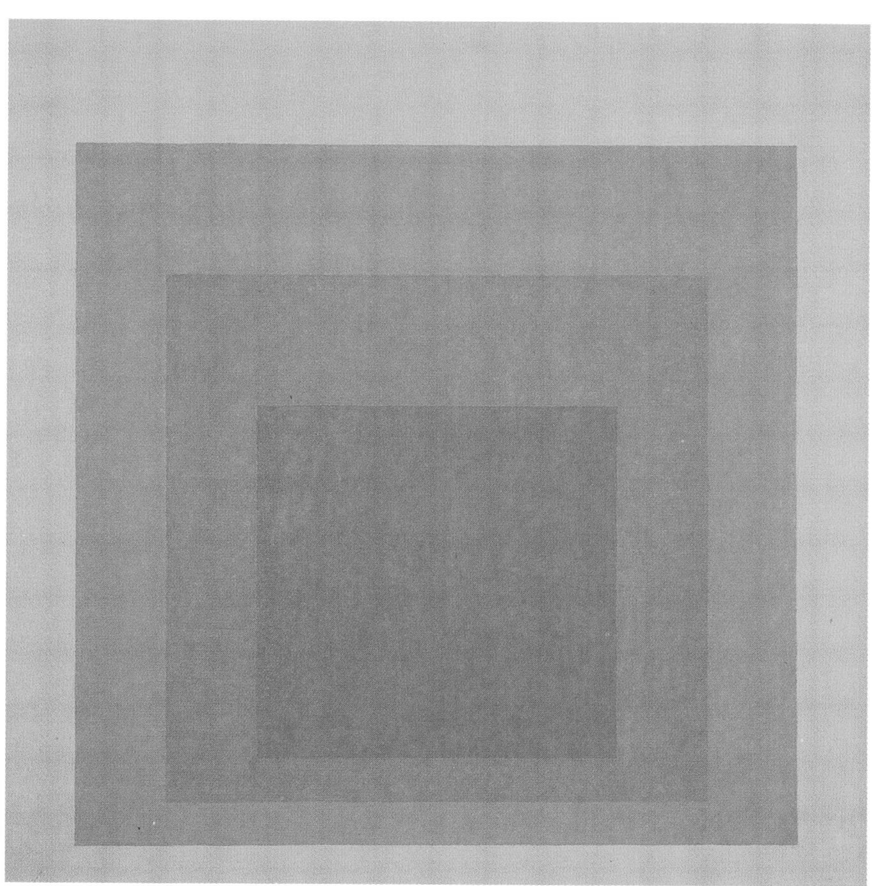

FIGURE 10.26 Albers had a strong influence on the development of American Hard-edge and Op art. He reduced line, shape, space, and texture to minimal importance and concentrated on color relationships. He created optical effects by changing the colors in the squares.

Josef Albers. *Homage to the Square: Glow.* 1966. Acrylic on fiberboard. 121.7 × 121.7 cm (48 × 48″). Hirshhorn Museum and Sculpture Garden, Smithsonian Institution, Washington, D.C. Gift of Joseph H. Hirshhorn, 1972.

FIGURE 10.27 Notice the architect's symmetrical arrangement of shapes on the front of this house. Imagine a vertical axis through the center. Do you see how the balance has been achieved?

John Vassall (Longfellow) House. 1759. Piazzas added later. Cambridge, Massachusetts. Façade. Photography by Sandak, Inc., Stamford, Connecticut.

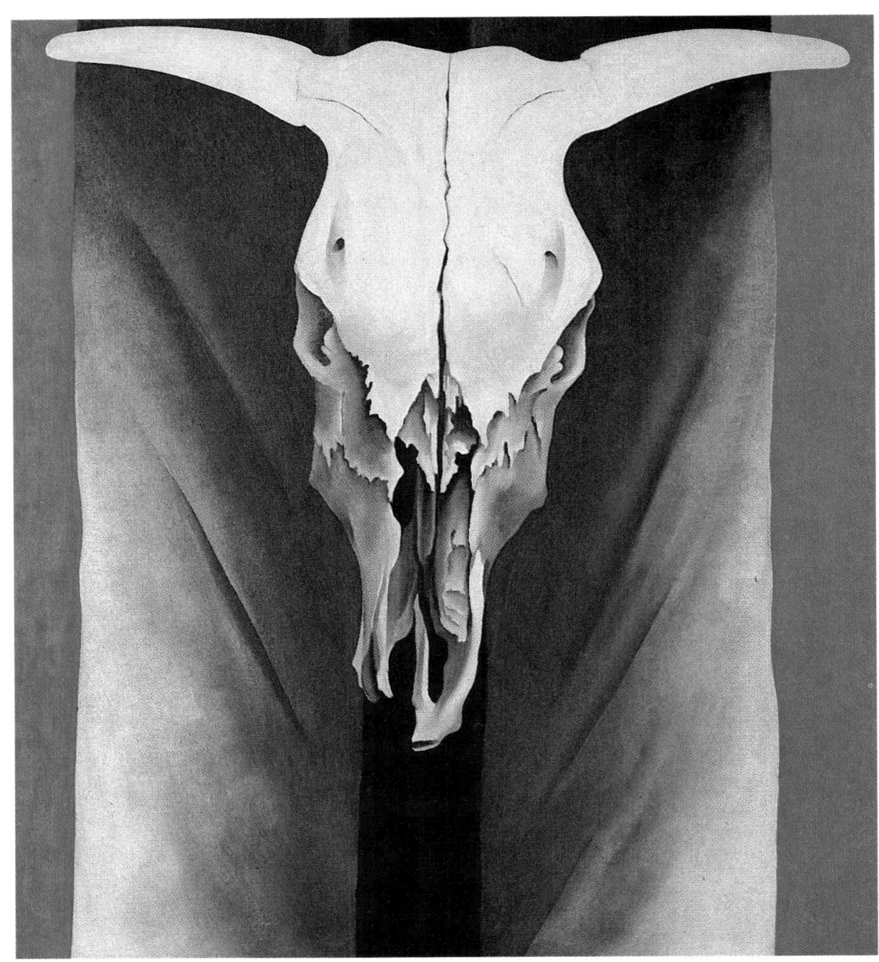

FIGURE 10.28 How has O'Keeffe arranged the shapes in this painting to create approximate, not absolute, symmetry? Would you like the painting more if it were perfectly symmetrical? Why or why not?

Georgia O'Keeffe. *Cow's Skull: Red, White, and Blue.* 1931. Oil on canvas. 101.3 × 91.1 cm (39⅞ × 35⅞″). The Metropolitan Museum of Art, New York, New York. The Alfred Stieglitz Collection, 1952.

FIGURE 10.29 The edges of the building and sidewalks, as well as the implied lines in the rows of windows and trees, radiate loosely from the vanishing point in this painting.

Maurice Utrillo. *Street at Corte, Corsica.* 1913. Oil on canvas. 60.8 × 80.7 cm (24 × 31¾″). National Gallery of Art, Washington, D.C. Ailsa Mellon Bruce Collection.

FIGURE 10.30 Notice how the large, dead tree on the left is balanced by the mass of trees in the distance on the right. Church is famous for large-scale paintings of exotic scenes such as icebergs and tropical jungles. This small painting was inspired by a sunrise he saw during the first weeks of the Civil War. It is a patriotic expression of his personal feelings about the war. He sold the rights of this image to a printmaker, and it was circulated throughout the North as a mass-produced color print.

Frederic Edwin Church. *Our Banner in the Sky.* 1861. Oil on paper mounted on cardboard. 19 × 28.9 cm (7½ × 11⅜"). Terra Museum of American Art, Chicago, Illinois. Terra Foundation for the Arts, Daniel J. Terra Collection, 1992.

Identifying Balance

1. Applying Your Skills. Look through the other chapters in this book to find examples of both formal and informal balance. Be sure to include symmetry, approximate symmetry, and radial balance. List the name of the work and describe how the type of balance used affects the feelings expressed.

2. Further Challenge. Look around your neighborhood for buildings that have been constructed using formal or informal balance. Make a rough sketch of one building and describe the feeling it gives you. If you live in the city and all the buildings are too tall, look at the entrances to the buildings and sketch one of them. The entrance includes the door and all the decorative shapes around the doorway.

3. Computer Option. Use the tools of your choice to create a complex design illustrating one of the following: formal balance, informal balance, symmetry, approximate symmetry, radial balance. Save your work and print it if possible. If your printer only prints in black and white, use colored pencils to add color. Evaluate your design. Does it meet the criteria for the kind of balance you chose to illustrate?

STUDIO LESSON: FORMAL PORTRAIT

FIGURE 10.31 Artist unknown. *Winxiang, Prince Yi.* Qing dynasty. 1644–1911. Ink and color on silk. 186.7 × 121.9 (73½ × 48″). Arthur M. Sackler Gallery, Smithsonian Institution, Washington, D.C. Gift of Richard G. Pritzlaff.

Supplies

- Sketchbook and pencil
- Large sheet of white paper
- Yellow chalk
- Black fine-line marker
- Acrylic paints and brushes

This portrait of a Chinese prince is very different from Chinese landscape painting that one usually sees. The pose is dictated by tradition (Figure 10.31).

Notice the details in this formal portrait and think about how you can use them.

Design and create a formal portrait of a person from history or from current events. Arrange the person in a symmetrical pose in the

FIGURE 10.31A Student work.

center of the composition. The figure should fill the page. Use approximate symmetry to place objects that symbolize important events in that person's life on and around the figure. Choose a color scheme that expresses a specific mood.

FOCUSING

Choose a person you have studied in history or in current events that you admire. Research information about this person. If this person is from past history, you will find information in encyclopedias or in biographies. If your subject is involved in current events, look through newspapers and the *Readers' Guide to Periodicals* for magazines that will provide information about your subject. Make visual and verbal notes about your subject in your sketchbook.

CREATING

Make rough sketches for your composition. Remember that the figure must be organized in a symmetrical pose and that it must fill most of the paper. Make some accurate sketches of details needed for the portrait such as clothing of the historical period, furniture, symbols that will surround or cover the figure, and an appropriate background setting. Choose your best design and sketch it lightly with yellow chalk on the large white paper.

Choose a color scheme that expresses the appropriate mood. Paint your composition. Use large brushes to fill in the largest shapes. Use small brushes to paint the symbols and clothing details. If necessary, use a fine-line black marker to define some of your details and labels.

Write a paragraph about your subject. Mount or mat your portrait for display. Integrate the written paragraph into your display.

CRITIQUING

Describe Name the subject of your portrait. What symbols did you select to represent the events in that person's life? How did you do visual and verbal research? Where did you look and what kind of information did you find? How did you prepare your work for display? Did you include a paragraph about the subject? How did you incorporate it into the display?

Analyze What kinds of balance did you use in your composition? Explain. Describe the color scheme you selected for this work and explain why you chose it.

Interpret What does your painting express about the subject of your portrait? Did the kinds of balance and the color scheme affect the mood? Give this work a poetic title.

Judge Which aesthetic theories would you use to judge this work? If you were to do this over, what would you do to improve it?

STUDIO LESSON: INFORMAL GROUP PICTURE

FIGURE 10.32 Mary Cassatt. *Five O'Clock Tea.* 1879. Oil on canvas. 65 × 93 cm (25½ × 36½″). Courtesy of Museum of Fine Arts, Boston, Massachusetts. M. Theresa B. Hopkins Fund.

Supplies

- Sketchbook and pencil
- Snapshots you have taken
- Large sheet of white paper
- Acrylic paints and an assortment of brushes

Many late-nineteenth-century American artists painted in the Impressionist style, but Mary Cassatt was the only one who actually joined the radical French artists to show her artwork in their independent exhibitions in Paris. She followed their practice of capturing a moment of everyday life as it would look in a snapshot—one single moment in time. Like snapshots, her compositions were asymmetrical and closely cropped (Figure 10.32).

The Japanese print, which had arrived in Paris in the late 1800s, was one source of inspiration for the Impressionists' asymmetrical compositions. The Japanese printmakers were not afraid to cut off part of a figure. European artists, who had never done this, began to use this technique.

The new art of photography also influenced the compositions of the Impressionists. The camera presented them with candid, or unposed, views of people. Snapshots showed familiar subjects from new and unusual points of view. Look at Cassatt's painting. Observe how she used balance, cropped figures, and color.

Plan and create a painting in the Impressionist style using asymmetrical balance, a close-cropped composition, loose brushstrokes that look like dabs and dashes, and the colors of the Impressionists. This painting must be based on an unposed snapshot you have taken of your friends or family. It must include two or more people.

FOCUSING

Collect snapshots you have taken. Select one that you think will make an interesting painting. Remember that it must show asymmetrical balance, two or more people must be visible, and part of each figure must be cropped off, as are the two young women in *Five O'Clock Tea*.

CREATING

Make a large, rough sketch in your sketchbook based on the snapshot. Work on your first sketch to improve the composition as needed. Do not worry about whether the faces in the sketch and the painting look like the real people in the snapshot.

Practice using the colors of the Impressionists in your sketchbook. Use only spectral colors and white. Blues and violets replace grays, browns, and blacks even in the shadows. Apply the colors using short dabs and dashes of color. Make grays by placing complements side by side. Use white side by side with your colors and add white to some of your colors to create light values.

Using a brush and a very light value of yellow, sketch the final composition loosely onto the large sheet of white paper. Use what you have learned during practice in your sketchbook to paint your composition. Create an expressive title for your work.

Mount or mat your work for display.

FIGURE 10.32A Student work.

CRITIQUING

Describe What is the subject matter of your work? How many people have you used? What other objects are important in the composition?

Analyze Did you use asymmetry? Which kind of informal balance did you use? Did you keep the effect of a snapshot by cropping off parts of the figures? Did you use Impressionists' colors? How many ways did you employ white?

Interpret Describe the difference between the look of the snapshot and the look of your finished painting. How did style affect the look of your work? Give your work a title that expresses the mood of your work.

Judge Which aesthetic theories would you use to judge this work? If you were to do this over, what, if anything, would you do differently?

STUDIO LESSON: LINOLEUM PRINT USING RADIAL BALANCE

FIGURE 10.33 Beau Dick. *Sacred Circles.* 1991. Serigraph 98/155. 50 × 50 cm (19¾″ × 19¾″). Private collection.

Supplies

- Sketchbook and pencil
- Ruler, compass, and scissors
- Tracing paper and carbon paper
- Linoleum and dark marker
- Linoleum cutting tools
- Bench hook or C clamp
- Water-base printing ink
- Brayer and inking plate
- Printmaking paper

Beau Dick was born in 1955 in the isolated village of Kingcome in British Columbia, Canada. He is a Northwest Coast Native American of the Southern Kwakiutl tribe.

The making of serigraphs (limited-edition silk-screen prints) is a new art form for the Northwest Coast artists. These artists started making serigraphs around 1970. *Sacred Circles* (Figure 10.33) was originally designed for a drum. Dick's daughter, who is a teacher in Queen Charlotte, British Columbia, asked him to design something for her students for Rediscovery Week. The Rediscovery program in Canada was begun to teach young Native Americans to rediscover their heritage as a source of self-esteem.

Beau Dick believes that the children are the future, that they are the ones to keep the traditions alive and strong. This design shows a group of young people holding hands and sitting in a circle. He depicts them holding hands to show unity and friendship. The dark round shapes in the center are stones, inside of which a bonfire is to be built. He believes the children are the ones who will rekindle the fires and the traditions of the tribes.

Select symbols from your cultural heritage to create one or more motifs for a relief print. Produce an edition of five relief prints. Sign, date, and number your prints using proper printmaking procedures.

FOCUSING

Brainstorm with your classmates about well-known symbols for different cultures. Then discuss your cultural heritage with members of your immediate family. Choose symbols that represent your cultural identity. Select the ones you prefer and make some rough sketches for arranging them into a radial design.

CREATING

Trace the shape of your piece of linoleum onto a page in your sketchbook. Using the ruler, connect the opposite corners of the rectangle to find the center of the shape. Place the point of the compass on that center and draw the largest circle possible within that shape. Select your best design and draw it in the circle.

Trace your finished design onto the tracing paper. Use a piece of carbon paper to transfer the design from the tracing paper to the piece of linoleum.

Use a dark marker to color the lines and shapes on the areas of linoleum that will not be cut away.

Use a bench hook to hold your linoleum safely in place. You have left the linoleum in the shape of a rectangle so that it can be held in place by the bench hook. Do not cut it into a circle until all your linoleum cuts are finished. Use the narrow V-gouge to outline the shapes. To prevent injury during cutting, always move the cutting tool in an outward motion away from your body. Then use wider U-gouges to cut away the negative areas. The pattern of your cuts will show in the final print. Plan the direction of the cuts as carefully as you plan the positive shapes in your design. Finally, use the V-gouges to cut the fine lines on the positive shapes.

FIGURE 10.33A Student work.

Squeeze out an inch (2.5 cm) of ink onto the inking plate. Roll the brayer in both directions until it is loaded with ink. Ink the linoleum.

Select your paper to make an edition of five prints. When they are dry, sign each one in pencil at the bottom of the print. Write the title on the left, the number in the center, and your name and date on the right. The number of your print is a fraction. The denominator represents the total number of the edition, and the numerator is the number of the print. Your first print should be numbered 1/5.

CRITIQUING

Describe List and describe the symbols you used to create the motifs for your personal radial design.

Analyze Did you use radial balance to organize the motifs? Did you use size to indicate the dominant motif? Did you use radial lines to help organize the motifs?

Interpret What is the expressive quality of your personal print? Does it represent your family heritage?

Judge Which aesthetic theories would you use to judge this work? If you were going to do this one more time, what, if anything, would you change?

STUDIO LESSON: CLAY POT DECORATED WITH RADIAL DESIGNS

FIGURE 10.34 Maria and Julian Martinez. Black-on-black storage jar. 1942. Clay shaped by Maria and design painted by Julian. 47.6 x 56 cm (18¾ x 22"). Signature: Maria and Julian. Courtesy of the Museum of New Mexico, Sante Fe, New Mexico. School of American Research Collection.

Supplies

- Sketchbook, pencil, and ruler
- Clay
- Metal scraper or damp sponge
- Plastic bag (large enough to store work in progress)
- Clay tools
- Slip of a contrasting color
- Brushes

Maria Montoya Martinez, a Native American artist from the San Ildefonso Pueblo in New Mexico, learned to make pottery when she was a little girl by watching and helping her aunt and other women from the community. She met her husband, Julian, while they were attending St. Catherine's Indian School in Santa Fe, New Mexico. In addition to their community, ceremonial, and home responsibilities, Julian and Maria worked together to make pottery. She formed and polished the pottery, and he painted the surface designs.

As early as 1915, Maria's pottery stood out above all the others that were made in the area. One early critic wrote that Maria did the best polishing because she was the swiftest polisher. From the moment she picked up the pot to apply the slip, she did not put it down until the polishing was completed. In 1919 Maria and Julian began to experiment with the matte-black-on-shiny-black decorative process. This process became very popular, and by 1925 all of the San Ildefonso potters were making black-on-black ware.

After Julian died in 1943, Maria worked with Santana, her daughter-in-law, and later with her son, Popovi Da. Many experts felt that the Maria/Popovi Da period expressed the highest level of Maria's aesthetic achievement.

Near the end of her life, Maria told her great-granddaughter that other people owned her pots, but she saved her greatest achievement—the ability to create—for her family. Look at Maria and Julian's pot in Figure 10.34 and begin to think of ideas for your clay pot decorated with radial designs.

Using clay, build a coil or pinch pot, smooth the outside surface, and decorate it with a design that is organized using radial balance. The radial balance will be visible when viewed from above or below. When the pot has dried, fire it.

FOCUSING

Make some rough sketches in your sketchbook to plan the form of your pot. Plan the form so that you can see the radial design from the top or bottom.

CREATING

Build your pot using the pinch pot or the coil technique. See Technique Tips 17 and 18 on page 355 in the Handbook. When you have finished forming the pot, smooth the outside by scraping it with a metal scraper and/or rubbing with a damp sponge. Be sure to store your pot in the airtight plastic bag until you have finished forming it. Then you can cover it loosely until it becomes leather-hard. Do not let it dry too fast or it will crack.

Study your pot. Make drawings of it in your sketchbook showing different points of view. Using your pencil and ruler, plan a design for your pot that uses radial balance. You may use representational symbols, abstract shapes and lines, or a combination of both to create your design.

Decide which method you will use to apply the radial design to your pot. Decorate your pot. When your pot is bone dry, fire it in the kiln. Working with a team, plan a display of your pots. Consider the color of the fired clays so that you can select contrasting colors for the display.

FIGURE 10.34A Student work.

CRITIQUING

Describe Describe the form you selected for your pot. Explain why you chose that form. Explain which technique you used to create your pot. Did you have problems with the clay cracking? What technique did you use to apply the design to your pot? How did you arrange the display of your pot?

Analyze Did you create a smooth surface on which to apply the design? Did you use radial balance to create the decorative design? Did the design fit the form of the pot?

Interpret Compare your pot to the others in the class. Did you all use the same techniques? How did that affect the look of the different pieces? Are the surface designs alike or are they different? Can you explain why?

Judge Which aesthetic theory would you use to judge this piece? If you were to do this one more time, what, if anything, would you do differently?

ART CRITICISM IN ACTION

FIGURE 10.35 Diego Rivera. *Flower Day.* 1925. Oil on canvas. 147.4 × 120.6 cm (58 × 47½″). Los Angeles County Museum of Art, Los Angeles, California.

CRITIQUING THE WORK

1. **Describe** Read the credit line for the facts about *Flower Day* (Figure 10.35). Then describe the people in this work. What do they look like? What are they doing? What is the central figure carrying?
2. **Analyze** What kinds of line movement do you see? Does the painting look flat or does it have the illusion of three dimensions? How does the artist use space? Do the forms of the people look active or static? What kind of a color scheme has Rivera used? What kind of texture do you see in this work? Is rhythm important in this work? Explain. Why is balance an important principle in this painting?
3. **Interpret** Based on the visual clues you have collected and your personal experiences, write a brief paragraph explaining the meaning of this work. What do you think the artist is trying to tell us? Give the work a new title that sums up your interpretation.

FIGURE 10.36 Gianlorenzo Bernini. *David.* 1623. Marble. Life-size. Galleria Borghese, Rome, Italy.

4. Judge Do you think this is a successful work? Use one or more of the three aesthetic theories explained in Chapter 2 to defend your opinion.

COMPARING THE WORKS

Look at *Flower Day* (Figure 10.35) and *David* by Gianlorenzo Bernini (Figure 10.36). Rivera's work is a painting that looks sculptural, and Bernini's work is a freestanding, three-dimensional sculpture. Compare the central figure in *Flower Day* to the figure David. We know David represents the hero of the Old Testament story about David and Goliath. Does Rivera identify the man in his painting? Who do you think he is? List the similarities and differences between the two men. Notice their facial expressions, the movement of their bodies, the way they are dressed, and their muscles. How does balance affect the look of the two works?

MEET THE ARTIST

DIEGO RIVERA

Mexican, 1886–1957

Diego Rivera. *Self-Portrait.* 1941. Oil on Canvas. 61 × 43 cm (24 × 17″). Smith College Museum of Art, Northampton, Massachusetts.

In 1886 Diego Rivera was born in the small town of Guanajuato in central Mexico. Both his parents were teachers. His father also edited the local paper, *El Democratico,* a liberal newspaper concerned with the troubles and hardships of the workers. Rivera's concern for the workers, the poor, and the illiterate influenced all of his art.

As a young man, Rivera received a government grant to study art in Spain, and he traveled to France to study with Picasso. He also studied the fifteenth-century Italian murals of Raphael and Michelangelo and learned about fresco painting, later using those skills to paint his famous political murals.

When he returned to Mexico, he decided to paint only Mexican subjects. During the 1920s he received important commissions for monumental frescoes from the Mexican government. He used the simplified forms of pre-Columbian art in his work.

In 1929 he married the young artist Frida Kahlo. Her painting *Frida and Diego* (Figure 10.17, page 259) is their wedding portrait. Rivera painted many small paintings as well as murals, but he saw his murals as a way to teach people who could not read. Many of his murals have political themes. He combined the techniques of European art with the history of Mexico to create a new and individual way to portray his ideas about the people and the culture of his native land.

MORE PORTFOLIO IDEAS

Rivera painted the members of the working class, showing them with dignity. Think of an occupation that requires physical labor. Create a collage that depicts a person who performs such a service and does it well.

Rivera's painting depicts someone who is going to sell flowers at a festival in Mexico. Pick an exciting event where you have lots of fun, such as a ball game, a concert, or a festival. Create a painting of someone who has to work while everyone else is having fun. Try to express the worker's feelings about being left out of the fun.

CHAPTER 10 REVIEW

Building Vocabulary

On a separate sheet of paper, write the term that best matches each definition given below.

1. The principle of design concerned with equalizing visual forces, or elements, in a work of art.
2. A dividing line that works like the point of balance in the balance scale.
3. When equal, or very similar, elements are placed on opposite sides of a central axis.
4. A special type of formal balance in which two halves of a symmetrically balanced composition are identical, mirror images of each other.
5. When the forces or elements of a design come out (radiate) from a central point.
6. A balance of unlike objects.

Reviewing Art Facts

Answer the following questions using complete sentences.

1. Why is balance important to a work of art?
2. What are the visual forces, or weights, in art?
3. What is the difference between bilateral and approximate symmetry?
4. What factors in a work of art influence the visual weight of the art elements?
5. Which carry more weight, warm or cool colors?
6. How can value affect visual weight?
7. What does a formally balanced building express?

Thinking Critically About Art

1. **Extend.** Find a mural that is located in or near your community. Research the artist, the subject, and the inspiration for the mural. Photograph the mural to share with your classmates.
2. **Research.** The Leaning Tower of Pisa (Figure 10.2, page 252) is in serious trouble. Search the *Readers' Guide to Periodicals* for recent articles about the tower and encyclopedias for background information. What caused the tower to lean? When did it begin leaning? What has been done in the past to correct the lean? What would happen if the problem is not corrected? What has been done in recent years? Has the problem been solved? If so, how?
3. **Synthesize.** Grant Wood was an American Regionalist who created paintings about middle America such as *American Gothic* (Figure 10.8, page 254). Diego Rivera was a Mexican Muralist who created paintings about Mexican working people such as *Flower Day* (Figure 10.35, page 276). Find other works by each of the artists. Compare their styles. List the similarities and differences. Then write a paragraph explaining how each artist visually represents his own country.
4. **Analyze.** Edward Hopper, who painted *First Row Orchestra* (Figure 10.16, page 258), was not considered a member of the Regionalist school of painting. Find a book about him at the library, and look at his paintings. In what way does his subject matter and themes differ from those of the Regionalists? Explain your findings to the class using visual examples to illustrate your conclusions.

Making Art Connections

1. **Science.** Discuss balance with your science teacher to learn about the structure of life forms. Which life forms are symmetrical? Which have radial balance? Discover if any living things grow using informal balance.
2. **Math.** Discuss symmetry with your math teacher and report to the class about symmetry in mathematics.
3. **Social Studies.** Read about the "Balance of Power" and how it has affected the history of the world. What was it like in 1500, in 1914, in 1939? What is the balance of power today? Write a brief report explaining your findings.

FIGURE 11.1 The gigantic dancing figures seem to float across the mound of grass as they balance on three points. They visually defy the facts that they are 35 feet (10.6 m) tall and weigh 1200 pounds (544 kg).

Miriam Schapiro. *Anna and David.* 1987. Painted stainless steel and aluminum. 10.6 × 9.4 × .228 m (35′ × 31′ × 9″). Steinbaum-Krauss Gallery, New York, New York.

CHAPTER 11

Proportion

"I wish my nose weren't so big!"

"This desk is too small for me!"

"You put too much salt in the stew!"

All of these complaints are about problems with proportion. **Proportion** is *the principle of art concerned with the size relationship of one part to another.*

The size of an object by itself has no meaning (Figure 11.1). We can't tell how big or small an object is unless we can compare it with something else (Figure 11.2, page 282). If you are more than 6 feet (1.8 m) tall, you must approach a doorway with caution. When you are shopping for clothes, you look for the sizes designed to fit the proportions of your body. When you are cooking, you must be sure that the proportions in your recipes are correct.

In this chapter you will learn about how artists use the elements of art to create different kinds of proportion in their works. You will begin to understand why proportion is important in both two-dimensional and three-dimensional art, and you will learn how to use proportion in your own works of art.

FIRST IMPRESSIONS

Look at *Anna and David* by Miriam Schapiro. Do the figures have the proportions of average people? Read the credit information to discover the height of this sculpture. Notice the windows in the building behind the figures. That gives you an indication of the scale of the figures. How do you think this sculpture affects the mood of the people who pass it every day? How do the elements of line and color affect this mood? Why is negative space an important factor in this work?

Objectives

After completing this chapter, you will be able to:

- Explain and recognize the Golden Mean.
- Understand how we perceive proportion and scale.
- Measure and draw human faces and bodies with correct proportions.
- Understand how artists use proportion and distortion to create meaning.

Words to Know

distortion
exaggeration
foreshortening
Golden Mean
hierarchical proportion
proportion
scale

FIGURE 11.2 Look carefully at what seem to be cliffs. There is nothing in this picture to tell you that these are merely small piles of sand. Without anything to compare them with, you cannot tell how tall they are.

THE GOLDEN MEAN

You have just read about the importance of proportion to the function of products. Proportion is also important in creating the beauty of art objects (Figure 11.3).

Through the ages, people have sought an ideal of harmony and beauty. They have looked for a ratio (a mathematical comparison of sizes) that would produce an ideal form for figures and structures.

The ancient Greek philosopher Pythagoras found that he could apply mathematical equations to both geometric shapes and musical tones. If this is so, he thought, there must also be a way to explain other things—even the universe—in mathematical terms.

Euclid, a Greek mathematician, discovered what he considered a perfect ratio, or relationship of one part to another. He called this ratio the Golden Section, or **Golden Mean,** *a line divided into two parts so that the smaller line has the same proportion, or ratio, to the larger line as the larger line has to the whole line* (Figure 11.4). With this ratio, the ancient Greeks felt they had found the ideal proportion. It was used to control the relationship of parts in their sculpture, architecture, and even in their pottery. In math, this ratio is written 1 to 1.6. It is also written 1:1.6.

The Golden Rectangle (Figure 11.5) had sides that matched this ratio. The longer sides were a little more than half again as long as the shorter sides. This ratio was thought to be the most pleasing to the eye.

One of the many fascinating facts about the Golden Mean is its relationship to the human figure. If you divide the average adult male body horizontally at the navel, the two body measurements

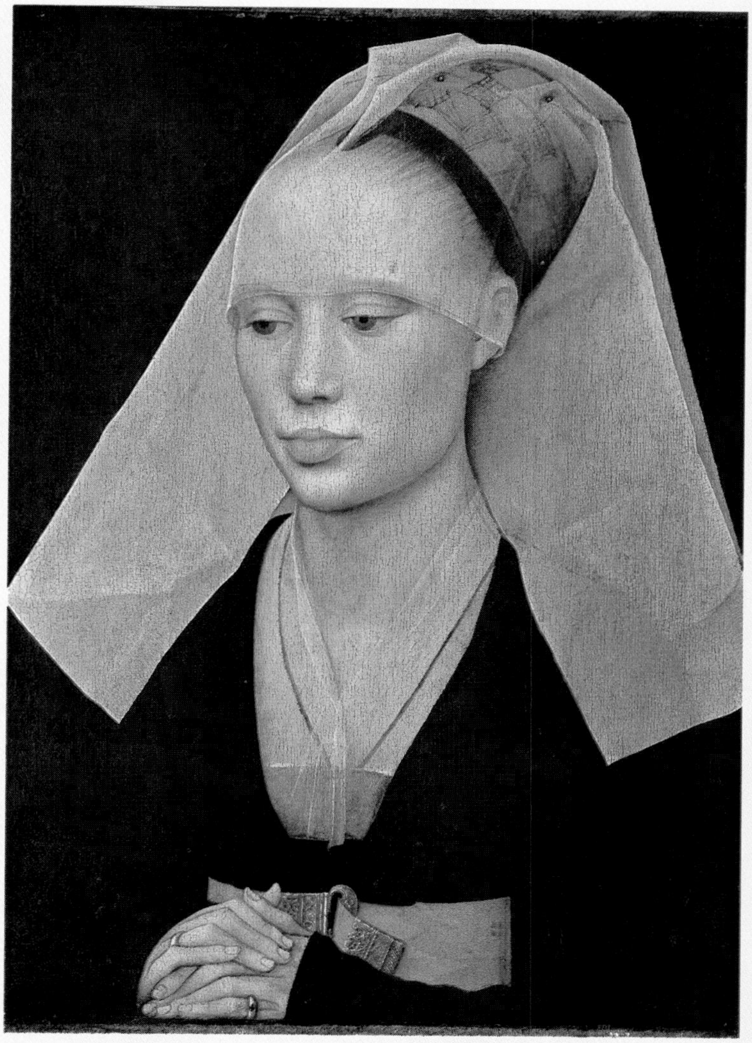

LOOKING CLOSELY

FIGURE 11.3 This heiress from the fifteenth century has some odd proportions. The red silk belt emphasizes her thin, high waist. If you use a ruler to measure, you will notice that her waist is not much wider than her head. Her lips are very full. This is supposed to symbolize a sensuous person. Notice the high forehead, which is thought to be a symbol of an intellectual person. Are these conflicting symbols? Do you think she looked like this or did the painter exaggerate her proportions to make her look more interesting?

Rogier van der Weyden. *Portrait of a Lady.* c. 1460. Oil on wood. 34 × 25.5 cm (13⅜ × 10 1/16″). National Gallery of Art, Washington, D.C. Andrew W. Mellon Collection.

FIGURE 11.4 The ratio of the Golden Mean is 1 to 1.6.

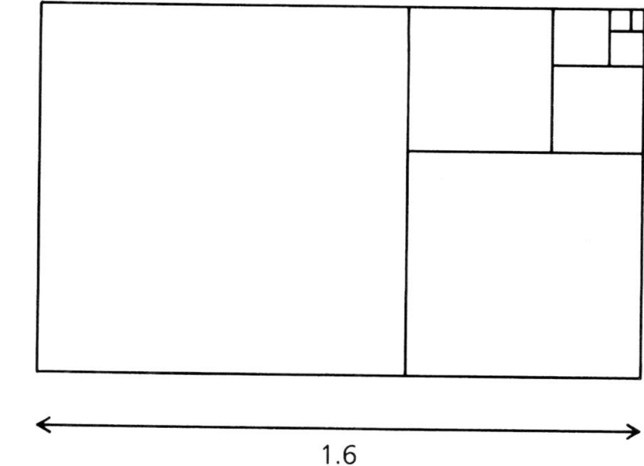

FIGURE 11.5 The Golden Rectangle is interesting to study. If you divide it into two shapes, one of which is a square, the remaining shape will always be a smaller Golden Rectangle. This new Golden Rectangle can be divided again and again.

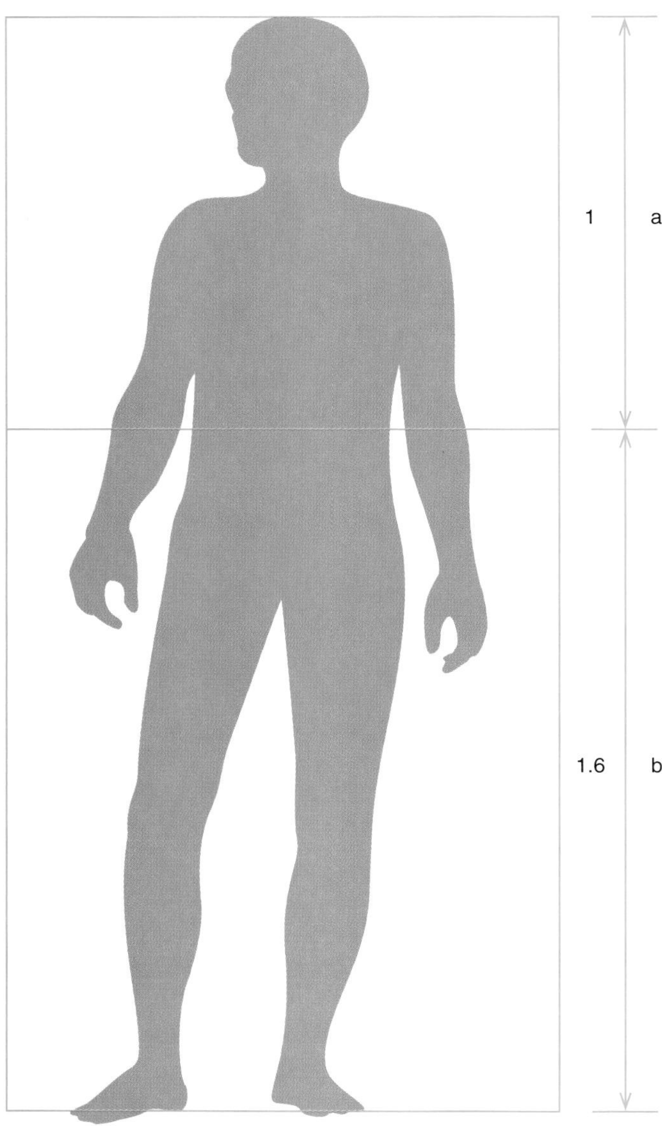

FIGURE 11.6 The relationship of the Golden Mean to the human body.

that result (head to navel = a, navel to toes = b) have a ratio of 1 to 1.6 (Figure 11.6).

The secret of the Golden Mean was forgotten with the fall of Ancient Greece. The ratio was rediscovered, however, during the Renaissance, and a book was written about it. This time the ratio was called the Divine Proportion, and it was thought to have magical qualities.

Since that time, some artists have chosen to use the Golden Mean as the basis for their compositions. Others, unaware of the mathematical ratio, used the Golden Mean just because that arrangement of parts looked good. Most artists now reject the idea that only this one rule can fit the "correct" proportions for all works of art. The ratio, however, is found in visual art so often that it is hard to ignore its importance (Figure 11.7).

Many people looked at the human body as a source for perfect proportions. As you know, artists during the Golden Age of Greece believed that the human body was the true expression of order. Statues created during that time were not realistic portraits of real people. The artists of the period showed the ideal form rather than the real form (Figure 11.8).

FIGURE 11.7 Can you find the proportions of the Golden Mean in this work?

Reginald Marsh. *Why Not Use the "L"?* 1930. Egg tempera on canvas. 91.4 × 121.9 cm (36 × 48″). Collection of Whitney Museum of American Art, New York, New York.

In the first century B.C., Vitruvius, a Roman writer, set down ratios for human proportion. These were later used by Leonardo da Vinci and other artists. The modern-day architect Le Corbusier applied human dimensions to architecture and city planning (Figure 11.9).

SCALE

Scale is much like proportion, but there is a difference. Proportion refers to the relationship of one part to another. **Scale**, on the other hand, *refers to size as measured against a standard reference,* such as the human body. A 7-foot (2.1-m) basketball player may not look big next to other basketball players. The player will look big, however, when

FIGURE 11.8 This sculpture is idealized. The facial features and all the proportions are so perfect that you would not recognize the model even if she stood next to the work.

Greece (from Alexandria?). *Dancing Lady.* c. 50 B.C. Peloponnesian marble. 85.4 cm (33⅝″) high with base; 78.7 cm (30 15/16″) high without base. The Cleveland Museum of Art, Cleveland, Ohio. John L. Severance Fund.

FIGURE 11.9 The sculptural form of this building is based on human dimensions.

Le Corbusier. *Chapelle Notre-Dame-du-Haut.* Ronchamp, France. 1955.

you see him in scale—that is, compared with a crowd of people of average height.

In art there are two kinds of scale to consider. One is the scale of the work itself. The other is the scale of objects or elements within the design.

The pyramids of Egypt are of such large scale that ordinary people are overwhelmed by their size. These pyramids were designed to be large to express the eternal strength of Egypt.

Wall paintings inside a pyramid depict the body of the pharaoh in very large scale. His servants, however, are very small in scale to emphasize their low status (Figure 3.4, page 44). When *figures are arranged in a work of art so scale indicates importance,* the artist is using **hierarchical proportion.** This arrangement disregards the actual size of figures and objects in order to indicate rank in a society. Use of scale to emphasize rank appears in the art of many cultures.

Actual works of art are usually much larger or much smaller than they appear to be when you look at photographs of them. You may have seen photos with a human hand or a human figure added for the purpose of showing the size of the objects in relation to human scale. Without some sort of measure, no illustration in any book can convey the effect of the scale of a work of art.

Some works that seem monumental in quality are really quite small in size. This is why the dimensions are always listed in the credits of the work. Try to visualize the size of a work in relation to your size. Imagine how it would look if it were in the room with you.

The picture of Claes Oldenburg's *Shoestring Potatoes Spilling from a Bag* (Figure 11.10) is not very impressive until you realize that the sculpture is 9 feet (2.7 m) tall. If you could stand beside it, the potatoes would be as tall or taller than you are, and the bag would tower an additional 3 feet (.9 m) above you. The scale of this work compared with a real bag of french fries is enormous. It is also big compared with a human being.

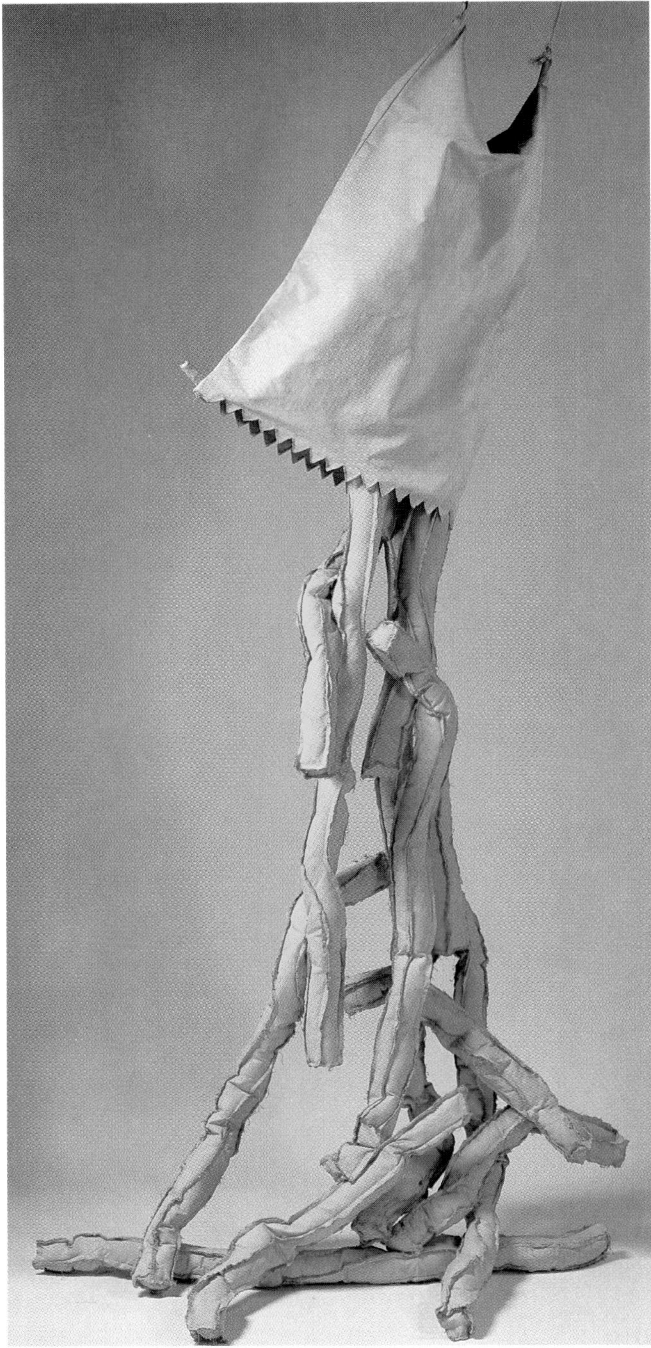

FIGURE 11.10 This soft sculpture is 9 feet (2.7 m) tall. This type of exaggerated scale is one method Pop artists used to make viewers see ordinary objects in a new way.

Claes Oldenburg. *Shoestring Potatoes Spilling from a Bag.* 1966. Acrylic, canvas, kapok, and glue. 274.3 × 116.8 × 106.7 cm (108 × 46 × 42"). Walker Art Center, Minneapolis, Minnesota. Gift of the T. B. Walker Foundation, 1966.

Variations in scale within a work can change the work's total impact. For example, interior designers are concerned with the scale of the furniture that is to be placed in a room. The designer considers the scale of the space into which the furniture will be placed. The needs of the people who will use the space must also be considered. An oversized, overstuffed sofa would crowd a small room with a low ceiling. However, the same sofa would fit comfortably in a large hotel lobby with a four-story ceiling. The large scale of the lobby would make the size of the sofa look right.

ACTIVITY Experimenting with Scale

1. Applying Your Skills. Create a small collage scene using magazine cutouts of people, furniture, and hand-held objects such as books, combs, pencils, hair dryers, and dishes. Arrange the cutouts on a small sheet of paper using realistic, accurate scale. All the things in the scene are in scale with the people, and all the people are in correct proportion to each other (Figure 11.11). You may have to employ perspective techniques and arrange things in depth to use all of your cutouts. Draw a background environment for the scene using water-base markers, colored pencils, or crayons.

2. Further Challenge. Create a collage using the same kinds of cutouts but use unrealistic scale. The objects and furniture will not be in scale with the people (Figure 11.12). A mysterious or humorous effect is created through the change in normal scale relationships. Create a background using water-base markers, colored pencils, or crayons.

FIGURE 11.12 Student work. Unrealistic scale.

FIGURE 11.11 Student work. Realistic scale.

3. Computer Option. Draw a figure with proportion based on average body proportions: 7½ heads high. The Line and Select tools and the Copy and Paste options can be used to quickly make the 7½-head grid that will guide your drawing. When the figure is completed, Copy and Paste the figure and then use the Resize option to change height and width of the figure. Repeat this three or four times. Have some figures that are tall and thin, others that are tall and fat, short and thin, and so on. Measure the head size of each figure you have resized. Even though the figures look very different based on height and width, the proportion related to head size will still be the same.

DRAWING HUMAN PROPORTIONS

Different cultures have set different standards for human beauty. People from the Middle Ages would view us as giants (Figure 11.13). The rounded females in Rubens's Baroque paintings

FIGURE 11.13 The man who wore this armor was about 5′ 9½″ (1.7 m) tall. Would many men today fit into this armor?

English (Greenwich School). Armor of George Clifford, Third Earl of Cumberland, K. G. c. 1580–85. Steel and gold. 176.5 cm (69½″). The Metropolitan Museum of Art, New York, New York. Munsey Fund, 1932.

FIGURE 11.14 Rubens's Virgin looks much chubbier than those in most other paintings of the Virgin Mary, but hefty proportions were the favored style in the time of Rubens, so he painted Mary in that manner.

Peter Paul Rubens. *The Assumption of the Virgin*. c. 1626. Oil on wood. 125.4 × 94.2 cm (49⅜ × 37⅛″). National Gallery of Art, Washington, D.C. Samuel H. Kress Collection.

would seem overweight by today's standards (Figure 11.14). Even today there are dramatic differences between the proportions of a high-fashion model and those of the average person.

Figures

People come in a variety of sizes and shapes. Categories for clothes sizes—slim, husky, petite, tall—are just one indication of the many different shapes and sizes of people.

Although they vary in size and shape, most people do not vary with regard to proportion. The 7-foot (2.1-m) basketball player and the 5-foot (1.5-m) dancer might have the same proportions. The tall basketball player's arms, legs, and torso have the same ratio to each other as the arms, legs, and torso of the dancer. Body proportions cannot be defined only in ratios of one body part to another.

The unit usually used to define the proportions of an individual figure is the length of the head from the chin to the top of the skull. The average adult is seven and one-half heads tall (Figure 11.15); a young child is five or six heads tall; and an infant is only three heads long (Figure 11.16). Many amateur paintings of children look strange because the artist has drawn the head too small in proportion to the rest of the body. When this happens, the child looks like a miniature adult.

There is one instance in which an artist may purposely distort proportion to make a drawing look more realistic. If a model is pointing at you, the arm from the fingertips to the shoulder will look shorter than it actually is. The artist will use a technique to visually shorten the arm. **Foreshortening** is *to shorten an object to make it look as if it extends backward into space* (Figure 11.17, page 290).

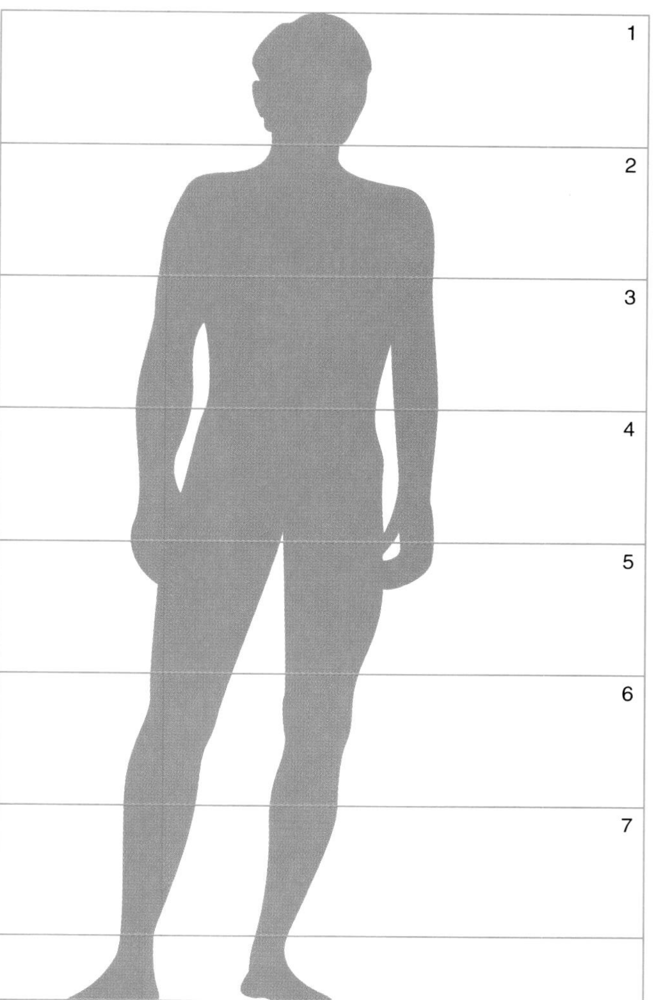

FIGURE 11.15 Average body proportions.

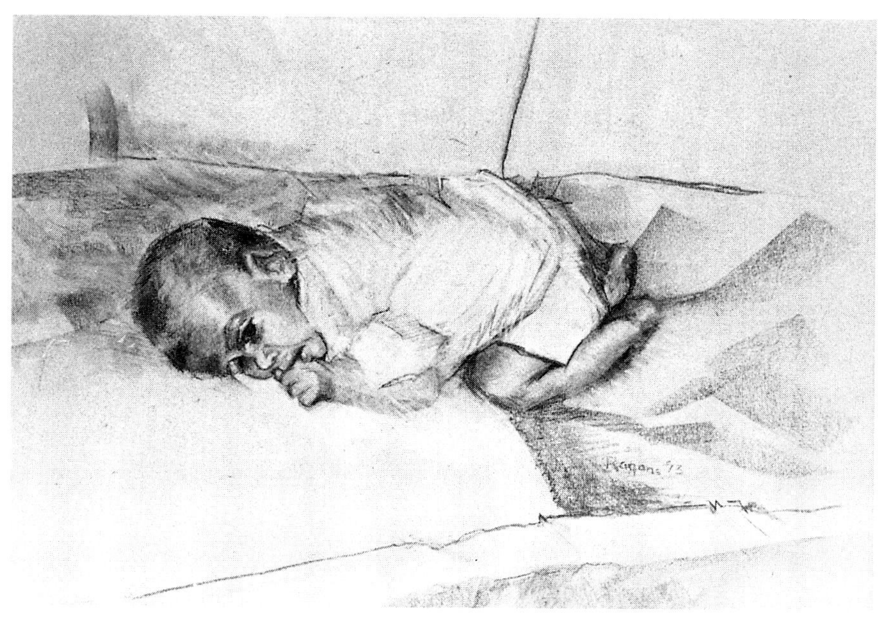

FIGURE 11.16 Notice the ratio of head to body in this sketch of an infant. Does the ratio differ from the usual adult ratio?

FIGURE 11.17 Siqueiros used foreshortening in this painting to dramatically exaggerate his reach to grab everything he can. His hand becomes a burst of superhuman energy.

David Alfaro Siqueiros. *Self-Portrait (El Coronelazo).* 1945. Pyroxylin on Masonite. 91 × 121 cm (35⅞ × 47⅝″). Museo de Arte Moderno, Mexico City, Mexico.

Human Proportions

1. Applying Your Skills. Measure your head from the top of your skull to the bottom of your chin. Because the top of your head is round, hold something flat, such as a piece of cardboard, across the top of your head to obtain an accurate measurement.

Use the length of your head as a unit against which to measure the rest of your body. In this way you can figure the relationship, or ratio, of all parts of your body to your head. You may need a friend to help you obtain accurate measurements. Determine the number of head lengths that each of the following represents: total height, chin to waist, waist to hip, knee to ankle, ankle to bottom of bare heel, underarm to elbow, elbow to wrist, wrist to tip of finger, and shoulder to tip of finger. Record the ratios and create a diagram or chart to show your findings. Compare your findings with those of your classmates. Find averages for the class, because the ratios will not be exactly alike.

2. Further Challenge. Make a series of figure drawings using a live model. Use the sighting technique to help you see proportions. (See Technique Tip 5 on page 350 in the Handbook.) Remember, as your model's poses change, the proportions will look different. Measure what you see, not what you think you should see.

If your model is sitting facing you, the length from hip to knee may be foreshortened. This means that the amount of leg you see from hip to knee will depend upon your point of view (Figure 11.17).

3. Computer Option. Use video digitizing software and a video camera or a scanner to capture a variety of photographs of students and objects. Use the Select tool and the Copy and Paste options to assemble a computer collage using unrealistic scale. Use the tools of your choice to manipulate the images. Images can be captured from many other sources such as videodisc. If you do not have these capabilities, use the drawing tools of your choice to create your own. Create a surrealistic scene.

Heads and Faces

As you read this section, look in a mirror or at a friend to check the examples discussed.

FIGURE 11.21 As with body proportions, the facial proportions of infants are different from those of adults. The skull is large. The infant's features seem to be squeezed together in the lower half of his face.

Albrecht Dürer. *Virgin and Child with Saint Anne.* 1519. Tempera and oil on canvas, transferred from wood. 60 × 49.9 cm (23⅝ × 19⅝″). The Metropolitan Museum of Art, New York, New York. Bequest of Benjamin Altman, 1913.

2. Further Challenge. Use a mirror to study the proportions of your head. Draw a self-portrait with charcoal or pencil. Use sighting to help find accurate size and shape relationships.

3. Computer Option. Gather some pictures of the faces of babies, young children, and adults. Notice that facial proportions change with age. Use the drawing tools of your choice to draw a human face using average facial proportions. Save your work. Use the Selection tool and the Copy and Paste options to duplicate the first face you drew. To experiment with the size of facial features, use the Selection tool to select the features of the face but not the outline of the head itself. Use the Resize option to create the correct feature size for a young child. Save your work. Reduce the size even more to create the correct feature size for an infant. The features need to be small and in the lower third of its face. Save your work. If possible, save all three faces on the same screen. Compare the three faces you have created.

How Artists Use Proportion and Distortion

Many artists use correct proportions in their work. They want every viewer to recognize the person, place, or thing being shown. These artists use correct proportion to create illusions of reality.

FIGURE 11.22 In this painting, Copley not only tells us what Paul Revere looked like, but he also tells us the man's profession. Revere was a silversmith, and the artist shows Revere holding a finished piece of work. The tools on the table were those used by Revere to engrave designs on the surface of his finished forms.

John Singleton Copley. *Paul Revere.* c. 1768–70. Oil on canvas. 88.9 × 72.3 cm (35 × 28½"). Museum of Fine Arts, Boston, Massachusetts. Gift of Joseph W., William B., and Edward H. R. Revere.

This ability to show objects as though they were real seems magical to many viewers.

Most Americans have favored works of art that are accurate, realistic views of life. Early American artists were hired to paint portraits—not so much to create art as to record accurate information about real people (Figure 11.22). George Catlin recorded the life of the Native American (Figure 11.23).

Some artists use exaggeration and distortion rather than real proportion to convey their ideas and feelings. **Exaggeration** and **distortion** are *deviations from expected, normal proportions.* They are powerful means of expression. Artists can lengthen, enlarge, bend, warp, twist, or deform parts or all of the human body. By making these changes, they can show moods and feelings that are easily understood by viewers (Figure 11.24).

In the past, movie stars of the silent screen had to exaggerate facial expressions and body language

FIGURE 11.23 As a young man, Catlin visited forty-eight Indian tribes, and he lived with Indians in both North and South America. His paintings are an accurate record of Indian life.

George Catlin. *See-non-ty-a, an Iowa Medicine Man.* c. 1845. Oil on canvas. 71.1 × 58.1 cm (28 × 22⅞"). National Gallery of Art, Washington, D.C. Paul Mellon Collection.

FIGURE 11.24 The intensity of feeling in this painting is almost unbearable. The twisted, tortured hands and feet of Christ are visual symbols of the entire Crucifixion. Grünewald has used just enough distortion to express the suffering without losing the reality of the moment.

Matthias Grünewald. *The Small Crucifixion*. c. 1511–20. Oil on wood. 61.6 × 46 cm (24¼ × 18⅛"). National Gallery of Art, Washington, D.C. Samuel H. Kress Collection.

to convey meaning without words. If you have ever seen an old silent movie, you have probably laughed at the exaggerated eyelid movements used to express meaning. Similarly, mimes move with graceful control that comes from years of training. Even though exaggerated or distorted, a mime's movements can convey a sense of truth (Figure 11.25 on page 296).

It takes study and skill to use exaggeration and distortion effectively. Artists who do so have first practiced the use of accurate proportion.

Edvard Munch (**ed**-vard moonk) and Pablo Picasso are two artists who used exaggeration and distortion in their work. Munch exaggerates the unity of the couple in love by eliminating all negative space between the figures (Figure 11.26 on page 296). Picasso's poor, undernourished couple in *The Frugal Repast* is not depressing because the long hands and arms of the lovers weave the withered bodies into an expression of tender togetherness (Figure 11.27 on page 297). Look for other ways in which the artist used distorted proportions.

FIGURE 11.25 A mime.

Chagall uses distortion to present a happier theme in his painting *Birthday* (Figure 11.28, page 298). The subjects of this work are the artist himself and Bella, his fiancée. The birthday is the artist's. Instead of simply showing himself leaning over to kiss Bella, Chagall used distortion. In the painting he appears to leap backward, stretch his neck like a swan, curve it around, and give Bella a kiss as he floats by. Do you think Chagall might have been thinking, "I'm so happy, I'm floating on air," when he created this work?

Artists can create feelings of great stability and calm by placing a small head on a large body. A monumental, or large and imposing, quality results. This is due mainly to placing a small head on a large, stable base. The monumental quality of Gaston Lachaise's *Walking Woman* (Figure 11.29, page 298) is created through exaggerated proportions and spacing rather than through large scale.

FIGURE 11.26 Munch has melted the two figures into one. He exaggerates the roundness of the embrace by drawing the arms as smooth curves without any elbows.

Edvard Munch. *The Kiss.* 1897–1902. Woodcut, printed in black. 46.6 × 47.4 cm (18⅜ × 18⅝"). The Museum of Modern Art, New York, New York. Gift of Abby Aldrich Rockefeller.

Pablo Picasso. *The Frugal Repast.* 1904 (printed 1913). Etching. 46.3 × 37.6 cm (18¼ × 14¹³⁄₁₆″). The Museum of Modern Art. New York, New York. Gift of Abby Aldrich Rockefeller.

LOOKING CLOSELY

FIGURE 11.27 Notice how Picasso used distortion and exaggeration to create the atmosphere of poverty and starvation. Look at the man's face. See how the shadows under his cheekbone and around his eye are exaggerated. Notice how the tendons in his neck protrude. You can see the bones sticking out of his shoulder and elbow. Observe the elongated arms, fingers, and torsos of both figures. Why is there an empty bowl on the table? Why is there liquid in only one glass? Notice that the filled glass, the piece of bread, and the lump of food are on the woman's side of the table. Why?

Another use of exaggeration can be seen in the features of a mask. Masks have been used in all societies, from early primitive tribes to our modern computer age (Figure 11.30, page 299). A mask allows a person to hide his or her real self and become someone, or something, else.

Masks are used in many cultures as part of religious ceremonies and rituals. In many cases the features of the mask are exaggerated for expressive purposes. There are different procedures for making and using masks. Each culture has specific traditions that are followed. Sometimes the mask appears to the person in a dream. Sometimes the mask is part of a cultural tradition. In most cases the mask is intended to aid efforts to communicate with the spirit world.

Cartoons are another way in which exaggeration can be used. Editorial cartoonists use this technique to make caricatures of famous people. The caricatures emphasize unusual facial features. Similarly, characters in comic strips are often made by using proportions that are larger than life. The most distorted comic-strip characters are often the funniest ones.

FIGURE 11.28 Chagall's painting shows a childlike belief in love's power to conquer all. He created distorted fantasies full of bright colors that looked like joyful dreams.

Marc Chagall. *Birthday*. 1915. Oil on cardboard. 80.6 × 99.7 cm (31¾ × 39¼"). Collection, The Museum of Modern Art, New York, New York. Acquired through the Lillie P. Bliss bequest.

Distorting Proportions

1. Applying Your Skills. Cut two ovals about 9 inches (23 cm) long from any color of construction paper. Using parts cut from magazines, create one face using accurate proportions. On the second oval, create a distorted face (Figure 11.31).

2. Further Challenge. Find caricatures (cartoons in which certain features are exaggerated) of one well-known person done by two different artists. The editorial page of a newspaper is a good source. Find a photograph of the same person. Compare the three pictures by describing similarities and differences.

FIGURE 11.29 This sculpture is only 19¼ inches (48.8 cm) high and yet it has a monumental quality, because Lachaise has made the head small.

Gaston Lachaise. *Walking Woman*. 1922. Bronze. 48.8 × 26.9 × 18.9 cm (19¼ × 10⅝ × 7½"). Hirshhorn Museum and Sculpture Garden, Smithsonian Institution, Washington, D.C. Gift of Joseph H. Hirshhorn, 1966.

FIGURE 11.30 Some masks were worn and some were held, but most were created for ceremonial purposes.

(left) Kwakiutl. *Wolf Mask.* Northwest Coast. 1900. Wood, copper eyes and upper teeth, haliotis shell, and paint. Height: 43 cm (17"). Milwaukee Public Museum, Milwaukee, Wisconsin.

(middle) *Mask.* New Ireland. c. 1920. Wood, paint, fiber, seashells. Height: 38 cm (15"). Milwaukee Public Museum, Milwaukee, Wisconsin.

(right) Bella Coola. *Cockle Hunter Mask.* Northwest Coast. c. 1900. Wood, horsehair, paint. Height: 33 cm (13"). Milwaukee Public Museum, Milwaukee, Wisconsin.

3. Computer Option. Use the drawing tools of your choice to draw a human face using average facial proportions. Use the Select tool and the Copy and Paste options to make four or five copies of the head and face on the same screen. Use the Select tool to experiment with the whole head and with individual facial features. Resize, Distort, Rotate, and Bend are some options that may prove useful to you. If your software does not have these options, draw the changes with drawing tools of your choice. Save your work. Compare the faces you have distorted and changed. How does the distortion affect the way you would use each face in a piece of artwork?

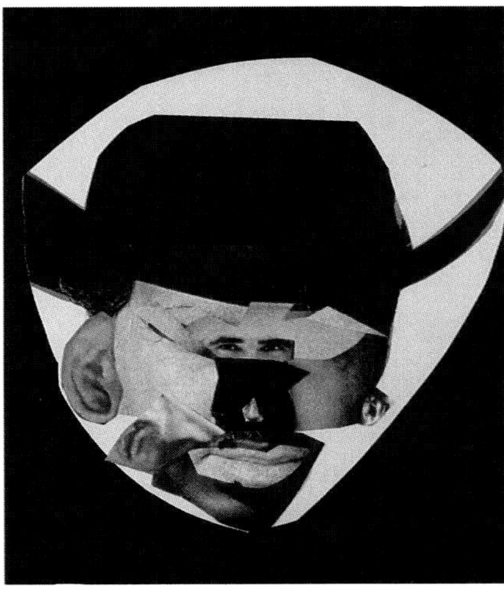

FIGURE 11.31 Student work. Accurate and distorted proportions.

STUDIO LESSON: STORYTELLER FIGURE

FIGURE 11.32 Annette Romero of the Cochiti Pueblo. *Storyteller Doll.* 1993. Clay and earth pigments. 20 × 10 × 17.7 cm (8 × 4 × 7″). Private collection.

Supplies

- Sketchbook and pencil
- Clay
- Clay modeling tools
- Slip and brush
- Plastic bag
- Tray or board
- Acrylic paints and assorted brushes
- Fine-line black markers

When Helen Cordero of the Cochiti Pueblo shaped the first Storyteller doll in 1964, she brought the Singing Mother, one of the oldest forms of Native American self-portraiture, into the twentieth century. In doing so, she reinvented a dying Cochiti tradition of figurative pottery.

Helen Cordero began making clay people in the late 1950s. Eventually little people came to life in her hands (Figure 11.32).

The first time Helen exhibited her work at a Santo Domingo feast day, a folk art collector named Girard bought all her little people. He asked her to make an even larger seated figure with children, and Helen thought about her grandfather, who had been a very good storyteller.

It is impossible to determine how many Storytellers Helen Cordero has shaped since 1964. It is also impossible to measure the influence of her invention, which began a revival of figurative pottery in both her own and other New Mexico pueblos. All sorts of variations have appeared. Mary E. Toya from the Jemez Pueblo made a female Storyteller in 1984 with 115 children, ten miniature pots, three baskets, two dogs, two balls, a drum and two dolls (one of which is a miniature Storyteller, less than an inch tall, with six babies). Create a clay Storyteller sculpture involving one adult interacting with many children, using proper clay construction techniques. After firing, add color.

Brainstorm with your friends to think up variations for the Storyteller project. You may depict a male or female person or an animal as the adult. The children must match the adult; for example, if you chose a bear as the adult, the children must be bear cubs. Use exaggerated scale to illustrate how an adult can enthrall children with storytelling.

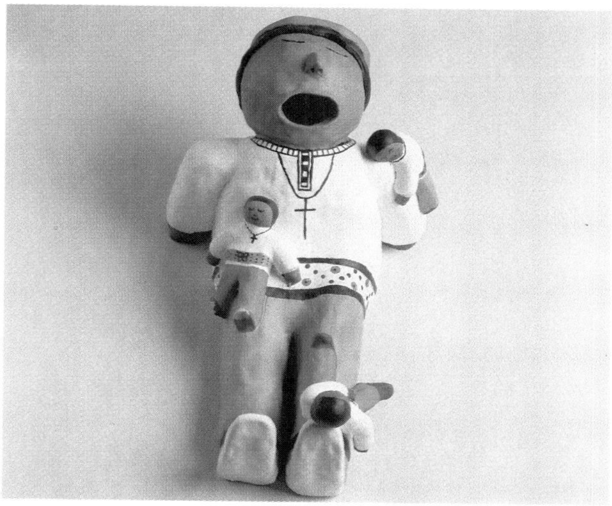

FIGURE 11.32A Student work.

CREATING

When you have selected the subject of your sculpture, make several sketches of the adult. Draw different views of your adult. Then make some rough sketches to help you think through how you will arrange the children on the adult.

Review clay construction procedures by reading Technique Tip 15 on page 354 in the Handbook. Decide which process you will use to build the adult figure. Remember that it needs to be hollow, and it needs an opening to allow the air to get inside. The storyteller's mouth would be appropriate. Decide which process will you use to create the smaller figures. Make notes about your construction plans in your sketchbook.

Collect your construction materials. Build the adult first, adding all three-dimensional details. Keep the adult stored tightly in the plastic bag while you construct the children. When you have attached all the children using scoring and slip, cover the sculpture loosely and let it dry. Check it every day to be sure that the little people are not drying too fast. They might shrink faster than the adult and crack off. When the sculpture is bone dry, fire it in the kiln.

After firing, paint the sculpture with acrylic paints. Use small brushes or fine-line markers to add linear details. You do not have to cover all the clay. Use the color of the clay as one of the predominant colors in your sculpture.

Write the story that your storyteller is narrating. Record it on tape. Arrange the Storyteller sculpture in a display. Use a tape player to tell the story to your viewers.

CRITIQUING

Describe Explain the subject of your Storyteller sculpture. How many children did you make? Which clay construction processes did you use?

Analyze How much did you exaggerate scale in your sculpture? Did you use accurate or distorted proportions? How did you incorporate the color of the fired clay into the color scheme?

Interpret What is the theme of your story? Does it match the mood of the sculpture?

Judge Which aesthetic theories would you use to judge this work? If you were to do it one more time, what, if anything, would you change?

STUDIO LESSON: USING DISTORTION FOR EXPRESSIVE EFFECT

FIGURE 11.33 Fernando Botero. *The Pinzon Family.* 1965. Oil on canvas. 173 × 173 cm (68 × 68″). Museum of Art, Rhode Island School of Design, Providence, Rhode Island. Nancy Sayles Day Collection of Modern Latin-American Art. © Fernando Botero/VAGA, New York. 1994.

Fernando Botero is a native of Colombia. He is one of the most popular artists in the world. After you have seen a Botero you will always recognize a Botero work. When asked about the plump proportions of the subjects in his work, he declares that he doesn't paint fat people. He gives everything in his world equal weightiness, a serious roundness he calls plasticity.

Botero has always worked in this distorted representational style. He says that if he were an abstract painter he would put a line or a spot where he needed it, but because he is a figurative painter he needs something real in order to add a particular color or form. Notice how he has used the dog's chew stick, the ball, and the lavender rod as abstract elements in this painting.

The great generals, ministers of war, dictators, and wealthy landowners in Botero's paintings look like toys. Botero has taken

Supplies

- Selected reproduction for study
- Sketchbook and pencil
- Large sheet of white paper
- Yellow chalk and soft eraser
- Painting medium of your choice

away the dignity of the rich and powerful and turned them into harmless playthings by giving them facial proportions that make them resemble infants.

In Botero's portrait of the Pinzon family, he has reduced a formal family portrait to a picture of toylike people by distorting facial and body proportions (Figure 11.33).

Choose a reproduction of a two-dimensional work in this book and change the mood and meaning by altering the proportions. All the people, animals, and objects in the work must be distorted in the same way. Choose a new color scheme to match the new mood and paint your distorted interpretation of the work.

Choose a reproduction of a realistic, two-dimensional work of art in *ArtTalk* that includes at least one person. (Do not select a student work.)

FOCUSING

Study it to see how you can alter the mood and meaning of the work by distorting its proportions. For example, what would be the effect if Picasso's couple in *The Frugal Repast* (Figure 11.27, page 297) were as plump as Botero's people?

CREATING

Make a small sketch in your sketchbook of the reproduction you have chosen. Then make a second sketch distorting the original proportions. All figures in the work should be distorted in the same style. Animals and objects may be distorted, if appropriate, to match the figures. Try a few more sketches, experimenting with different amounts and methods of distortion.

Select your best sketch. Draw it freely on the large sheet of white paper using the yellow chalk. Choose a new color scheme that will strengthen the expressive quality of your new composition. Paint your work using a paint medium of your choice.

Mount or mat your work for display.

FIGURE 11.33A Student work.

CRITIQUING

Describe Identify the reproduction you selected for this assignment. List the people, animals, and/or objects that you changed using distortion. Explain how you prepared the work for display.

Analyze Explain how and why you altered the proportions in your interpretation of the original work. Describe the color scheme and explain how it is different from the original and why you chose it.

Interpret Explain how changing proportions and color transformed the expressive effect of the work. Give your work a title that expresses the new mood of the work or one that expresses the transformation of the work through distortion.

Judge Which aesthetic theories would you use to judge this work? If you were to do this work again, what would you change?

STUDIO LESSON: PAPIER-MÂCHÉ MASK

FIGURE 11.34 Henry Hunt, Southern Kwakiutl. *K'umugwe' (Komokwa) Mask.* 1970. Wood, copper, paint. 31.6 × 28.7 × 20.7 cm (12⅜ × 11⅛ × 8″). Royal British Columbia Museum, Victoria, British Columbia, Canada. #13215.

Supplies

- Sketchbook and pencil
- Newspaper and paper towels
- Nontoxic papier-mâché paste
- Acrylic paints and a variety of brushes
- Scissors and white glue
- Found material for decorations such as yarn and foil

The mask shown in Figure 11.34 represents the chief of the undersea world, K'umugwe' (Komokwa). The copper teeth, eyes, and eyebrows on this mask are indications of great wealth. This creature, whose dance is part of the Red Cedar Bark dance series, is a monster who causes trouble in the waters. He can stop rivers, create great waves on bodies of water, and swallow or overturn canoes. This mask was designed to be viewed on the head of a costumed figure dancing around a flickering firelight. The movements used in the dance of the K'umugwe' imitate those of a sea mammal in water, including surfacing to breathe. Notice how the wood has been carved into high relief. This is done so that the viewer will see changing shadows alternating with bright light.

Just as the K'umugwe' was used to explain things that happened in the water, you will create a myth that explains something about modern technology. Each member of the team will be an actor in the drama. Each will design and create a high-relief papier-mâché mask using distortion and exaggeration to make the mask expressive. Choose a color scheme that matches the character of the mask. Paint and decorate the mask.

FOCUSING

Brainstorm with your classmates to list mysteries of modern technology. Make a list of possible themes that could be explained in a storytelling dance drama.

Divide into work teams for a planning conference. Keep notes from the conference.

Select a specific theme or topic. Choose music. Name and define the character of each participant. Write the story. Decide how you will communicate with the audience. Will you all speak lines, will a narrator tell the story, or will you act it out in pantomime? List the props and setting you will need. Plan body movements to match the music.

CREATING

Draw several ideas for your mask. Plan the side view as well as the front view. Use exaggeration and distortion to create the mood you wish your character to express.

Meet with the team to make final decisions about the masks. At this time decide on colors and the extra materials you will need for decorations. Decide if you need costumes.

Draw the final plan for your mask in your sketchbook. List the colors and special decorations you plan to add. Collect the extra materials such as yarn, costume jewelry, and fabrics.

Construct your mask. See the different directions for papier-mâché construction in Technique Tip 19 on page 355 in the Handbook. Use high relief. Make some ridges rise 2 inches (5 cm) from the surface of the mask. Plan how you will hold the mask on your head. You must be able to see through it when you are wearing it. The holes for your eyes do not have to be the eyes of the mask.

FIGURE 11.34A Student work.

When the papier-mâché is dry, paint your mask with acrylic paints. Glue on the additional decorations.

Rehearse with your group using all the props you will need for the performance, including special lighting. Perform your dance drama for the class.

CRITIQUING

Describe Explain the theme and story of your dance drama. Describe the music you used and explain why you chose it. List and explain all the characters in your drama. Describe your mask.

Analyze Did you use high relief? Explain the shadows and highlights that resulted. Explain your color scheme. Which parts of the mask did you exaggerate and distort? Did the body movements match the character of the mask and the music?

Interpret What was the message of your production? Did the audience understand the message?

Judge Which aesthetic theories would you use to judge the entire production? Are they different from the theories you would use to judge the mask? Why?

STUDIO LESSON: SOFT SCULPTURE

FIGURE 11.35 Faith Ringgold. *Mrs. Jones and Family.* 1973. Mixed media. Mrs. Jones: 152 × 30 × 41 cm (60 × 12 × 16″). Andrew: 122 × 30 × 30 cm (48 × 12 × 12″). Barbara: 58 × 16 × 28 cm (23 × 6½ × 11″). Faye: 63 × 14 × 30 cm (25 × 5½ × 12″). Faith Ringgold, Inc.

Faith Ringgold is an African-American artist. She is a painter, soft sculptor, and performance artist. *Mrs. Jones and Family* (Figure 11.35) represents Ringgold's family. Mrs. Jones is her mother, and Andrew is her father.

Ringgold started as a traditional painter. Her education, like that of any other art student in the 1950s, was in the European tradition. In the late 1960s, during a period when she was incorporating African designs and motifs into her painted canvases, Ringgold began to experiment first with masks and later with soft sculpture. These media enabled her to work in the center of her family. The interaction of the people in her family nourished her spirit. Notice in the sculpture *Mrs. Jones and Family* that all the dolls have their mouths open. They are all talking at once!

Look closely at the figures in Ringgold's work to see how she used media, distortion, and exaggeration to create her sculpture. Think about the techniques you can use to create yours.

Supplies

- Sketchbook and pencil
- Paper for patterns
- Scissors and pins
- Sewing and embroidery threads
- Variety of sewing needles
- Assorted fabrics
- Stuffing material such as fiberfill
- Yarns and other trims
- Sewing machine (optional)

Design and construct a soft sculpture symbolizing a person from history, art history, literature, or current events. Ringgold made the faces large according to African traditions. She made all the mouths open to indicate that her family was very talkative. Use distortion and exaggeration to emphasize the most important attributes of the person you have chosen. Select colors and fabrics to fit the personality of your sculpture and add details using stitchery and/or appliqué.

FIGURE 11.35A Student work.

FOCUSING

Brainstorm with classmates about subjects to consider for your soft sculpture. Select the person you will symbolize. Do some research about this person. Make visual and written notes in your sketchbook. What is your person famous for? What kind of clothing is appropriate? Which features will you exaggerate? For example, if you are doing a track star, you may make the feet oversized; if you are representing a rock star, you may wish to exaggerate the mouth.

CREATING

Draw a plan for constructing your sculpture in your sketchbook. Draw your sculpture from the front, back, and sides. On a sheet of paper, make a pattern for cutting the body fabric. Cut out fabric and pin the pieces, right sides together. Sew the body together on the inside, leaving a small opening. Then turn it inside out and stuff it. You may shape a three-dimensional face, or you may use stitches and appliqué as Ringgold did. Use yarn or other material to make hair. Make clothes to fit your sculpture, or use doll clothes. Add details with stitchery. See Technique Tip 22 on pages 357–58 of the Handbook.

Arrange your soft sculpture for display. You may add props and a setting if desired. Write a few paragraphs about your sculpture and include the writing in your display.

CRITIQUING

Describe Name the subject of your soft sculpture and explain why you selected that person. Describe the procedures you followed to construct this sculpture. List the attributes of your subject that you chose to emphasize and explain why.

Analyze Explain how, where, and why you used distortion and exaggeration. Which colors did you select for your sculpture?

Interpret What kind of a mood does your sculpture express? Give it a title that symbolizes the character of your subject. Do not use the subject's name.

Judge Which aesthetic theories would you use to judge this work? If you were to do it over, what would you change?

ART CRITICISM IN ACTION

FIGURE 11.36 Isabel Bishop. *Waiting.* 1938. Oil and tempera on gesso panel. 73.6 × 56.5 cm (29 × 22¼"). Collection of The Newark Museum, Newark, New Jersey. Purchase, 1944. Arthur F. Egner Memorial Fund.

CRITIQUING THE WORK

1. **Describe** Read the credit line for Figure 11.36. What is unusual about the media? Describe the subject matter of the work. Can you tell what the people are wearing?
2. **Analyze** Where do you see lines? What kind of lines are they? Has the artist created the illusion of three dimensions? What kind of shapes do you see? What shape do the two overlapping figures form? What is unusual about the artist's treatment of space and depth? What is the scale of the artwork itself? Can you tell the scale of the figures in relation to other objects? Using each head to measure, are the proportions of the child the same as those of the woman?

3. **Interpret** Based upon the clues you have collected and your own ideas, write a brief paragraph explaining the meaning of the work. Then give the work a new title that sums up your interpretation.
4. **Judge** Do you think this is a successful work of art? Use one or more of the three aesthetic theories explained in Chapter 2 to defend your opinion.

COMPARING THE WORKS

Look at *Waiting* (Figure 11.36) and look at the *Pietà* by Michelangelo (Figure 11.37). In what ways are these two works similar and in what ways do they differ? Notice the subject matter. Pay attention to the way the two artists use proportion in the works and the moods expressed by the works.

FIGURE 11.37 Michelangelo. *Pietà*. c. 1500. St. Peter's Basilica, Rome, Italy.

FYI Michelangelo thought of himself as a sculptor. He thought that the creation of people from hard marble was, in some small way, related to divine creation. He loved to "liberate" human forms from cold stone. In spite of that, one of his most important achievements was a painting: the ceiling of the Sistine Chapel.

MEET THE ARTIST

ISABEL BISHOP

American, 1902–88

Isabel Bishop. *Self-Portrait.* 1927. Oil on canvas. 36 × 33 cm (14⅛ × 13″). Wichita Art Museum, Wichita, Kansas. Gift of the Friends of the Wichita Art Museum, Inc.

In 1920, with financial support from an inheritance, Isabel Bishop enrolled at the Art Students' League in New York City. She had a small studio apartment on Union Square in Manhattan. After marrying and moving to Riverdale, she made the daily trip to Grand Central Station by train and then transferred to the subway, which took her to the studio. During the trips she sketched.

The subjects of her paintings were the working women she saw in the trains and from her studio window. Her concern was composition, and the subjects were a means to attack the abstract problem of time and space. She tried to express the possibility of momentary change. To her, the young women did not belong to a specific class.

The procedures she followed were unusual. First she sketched from life. From her sketchbook ideas, she selected some to become etchings. From those she selected the compositions of her paintings. She then treated a panel with eight coats of gesso, front and back. She painted a ground of loose, uneven, horizontal, gray stripes to create an undersurface that gave her paintings a sense of vibration. Then she painted on the surface with tempera. Finally, she added glazes of oil paint. The stripes always showed through. She applied the highlights with thick opaque paint and kept the shadows thin and transparent. She half concealed the people in thin shifting shadows and sparkles of light.

Her paintings took months and sometimes years to complete. There was never any point at which she felt a work was complete.

MORE PORTFOLIO IDEAS

I. Using tempera paint, cover a sheet of white paper with uneven, gray, horizontal stripes. Allow some white paper to show between the stripes. Make a crayon drawing based on one of the drawings in your sketchbook. Color it lightly with crayon so that the underpainting shows through.

II. Using acrylics, prepare a sheet of white paper with gray stripes as above. Using a brush and thinned acrylics, make a drawing over the stripes, based on a drawing in your sketchbook. Paint it using thin glazes of acrylic in the shadows. Accent the highlights using thick opaque light colors in the manner of Isabel Bishop.

CHAPTER 11 REVIEW

Building Vocabulary

On a separate sheet of paper, write the term that best matches each definition given below.

1. The principle of art concerned with the size relationship of one part to another.
2. A line divided into two parts so that the smaller line has the same proportion, or ratio, to the larger line as the larger line has to the whole line.
3. When figures are arranged in a work of art so scale indicates importance.
4. To shorten an object to make it look as if it extends backward into space.
5. Refers to size as measured against a standard reference.
6. Deviations from the expected, normal proportions.

Reviewing Art Facts

Answer the following questions using complete sentences.

1. What is the Golden Mean ratio?
2. Explain the difference between scale and proportion.
3. What was the name for the geometric form that had sides matching the ratio of the Golden Mean?
4. What are the two kinds of scale in art?
5. What unit is usually used to define the proportions of any individual figure?

Thinking Critically About Art

1. **Extend.** Do some library research to determine how hierarchical proportions have been used in the art of different cultures. Photocopy examples to show and report your findings to the class.
2. **Analyze.** Schapiro's sculpture *Anna and David* (Figure 11.1, page 280) was based on a painting she created in 1986 called *Pas de Deux.* Find a color reproduction of the painting. Compare the sculpture to the original painting. List the similarities and differences. Explain the changes that were made to transform the work from one medium to another.
3. **Analyze.** Study the illustration of the Golden Rectangle in Figure 11.5, page 283. Look through this book to find works of art that have been organized using those proportions. Choose at least one to diagram.
4. **Apply.** Apply the four steps of art history to Albrecht Dürer's *Virgin and Child with Saint Anne* (Figure 11.21, page 293). Describe when and where it was painted. Analyze the unique features of the work. Interpret how Dürer was influenced by other artists and the world in which he lived. Finally, make a conclusion about the importance of this work.
5. **Synthesize.** Research the life and work of George Catlin. What kind of paintings did he make? What was his purpose? How did he go about accomplishing his goals? Write a report about Catlin and explain his position in the history of America as well as his place in the history of American art. Which was more important, history or art history? Why?

Making Art Connections

1. **Music.** Read about the Pythagorean theories of music. Ask your music teacher for help if necessary. Use charts, diagrams, and/or pictures to report your findings to the class.
2. **Math.** Do more in-depth research about the Golden Mean. Find out what Fibonacci's number sequence has to do with the Golden Mean. Consult your math teacher for help if necessary.
3. **Health.** The man who wore the suit of armor shown in Figure 11.13, page 288, was only 5 feet 9½ inches (176.5 cm) tall. The average man is taller than that today. What do you think nutrition has to do with the change in size?

FIGURE 12.1 Jacquette makes sketches and takes photos from airplanes or tall buildings to use as references. She captures the contrast between the natural and the manufactured environment.

Yvonne Jacquette. *Town of Skowhegan, Maine V.* 1988. Oil on canvas. 198.6 × 163 cm (78³⁄₁₆ × 64³⁄₁₆″). Courtesy Brooke Alexander Gallery, New York, New York.

CHAPTER 12

Variety, Emphasis, Harmony, and Unity

You have already learned about the principles of rhythm, balance, and proportion. In this chapter you will learn about three additional principles: *variety, emphasis,* and *harmony.* Even more important, you will learn about the principle of *unity.* It is only when all the elements and all the principles work together that you achieve a unified work of art.

Emphasis is a principle that enhances variety, because it creates a feeling of dominance and subordination. The dominant area is usually a focal point that attracts the attention of the viewer before the subordinate areas. Harmony enhances unity because it uses similarities and relatedness to tie elements together.

Unity and variety complement one another in the same way that positive and negative spaces complement one another. Unity and variety are like two sides of one coin. Unity controls and organizes variety, while variety adds interest to unity.

In this chapter you will see how artists have used the elements of art to create unity in their works. As you read, you will learn how to use the elements to create variety, emphasis, harmony, and unity in your own works of art.

First Impressions

Look at Figure 12.1, *Town of Skowhegan, Maine V.* How does the water affect the town in this painting? What kind of buildings do you see at the very top of the painting? Are the buildings on the right and at the bottom of the picture the same? How does the artist use the road to divide as well as unify the composition? How has she indicated the difference between the cars that are speeding on the highway and the cars that are parked? How does she unite the various conflicting factors in this painting?

Objectives

After completing this chapter you will be able to:

- Identify and describe variety, emphasis, harmony, and unity in your environment and in a work of art.
- Understand how artists use variety and emphasis to express their ideas and feelings.
- Understand how artists use the elements and principles of art to create unified works of art.
- Use variety, emphasis, and harmony to create your own unified works of art.

Words to Know

emphasis
focal point
harmony
unity
variety

VARIETY

People need variety in all areas of their lives. Imagine how boring it would be if daily routines were exactly the same every day of the week for a whole year. Imagine how visually boring the world would be if everything in it—everything—were the same color.

People put a great deal of time and effort into creating variety in their environment. They may buy new furniture or paint the walls, not because the furniture is old or the paint is peeling, but simply because they need a change. New clothes, new foods, new friends—the list of items people seek out to relieve the sameness or boredom in life is endless.

Just as people must add variety to their lives to keep it interesting, so must artists add variety to their works. **Variety** is *the principle of design concerned with difference or contrast.*

A work that is too much the same can become dull and monotonous. For example, a work composed of just one shape may be unified, but it will not hold your attention. Variety, or contrast, is achieved by adding something different to a design to provide a break in the repetition (Figure 12.2). When different elements are placed next to each other in a work of art, they are in contrast (Figure 12.3). This type of contrast, or variety, adds interest to the work of art and gives it a lively quality.

Almost every artist uses contrasting elements to balance unifying elements. Wide, bold lines complement thin, delicate lines. Straight lines contrast with curves. Free-form shapes differ from geometric shapes. Rough textures add interest to a smooth surface. The number of contrasts that can be introduced through color are limitless. The degree of contrast may range from bold to subtle. The amount of difference between the elements depends on the artist's purpose.

FIGURE 12.2 MTV has used variety to maintain interest in its logo. The shape of the logo is always the same: a heavy, solid **M** decorated with a small, thin TV, but every time you see the logo, the colors and patterns on it change. Repetition reassures the viewer that this is the same station, but variety stirs the viewer's curiosity.

Courtesy of MTV Networks.

FIGURE 12.3 Which elements has Pereira used to create variety in this painting? Which element do you think shows the strongest contrast?

Irene Rice Pereira. *Untitled*. 1951. Oil on board. 101.6 × 61 cm (40 × 24″). Solomon R. Guggenheim Museum, New York, New York. Gift of Jerome B. Lurie, 1981.

Variety and Contrast

1. Applying Your Skills. Look through the works you have produced in this course. Find one that seems dull. Study it and tell how you could add variety without destroying the unity.

2. Further Challenge. Look through *ArtTalk* for works of art that show bold contrast of line, shape, color, value, and texture. List one work for each kind of contrast. Explain how the contrast was created.

3. Computer Option. Draw a simple design using five or six shapes. Use the Select tool and the Copy and Paste options to make five copies of the design on the same screen. Leave one design unchanged; alter the others to show a variety of contrasts. Vary contrast in color, value, and textures by using the Fill Bucket tool. Save your work.

EMPHASIS

Have you ever underlined an important word or phrase several times in a letter? Have you ever raised the volume of your voice to make sure the person you were talking to understood a key point? These are just two ways that people use emphasis to focus attention on the main points in a message. In advertisements, music, news stories, your lessons at school, and your day-to-day communications, you see and hear certain ideas and feelings being emphasized over others.

Emphasis is *the principle of design that makes one part of a work dominant over the other parts.* Artists use this principle of emphasis to unify a work of art. Emphasis controls the sequence in which the parts are noticed. It also controls the amount of attention a viewer gives to each part.

There are two major types of visual emphasis. In one type, an *element of art* dominates the entire work. In the other type of emphasis, an *area* of the work is dominant over all the other areas.

Emphasizing an Element

If the artist chooses to emphasize one element, all the other elements of the work are made *subordinate,* or less important. The *dominant,* or most important element affects the viewer's perception of the total work. This element also affects the way in which all the separate items and elements in the work are perceived.

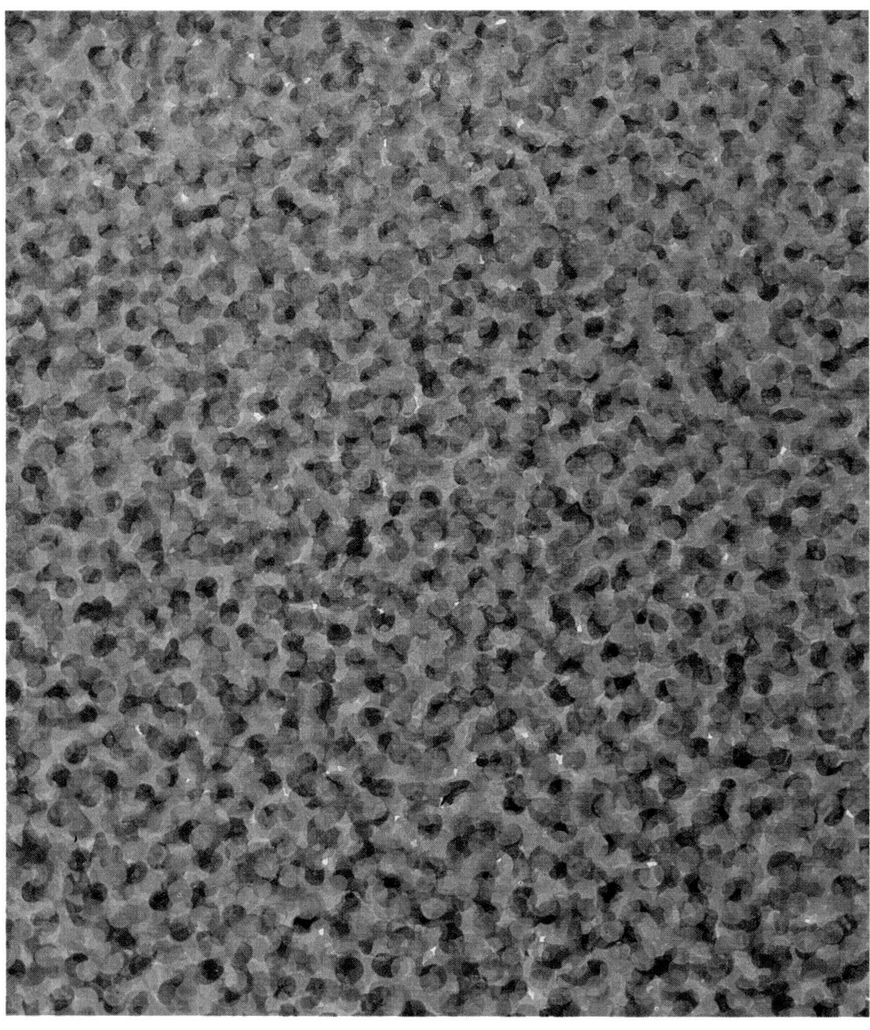

FIGURE 12.4 Redness overwhelms this painting. There is no focal point—your eyes dance from one red to another.

Bronislaw Bak. *Interpenetrations in Red.* 1980. Oil on canvas. 122 × 152.4 cm (4 × 5′). Private collection.

Sometimes the dominant element is made so strong that the whole work seems to be drenched in that element. For instance, Bronislaw Bak's *Interpenetrations in Red* (Figure 12.4) is saturated with the color red. In this painting the redness takes on a meaning all its own. It affects the viewer's perception of the painting as a whole as well as the viewer's perceptions of the separate parts.

Emphasizing an Area

Sometimes a specific area in a work of art is emphasized. This area, called the **focal point,** is *the first part of a work to attract the attention of the viewer.* The other areas are subordinate to the focal point (Figure 12.5).

It is possible for a work of art to have more than one focal point. Artists must be careful about this, however. Too many focal points cause the eye to jump around and will confuse the viewer.

Artists must decide on the degree of emphasis needed to create a focal point. This usually depends on the purpose of the work. Of course, a focal point is not necessary, and many artists don't create one in their works (Figure 12.6, page 318).

When artists do create focal points, they are usually careful not to overdo the emphasis. They make certain that the focal point is unified with the rest of the design.

Artists use several techniques to create a focal point in a work of art. Following are some examples of these techniques.

Contrast. One way to create a focal point is to place an element that contrasts with the rest of the work in that area. One large shape, for example, will stand out among small ones. One angular, geometric shape will be noticed first among rounded, free-form shapes. A bright color will dominate low-intensity colors, while a light area will dominate a dark design (Figure 12.7, page 318).

FIGURE 12.5 Rembrandt uses value contrast to create a focal point in this work. Only the head and the area immediately around it are painted in light values. The background sinks into darkness.

Rembrandt van Rijn. *Self-Portrait.* 1650. Oil on canvas. 92 × 75.5 cm (36¼ × 29¾″). National Gallery of Art, Washington, D.C. Widener Collection.

FIGURE 12.6 The artist has designed this work without a focal point. In this detail you can see how one shape leads your eyes to another. Your eyes cannot find one place to rest that is more important than another.

Lois Dvorak. *The Lizards.* 1982. Handmade, hand-dyed papers and opera cloth stitched and interwoven on four layers of dowels, accented with metallic marking pen and metallic threads. 81.3 × 101.6 cm (32 × 40″). Courtesy of the artist.

FIGURE 12.7 Notice how the bright red shapes in the lower right corner catch your attention.

Horace Pippin. *Asleep.* 1943. Oil on board. 22.9 × 30.5 cm (9 × 12″). The Metropolitan Museum of Art, New York, New York. Bequest of Jane Kendall Gingrich, 1982.

An object with rough texture becomes a focal point in a design of smooth textures.

Isolation. Artists sometimes use isolation to create a focal point and thereby emphasize one part of their work. They do this by putting one object alone, apart from all the other objects (Figure 12.8). This draws the viewer's eye to the isolated object.

Alice Neel. *Loneliness*. 1970. Oil on canvas. 203.2 × 96.5 cm (80 × 38″). Robert Miller Gallery, New York, New York. Collection, National Gallery of Art, Washington, D.C. The estate of Alice Neel.

LOOKING CLOSELY

FIGURE 12.8 Neel has isolated the red chair to make it the focal point in this painting. How does the black line help? What about the color? Notice line direction. The walls, the curtains, the window, the shade, and even the windows across the street are all drawn with static lines. What kind of lines do you see around the chair? Notice how the woodwork behind the chair has been blurred. Why do you think Neel did that?

FIGURE 12.9 The young woman appears to be in the center of this painting. If you measure, however, you will see that her head is to the left of the vertical axis and far above the horizontal axis. What devices has Morisot used to make the woman's face the center of interest?

Berthe Morisot. *In the Dining Room.* 1886. Oil on canvas. 61.3 × 50 cm (24⅛ × 19¾″). National Gallery of Art, Washington, D.C. Chester Dale Collection.

FIGURE 12.10 In this painting all the people are staring at the preacher and the girl. The viewer becomes one of the crowd and stares too. Can you find lines in this painting that are also pointing to the two figures?

John Steuart Curry. *Baptism in Kansas.* 1928. Oil on canvas. 101.6 × 127 cm (40 × 50″). Collection of Whitney Museum of American Art, New York, New York. Gift of Gertrude Vanderbilt Whitney.

Location. *Location* is another method used to create a focal point for emphasis. A viewer's eye is normally drawn toward the center of a visual area. Thus, something near this center will probably be noticed first. Because the exact center is a dull location, most artists place the objects they wish to emphasize a bit off center. They select a location a little to the left or right of center and a little above center (Figure 12.9).

Convergence. When many elements in a work point to one item, that item becomes the focal point. This technique, called convergence, can be created with a very obvious radial arrangement of lines. It can also be achieved through a more subtle arrangement of people who are staring and pointing at the point of emphasis (Figure 12.10).

The Unusual. In a work of art, an object that is out of the ordinary can become the focal point (Figure 12.11 on page 322). In a row of soldiers standing at attention, the one standing on his head will be noticed first. The unexpected will always draw the viewer's attention.

FIGURE 12.11 In this painting the artist has chosen a point of view that is at the eye level of the child. We see only the skirt and the hand of Ernesta's nurse.

Cecilia Beaux. *Ernesta (Child with Nurse).* 1894. Oil on canvas. 128.3 × 96.8 cm (50½ × 38⅛″). The Metropolitan Museum of Art, New York, New York. Maria DeWitt Jesup Fund, 1965.

Using Emphasis

1. Applying Your Skills. Collect a set of five magazine or newspaper advertisements that have a strong focal point. Identify the focal point in each.

2. Further Challenge. Make a series of small designs with strong focal points using each of the following: contrast of shape, contrast of color, contrast of value, contrast of texture, isolation, location, convergence, and the unusual.

3. Computer Option. Use the drawing tools of your choice to create a series of small designs with strong focal points, using each of the following: contrast of shape, contrast of color, contrast of value, contrast of texture, isolation, location, and convergence.

One advantage in using computers to create art is the ease with which images can be manipulated. You will be able to transform some designs to others by using the Fill Bucket tool. Others can be changed by using the Selection tool and rearranging the shapes. See if you can create all seven designs by starting with only three designs and making alterations to them. Save your work.

HARMONY

Harmony is *the principle of design that creates unity by stressing the similarities of separate but related parts.*

FIGURE 12.12 Notice how often Degas repeats round shapes in this work: the hats, the ring of flowers, the round-looking bows, the young woman's head, her bodice, and her skirt. He then creates a second harmony of vertical lines. He uses thin lines in the foreground and thick ones in the background.

Edgar Degas. *The Millinery Shop.* c. 1879–84. Oil on canvas. 100 × 110.7 cm (39⅜ × 43⅞"). Art Institute of Chicago, Chicago, Illinois. Mr. and Mrs. Lewis Larned Coburn Memorial Collection, 1933.

In musical harmony, related tones are combined into blended sounds. Harmony is pleasing because the tones complement each other. In visual harmony, related art elements are combined. The result looks pleasing because the elements complement each other.

Used in certain ways, color can produce harmony in a work of art. Repetition of shapes that are related, such as rectangles with different proportions, produces harmony (Figure 12.12). A design that uses only geometric shapes appears more harmonious than a design using both geometric and

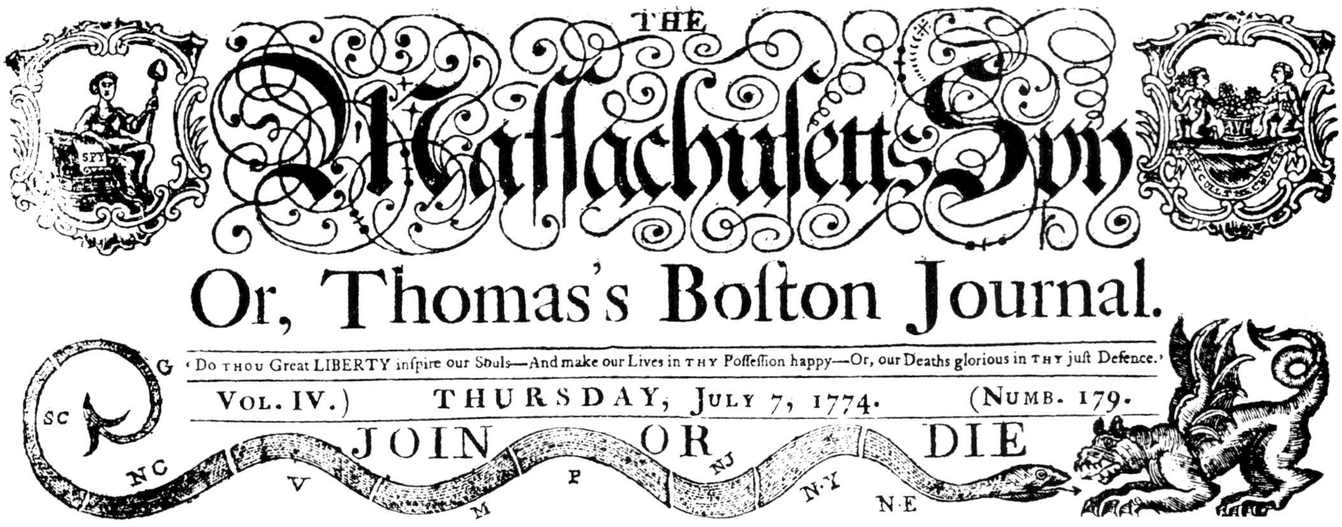

THE Massachusetts Spy Or, Thomas's Boston Journal.

'Do THOU Great LIBERTY inspire our Souls—And make our Lives in THY Possession happy—Or, our Deaths glorious in THY just Defence.'

VOL. IV.) THURSDAY, JULY 7, 1774. (NUMB. 179.

JOIN OR DIE

FIGURE 12.13 It is said that this cartoon was drawn by Ben Franklin. How did he use unity to convey his message? What do the parts of the snake symbolize?

Ben Franklin (attributed to). *Join or Die.* Cartoon. 1774. 5 × 7.25 cm (2 × 2⅞"). Courtesy of the Library of Congress, Washington, D.C.

free-form shapes. Even space used in a certain way can produce harmony. If all the parts in a work of art are different sizes, shapes, colors, and textures, the space between the parts can be made uniform to give the work a sense of order.

UNITY

Unity is oneness. It brings order to the world. Without it, the world would be chaotic.

Countries made up of smaller parts are political unities: the United States is such a country. Its fifty states are joined by a single federal government. As a whole unit, the United States is a world power far stronger than the combined power of the separate states (Figure 12.13).

A tree is an example of unity in nature. It is composed of roots, trunk, bark, branches, twigs, and leaves. Each part has a purpose that contributes to the living, growing tree. An electric lamp is a manufactured unit composed of a base, electric wire, sockets, bulbs, shades, and so on. All the separate parts of the lamp work together as a unified whole to provide light. If any part does not work, the unity of the lamp is impaired.

CREATING VISUAL UNITY

In art, **unity** is *the quality of wholeness or oneness that is achieved through the effective use of the elements and principles of art.* Unity is like an invisible glue. It joins all the separate parts so they look as if they belong together.

Unity is difficult to understand at first because it is not easily defined. It is a quality that you feel as you view a work of art (Figure 12.14). As you study a work, you may think that you would not change one element or object. When this happens, you are receiving an impression that the work is a unified whole.

Unity helps you concentrate on a visual image. You cannot realize how important this is until you study a work that lacks unity. Looking at a work that lacks unity is like trying to carry on a serious

FIGURE 12.14 Rodin created this monument to honor six citizens who gave their lives in 1347 to save the city of Calais, France. Rodin showed the six men getting ready to see the king, who was laying siege to the city. Rodin spent two years modeling faces and bodies to express the men's tension and pain. Each figure would be successful as an individual statue, but Rodin has place them so that unity results. The work was designed to be placed at street level, not on a pedestal above the heads of the people.

Auguste Rodin. *The Burghers of Calais*. 1886, cast 1930s. Bronze. 2 × 2 × 1.9 m (79⅜ × 80⅞ × 77⅛″). Hirshhorn Museum and Sculpture Garden, Smithsonian Institution, Washington, D.C. Gift of Joseph H. Hirshhorn, 1966.

discussion while your little sister is practicing the violin, your brother is listening to the stereo, and your mother is running the vacuum cleaner. It would be difficult to concentrate on your conversation with all these distractions. It is the same with a work of art that lacks unity. You can't concentrate on the work as a whole, because all the parts demand separate attention.

To create unity, an artist adjusts the parts of a work so they relate to each other. A potter adjusts

FIGURE 12.15 The decorations on these containers were created by drilling small holes into which short lengths of wire were inserted to form the various designs. The polished surface is the result of frequent handling and an occasional application of oil.

Possibly Thonga or Shona peoples. Mozambique and Zimbabwe. *Snuff Containers.* Hard fruit shell with copper, brass, and iron wire. Largest: 6 × 7.6 cm (2⅜ × 3″). National Museum of African Art, Smithsonian Institution, Washington, D.C. Acquisition Grant from the James Smithson Society.

FIGURE 12.16 The designer of these clothes travels around the world looking for fabrics with unusual colors and textures. She then designs and creates unique patterns for her wearable art.

Florence Bayless. *Haori Coat.* 1992. Silk peau de soir, Thai silk, and silk lamé. Private collection.

FIGURE 12.17 Johns combines the loose brushwork of Abstract Expressionism with the commonplace objects of American Realism. His map of the United States could be pulled apart by the wild action painting, but it is unified by the harmonious, limited color scheme of a primary triad.

Jasper Johns. *Map.* 1961. Oil on canvas. 198.2 × 312.7 cm (78 × 123⅛"). Collection, Museum of Modern Art, New York, New York. Gift of Mr. and Mrs. Robert C. Scull. © Jasper Johns/VAGA, New York 1994.

decorations on a bowl to complement the bowl's shape, size, and purpose (Figure 12.15). Clothing designers choose fabrics that complement the design and purpose of each outfit (Figure 12.16). Painters adjust the elements in a work to each other. A "busy" work with a variety of shapes and textures can be unified with a limited color scheme, for example (Figure 12.17).

Simplicity

Another way to create unity is through *simplicity.* Simplicity is not, however, easy to achieve. An artist must plan very carefully to create a good, simple design. This is done by limiting the number of variations of an element. The fewer variations the artist uses, the more unified the design will seem (Figure 12.18, page 328).

A painting in which the entire surface is covered with a single, even layer of one hue will appear strongly unified. A sculpture of a single person expresses a simple unity (Figure 12.19, page 328).

Repetition

The repetition of objects and elements can be an effective way to unify a work of art. Louise Nevelson's assemblages are a good example. As you know from reading Chapter 6, Nevelson collects objects that are not alike. This presents a problem of unity, which she solves in one or more ways. Often, she places the objects in a series of boxlike containers (Figure 12.20 on page 329). The boxes help to unify the work. She sometimes paints the entire structure the same color. Sometimes she repeats both container shape and color to unify her assemblages.

FIGURE 12.18 Carr has used simplification to eliminate the details of bark, grass, and leaves. The foliage seems to be solidified into diagonally flowing living forms.

Emily Carr. *Forest, British Columbia.* c. 1931–32. Oil on canvas. 129.5 × 86.4 cm (51 × 34″). Collection of Vancouver Art Gallery, Vancouver, British Columbia, Canada. Emily Carr Trust.

FIGURE 12.19 Why was it much easier for Barlach to unify this sculpture than it was for Rodin to unify *The Burghers of Calais* (Figure 12.14)?

Ernst Barlach. *Singing Man.* 1928. Bronze. 49.5 × 55.6 × 35.9 cm (19½ × 21⅞ × 14 ⅛″). Collection, The Museum of Modern Art, New York, New York. Abby Aldrich Rockefeller Fund.

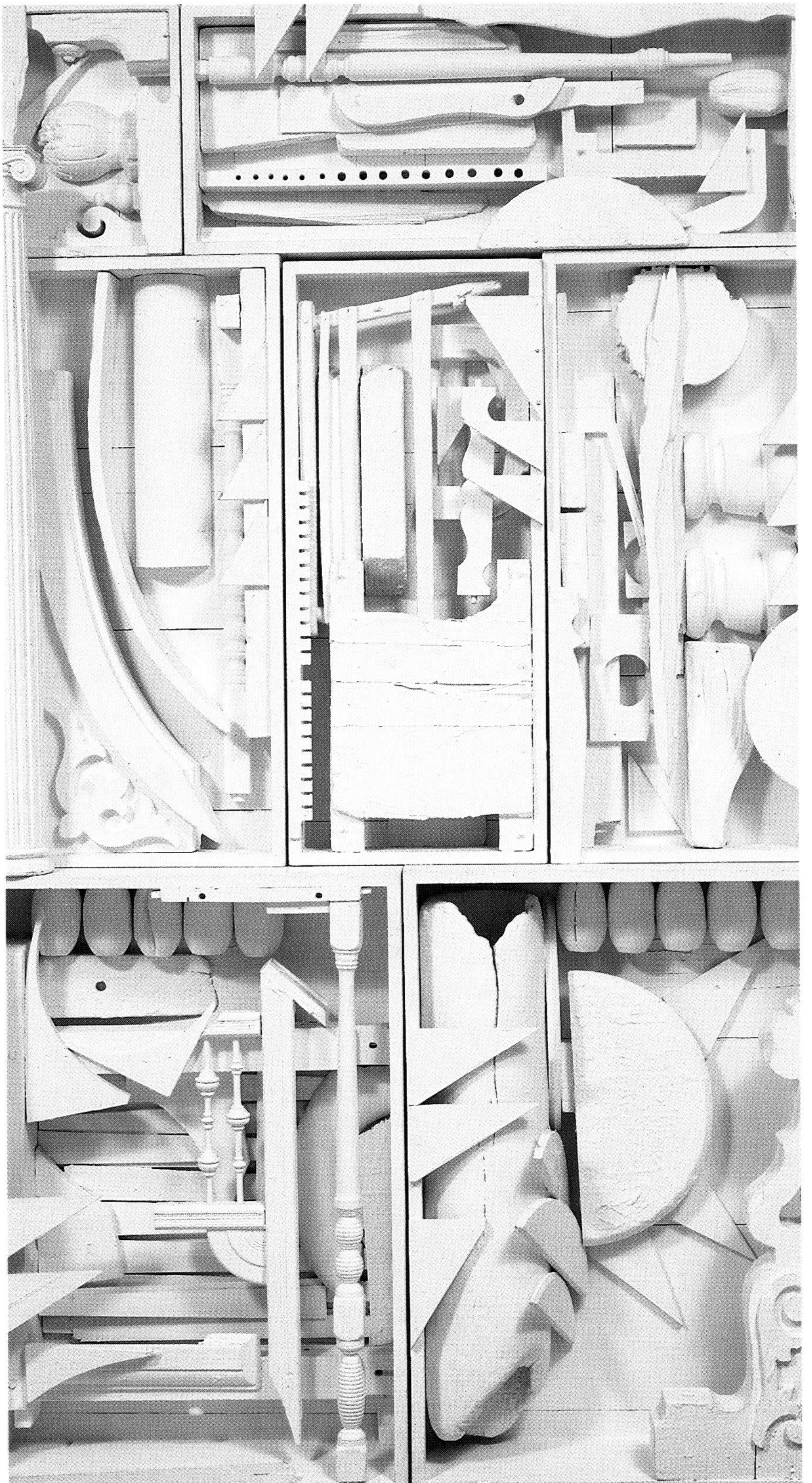

FIGURE 12.20 The use of one color and the repetition of the box shapes add to the unity of this work.

Louise Nevelson. *Dawn's Wedding Chapel I.* 1959. Wood painted white. 228 × 129 × 15 cm (90 × 51 × 6″). The Pace Gallery, New York, New York.

FIGURE 12.21 Wright was a genius who dared to be different. In 1936 he was asked to design a house close to this waterfall. Instead, he placed the house right over the falls. Terraces hang suspended over the running water. Even though they are made of reinforced concrete, the terraces repeat the shapes of the natural stone terraces below. The stones that make up the walls come from the building site, which ties the house more closely to its surroundings.

Frank Lloyd Wright. *Falling Water House. Bear Run, Pennsylvania.* 1936. Photography by Sandak, Inc., Stamford, Connecticut.

FIGURE 12.22 The artist has created unity by grouping the women and children close together. There is no negative space between the figures. Each one touches the next.

Élisabeth Vigée-Lebrun. *The Marquise de Peze and the Marquise de Rouget with Her Two Children.* 1787. Oil on canvas. 123.4 × 155.9 cm (48⅝ × 61⅜″). National Gallery of Art, Washington, D.C. Gift of the Bay Foundation in memory of Josephine Bay Paul and Ambassador Charles Ulrick Bay.

Georgia Mills Jessup. *Rainy Night, Downtown.* 1967. Oil on canvas. 112 × 122 cm (44 × 48″). National Museum of Women in the Arts, Washington, D.C.

LOOKING CLOSELY

FIGURE 12.23 Jessup has created a unified composition using many techniques. What has she simplified to unify the work? What has been repeated? Look for examples of proximity and continuity. Which area is the focal point of this work? How has the artist used variety? Notice the two people in the lower right of the work. Do you see any other hints of people in the work? What do you think the bright, round shapes represent?

Many architects are concerned with unity. Their goal is to design homes that blend with the land (Figure 12.21). They may use materials that repeat the colors and textures found in the home's environment. They may also use materials that reflect the surroundings. For instance, mirrored outside walls have been used on skyscrapers. The mirrors reflect the shapes and colors of the clouds and sky, and the buildings seem to blend with their surroundings and the atmosphere.

Proximity

Proximity, or closeness, is another way of unifying very different shapes in a work (Figures 12.22 and 12.23). This is achieved by limiting the negative space between the shapes. Clustering the shapes in this way suggests unity and coherence. The sense of unity can be made even stronger if the cluster of unlike items is surrounded by an area of negative space.

Continuation

Sometimes shapes can be arranged so that a line or edge of one shape continues as a line or edge of the next shape (Figure 12.24, page 332). This type of arrangement allows the viewer's eye to flow smoothly from one shape to the next along the continuing contour. This continuity links the different parts into a unified group.

Creating Unity

1. Applying Your Skills. Using any media you wish, create small designs to illustrate the following unifying devices: simplicity, harmony of color, harmony of shape, harmony through space, proximity, and continuation.

2. Further Challenge. Suppose you have been hired to create a window display for a gift shop that sells many unrelated objects. From magazines, cut out photographs of fifteen unrelated objects that represent the merchandise to be displayed. Use as many unifying techniques as you can to create the display. Draw the window and the design for the display and glue the cutouts where the objects would be placed in the design (Figure 12.25).

3. Computer Option. Create small designs to illustrate the following unifying devices: simplicity, harmony of color, harmony of shape, harmony through space, proximity, and continuation. Take advantage of your software tools and options to make this task easier. Can you use one illustration as the basis for another? Decide which tools and options you will need to make the necessary changes. Save your work.

FIGURE 12.24 Gris uses continuity to tie this composition together. Find out how many lines have been continued. Hold the straight edge of a ruler over a strong line direction to see how many times that line is continued throughout the painting.

Juan Gris. *Guitar and Flowers.* 1912. Oil on canvas. 112.1 × 70.2 cm (44⅛ × 27⅝"). Collection, The Museum of Modern Art, New York, New York. Bequest of Anna Erickson Levene in memory of her husband, Dr. Phoebus Aaron Theodor Levene.

HOW ARTISTS USE VARIETY, EMPHASIS, AND HARMONY TO ENHANCE UNITY

As you know, artists use variety, emphasis, and harmony to make their works more interesting and appealing. If carried to extremes, however, these principles can destroy the unity of a visual work. This means that artists must be careful to balance the contrasting qualities of variety and emphasis with harmonizing and unifying techniques to create a unified work.

Jane Wilson has successfully balanced the harmonizing and varying devices in *Solstice* (Figure 12.26). She has divided the work into two contrasting rectangles. The sky in the upper rectangle is painted with both light and dark values. The focal point of the work is the bright yellow glow of sunlight peeking through the dark clouds.

You cannot see any specific shapes in the water, shown in the lower rectangle, yet the sky is full of loose triangular shapes. These contrasting factors would pull the work apart if the artist had not used a harmonious color scheme. The entire work is composed of various values of blue, green, and yellow. She has simplified this work, showing nothing but clouds, sky, and water. She has tied the work together using repetition. The clear triangle of sky repeats the color of the water. The bright yellow of the sun is reflected along the edge of the clouds and in the water below. The active clouds are repetitions of loose triangular shapes. Without the repetitions and simple color scheme, this work might not be the unified composition that it is.

FIGURE 12.25 Student work. A unified window display.

FIGURE 12.26 Analyze the ways in which the artist has balanced the harmonizing and varying devices in this painting.

Jane Wilson. *Solstice.* 1991. Oil on linen. 152.4 × 178 cm (60 × 70″). Fischbach Gallery, New York, New York.

STUDIO LESSON: ASSEMBLAGE WITH HANDMADE PAPER

FIGURE 12.27 Lois Dvorak. *Spirit Boxes I*. 1985. Assemblage with handmade paper, construction paper, tree bark, colored pencils, pastels, and embroidery thread. 51 × 76.2 × 5.1 cm (20 × 30 × 2″). Private collection.

Spirit Boxes I is a mixed-media assemblage (Figure 12.27). The background is a sheet of paper Lois Dvorak made from cotton pulp. The swirling pattern is drawn with colored pencils and pastels. The dark tree shape is made from construction paper with pastel shading that continues the movement of the design in the background. The boxes are made from bark that was soaked and beaten into a very strong, thin paper, which was then glued and sewn together. Inside the boxes are bits of bark paper embroidered with colored threads. Notice that in some places the details in the boxes are unified with the background. Across the front of the boxes you can see very thin, transparent paper that has bits of homemade and construction paper glued in strategic places to unite the rhythmic repetition of the boxes.

Dvorak is always searching for little treasures in the environment to put in her spirit boxes, such as pieces of mica, yucca seeds, bits of bird eggshells, locust wings, hornet's nest paper, and dried-out lizards. Begin to think about how you can adapt Dvorak's techniques to your own assemblage.

Create a relief assemblage that contains symbols of your life. Each symbol should be protected in a handmade paper container just as Dvorak has protected each symbol in a spirit box. Use the principle of harmony to join the various symbols and containers into a unified composition. Use handmade papers, other papers, fabrics, fibers, and small found objects to construct the relief. Like Dvorak, add details using pencil, crayon, markers, and/or fibers.

Supplies

- Sketchbook and pencils
- Large strong sheet of paper for background
- Your own handmade paper
- Variety of paper and fabric
- Fibers and needles
- Personal symbols
- Other found materials
- White glue
- Scissors
- Pencils, markers, and/or crayons

FOCUSING

Study Dvorak's assemblage, *Spirit Boxes I.* She has used several different ways to unify her work. Notice how the forms of the spirit boxes are related. Observe how the paths that weave over and under each other in the background are alike, and most of the shapes between the paths are covered with an invented texture. The boxes are placed close to each other and are held together in the branches of the tree. Can you find other ways that the artist has created unity?

Brainstorm with your classmates about objects that can be used to symbolize aspects of your life.

CREATING

Working in small groups, make handmade paper to use in this project. See the instructions for making paper in Technique Tip 21 on page 356 in the Handbook. Plan the colors you will use when making the paper, because they will be some of the colors in your final project. Collect the other materials and symbolic objects you plan to use.

Make plans for your relief assemblage in your sketchbook. List and sketch the symbolic objects you will use and explain what each represents. Design the forms of the containers. Draw each container from two or more views. List the ways that you will use harmony to unify your project.

Draw several plans for your mixed-media relief. As you draw, think about the materials you will use for construction and how you will alter them using drawing or stitching materials. Choose the best design.

Plan the procedures you need to follow to construct your work and follow your plan. Prepare your finished product for display.

FIGURE 12.27A Student work.

CRITIQUING

Describe Explain the process, step by step, that you used to make paper. Describe the three-dimensional containers you made to hold the symbolic objects and explain how you constructed them.

Analyze Which elements did you emphasize in this project? List and describe the methods you used to create harmony. Does the work have visual rhythm? Describe.

Interpret Do the symbols you used represent only one part of your life or all of it? Are the symbols obvious or are they private and personal?

Judge Does your work have a strong sense of unity? Which of the aesthetic theories would you use to judge this work? What, if anything, would you change to give it more unity?

STUDIO LESSON: ENLARGE ONE FRAME FROM A COMIC STRIP

FIGURE 12.28 Roy Lichtenstein. *Blam.* 1962. Oil on canvas. 172.7 × 203.2 cm. (68 × 80″). Yale University Art Gallery, New Haven, Connecticut. Richard Brown Baker Collection.

Supplies

- One frame cut from a comic strip
- Sketchbook, pencils, tape
- Crayons or markers
- Large sheet of white paper
- Ruler and yardstick
- Soft eraser
- Acrylic or tempera paints and brushes
- Stipple brush (optional)

When Roy Lichtenstein's paintings appeared on the scene in the early 1960s, art critics assumed that he had copied his work from the comics. Lichtenstein does not copy his subject matter. He starts with reality and then uses his excellent sense of design to reorganize the original elements into a very well-organized, strong composition (Figure 12.28). He calls what he does "quotation."

The source of his first painting was not comic strips, but bubble-gum wrappers that Lichtenstein got from his children. He continued by doing a series based on different comics. The use of strong black lines, limited color schemes, and dot patterns make his work instantly recognizable. The dots represented the benday dots used in comic strips to create light values or mixed colors.

Observe Lichtenstein's techniques and think about the comic strips you see in your daily newspaper. Consider how you can use these techniques to create your own adaptation.

Select one frame from your favorite comic strip and, in the style of Roy Lichtenstein, reorganize and redraw it. Use harmony to improve the composition of the original frame employing repetition, simplification, and continuation of line to make it a stronger, more unified work. To keep it interesting, add variety through the use of emphasis.

FOCUSING

Study Lichtenstein's painting *Blam*. It looks like he copied a comic strip frame, but what he did was use the comic strip as the subject matter for his painting. Lichtenstein simplified the original. He omitted all the writing except *BLAM* and the numeral 3. He limited the colors to the three primaries. He repeated curved shapes such as the ovals used in the nose of the airplane and the cockpit. He has used line continuation in several places. For example, the bottom line of the wing on the right is continued in the bold, black line of the yellow explosion on the left. All the positive shapes are smooth, but the negative spaces in the background have been textured in an exaggerated imitation of the dots used to print color.

CREATING

Select one frame from your favorite comic strip, with or without color. Tape the original frame into the corner of a page in your sketchbook. With a ruler, draw a rectangle the same proportions as the original. Sketch a more unified version of the original in your rectangle. Use different methods of emphasis for variety. Make several variations of the original design. Choose the strongest, most unified composition for your final work.

Select a limited color scheme that enhances the expressive feeling of your composition. Test it in your sketchbook using crayons or markers. Plan areas of light value.

Enlarge the composition you have selected onto a large sheet of white paper using a grid. (See Technique Tip 8 on page 352 in the Handbook.) Make the final composition as large as possible.

Paint your work following the plan you made in your sketchbook. To create textured areas of light value, use stippling. Be sure to practice stippling before you use it in your final composition. Prepare your finished work for display.

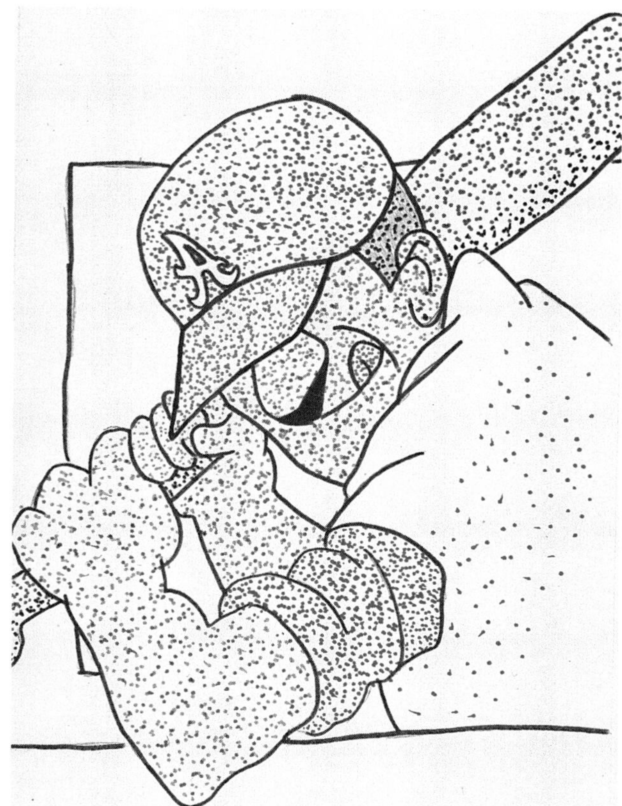

FIGURE 12.28A Student work.

CRITIQUING

Describe Name the comic strip you used for this project. List the objects in the frame you selected and then list the things you eliminated in your final composition.

Analyze Explain how you used repetition, simplification, and line continuation to create harmony. Describe how you used emphasis.

Interpret Did you change the expressive effect of the comic strip frame when you made the composition stronger and more unified? If so, how? Give this work an expressive title.

Judge Which aesthetic theories would you use to judge this work? If you were to do this one more time, what would you change?

STUDIO LESSON: CLAY SCULPTURE UNIFYING TWO IDEAS

FIGURE 12.29 Artist unknown. Folk art from the town of Acallan, State of Puebla, Mexico. *Fiesta Rodeo.* 1975. Ceramic with nichrome wire and acrylic paint. 55.8 × 33 × 33 cm (22 × 13 × 13″). Private collection.

Supplies

- Sketchbook and pencil
- Clay and clay tools
- Slip and brush
- Cloth-covered clay board
- Plastic bags
- Glaze or acrylic paint (optional)

Contemporary Mexican folk artists do not sign their work individually. The piece shown in Figure 12.29 comes from the town of Acallan in the State of Puebla in Mexico.

What makes this particular work so unusual is that the artist has taken two themes that are not really related and tied them together by using a balance between harmony and variety. The artist took two different themes of celebration: the secular rodeo and the religious tree of life, and carefully organized the elements of art so that the two themes merged into a unified whole. The rodeo is a worldly event. The tree of life represents the tree in the Garden of Eden from which Adam and Eve gained knowledge.

Notice how the artist has used contrast. The negative spaces in the rodeo fence are small rectangles, but when your eyes move up to the tree area the lines explode into active, blossoming curves.

Observe the ways in which the two themes have been related in this sculpture and think about how you will relate two themes.

Like the Mexican folk artist who combined two different themes in the sculpture, *Fiesta Rodeo,* you will create a clay sculpture that combines two unrelated objects. Create unity in your work by using a balance between variety and harmony. Use some of the following harmonizing techniques: simplification, repetition, proximity, and continuation. To help you tie the two parts together, use emphasis of an element and/or emphasis of an area.

FOCUSING

Study *Fiesta Rodeo.* Notice how the artist has unified two different themes. In your sketchbook describe how the artist has used a balance between variety and harmony to create unity. List which elements are the most important and explain why. Discuss your findings with your classmates.

Brainstorm with your classmates about different themes or objects that could be unified in a sculpture as the artist has done with *Fiesta Rodeo.* Think of your favorite school subject, your favorite after-school activity, or a hobby. Write the two ideas in your sketchbook. Make verbal and visual notes about how you could create your sculpture. Make some sketches based on your ideas. Choose your best idea. List the harmonizing techniques you want to use and which elements you will use. Then list the way you will use emphasis.

CREATING

Construct your sculpture. For proper clay construction techniques see Technique Tip 16 on page 354 in the Handbook. Between work sessions, cover your sculpture tightly with a plastic bag so the clay does not dry. When you are finished with construction, cover your work loosely so the clay does not dry too quickly. Remember that thin clay will dry and shrink more quickly than thick clay, so cover thin areas very carefully.

FIGURE 12.29A Student work.

When your work is bone dry, fire it in the kiln. After your sculpture is fired, you may decorate it by glazing and glaze firing the piece or painting it with acrylic paints. Prepare your work for display.

CRITIQUING

Describe List the two different themes or objects you combined in your sculpture. Describe the clay-building techniques you used to construct your work. How did you prepare your work for display?

Analyze Which harmonizing techniques did you use to unify your work? Describe how you used emphasis to pull the piece together visually. Does your finished product look unified?

Interpret What is the expressive effect of your sculpture? Give your work an expressive title. Write a poem or a brief paragraph about your sculpture that expresses your feelings toward this work.

Judge Which aesthetic theories would you use to judge this work? If you were to do this over, what would you change?

STUDIO LESSON: DESIGNING A MURAL

FIGURE 12.30 John Yancy. *Celebration of Arts: Vibrations of Life.* 1991. Permanent exterior mural, acrylic on panels. 2.4 × 9.7 m (8′ × 32′). Located at 1531 West 60th Street, Chicago, Illinois.

Supplies

- Sketchbook, pencil, and ruler
- Photograph of proposed site
- Enlarged photocopy of photograph
- Large sheet of white paper
- Tempera or acrylic paints
- Brushes

John Yancy received his first mural commission during his senior year in high school. He liked murals because of their scale and visibility. During his studies at The Art Institute of Chicago, he began to realize that murals inform, enlighten, and motivate people. His *Celebration of the Arts* mural depicts the programs and contributions of the Boulevard Art Center and expresses the excitement and vitality of all the visual and performing arts (Figure 12.30). The patterns on the mural portray textile designs that are seen in the masquerade ceremonies of the Yoruba people of Africa. The dancers in the mural function as dynamic, formal elements to increase movement and drama. The mural was completed with the help of a small crew of 16- to 20-year-old participants who had exhibited interest in a career in the arts.

Yancy created the mural to let people know what was going on in the Center. Notice which elements he used to create variety and which ones he used to create harmony in the composition so that the mural became a unified whole.

Design and create a presentation painting of a mural for a specific site. Yancy used the events in the building as a theme for his mural. Choose a theme and design a mural by using subject matter that is linked to the site. Use a balance between the principles of variety, emphasis, and harmony to create a unified composition. Make your final painting to scale.

FIGURE 12.30A Student work.

FOCUSING

Brainstorm with classmates about sites and themes for your mural designs. Decide whether you all want to work on the same theme such as the environment or the history of the community, or whether you all want to use independent themes. Then find an interesting site for your mural and choose your individual idea. Think of the subject matter you will use to express your theme.

CREATING

Photograph your site and enlarge the photograph using a photocopier. Measure the area of the photocopy on which you will place your mural. Make some rough sketches in your sketchbook. Create a unified composition by balancing the varying and unifying techniques. Because this is a plan for a large mural, you may not want to have a single focal point; you may decide to create several centers of interest. Plan your color scheme.

Select your best idea and draw it carefully with pencil on the measured area of the photocopy. Enlarge your mural plan, to scale, onto a large sheet of white paper. See Technique Tip 8 on page 352 of the Handbook for directions on using a grid to enlarge a work to scale. Paint the enlarged presentation drawing.

Arrange a display that includes the photograph, the enlarged photocopy with the drawing for the mural, the presentation painting, and a brief written statement that explains your theme, the subject matter, and why you selected them for that specific site.

CRITIQUING

Describe Tell the theme, the subject matter, and the site you selected for your mural.

Analyze Explain which principles of design you used to create a unified composition. Explain which color scheme you chose and why you chose it.

Interpret What kind of a mood does your mural express? How do you think the mural would affect the site for which it was planned? Give your work an expressive title.

Judge Which aesthetic theories would you use to judge this mural? What, if anything, would you change before you painted it on the final site?

ART CRITICISM IN ACTION

FIGURE 12.31 Wayne Thiebaud. *Apartment Hill.* 1980. Oil on linen. 165.1 × 122 cm (65 × 48″). Nelson-Atkins Museum of Art, Kansas City, Missouri. Acquired through the generosity of the Friends of Art and Nelson Gallery Foundation.

CRITIQUING THE WORK

1. **Describe** Read the credit line for Figure 12.31. What is the size of this work? Describe the subject matter. Do you see any people?
2. **Analyze** Has Thiebaud created a unified composition? Which elements has he used to produce harmony? Which ones were used to introduce variety? Do you see the principle of emphasis? If you see a focal point, where is it? How did he create it?
3. **Interpret** What message is the artist trying to express in this work? Write a brief paragraph explaining your interpretation.

FIGURE 12.32 Rembrandt. *The Mill.* c. 1650. Oil on canvas. 87.6 × 105.6 cm (34½ × 41⅝″). National Gallery of Art, Washington, D.C. Widener Collection.

4. Judge Do you think this is a successful work of art? Use one or more of the three aesthetic theories explained in Chapter 2 to defend your opinion.

COMPARING THE WORKS

Look at Thiebaud's *Apartment Hill* (Figure 12.31). Now study Rembrandt's *The Mill* (Figure 12.32). Compare the two works. List the similarities and differences. Notice the color schemes, the architectural structures, transportation, and the treatment of the land masses. Notice how each artist has used isolation to create a focal point. What other principles can you find that have been used in the same way by each artist?

FYI *The Mill* is considered Rembrandt's greatest landscape painting. Many myths were told about this work. One was that it belonged to Rembrandt's father. Another was that the dark, gloomy sky was foretelling Rembrandt's financial difficulties. In truth, the sky was gloomy because the varnish had yellowed. The recent restoration of the painting has revealed the blue sky you see in this reproduction.

MEET THE ARTIST

WAYNE THIEBAUD

American, b. 1920

Wayne Thiebaud, one of California's most famous painters, has earned as many awards for excellence in teaching as he has for his painting and printmaking. He became interested in drawing in high school and later worked as a freelance cartoonist and illustrator. He continued his artwork during military service in World War II, drawing cartoons for the military base newspaper.

In 1949 he decided to become a painter. His first one-person show in New York was praised by the critics. At that time his subject matter was mass-produced consumer goods, particularly junk food, and he was considered a Pop artist. Later he became classified as an American Realist.

Since the 1970s he has concentrated on the urban landscapes of San Francisco. His primary concern is changing realistic subject matter into abstract compositions. He turns cakes into circles and figures into arrangements of spheres, triangles, and cylinders. Today Thiebaud lives and works in Sacramento and San Francisco and transforms street scenes into compositions of arcs, cubes, and networks of lines. He creates compositions that symbolize the essence of San Francisco by simplifying forms.

MORE PORTFOLIO IDEAS

I. Collect images that symbolize a place you know well. Organize them into a collage that expresses the essence of the place. Photocopy the collage into a black-and-white composition. Then, using a simple color scheme, paint the copy of your collage. Which looks better, the original collage or the painted photocopy?

II. Make some sketches of objects that symbolize your community. Then decide which abstract elements such as lines, shape, and colors symbolize your community. Create a painting simplifying details of the objects in a composition that emphasizes the abstract qualities you selected.

CHAPTER 12 REVIEW

Building Vocabulary

On a separate sheet of paper, write the term that best matches each definition below.

1. The principle of design concerned with difference, or contrast.
2. The principle of design that makes one part of a work dominant over the other parts.
3. The first part of a work to attract the attention of the viewer.
4. The principle of design that creates unity by stressing the similarities of separate but related parts.
5. The quality of wholeness or oneness that is achieved through the effective use of the elements of art and the principles of design.

Reviewing Art Facts

Answer the following questions using complete sentences.

1. Name the two major types of visual emphasis.
2. What word is used to describe an element that is made the most important element in a comparison?
3. What must an artist consider when creating a focal point?
4. Name the five ways in which artists create a focal point.
5. Name four techniques that artists use to create unity in a work of art.

Thinking Critically About Art

1. **Analyze.** Rembrandt is known for his many self-portraits. Look through this book and list the self-portraits you find. You will have to look at the works themselves. The titles of Figures 1.1, page 4,and Figure 3.1 on page 40 do not tell you that the works are self-portraits. What do the self-portraits tell you about the different artists?
2. **Synthesize.** Artists from the past, such as Rembrandt, are easy to classify as a member of a school or movement. Contemporary artists, such as Wayne Thiebaud, move through several movements before they are finally classified. Certain artists, like Picasso, are never classified. Write a brief paper explaining why artists from the past are easy to classify, while twentieth-century artists are so difficult to classify. Select at least two artists to use as examples. Give your opinion on whether or not classifying an artist is important.
3. **Analyze.** Look through the other chapters of this book to find three examples of works in which the artist has emphasized one element, making all the others subordinate to it. List the works and explain which element has been emphasized.

Making Art Connections

1. **Music.** Do the principles of variety, emphasis, harmony, and unity play an important role in music? Bring a recording to class that illustrates each of the principles you consider important. Play it for the class and explain how the principles are used in the piece you selected.
2. **Language Arts.** Which principles of design are important in the creation of poetry? Create a poem that illustrates at least one principle discussed in this chapter. Share it with classmates.
3. **Social Studies.** Is this world moving toward a unified planet? Write a brief paper explaining your conclusions. Cite examples from ancient history, from one hundred years ago, and from the things that are happening today.
4. **Math.** Do you find examples in mathematics where unity and variety are important? Explain.

Elena Bonafonte Vidotto. *Eggs.* (Detail.) 1977. Oil on panel. 25.4 × 30.5 cm (10 × 12″). National Museum of Women in the Arts, Washington, D.C. Gift of Wallace and Wilhelmina Holladay.

TECHNIQUE TIPS HANDBOOK

In the past, a young person who wished to become an artist had to spend time as an apprentice to a master artist. The first assignment given to the beginner was to prepare art materials for the use of the artist.

No one taught the apprentice how to appreciate art or how to use the elements of art and the principles of design. The student learned by listening and observing. If the apprentice did not learn to handle the media of art correctly, the art career was discontinued.

This unit is a reference unit. It is here to help you use the media of art. It is a collection of helpful suggestions for using a variety of tools and techniques. By referring to the information in this Handbook as you prepare your Activities and Studio Lessons, you will sharpen your skills and master the techniques needed for creating successful art projects.

TECHNIQUE TIPS HANDBOOK

TABLE OF CONTENTS

DRAWING TIPS

1. Making Contour Drawings

When you make a contour drawing, your eye and hand must move at the same time. You must look at the object, not at your drawing. You must imagine that your pencil is touching the edge of the object as your eye follows the edge. Don't let your eye get ahead of your hand. Also, do not lift your pencil from the paper. When you move from one area to the next, let your pencil leave a trail. If you do lift your pencil accidentally, look down, place your pencil where you stopped, and continue.

a. To help you coordinate your eye-hand movement, try this: First, tape your paper to the table so it will not slide around. Then, hold a second pencil in your nondrawing hand and move it around the edges of the object. With your drawing hand, record the movement.

b. If you have trouble keeping your eyes from looking at the paper, ask a friend to hold a piece of stiff paper between your eyes and your drawing hand so the drawing paper is blocked from view. You might also place your drawing paper inside a large paper bag turned sideways. A third method is to put the object on a chair and place the chair on a table. When you are standing, the object should be at your eye level. Then, place your drawing paper on the table directly under the chair. In this way you will be unable to see the paper easily.

c. When you draw without looking at the paper, your first sketches will look strange. Don't be discouraged. The major purpose of blind contour drawing is to teach you to concentrate on directions and curves. The more you practice, the more accurate your drawings will become.

d. As you develop your skills, remember that in addition to edges, contours also define ridges. Notice the wrinkles you see at the joints of fingers and at a bent wrist or bent elbow. Those wrinkles are curved lines. Draw them carefully; the lines you use to show these things will add the look of roundness to your drawing.

e. After you have made a few sketches, add pressure as you draw to vary the thickness and darkness of your lines. Some lines can be emphasized and some can be made less important through the right amount of pressure from your hand.

2. Making Gesture Drawings

Unlike contour drawings, which show an object's outline, gesture drawings show movement. They should have no outlines or details.

a. Using the side of a piece of unwrapped crayon or a pencil, make scribble lines that build up the shape of the object. Do not use single lines that create stick figures.

b. Work very quickly. When drawing people, do the head, then the neck, and then fill in the body. Pay attention to the direction in which the body leans.

c. Next, scribble in the bulk of the legs and the position of the feet.

d. Finally, add the arms.

3. Drawing Calligraphic Lines with a Brush

Mastering the technique of drawing with flowing, calligraphic lines takes practice. You will need a round watercolor brush and either watercolor paint or ink. First, practice making very thin lines.

a. Dip your brush in the ink or paint and wipe the brush slowly on the side of the ink bottle until the bristles form a point.

b. Hold the brush at the metal ferrule so the brush is vertical rather than slanted above the paper. Imagine that the brush is a pencil with a very sharp point—if you press down, you will break the point (Figure T.1).

FIGURE T.1

c. Touch the paper lightly with the tip of the brush and draw a line.

d. When you are able to control a thin line, you are ready to make calligraphic lines. Start with a thin line and gradually press the brush down to make the line thicker. Pull up again to make it thinner (Figure T.2, page 350). Practice making lines that vary in thickness.

TECHNIQUE TIPS

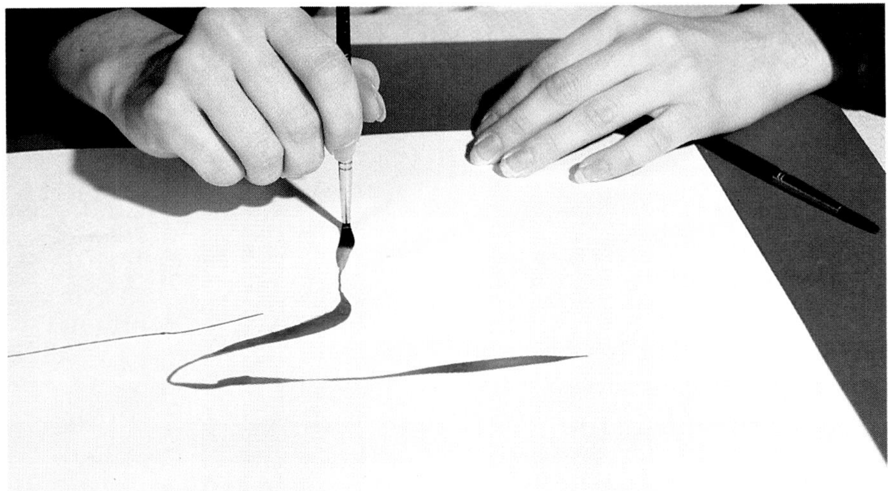

FIGURE T.2

4. Using Shading Techniques

The following techniques help create shading values.

- **Hatching:** Use a series of fine parallel lines.
- **Crosshatching:** Use two or more intersecting sets of parallel lines.
- **Blending:** Use a smooth, gradual application of an increasingly dark value. Pencil lines may be blended.
- **Stippling:** Create shading with dots.

To be effective in forming the shaded areas, your lines and strokes must follow the form of the object. Use lines to show the surface of a flat surface. Let the lines run parallel to one edge of the surface. To show a curved surface, draw a series of parallel curved lines to give the illusion of roundness. The lines should follow the curve of the object.

Lines or dots placed close together create dark values. Lines or dots spaced farther apart create lighter values. To show a gradual change from light to dark, begin with lines or dots far apart and bring them closer together. (Figure T.3.)

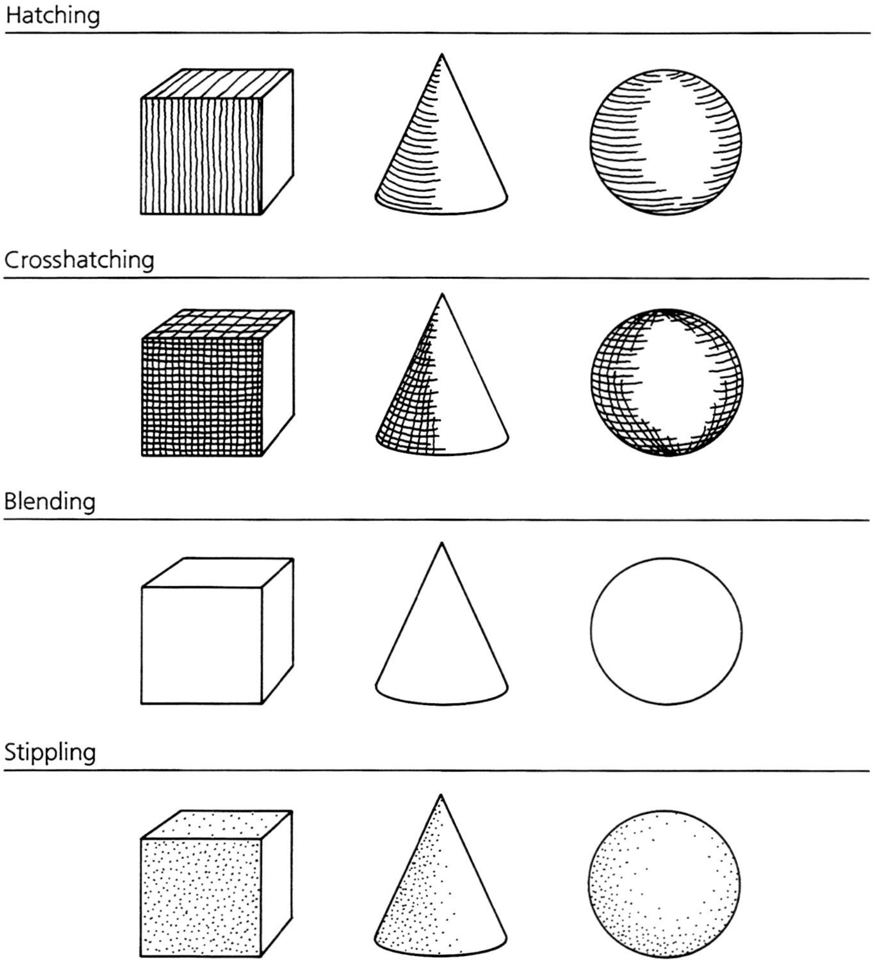

Hatching

Crosshatching

Blending

Stippling

FIGURE T.3

5. Using Sighting Techniques

Sighting is a method that will help you determine proportions.

a. Hold a pencil vertically at arm's length in the direction of the object you are drawing. Close one eye and focus on the object you are going to measure.

b. Slide your thumb along the pencil until the height of the pencil above your thumb matches the height of the object (Figure T.4).

c. Now, without moving your thumb or bending your arm,

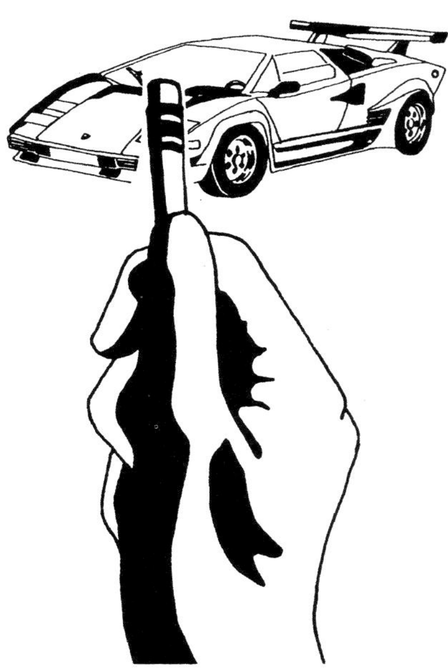

FIGURE T.4

hold the pencil parallel to the widest part of the object. Compare the height of the object with its width. You can determine the ratio of height to width by seeing how many times the smaller measure fits into the larger measure. This method can be applied either to different parts of the same object or to two or more different objects. Use one measurement as a base measurement and see how the other measurements relate to it.

6. Using a Viewing Frame

A viewing frame helps you to zero in on an area or object you intend to draw. To make a viewing frame, do the following:

a. Cut a rectangular hole in a heavy sheet of paper (Figure T.5).

b. Hold the frame at arm's length and look through it at your subject. Imagine that the opening represents your drawing paper.

c. You can decide how much of the subject you want to include in your drawing by moving the frame up, down, or sideways.

d. You can also move the frame closer or farther away to change the focus of your drawing.

7. Using a Ruler

There are times when you need to draw a crisp, straight line.

a. Hold the ruler with one hand and the pencil with the other.

b. Place the ruler where you wish to draw a straight line.

c. Hold the ruler with your thumb and first two fingers. Be careful that your fingers do not stick out beyond the edge of the ruler.

d. Press heavily on the ruler so it will not slide while you're drawing.

e. Hold the pencil lightly against the ruler.

f. Pull the pencil quickly and lightly along the edge of the ruler. The object is to keep the ruler from moving while the pencil moves along its edge.

FIGURE T.5

TECHNIQUE TIPS

8. Making a Grid for Enlarging

Sometimes you must take a small drawing and enlarge it. To do this, you must first measure the size that the large, finished drawing will be. Then, using proportional ratios, reduce that size to something you can work with.

a. For example: If you want to cover a wall 5 feet high and 10 feet wide, let 1 inch equal 1 foot. Then make a scale drawing that is 5 inches high and 10 inches wide. You may work either in inches or centimeters.

b. After you have completed your small drawing, draw vertical and horizontal grid lines 1 inch apart on the drawing. Number the squares (Figure T.6).

c. On the wall, draw vertical and horizontal grid lines one foot apart.

d. Number the squares on the wall to match the squares on the paper and enlarge the plan by filling one square at a time.

9. Measuring Rectangles

Do you find it hard to create perfectly formed rectangles? Here is a way of getting the job done:

a. Make a light pencil dot near the long edge of a sheet of paper. With a ruler, measure the exact distance between the dot and the edge. Make three more dots the same distance in from the edge. (See Figure T.7.)

b. Line a ruler up along the dots. Make a light pencil line running the length of the paper.

c. Turn the paper so that a short side is facing you. Make four pencil dots equally distant from the short edge. Connect these with a light pencil rule. Stop when you reach the first line you drew.

d. Do the same for the remaining two sides. Erase any lines that may extend beyond the box you have made.

e. Trace over the lines with your ruler and pencil. The box you have created wil be a perfectly formed rectangle.

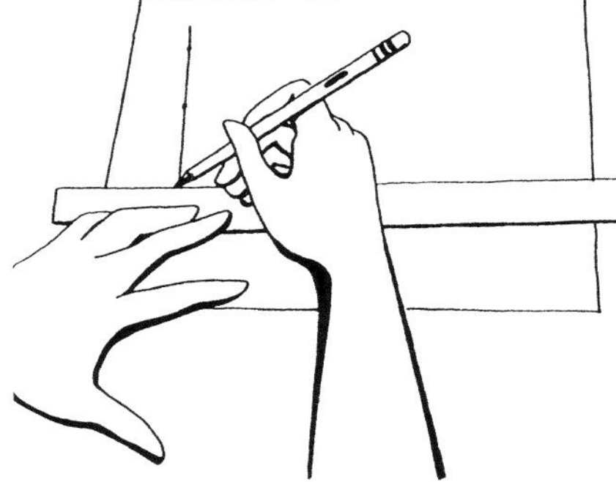

FIGURE T.7

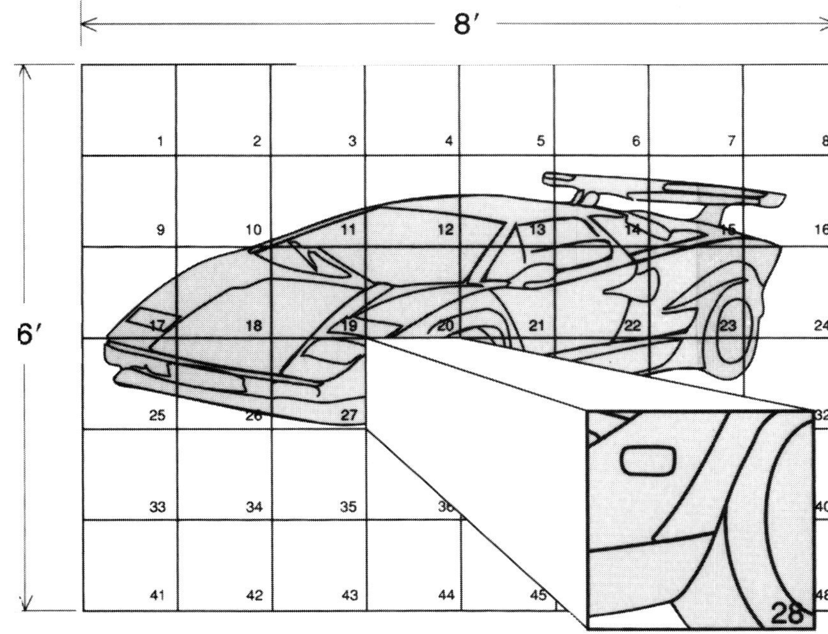

FIGURE T.6

PAINTING TIPS

10. Mixing Paint to Change the Value of Color

You can better control the colors in your work when you mix your own paint. In mixing paints, treat opaque paints (for example, tempera) differently from transparent paints (for example, watercolors).

a. *For light values of opaque paints.* Add only a small amount of the hue to white. The color can always be made stronger by adding more of the hue.

b. *For dark values of opaque paints.* Add a small amount of black to the hue. Never add the hue to black.

c. *For light values of transparent paints.* Thin a shaded area with water. This allows more of the white paper to show through.

d. *For dark values of transparent paints.* Carefully add a small amount of black to the hue.

11. Making Natural Earth Pigment Paints

Anywhere there is dirt, clay, and sand, you can find natural earth pigments.

a. Collect as many different kinds of earth colors as you can find (Figure T.8).

FIGURE T.8

b. Grind them as finely as possible. If you can, borrow a mortar and pestle from the science lab (Figure T.9). Regardless of the method you use, your finished product will still be a little gritty. It will not have the smooth texture of commercial pigment.

c. For the binder, use one part white glue to one part water. Put a few spoons of pigment into a small container and add some of the binder. Experiment with different proportions of pigment and binder.

FIGURE T.9

d. When you have found the best proportion, apply the mixture to paper with a variety of brushes. Do not allow the brushes you use to dry before you wash them, because the glue will solidify.

e. Keep stirring your paint as you work to keep the pigment from settling. The pigment will keep indefinitely. Mix a fresh batch each time you paint, because the mixed paint is difficult to store for more than a few days.

12. Working with Watercolors

Here are some tips to control watercolor paints.

a. If you apply wet paint to damp paper, you create lines and shapes with soft edges.

b. If you apply wet paint to dry paper, you create lines and shapes with sharp, clear edges.

c. If you dip a dry brush into damp paint and then brush across dry paper, you achieve a fuzzy effect.

d. School watercolors come in semi-moist cakes. Before you use them, place a drop of water on each cake to let the paint soften. Watercolor paints are transparent. You can see the white paper through the paint. If you want a light value of a hue, dilute the paint with a large amount of water. If you want a bright hue, you must dissolve more pigment by swirling your brush around in the cake of paint until you have dissolved a great deal of paint. The paint you apply to the paper can be as bright as the paint in the cake.

13. Cleaning a Paint Brush

Rinsing a paint brush under running water will not clean it completely. Paint will remain inside the bristles and cause the brush to lose its shape. Use the following procedure to help your brushes last a long time.

a. Rinse the thick paint out of the brush under running water.

b. Do not use hot water. Gently "paint" the brush over a cake of mild soap or dip it into a mild liquid detergent (Figure T.10).

c. Gently scrub the brush in the palm of your hand to work the soap into the center of the brush. This will remove paint that you did not realize was still in the brush (Figure T.11).

d. Rinse the brush under running water while you continue to scrub your palm.

e. Repeat steps b, c, and d.

FIGURE T.10

FIGURE T.11

FIGURE T.12

f. When your brush is thoroughly rinsed, shape it into a point with your fingers (Figure T.12).

g. Place the brush in a container with the bristles up so it will keep its shape as it dries.

PRINTMAKING TIP

14. Making a Stamp Print

A stamp print is an easy way to make repetitive designs. The following are a few suggestions for making a stamp and printing with it. You may develop some other ideas after reading these hints. Remember, printing reverses your design, so if you use letters, be certain to cut or carve them backward.

- Cut a simple design into the flat surface of a rubber eraser with a knife that has a fine, precision blade.
- Glue yarn to a bottle cap or a jar lid.
- Glue found objects to a piece of corrugated cardboard. Make a design with paperclips, washers, nuts, leaves, feathers, or anything else you can find. Whatever object you use should have a fairly flat surface. Make a handle for the block with masking tape.
- Cut shapes out of a piece of inner tube material. Glue the shapes to a piece of heavy cardboard.

There are several ways to apply ink or paint to a stamp:

- Roll water-base printing ink on the stamp with a soft brayer.
- Roll water-base printing ink on a plate and press the stamp into the ink.
- Apply tempera paint or school acrylic to the stamp with a bristle brush.

SCULPTING TIPS

15. Working with Clay

To make your work with clay go smoothly, always do the following:

a. Dip one or two fingers in water.

b. Spread the moisture from your fingers over your palms.

Never dip your hands in water. Too much moisture turns clay into mud.

16. Joining Clay

Use these methods for joining clay.

a. First, gather the materials you will need. These include clay, slip (a creamy mixture of clay and water), brush, a scoring tool (such as a fork), and clay tools.

b. Rough up or scratch the two surfaces to be joined (Figure T.13).

c. Apply slip to one of the two surfaces using a brush or your fingers (Figure T.14).

d. Gently press the two surfaces together so the slip oozes out of the joining seam (Figure T.15).

e. Using clay tools and/or your fingers, smooth away the slip that has oozed out of the seam (Figure T.16). You may wish to smooth out the seam as well,

FIGURE T.13

FIGURE T.14

FIGURE T.15

FIGURE T.16

or you may wish to leave it for decorative purposes.

17. Making a Pinch Pot

To make a pot using the pinch method, do the following:

- **a.** Make a ball of clay by rolling it between your palms until it is round.
- **b.** Set it on the working surface and make a hole in the top by pushing both thumbs into the clay. Stop pushing before your thumbs reach the bottom.
- **c.** Begin to pinch the walls between your thumb and fingers, rotating the pot as you pinch.
- **d.** Continue pinching and shaping the walls of the pot until they are an even thickness and the pot is the desired shape.

18. Using the Coil Technique

Collect all the materials you will need. These include clay, a cloth-covered board, slip and brush, scoring tool, small bowl of water, and pattern for a circular base.

- **a.** Make a base by flattening a piece of clay to about ½ inch thick. Using the pattern as a guide, cut the base into a circle.
- **b.** Begin a clay coil by shaping a small ball of clay into a long roll on the cloth-covered board until the roll is about ½ inch thick (Figure T.17). Your hands should be damp so the clay remains damp.
- **c.** Make a circle around the edge of the clay base with the roll of clay. Cut the ends on a diagonal and join them so the seam does not show. Using scoring and slip, join this first coil to the base.
- **d.** Make a second coil. If you want the pot to curve outward, place the second coil on the outer edge of the first coil. Place coil on the inner edge for an inward curve. Use proper joining techniques for all coils.

FIGURE T.17

19. Papier-Mâché

Papier-mâché is a French term that means mashed paper. It refers to sculpting methods that use paper and liquid paste. The wet paper and paste material are molded over supporting structures such as a wad of dry paper or crumpled foil. The molded paper dries to a hard finish. The following are the three basic methods for working with papier-mâché.

Pulp Method

- **a.** Shred newspaper, paper towels, or tissue paper into tiny pieces and soak them in water overnight. (Do not use slick magazine paper as it will not soften.)
- **b.** Mash the paper in a strainer to remove the water or wring it out in a piece of cloth.
- **c.** Mix the mashed paper with prepared paste or white glue until the material is the consistency of soft clay. Use the mixture to model small shapes.
- **d.** When papier-mâché is dry, it can be sanded, and holes can be drilled through it.

Strip Method

- **a.** Tear paper into strips.
- **b.** Either dip the strips in a thick mixture of paste or rub paste on the strips with your fingers. Decide which method works best for you.
- **c.** Use wide strips to cover wide forms. Very thin strips will lie flat on a small shape.
- **d.** If you do not want the finished work to stick to the support structure, first cover the form with plastic wrap or a layer of wet newspaper strips. If you are going to remove the papier-mâché from the support structure, you need to apply five or six layers of strips. Rub your fingers over the strips so that no rough edges are left sticking up (Figure T.18). Change directions with each layer so that you can keep track of the number. If you are going to leave the papier-mâché over the support structure, then two or three layers may be enough.

Sheet Method

- **a.** Brush or spread paste on a sheet of newspaper or newsprint (Figure T.19). Lay a second

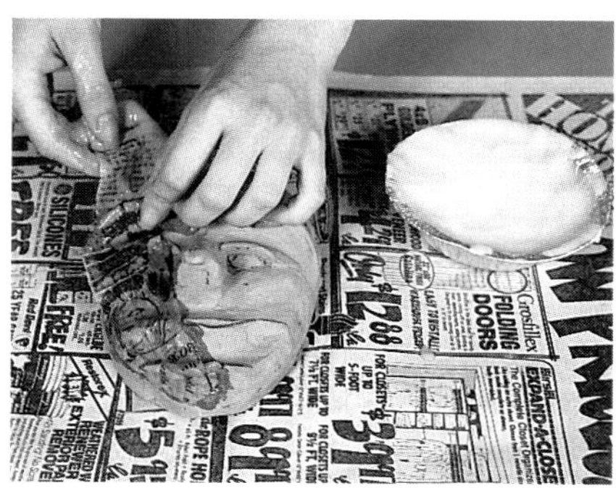

FIGURE T.18

FIGURE T.19

TECHNIQUE TIPS

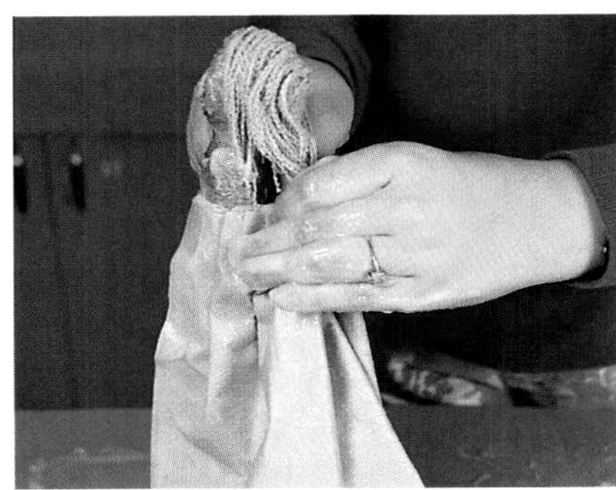

FIGURE T.20

sheet on top of the first and smooth out the layers. Add another layer of paste and another sheet of paper. Repeat this process until you have four or five layers of paper. This method is good for making drapery on a figure (Figure T.20).

b. If you let the layers dry for a day until they are leathery, they can be cut and molded any way you wish. Newspaper strips dipped in the paste can be used to seal any cracks that may occur.

Support Structures

a. Dry newspaper can be wadded up and wrapped with string or tape (Figure T.21).

b. Wire armatures can be padded with rags before the outside shell of papier-mâché is added.

c. Found materials such as boxes, tubes, and plastic bowls, can be arranged and taped together to form a base (Figure T.22).

d. For large figures, a wooden frame covered with chicken wire makes a good support. Push and pinch the wire into the shape you want.

FIGURE T.21

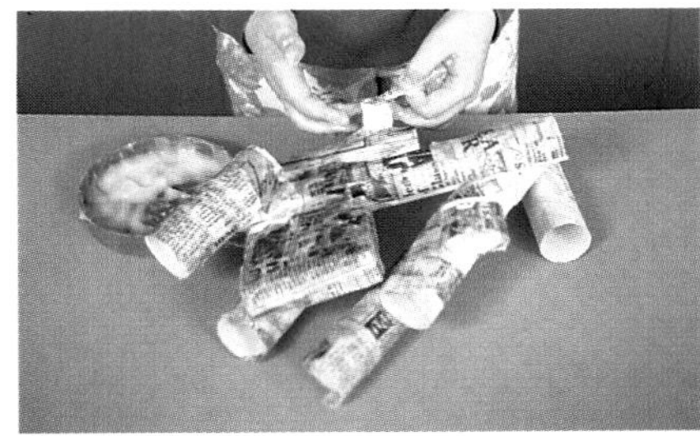

FIGURE T.22

20. Making a Paper Sculpture

Another name for paper sculpture is origami. The process originated in Japan and means "folding paper." Paper sculpture begins with a flat piece of paper. The paper is then curved or bent to produce more than a flat surface. Here are some ways to experiment with paper.

- **Scoring.** Place a square sheet of heavy construction paper on a flat surface. Position the ruler on the paper so that it is close to the center and parallel to the sides. Holding the ruler in place, run the point of a knife or a pair of scissors along one of the ruler's edges. Press down firmly but take care not to cut through the paper. Gently crease the paper along the line you made. Hold your paper with the crease facing upward. You can also score curved lines, but you must do this with gradually bending curves or wide arcs. If you try to make a tight curve, such as a semicircle, the paper will not give. For a tight curve you will have to make cuts to relieve the tension.
- **Pleating.** Take a piece of paper and fold it 1 inch from the edge. Then fold the paper in the other direction. Continue folding back and forth.
- **Curling.** Hold one end of a long strip of paper with the thumb and forefinger of one hand. At a point right below where you are holding the strip, grip it lightly between the side of a pencil and the thumb of your other hand. In a quick motion, run the pencil along the strip. This will cause the strip to curl back on itself. Don't apply too much pressure, or the strip will tear. (See Figure T.20.)

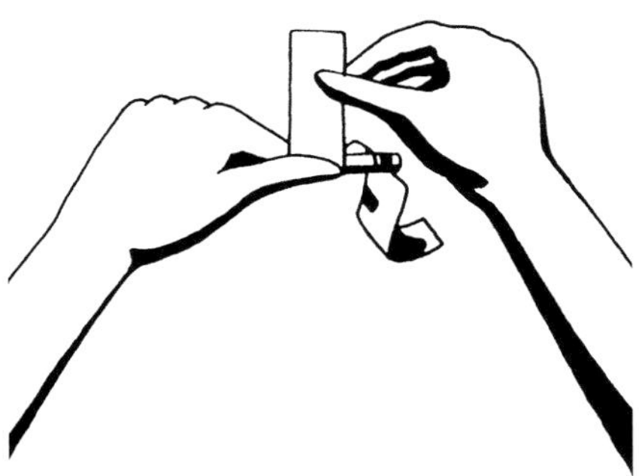

FIGURE T.20

OTHER TIPS

21. Making Paper

Papermaking is a process in which fibers are broken down and reformed as a sheet. In order to make paper, collect all the materials you will need. These include a food blender, two matching stretcher frames approximately 9 x 12 inches each, rustproof window screen slightly larger than the stretchers, staple gun, duct tape, Handi Wipes towels, large pan 5 to 8 inches deep, newspapers, assorted papers, and water.

a. Make the mold by stretching the screen over the frame, stapling it at the edges, and covering the rough edges with duct tape. The second frame is the deckle, the frame that keeps the pulp in place on the mold.

b. Tear paper into 1-inch squares. Put 4 cups water and $^1/_2$ cup paper scraps into the blender and blend for several minutes until the mixture is the consistency of watery cooked oatmeal.

c. Pour pulp into pan. Continue making pulp until there is about 4 inches of pulp in the pan. Additional water may be added to aid in the papermaking process.

d. Make a pad of newspapers $^1/_4$ inch thick. Unfold Handi Wipes towels and lay one on the pad; this is the blotter.

e. Align deckle on top of mold. Stir pulp to suspend paper fibers. Scoop mold and deckle under surface of water and shake to align fibers. Lift to drain excess water.

f. Remove the deckle and flip the mold and pulp onto the blotter, pulp side down against the Handi Wipes towel. Blot back of molds with a sponge to remove excess water and to compress the fibers. Remove the mold, using a rocking motion.

g. Lay another Handi Wipes towel on top of the sheet of paper and add more newspapers. Repeat the layering process.

h. Let paper dry slowly for 1–3 days. When dry, peel off the Handi Wipes.

i. To clean up, drain pulp through the mold or a sieve. Squeeze excess water from pulp and save pulp in a plastic bag for one to three days or discard it.

22. Basic Embroidery Stitches

The charts below and on the next page show the most common embroidery stitches.

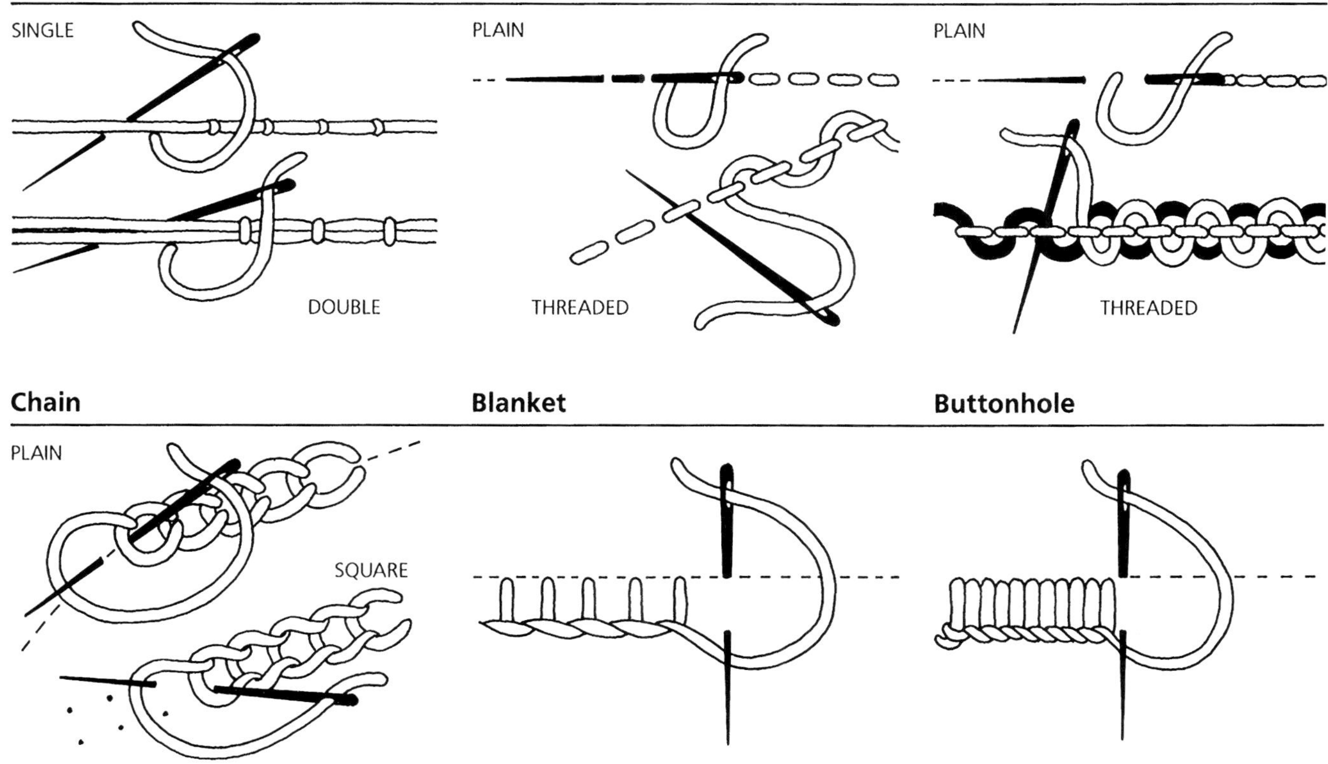

FIGURE T.24

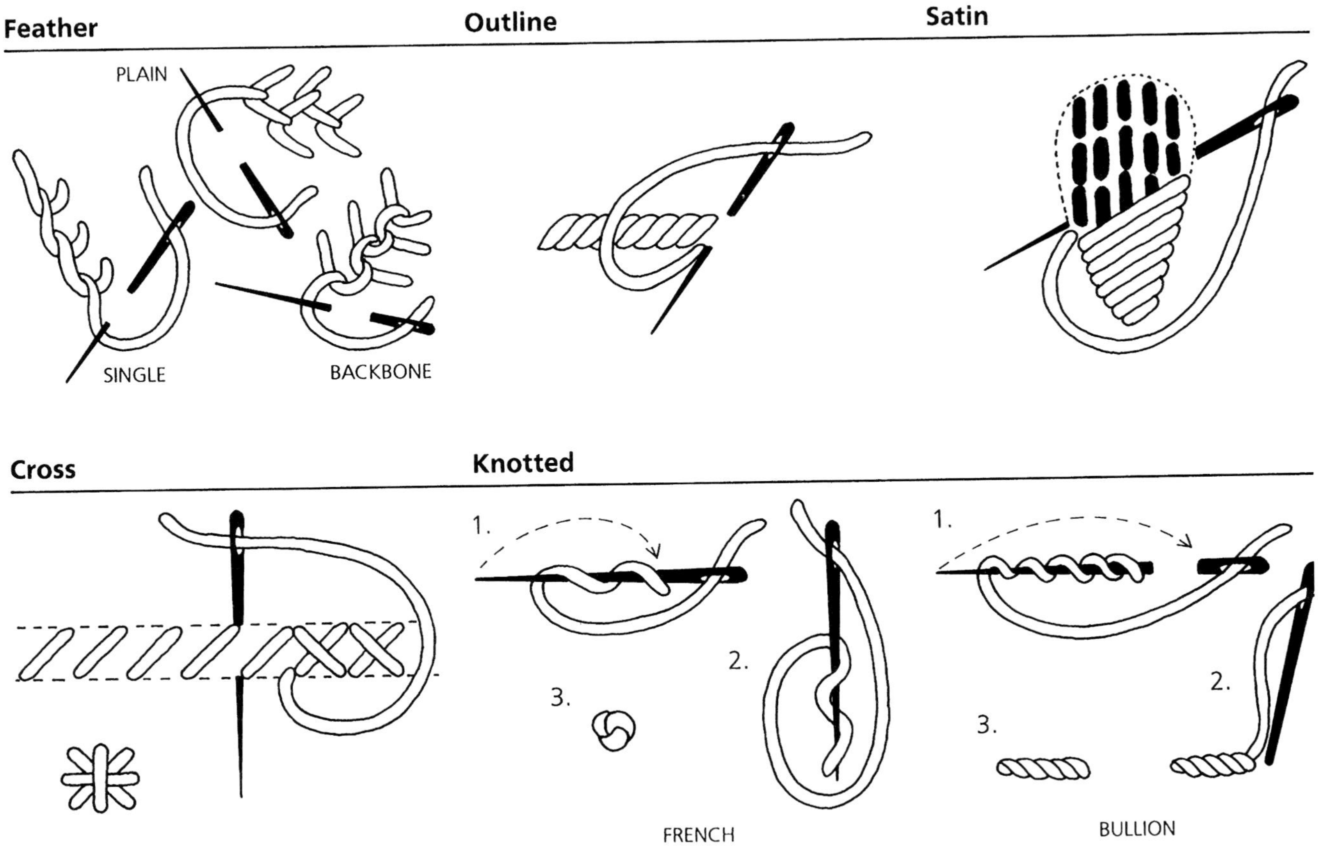

TECHNIQUE TIPS

Feather

PLAIN

SINGLE

BACKBONE

Outline

Satin

Cross

Knotted

1.

2.

3.

FRENCH

1.

2.

3.

BULLION

FIGURE T.24 (continued)

23. Weaving Techniques

To make a cardboard loom, gather the materials you will need. They include cardboard, ruler, pencil, scissors, strong, thin yarn for warp, various yarns and fibers for weft, tapestry needle, comb, and dowel.

- **a.** Measure and cut notches 1/4 inch apart and 1/2 inch deep on opposite sides of the cardboard.
- **b.** Tape warp thread to back of loom. Bring it to the front through the top left notch. Pull it down to the bottom of the loom and pass it through the bottom left notch to the back. Move one notch to the right and continue until you reach the last notch. Then tape the end of the warp thread to the back. (Figure T.25)
- **c.** Start to weave at the bottom of the loom, using a thin yarn. The weft yarns are the horizontal yarns; the easiest way to pull the weft yarn through the warp threads is to use an over-one-under-one motion. At the end of the row, reverse directions. (Figure T.26)
- **d.** Do not pull the weft threads too tight. Let them balloon, or curve slightly upward (Figure T.27).

FIGURE T.25

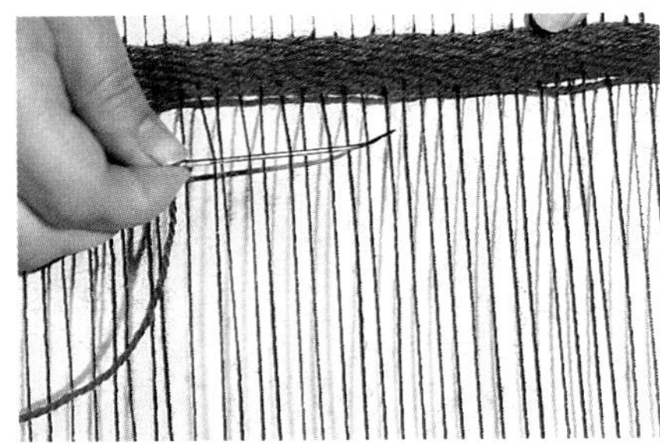

FIGURE T.26

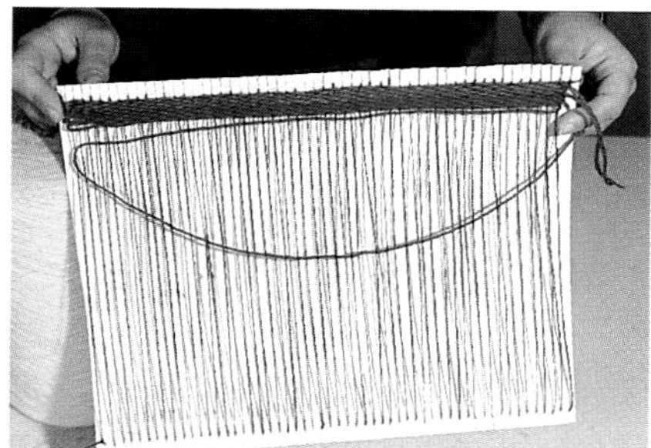

FIGURE T.27

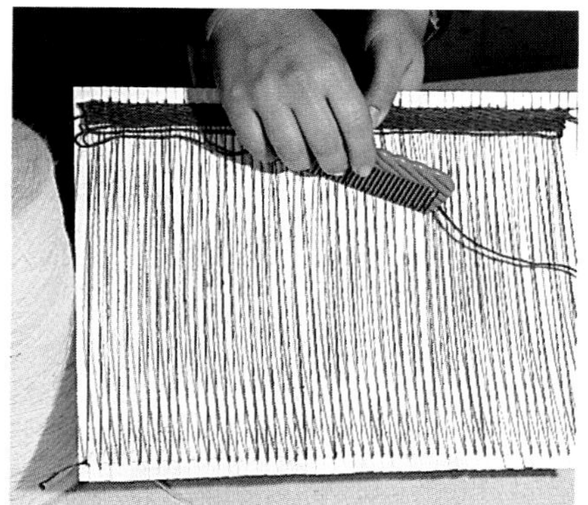

FIGURE T.28

e. After weaving several rows, pack the weft threads with a comb (Figure T.28). The tighter the weave, the stronger it will be.

f. After there is about 1 inch of tight weave, begin varying weave and materials (Figure T.29). End the process with another inch of thin, tight weave.

g. Before removing the fabric from the loom, weave in the loose ends. Cut the warp threads from the loom carefully and tie two at a time so they will not unravel.

h. Tie or sew the finished fabric to a dowel.

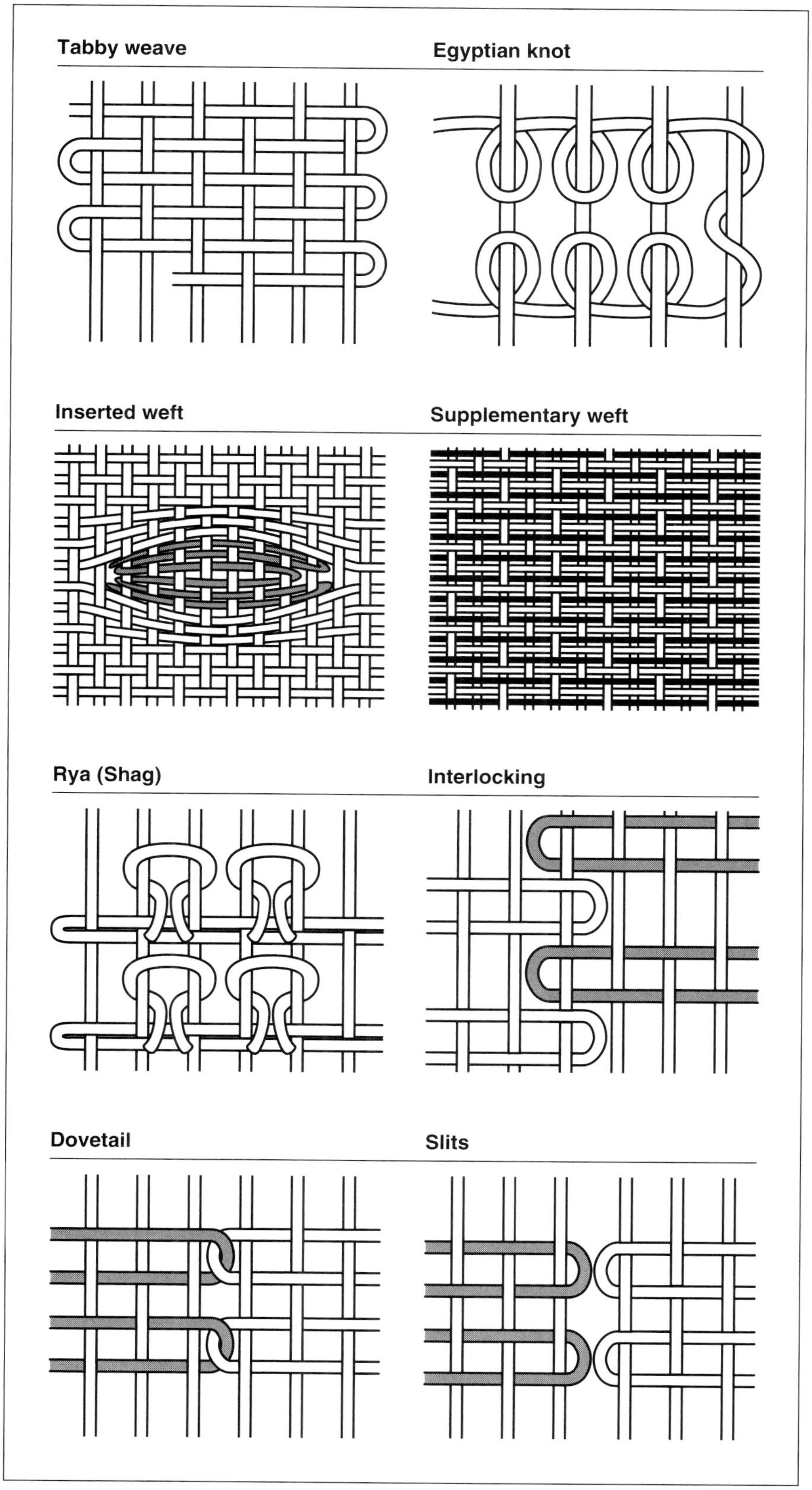

Tabby weave

Egyptian knot

Inserted weft

Supplementary weft

Rya (Shag)

Interlocking

Dovetail

Slits

FIGURE T.29

TECHNIQUE TIPS

24. Making a Coiled Basket

Mastering the technique of making a coiled basket takes practice. You will need *core* material (such as heavy cord), weft wrapping materials (such as yarns and fibers), a tapestry needle, scissors, and tape.

Coiling is a stitching technique in which the continuous coils of the *core* material are stitched together with a binding material called the *weft.* The first time you try this your binding and stitches probably will not look neat. Undo the work and begin again. You want to cover the core material completely, and all your weft binding and stitches must be even and tight.

a. Trim the end of the core so it tapers. Thread the tapestry needle with a 3-foot length of weft. Using the loose weft end, begin to wind it around the core starting about 2 inches from the end. Overlap the end as you wind to anchor it. Wind the weft to about 1/2 inch from the tapered end of the core (Figure T.30).

b. Bend the core, catch the tapered end, and make a loop (Figure T.31).

c. Continue winding for about 2 inches, being sure that the tapered core is attached securely to the solid section of core material. Push the tapestry needle through the center of the loop (Figure T.32).

d. Bend the core to form a coil and bring the weft between the core and the coil. (Figure T.33) Begin winding the weft around the core from front to back. You are now ready to begin the Lazy Squaw stitch.

e. Wind the weft around the core from front to back four times. Then, bringing the weft from behind and over the core, push the needle into the center of the coil (Figure T.34). Pull tightly and hold. Continue to wrap the weft four times around the core and pull the fifth stitch into the center until you complete two coils. Hold them flat between your fingers while you work.

f. As the coiling progresses, you may wrap the weft more than four times between stitches. After the first two coils, you will no longer bring the stitch back to the center; just take it over two coils (Figure T.35). Always insert the needle from the front. This way you can see exactly where you are placing the needle. If you want to create a pattern of long stitches, this is essential.

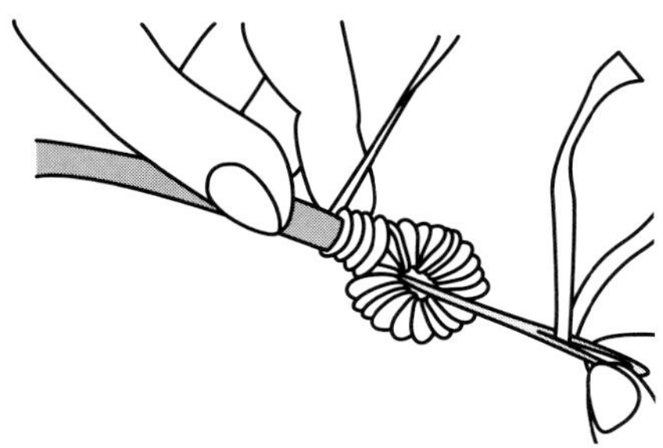

FIGURE T.32

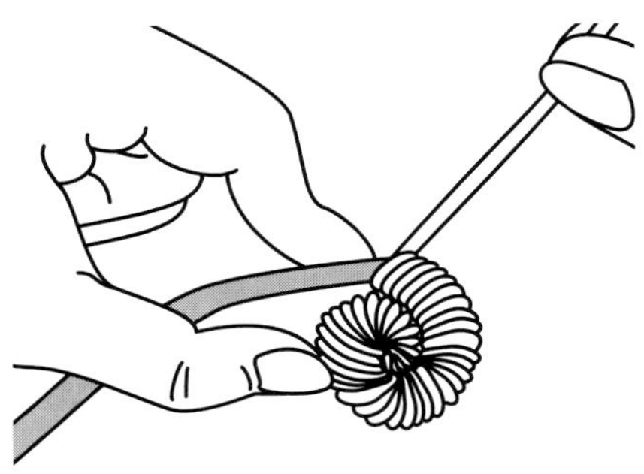

FIGURE T.33

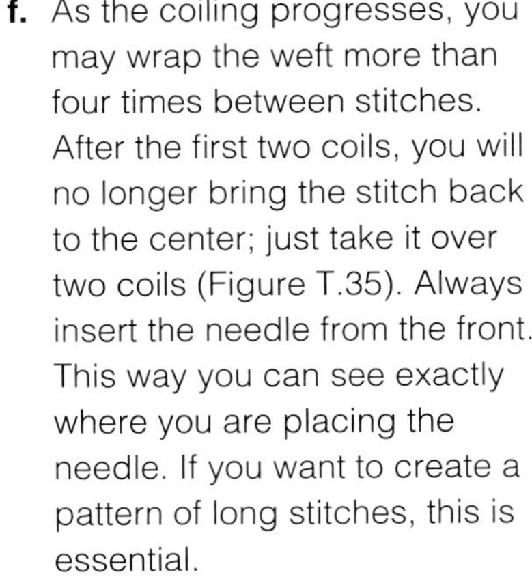

FIGURE T.30

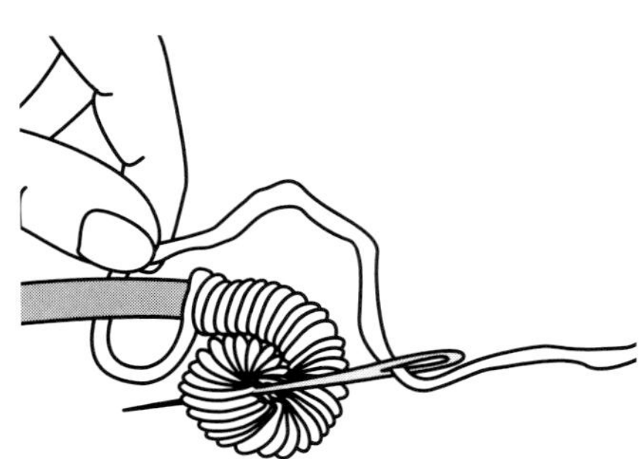

FIGURE T.34

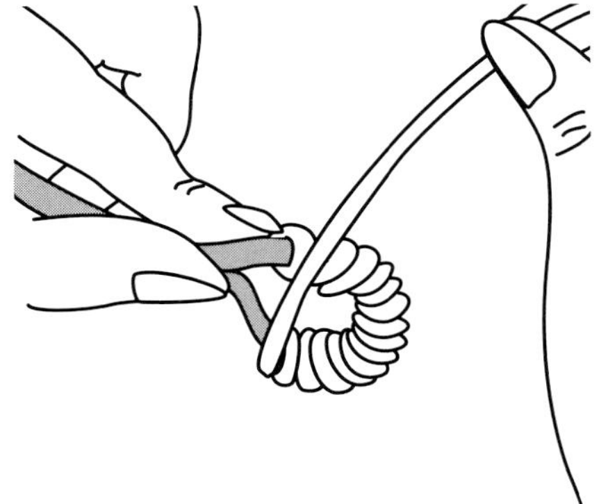

FIGURE T.31

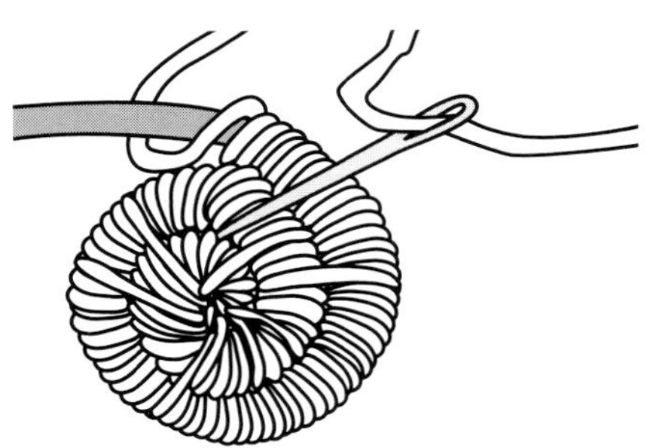

FIGURE T.35

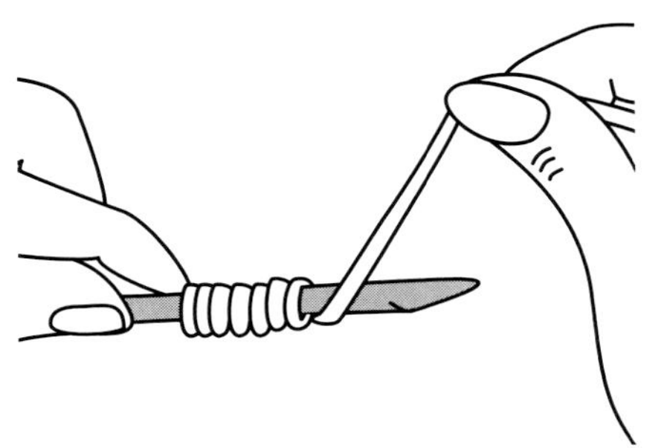

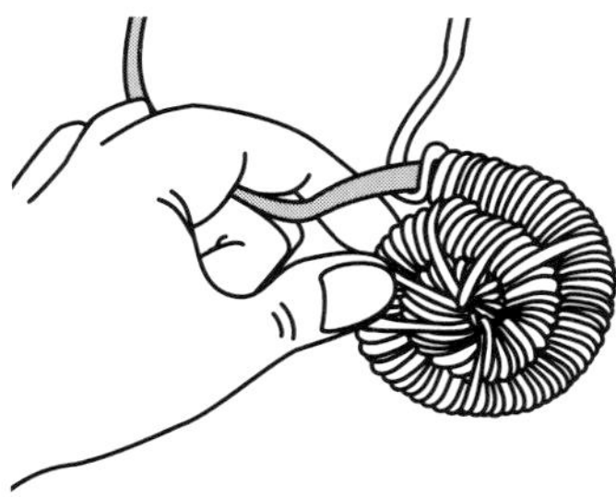

FIGURE T.36

g. Hold the coil with your left hand with the core material coming from the left, and wind the weft with your right hand so you do not tangle it with the core (Figure T.36). If you are left-handed, reverse the process. Always pull the weft very tight.

h. You will need to splice, or invisibly join, the ends of separate materials. To splice the core, taper the cut on the old and the new piece. Before working the weft, secure the spliced ends of the core by wrapping them with sewing thread or tape. Always hold the spliced area carefully until it is wrapped with the weft. Splice the weft during the wrapping, not during the stitching. Hold the tail ends of the old and the new weft together against the core as shown in Figure T.37. Wrap the new weft at least once before making a long stitch.

FIGURE T.37

i. When the base is the desired size, it is time to begin making the sides of the basket. If the side is to be perpendicular to the base, lay the first foundation coil directly on top of the last coil. If you want the basket to curve outward, place each new coil on the outer edge of the one below. To make an inward curve, place each coil on the inner edge of the previous coil. Use pressure from the nonstitching hand to keep the coils in place.

j. The best way to finish the basket is to taper the core and make several stitches around the last coil and the tapered coil. Then run the needle back through the wrapping stitches for about an inch and pull the weft thread through. Cut off the excess weft.

k. If you want to make a handle, simply wrap the end of the core until it is as long as you wish. Then attach it to the other side of the top of the basket following the instructions from Step j.

25. Making a Tissue Paper Collage

For your first experience with tissue, make a free design with the tissue colors. Start with the lightest colors of tissue first and save the darkest for last. It is difficult to change the color of dark tissue by overlapping it with other colors. If one area becomes too dark, you might cut out a piece of white paper, glue it over the dark area carefully, and apply new colors over the white area.

a. Apply a coat of adhesive to the area where you wish to place the tissue.

b. Place the tissue down carefully over the wet area (Figure T.38). Don't let your fingers get wet.

c. Then add another coat of adhesive over the tissue. If your brush picks up any color from the wet tissue, rinse your brush

FIGURE T.38

in water and let it dry before using it again.

d. Experiment by overlapping colors. Allow the tissue to wrinkle to create textures as you apply it. Be sure that all the loose edges of tissue are glued down.

DISPLAY TIPS

26. Making a Mat

You can add appeal to an artwork by making a mat, using the following steps.

a. Gather the materials you will need. These include a metal rule, a pencil, mat board, cardboard backing, a sheet of heavy cardboard to protect your work surface, a mat knife with a sharp blade, and wide masking tape.

b. Wash your hands. Mat board should be kept very clean.

c. Measure the height and width of the work to be matted. Decide how large a border you want for your work. (A border of approximately 2½ inches on three sides with 3 inches on the bottom is aesthetically pleasing.) Your work will be behind the window you will cut.

d. Plan for the opening, or window, to be ¼ inch smaller on all sides than the size of your work. For example, if your work measures 9 by 12 inches, the mat window should measure 8½ inches (9 inches minus ¼ inch times two) by 11½ inches (12 inches minus ¼ inch times two.) Using your metal rule and pencil, lightly draw your window rectangle on the back of the board 2½ inches from the top and left edge of the mat. (See Figure T.39). Add a 2½-inch border to the right of the window and a 3-inch border to the bottom, lightly drawing cutting guidelines.

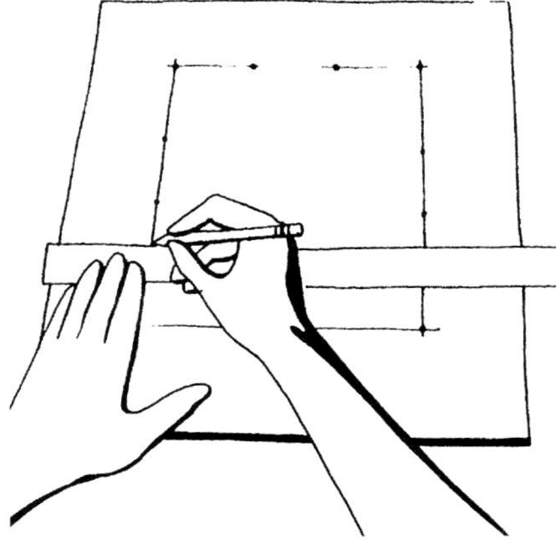

FIGURE T.39

Note: If you are working with metric measurements, the window should overlap your work by 0.5 cm (centimeters) on all sides. Therefore, if your work measures 24 by 30 cm, the mat window measures 23 cm (24−[2 x 0.5]) by 29 cm (30 − [2 × 0.5]).

e. Place the sheet of heavy, protective cardboard on your work surface. Place the mat board, pencil marks up, over the cardboard. Holding the metal rule firmly in place, score the first line with your knife. Always place the metal rule so that your blade is on the inside of the frame. (See Figure T.40.) In case you make an error you will cut into the window hole or the extra mat that is not used for the frame. Do not try to cut through the board with one stroke. By the third or fourth stroke, you should be able to cut through the board easily.

f. Working in the same fashion, score and cut through the board along all the window lines. Be careful not to go beyond the lines. Remove the window.

g. Cut a cardboard backing for your artwork that is slightly smaller than the overall size of your mat. Using a piece of broad masking tape, hinge the back of the mat to the backing. (See Figure T.41.) Position your artwork between the backing and the mat and attach it with tape. Anchor the frame to the cardboard with a few pieces of rolled tape.

FIGURE T.40

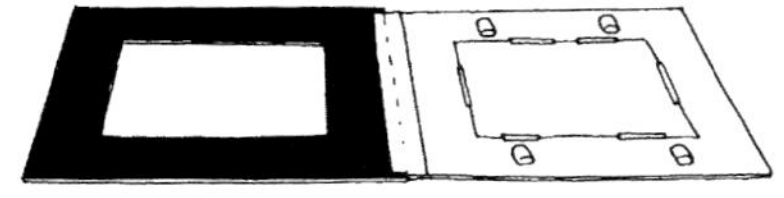

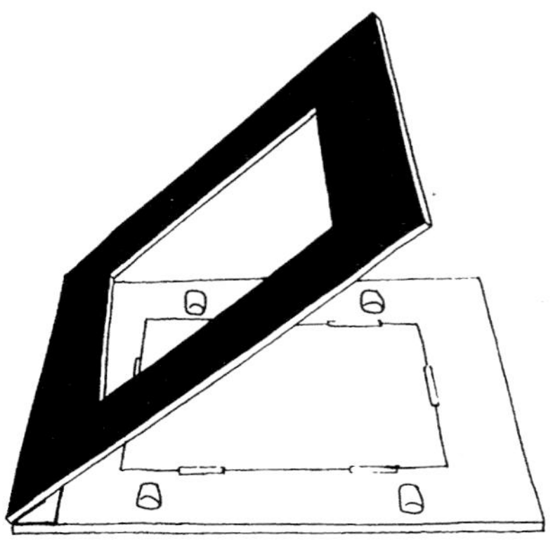

FIGURE T.41

27. Mounting a Two-Dimensional Work

Mounting pictures that you make gives them a professional look. To mount a work, do the following:

a. Gather the materials you will need. These include a yardstick, a pencil, poster board, a knife with a very sharp blade, a sheet of newspaper, and rubber cement.

b. Measure the height and width of the work to be mounted. Decide how large a border you want around the work. Plan your mount size using the work's measurements. To end up with a 3-inch border, for example, make your mount 6 inches wider and higher than your work. Record the measurements for your mount.

c. Using your yardstick and pencil, lightly draw your mount rectangle on the back of the poster board. Measure from the edges of the poster board. If you have a large paper cutter available, you may use it to cut your mount.

d. Place the sheet of heavy cardboard on your work surface. Place the poster board, pencil marks up, over the cardboard. Holding the yardstick firmly in place along one line, score the line with your knife. Do not try to cut through the board with one stroke. By the third try, you should be able to cut through the board.

e. Place the artwork on the mount. Using the yardstick, center the work. Mark each corner with a dot. (See Figure T.42)

FIGURE T.42

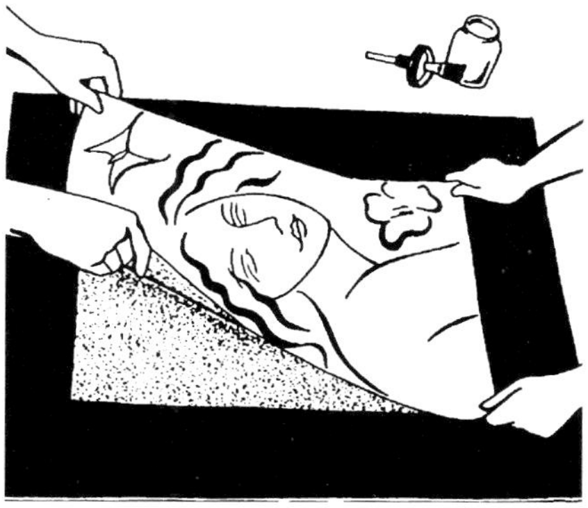

f. Place the artwork, face down, on a sheet of newspaper. Coat the back of the work with rubber cement. (Safety Note: Always use rubber cement in a room with plenty of ventilation.) If your mount is to be permanent, skip to Step h.

g. Line up the corners of your work with the dots on the mounting board. Smooth the work into place. Skip to Step i.

h. After coating the back of your artwork, coat the poster board with rubber cement. Be careful not to add cement to the border area. Have a partner hold your artwork in the air by the two top corners. Once the two glued surfaces meet, you will not be able to change the position of the work. Grasp the lower two corners. Carefully lower the work to the mounting board. Line up the two corners with the bottom dots. Little by little, lower the work into place (Figure T.43). Press it smooth.

FIGURE T.43

i. To remove any excess cement, create a small ball of dry rubber cement. Use the ball of rubber cement to pick up excess cement.

28. Working with Glue

When applying glue, always start at the center of the surface you are coating and work outward.

- When gluing papers together don't use a lot of glue, just a dot will do. Use dots in the corners and along the edges. Press the two surfaces together. Keep dots at least $\frac{1}{2}$ inch in from the edge of your paper.
- Handle a glued surface carefully with only your fingertips. Make sure your hands are clean before pressing the glued surface into place.
- Note: The glue should be as thin as possible. Thick or beaded glue will create ridges on your work.

SAFETY IN THE ART ROOM

Many artists, both students and teachers, come into daily contact with dangerous, possibly deadly materials. The unfortunate truth is that many art supplies contain high levels of chemicals, such as hexane, lead, toluene, and asbestos, and many people are unaware of the danger that these substances pose, both to art students and to teachers. In fact, the danger to art teachers, who are often exposed to toxins for several hours a day for many years, is often greater than to the students. Therefore, it is essential that all art teachers and students become aware of the potential hazards in using art materials.

Many art supplies contain materials that can cause acute illness (that is, a severe sudden illness that can be caused by a single exposure to a toxic substance and result in permanent disability or death). Long-term exposure to materials in many other art supplies can cause chronic illness (which develops gradually after repeated exposure) or cancer. Other chemicals in art supplies are sensitizers, causing allergies, particularly in children. Lead, for example, is acutely toxic and can be found in such commonly used supplies as stencil paint, oil paint, some acrylics, gessoes, ceramic glazes, copper enamels, and automotive paint in spray cans. Many highly toxic hydrocarbon-based solvents, including methyl alcohol, are used in school art programs. Other widely used art materials, such as preservatives, formaldehyde, epoxy glues, and dichromates, can contain dangerous chemicals like cadmium, nickel, silica, and pesticides.

There are three ways in which such chemicals can enter the body: absorption, inhalation, and ingestion. They can be absorbed through the skin from cuts or scrapes, resulting in burns or rashes, or into the bloodstream, moving to and damaging other parts of the body. Chemical irritants can be inhaled, causing lung problems like bronchitis and emphysema. Inhaling small particles, like the free silica in clay dust, can cause pulmonary fibrosis or asthma. Chemicals can be ingested through touching the mouth with the hands or fingers while working with supplies or unconsciously placing tools like paint brushes in or near the mouth. Since hazardous substances can easily enter the body, it is extremely important to make sure that the materials used are safe and are that they are used safely.

Labeling

Labeling can provide information on any potentially dangerous art supplies, but teachers need to be aware of what various labels mean. The label *nontoxic,* for example, does not guarantee a product's safety. According to federal regulations, toxicity means that a single exposure can be fatal to adults. The effect on young people, who are more likely to be harmed by dangerous substances, is not considered in this definition. Also, the chance of developing chronic or long-term illnesses is not addressed by the legal definition of toxicity. Repeated exposure to nontoxic materials is not always safe. Many dangerous substances, such as asbestos, can legally be defined as nontoxic. Also, some art supplies, particularly those manufactured by small or foreign companies, may be improperly labeled as nontoxic.

Not all products whose labels provide chemical components, but have no warnings or list no information at all, are safe to use. Since manufacturers are not required to disclose ingredients, products without this information or warnings are potentially hazardous.

For more complete information on the presence of hazardous substances in art supplies, teachers may request a Material Safety Data Sheet (OSHA Form 20) from the manufacturer. This sheet provides information on potential heath and fire hazards, a list of chemicals that might react dangerously with the product, and a list of all ingredients for which industrial standards exist. The manufacturer should supply this sheet on request, and a local public health official or poison control center technician can help interpret the information.

Art teachers can also take advantage of voluntary labeling standards developed by the art materials industry. The Art and Craft Materials Institute (ACMI) administers a voluntary testing and labeling program that helps to insure the safety of those who work with art materials. This system uses the labels CP, AP, and HL.

CP (Certified Product) and AP (Approved Product) labels are used mainly on products designed for younger children, while HL (Health Label) is used on products intended for older students and adults. Products labeled CP, AP, or HL (Nontoxic) are certified in a program of toxicological evaluation by a medical expert to contain no materials in sufficient quantities to be toxic or injurious to humans or to cause acute or chronic health problems. Products labeled CP, in addition, meet specific requirements of material, workmanship, working qualities, and color. HL (Cautions Required) means that the product is certified to be properly labeled in a program of toxicological evaluation by a medical expert. The Art and Craft Materials Institute makes available a list of institute-certified products. For a copy, or for more information on the institute's certification program, teachers can write to:

The Art and Craft Materials Institute
715 Boylston St.
Boston, MA 02116

Safety Rules

There are certain guidelines to be followed in selecting and using art supplies. Perhaps the most important is to know what the materials are made of and what potential hazards exist. If a material is improperly labeled, or if adequate information cannot be obtained about it, don't use it. The following rules are also helpful:

- Be sure that all materials used by younger students (ages 12 and under) have the CP or AP label and that materials used by older students and adults are marked HL.
- Don't use acids, alkalies, bleaches, or any product that will stain skin or clothing.
- Don't use aerosol cans because the spray can injure lungs.
- Use dust-producing materials (such as pastels, clays, plasters, chalks, powdered tempera, pigments, dyes, and instant papier-mâché, except the premixed cellulose type) with care in a well-ventilated area (or better yet, don't use them at all).
- Don't use solvents (including lacquers, paint thinners, turpentines, shellacs, solvent-based inks, rubber cement, and permanent markers) in the art room.
- Don't use found or donated materials unless the ingredients are known.
- Don't use old materials. Many art supplies formerly contained highly dangerous substances, such as arsenic, or raw lead compounds, or high levels of asbestos. Older solvents may contain chloroform or carbon tetrachloride.

Working conditions in the art room also affect safety. A disorderly art room leads to unsafe conditions, particularly when there are many people working close to each other. Controlling the buildup of litter and dust, insuring that tools are in good condition, and keeping workspace reasonably organized not only help prevent common accidents but also make it easier to recognize and eliminate other hazards. An orderly art room is absolutely essential to the students' and teacher's safety.

ARTISTS AND THEIR WORKS

This section contains an alphabetical list of the professional artists whose works appear in *ArtTalk*. Following each name is the nationality of the artist, birth or birth and death dates, artistic category, and the title and page reference for each work.

Abbot, Berenice, American, b. 1898, photographer
Façade, Alwyn Court, 129, Fig. 6.17

Albers, Josef, German, 1888–1976, painter
Homage to the Square: Glow, 265, Fig. 10.26

Albright, Ivan, American, 1897–1983, painter
The Farmer's Kitchen, 200, Fig. 8.16

Andrews, Benny, African-American, b. 1930, painter, printmaker
The Scholar, 101, Fig. 5.28

Apel, Marie, English, 1880–1970, sculptor
Grief, 141, Fig. 6.38

Arp, Jean (Hans), French, 1887–1966, painter, sculptor
Aquatique, 123, Fig. 6.9

Bak, Brunislaw M., American (born in Poland), 1922–1981, painter
Holocaust, 156, Fig. 7.3
Interpenetrations in Red, 316, Fig. 12.4

Bak, Hedi, American (born in Germany), b. 1924, painter
Grand Canyon #2, 194, Fig. 8.4

Balla, Giocomo, Italian, 1871–1958, painter
Dynamism of a Dog on a Leash, 236, Fig. 9.24
Street Light, 234, Fig. 9.20

Barlach, Ernst, German, 1870–1938, painter, sculptor
Singing Man, 328, Fig. 12.19

Bayless, Florence, American, b. 1922, craftsperson
Haori Coat, 326, Fig. 12.16

Bearden, Romare, African-American, 1914–1989, painter
Prevalence of Ritual: Baptism, 178, Fig. 7.37

Beaux, Cecilia, American, 1863–1942, painter
Ernesta (Child with Nurse), 322, Fig. 12.11

Benton, Thomas Hart, American, 1882–1975, painter
I Got a Girl on Sourwood Mountain, 98, Fig. 5.23
The Sources of Country Music, 61, Fig. 3.29

Bernini, Gianlorenzo, Italian, 1598–1680, sculptor
David, 277, Fig. 10.36

Bishop, Isabel, American, 1902–1988, painter
Two Girls, 292, Fig. 11.20
Waiting, 308, Fig. 11.36

Bonheur, Rosa, French, 1822–1899, painter
The Horse Fair, 224, Fig. 9.4

Botero, Fernando, Colombian, b. 1932, painter
The Pinzon Family, 302, Fig. 11.33

Botticelli, Sandro, Italian, 1445–1510, painter
The Adoration of the Magi, 135, Fig. 6.25

Brancusi, Constantin, Romanian, 1876–1957, sculptor
Torso of a Young Man, 140, Fig. 6.36

Burchfield, Charles, American, 1893–1967, painter
October Wind and Sunlight in the Woods, 223, Fig. 9.3

Calder, Alexander, American, 1898–1976, sculptor
Lobster Trap and Fish Tail, 237, Fig. 9.26
Varese, 108, Fig. 5.36

Carpenter, Miles Burkholder, American, 1889–1985, craftsperson, sculptor
Root Monster, 184, Fig. 7.40

Carr, Emily, Canadian, 1871–1945, painter
Above the Trees, 170, Fig. 7.27
Forest, British Columbia, 328, Fig. 12.18

Cassatt, Mary, American, 1845–1926, painter
Baby Reaching for an Apple, 24, Fig. 2.1
Five O'Clock Tea, 270, Fig. 10.32

Catlett, Elizabeth, African-American, b. 1915, printmaker, sculptor, painter
Sharecropper, 13, Fig. 1.9

Catlin, George, American, 1796–1872, painter
See-non-ty-a, an Iowa Medicine Man, 294, Fig. 11.23

Cézanne, Paul, French, 1839–1906, painter
Le Chateau Noir, 56, Fig. 3.23

Chagall, Marc, Russian, 1887–1985, painter
Birthday, 298, Fig. 11.28

Church, Frederic Edwin, American, 1826–1900, painter
Our Banner in the Sky, 267, Fig. 10.30

Clements, Bob, American, b. 1937, sculptor
Evening Up the Score, 263, Fig. 10.24

Clive, Carolyn, American, b. 1931, painter
Amplitude, 110, Fig. 5.37

Close, Chuck, American, b. 1940, painter
Janet, 246, Fig. 9.31

Copley, John Singleton, American, 1737–1815, painter
Paul Revere, 294, Fig. 11.22

Courtney-Clarke, Margaret, English, b. 1949, photojournalist
photo from *African Canvas,* 172, Fig. 7.30

D

E

G

H

Hepworth, Barbara, English, 1903–1975, sculptor
Figure for Landscape, 128, Fig. 6.15
Hiroshige, Andō, Japanese, 1797–1858, printmaker
Evening Rain on the Karasaki Pine, 48, Fig. 3.11
Hofmann, Hans, German (born in America), 1880–1966, painter
Flowering Swamp, 64, Fig. 3.32
Hokusai, Katsushika, Japanese, 1760–1849, printmaker
The Great Wave off Kanagawa, 262, Fig. 10.22
Homer, Winslow, American, 1836–1910, painter
Hound and Hunter, 12, Fig. 1.8
Sketch for Hound and Hunter, 12, Fig. 1.7
Hoover, John, Native American, Aleut, b. 1919, sculptor
Loon Song, 202, Fig. 8.20
Hopper, Edward, American, 1882–1967, painter
Early Sunday Morning, 98, Fig. 5.22
First Row Orchestra, 258, Fig. 10.16
Houser, Allan, Native American, b. 1914, sculptor
Coming of Age, 233, Fig. 9.19
Hua Yen, Chinese, c. 1682–1765
Conversation in Autumn, 47, Fig. 3.10
Hunt, Henry, Canadian Native American, Kwakiutl, 1923–1985, sculptor
K'umugwe' (Komokwa) Mask, 304, Fig. 11.34
Huntington, Anna Hyatt, American, 1876–1973, sculptor
Riders to the Sea, 142, Fig. 6.39

J

Jacquette, Yvonne, American, b. 1934, painter
East River Drive, 93, Fig. 5.6
Town of Skowhegan, Maine V, 312, Fig. 12.1
Jessup, Georgia Mills, American, b. 1926, painter
Rainy Night, Downtown, 331, Fig. 12.23
Jimenez, Luis, American, b. 1940, sculptor
Vaquero, 16, Fig. 1.12
Johns, Jasper, American, b. 1930, painter
Cups 4 Picasso, 124, Fig. 6.10
Map, 327, Fig. 12.17
Johnson, Philip, American, b. 1906, architect
Johnson House, 141, Fig. 6.37
Johnson, William H., African-American, 1901–1970, painter
Jitterbugs IV, 112, Fig. 5.38

K

Kahlo, Frida, Mexican, 1907–1954, painter
Frida and Diego Rivera, 259, Fig. 10.17
Self-Portrait Dedicated to Leon Trotsky, 264, Fig. 10.25
Keyser, Louisa (Dat So La Lee), Native American, 1850–1925, weaver
Basket, 244, Fig. 9.30
Kingman, Dong, American, b. 1911, painter
Higher, Faster, and Farther, 19, Fig. 1.15
Kollwitz, Käthe, German, 1867–1945, painter, printmaker, graphic artist
Self-Portrait, 58, Fig. 3.26

L

Lachaise, Gaston, French, 1882–1935, sculptor
Walking Woman, 298, Fig. 11.29
Lange, Dorothea, American, 1895–1965, photojournalist
Migrant Mother, 15, Fig. 1.11
Larraz, Julio, Cuban, b. 1944, painter
Papiamento, 8, Fig. 1.3
Lawrence, Jacob, African-American, b. 1917, painter
Parade, 238, Fig. 9.27
Study for the Munich Olympic Games Poster, 114, Fig. 5.39
Le Corbusier, Swiss, 1887–1965, architect
Chapelle Notre-Dame-du-Haut, 285, Fig. 11.9
Lee, Doris, American, b. 1905, printmaker, painter
Thanksgiving, 138, Fig. 6.33
Leonardo da Vinci, Italian, 1452–1519, painter, sculptor
Ginevra de' Benci, 67, Fig. 3.36
page from his sketchbook showing movement of water, 9, Fig. 1.5
Leyster, Judith, Dutch, 1609–1660, painter
Self-Portrait, 54, Fig. 3.20
Lichtenstein, Roy, American, b. 1923, painter
Blam, 336, Fig. 12.28
Loewy, Raymond, American (born in France), b. 1893, designer
Avanti, 74, Fig. 4.4

M

McKelvey, Lucy Leuppe, Native American, b. date unknown, ceramicist
Whirling Rainbow Goddesses, 237, Fig. 9.25
Magritte, René, Belgian, 1898–1967, painter
The Blank Signature, 148, Fig. 6.46
Marc, Franz, German, 1880–1916, painter
The Large Blue Horses, 175, Fig. 7.34
Marisol, Venezuelan (in America since 1950), b. 1930, sculptor
Poor Family I, 118, Fig. 6.1
Marsh, Reginald, American, 1898–1954, painter
Why Not Use the El?, 284, Fig. 11.7
Martinez, Maria and Julian, Native American, Maria: c. 1885–1980; Julian: c. 1885–1943, ceramicists
Black-on-black storage jar, 274, Fig. 10.34
Matisse, Henri, French, 1869–1954, painter
Beasts of the Sea, 132, Fig. 6.21
Michelangelo Buonarroti, Italian, 1475–1564, sculptor, painter
Pietà, 52, 309, Figs. 3.16, 11.37
Mitchell, Joan, American, 1926–1992, painter
Dirty Snow, 205, Fig. 8.25
Miyawaki, Ayako, Japanese, b. 1905, appliqué artist
The Red Crab, 212, Fig. 8.30
Mondrian, Piet, Dutch, 1872–1944, painter
Broadway Boogie Woogie, 176, Fig. 7.35

N

O

P

R

S

CHRONOLOGY OF ARTWORKS

In this section, the artworks that appear in *ArtTalk* have been arranged in chronological order. This list will enable you to see which artists were working at the same time and how the time and place in which they lived influenced their styles.

Prehistoric–1 B.C.

Artist Unknown, Altamira Caves, Spain
The Hall of the Bulls, 15,000 B.C., 43, Fig. 3.3

Artist Unknown
Statua di Donna, 2700–2600 B.C., 45, Fig. 3.5

Artist Unknown, Indian
Mohenjo-Daro, 2500 B.C., 46, Fig. 3.7

Artist Unknown, Egyptian
Methethy with His Daughter and Son, 2450 B.C., 44, Fig. 3.4

Artist Unknown, Egyptian
Figure of Hippopotamus, 1991–1786 B.C., 139, Fig. 6.34

Artist Unknown, Chinese
Ritual Wine Container, 1200 B.C., 45, Fig. 3.6

Myron, Greek, c. 480–440 B.C., sculptor
Discobolus, 450 B.C., 49, Fig. 3.12

Artist Unknown, Greco–Roman
Man of the Republic, 50 B.C., 49, Fig. 3.13

Artist Unknown, Greek
Dancing Lady, 50 B.C., 285, Fig. 11.8

Artist Unknown, Indian
Standing Vishnu, 9 B.C., 46, Fig. 3.8

A.D. 1–1399

Artist Unknown, Loma Negra, Peru
Nose Ornament, 1st–3rd centuries, 253, Fig. 10.5

Artist Unknown, Mexican, Gulf Coast
Figurine (Ball Player), 900, 53, Fig. 3.18

Artist Unknown, Coastal Huari, Tiahuanaco, Peru
Mantle, 600–1000, 225, Fig. 9.5

Artist Unknown, Southeastern Song dynasty
Carved Lacquer Circular Tray, 1127–1279, 255, Fig. 10.12

Artist Unknown, Southeast Asian
Temple at Angkor Wat, 1113–1150, 46, Fig. 3.9

Artist Unknown, Pisa, Italy
Bell Tower of the Cathedral at Pisa, 1174, 252, Fig. 10.2

Artist Unknown, French
Reims Cathedral, 1225–1299, 51, Fig. 3.15

Giotto di Bondone, Italian, c. 1266–1337, painter
Madonna and Child, 1320–30, 133, Fig. 6.22

1400–1499

van Eyck, Jan, Flemish, before 1395–1441, painter
The Annunciation, 1434–36, 187, Fig. 7.42

Ghiberti, Lorenzo, Italian, 1378–1455, sculptor
Gates of Paradise, 1425–52, 37, Fig. 2.10

van der Weyden, Rogier, Flemish, 1399–1464, painter
Portrait of a Lady, 1460, 283, Fig. 11.3

Leonardo da Vinci, Italian, 1452–1519, painter, sculptor
Ginevra de' Benci, 1474, 67, Fig. 3.36

Leonardo da Vinci, Italian, 1452–1519, painter, sculptor
page from his sketchbook c. 1475, 9, Fig. 1.5

Artist Unknown, Byzantine
Madonna and Child on Curved Throne, 1480, 50, fig. 3.14

Botticelli, Sandro, Italian, 1445–1510, painter
The Adoration of the Magi, 1481–82, 135, Fig. 6.25

Dürer, Albrecht, German, 1471–1528, painter, printmaker
An Oriental Ruler Seated on His Throne, 1495, 134, Fig. 6.23

1500–1599

Michelangelo Buonarroti, Italian, 1475–1564, sculptor, painter
Pietà, 1500, 52, 309, Figs. 3.16, 11.37

Giorgione, Italian, 1477–1511, painter
The Adoration of the Shepherds, 1505–10, 261, Fig. 10.20

Dürer, Albrecht, German, 1471–1528, painter, printmaker
Virgin and Child with Saint Anne, 1519, 293, Fig. 11.21

Grünewald, Matthias, German, c. 1470–1528, painter
The Small Crucifixion, 1511–20, 295, Fig. 11.24

Nizami (author). Artist unknown, Persian, c. 1524–25
Kamseh: Bahram Gur and the Chinese Princess in the Sandalwood Pavilion on Thursday, 1524–25, 52, Fig. 3.17

Musawwir, 'Abd Allah, Islamic, 16th century, painter
The Meeting of the Theologians, 1540–49, 240, Fig. 9.28

Tintoretto, Jacopo, Italian, c. 1518–1594, painter
Standing Youth with His Arm Raised, 102, Fig. 5.30

Fontana, Lavinia, Italian, 1552–1614, painter
Portrait of a Noblewoman, 1580, 24 125, Fig. 6.11

Artist Unknown, English
Armor of George Clifford, Third Earl of Cumberland, 1580–1585, 288, Fig. 11.13

Artist Unknown, Nigeria, Edo
Warrior Chief, Warriors and Attendants, 16th–17th centuries, 146, Fig. 6.45

1600–1699

Rubens, Peter Paul, Flemish, 1577–1640, painter
Daniel in the Lions' Den, 1615, 215, Fig. 8.32

Bernini, Gianlorenzo, Italian, 1598–1680, sculptor
David, 1623, 277, Fig. 10.36

Rubens, Peter Paul, Flemish, 1577–1640, painter
The Assumption of the Virgin, 1626, 288, Fig. 11.14

Leyster, Judith, Dutch, 1609–1660, painter
Self-Portrait, 1635, 54, Fig. 3.20

Gu Mei, Chinese, 17th century, painter
Orchids and Rocks, 1644, 104, Fig. 5.32

Rembrandt van Rijn, Dutch, 1606–1669, painter
The Mill, 1650, 343, Fig. 12.32

Rembrandt van Rijn, Dutch, 1606–1669, painter
Self-Portrait, 1650, 317, Fig. 12.5

Vermeer, Jan, Dutch, 1632–1675, painter
The Girl with the Red Hat, 1665, 247, Fig. 9.32

1700–1799

Haverman, Margareta, Dutch, 1693–1750, painter
A Vase of Flowers, 1716, 31, Fig. 2.6

Artist Unknown, Japanese
Footed Dish, 1700–1750, 229, Fig. 9.13

Hua Yen, Chinese, c. 1682–1765
Conversation in Autumn, 1762, 47, Fig. 3.10

Artist Unknown, Italian, Venice
Bedroom from the Sagredo Palace, 1725–1735, 100, Fig. 5.25

Copley, John Singleton, American, 1737–1815, painter
Paul Revere, 1768–70, 294, Fig. 11.22

Fragonard, Jean-Honoré, French, 1732–1806, painter
A Game of Hot Cockles, 1767–73, 260, Fig. 10.19

Franklin, Ben, American, 1706–1790, statesman, philosopher
Join or Die, 1774, 324, Fig. 12.13

Vigée-Lebrun, Élisabeth, French, 1755–1842, painter
Self-Portrait, 1781, 193, Fig. 8.3

David, Jacques Louis, French, 1748–1825, painter
Death of Socrates, 1787, 115, Fig. 5.40

Vigée-Lebrun, Élisabeth, French, 1755–1842, painter
The Marquise de Peze and the Marquise de Rouget with Her Two Children, 1787, 330, Fig. 12.22

Trumbull, John, American, 1756–1843, painter
The Sortie Made by the Garrison of Gibraltar, 1789, 18, Fig. 1.14

1800–1899

Goya, Francisco, Spanish, 1746–1828, painter
The Third of May, 1808, 1808, 83, Fig. 4.14

Hokusai, Katsushika, Japanese, 1760–1849, printmaker
The Great Wave off Kanagawa, 1823–29, 262, Fig. 10.22

Artist Unknown, Creek, Georgia or Alabama
Shoulder Bag, 1810–1830, 230, Fig. 9.14

Catlin, George, American, 1796–1872, painter
See-non-ty-a, an Iowa Medicine Man, 1845, 294, Fig. 11.23

Bonheur, Rosa, French, 1822–1899, painter
The Horse Fair, 1853–55, 224, Fig. 9.4

Olmstead, Frederick Law, American, 1822–1903, landscape architect
Central Park, 1858, 77, Fig. 4.8

Church, Frederic Edwin, American, 1826–1900, painter
Our Banner in the Sky, 1861, 267, Fig. 10.30

Eakins, Thomas, American, 1844–1916, painter
Baseball Players Practicing, 1875, 55, Fig. 3.21

Eakins, Thomas, American, 1844–1916, painter
Baby at Play, 1876, 257, Fig. 10.15

Renoir, Pierre Auguste, French, 1841–1919, painter
Madame Henriot, 1876, 199, Fig. 8.15

Cassatt, Mary, American, 1845–1926, painter
Five O'Clock Tea, 1879, 270, Fig. 10.32

Artist Unknown, Blackfeet, Montana
Man's Leggings, 1880, 121, Fig. 6.5

Degas, Edgar, French, 1834–1917, painter
Little Fourteen-Year-Old Dancer, 1880, 203, Fig. 8.21

Montata, Native American, b. date unknown, beadwork
Blackfeet Man's Leggings, 1880, 121, Fig. 6.5

Degas, Edgar, French, 1834–1917, painter
The Millinery Shop, 1879–84, 323, Fig. 12.12

Morisot, Berthe, French, 1841–1895, painter
In the Dining Room, 1886, 320, Fig. 12.9

Rodin, Auguste, French, 1840–1917, sculptor
The Burghers of Calais, 1886, 325, Fig. 12.14

van Gogh, Vincent, Dutch, 1853–1890, painter
Landscape at Saint-Rémy (Enclosed Field with Peasant), 1889, 200, Fig. 8.17

Artist Unknown, Chippewa, Minnesota
Man's Leggings, 1890, 121, Fig. 6.5

Artist Unknown, Northwestern Plains Indian
Feather Bonnet, 1890, 190, Fig. 8.1

Gauguin, Paul, French, 1848–1903, painter
Faaturuma (The Dreamer), 1891, 154, Fig. 7.1

Monet, Claude, French, 1840–1926, painter
Poplars, 1891, 173, 174, Figs. 7.32, 7.33

Homer, Winslow, American, 1836–1910, painter
Hound and Hunter, 1892, 12, Fig. 1.8

Homer, Winslow, American, 1836–1910, painter
Sketch for Hound and Hunter, 1892, 12, Fig. 1.7

Cassatt, Mary, American, 1845–1926, painter
Baby Reaching for an Apple, 1893, Fig. 2.1

Monet, Claude, French, 1840–1926, painter
Ice Floes, 1893, 161, Fig. 7.12

Beaux, Cecilia, American, 1863–1942, painter
Ernesta (Child with Nurse), 1894, 322, Fig. 12.11

Sullivan, Louis, American, 1856–1924, architect
Elevator Grille, 1893–94, 225, Fig. 9.6

Keyser, Louisa (Dat So La Lee), Native American, 1850–1925, weaver
Basket, 244, Fig. 9.30

1900–1949

Artist Unknown, Senufo Tribe, Ivory Coast
Equestrian Figure, 19th–20th centuries, 58, Fig. 3.25

Artist Unknown, Bella Coola, Northwest Coast
Cockle Hunter Mask, 1900, 295, Fig. 11.30

Artist Unknown, Iroquois
Corn Husk Mask, 1900, 53, Fig. 3.19

Artist Unknown, Kwakiutl
Wolf Mask, 1900, 299, Fig. 11.30

Steinlen, Théophile-Alexandre, French, 1859–1923, printmaker
Winter: Cat on a Cushion, 27, Fig. 2.3

Munch, Edvard, Norwegian, 1863–1944, painter, printmaker
The Kiss, 1897–1902, 296, Fig. 11.26

Picasso, Pablo, Spanish, 1881–1973, painter, sculptor
The Tragedy, 1903, 21, Fig. 1.19

Cézanne, Paul, French, 1839–1906, painter
Le Chateau Noir, 1900–04, 56, Fig. 3.23

Picasso, Pablo, Spanish, 1881–1973, painter, sculptor
The Frugal Repast, 1904, 297, Fig. 11.27

Artist Unknown, Bamum peoples, Cameroon
Male Figure, 1908, 57, Fig. 3.24

Monet, Claude, French, 1840–1926, painter
Palazzo da Mula, Venice, 1908, 56, Fig. 3.22

Balla, Giocomo, Italian, 1871–1958, painter
Street Light, 1909, 234, Fig. 9.20

Artist Unknown, Sundi group Kongo peoples, Congo, Zaire, and Angola
Bowl, before 1910, 226, Fig. 9.7

Perry, Lilla Cabot, American, 1848–1935, painter
Lady with a Bowl of Violets, 1910, 66, Fig. 3.35

Picasso, Pablo, Spanish, 1881–1973, painter, sculptor
Nude Woman, 1910, 59, Fig. 3.27

Marc, Franz, German, 1880–1916, painter
The Large Blue Horses, 1911, 175, Fig. 7.34

Balla, Giocomo, Italian, 1871–1958, painter
Dynamism of a Dog on a Leash, 1912, 236, Fig. 9.24

Gris, Juan, Spanish, 1887–1927, painter
Guitar and Flowers, 1912, 332, Fig. 12.24

Hassam, Childe, American, 1859–1935, painter, printmaker
Jelly Fish, 1912, 177, Fig. 7.36

Huntington, Anna Hyatt, American, 1876–1973, sculptor
Riders to the Sea, 1912, 142, Fig. 6.39

Utrillo, Maurice, French, 1883–1955, painter
Street at Corte, Corsica, 1913, 266, Fig. 10.29

Chagall, Marc, Russian, 1887–1985, painter
Birthday, 1915, 298, Fig. 11.28

Artist Unknown, New Ireland, Melanesia
Mask, 1920, 299, Fig. 11.30

Lachaise, Gaston, French, 1882–1935, sculptor
Walking Woman, 1922, 298, Fig. 11.29

Brancusi, Constantin, Romanian, 1876–1957, sculptor
Torso of a Young Man, 1924, 140, Fig. 6.36

Rivera, Diego, Mexican, 1886–1957, painter
Flower Day, 1925, 276, Fig. 10.35

Epstein, Sir Jacob, English (born in New York City), 1880–1959, sculptor
The Visitation, 1926, 28, Fig. 2.4

Kollwitz, Käthe, German, 1867–1945, painter, printmaker, graphic artist
Self-Portrait, 1926, 58, Fig. 3.26

Barlach, Ernst, German, 1870–1938, painter, sculptor
Singing Man, 1928, 328, Fig. 12.19

Curry, John Steuart, American, 1897–1946, painter
Baptism in Kansas, 1928, 321, Fig. 12.10

Hiroshige, Andō, Japanese, 1797–1858, printmaker
Evening Rain on the Karasaki Pine, 1929, 48, Fig. 3.11

Hopper, Edward, American, 1882–1967, painter
Early Sunday Morning, 1930, 98, Fig. 5.22

Marsh, Reginald, American, 1898–1954, painter
Why Not Use the El?, 1930, 284, Fig. 11.7

Wood, Grant, American, 1892–1942, painter
American Gothic, 1930, 254, Fig. 10.8

Artist Unknown, Asante people, Ghana
Wrapper, 228, Fig. 9.11

Calder, Alexander, American, 1898–1976, sculptor
Varese, 1931, 108, Fig. 5.36

Dali, Salvador, Spanish, 1904–1989, painter
The Persistence of Memory, 1931, 60, Fig. 3.28

Hartley, Marsden, American, 1877–1943, painter
Blueberry Highway, Dogtown, 1931, 165, Fig. 7.18

Kahlo, Frida, Mexican, 1907–1954, painter
Frida and Diego Rivera, 1931, 259, Fig. 10.17

O'Keeffe, Georgia, American, 1887–1986, painter
Cow's Skull, 1931, 266, Fig. 10.28

Orozco, José Clemente, Mexican, 1883–1949, painter
Barricade, 1931, 62, Fig. 3.31

Wood, Grant, American, 1892–1942, painter
Midnight Ride of Paul Revere, 1931, 91, Fig. 5.3

Carr, Emily, Canadian, 1871–1945, painter
Forest, British Columbia, 1931–32, 328, Fig. 12.18

Albright, Ivan, American, 1897–1983, painter
The Farmer's Kitchen, 1933–34, 200, Fig. 8.16

Bishop, Isabel, American, 1902–1988, painter
Two Girls, 1935, 292, Fig. 11.20

Lee, Doris, American, b. 1905, printmaker, painter
Thanksgiving, 1935, 138, Fig. 6.33

Wood, Grant, African-American, 1892–1942, painter
Return from Bohemia, 1935, 4, Fig. 1.1

Lange, Dorothea, American, 1895–1965, photojournalist
Migrant Mother, 1936, 15, Fig. 1.11

Wright, Frank Lloyd, American, 1867–1959, architect
Falling Water House, 1936, 330, Fig. 12.21

Hayden, Palmer, African-American, 1890–1973, painter
The Janitor Who Paints, 1937, 40, Fig. 3.1

Kahlo, Frida, Mexican, 1907–1954, painter
Self-Portrait Dedicated to Leon Trotsky, 1937, 264, Fig. 10.25

Abbot, Berenice, American, b. 1898, photographer
Façade, Alwyn Court, 1938, 129, Fig. 6.17

Artist Unknown, South American Indian
Featherwork Ornaments, 1938, 204, Fig. 8.24

Benton, Thomas Hart, American, 1882–1975, painter
I Got a Girl on Sourwood Mountain, 1938, 98, Fig. 5.23

Bishop, Isabel, American, 1902–1988, painter
Waiting, 1938, 308, Fig. 11.36

Rouault, Georges, French, 1871–1958, painter
Christ and the Apostles, 1937–38, 96, Fig. 5.17

Wright, Frank Lloyd, American, 1867–1959, architect
Taliesin West, 1938, 201, Fig. 8.19

Calder, Alexander, American, 1898–1976, sculptor
Lobster Trap and Fish Tail, 1939, 237, Fig. 9.26

Carr, Emily, Canadian, 1871–1945, painter
Above the Trees, 1939, 170, Fig. 7.27

Apel, Marie, English, 1880–1970, sculptor
Grief, 1940, 141, Fig. 6.38

Johnson, William H., African-American, 1901–1970, painter
Jitterbugs IV, 1939–40, 112, Fig. 5.38

Martinez, Maria and Julian, Native American, Maria: c. 1885–1980; Julian: c. 1885–1943, ceramicists
Black-on-black storage jar, 1942, 274, Fig. 10.34

Mondrian, Piet, Dutch, 1872–1944, painter
Broadway Boogie Woogie, 1942–43, 176, Fig. 7.35

Pippin, Horace, African-American, 1888–1946, painter
Asleep, 1943, 318, Fig. 12.7

Ernst, Max, German (in America after 1941), 1891–1976, painter
The Eye of Silence, 1943–44, 206, Fig. 8.27

Sheeler, Charles, American, 1883–1965, photographer and painter
Catastrophe No. 2, 1944, 99, Fig. 5.24

Siqueiros, David Alfaro, Mexican, 1896–1974, painter
Self-Portrait, 1945, 290, Fig. 11.17

Escher, M. C., Dutch, 1898–1972, printmaker
Other World, 1947, 127, Fig. 6.13

Wyeth, Andrew, American, b. 1917, painter
Christina's World, 1948, 33, Fig. 2.8

Moore, Henry, English, 1898–1986, sculptor
Family Group, 1948–49, 20, Fig. 1.18

Harrison, Wallace Kirkman, American, b. 1895, architect
United Nations Buildings, 1949, 128, Fig. 6.14

Johnson, Philip, American, b. 1906, architect
Johnson House, 1949, 141, Fig. 6.37

1950–1974

Matisse, Henri, French, 1869–1954, painter
Beasts of the Sea, 1950, 132, Fig. 6.21

Hopper, Edward, American, 1882–1967, painter
First Row Orchestra, 1951, 258, Fig. 10.16

Pereira, Irene Rice, American, 1907–1971, painter
Untitled, 1951, 315, Fig. 12.3

Wright, Frank Lloyd, American, 1867–1959, architect
The David Wright House, 1951, 62, Fig. 3.30

White, Charles, African-American, 1918–1979, painter
Preacher, 1952, 9, Fig. 1.4

Arp, Jean (Hans), French, 1887–1966, painter, sculptor
Aquatique, 1953, 123, Fig. 6.9

Artist Unknown, Mexican
Jaguar Mask, 250, Fig. 10.1

Shahn, Ben, American (born in Russia), 1898–1959, painter
The Blind Botanist, 1954, 140, Fig. 6.35

Le Corbusier, Swiss, 1887–1965, architect
Chapelle Notre-Dame-du-Haut, 1955, 285, Fig. 11.9

Rothko, Mark, American (born in Russia), 1903–1970, painter
Orange and Yellow, 1956, 166, Fig. 7.20

Tamayo, Rufino, Mexican, 1899–1991, painter
Toast to the Sun, 1956, 169, Fig. 7.26

Hofmann, Hans, German (born in America), 1880–1966, painter
Flowering Swamp, 1957, 64, Fig. 3.32

Saarinen, Eero, American, 1920–1961, architect
Armchair, 1957, 32, Fig. 2.7

Nevelson, Louise, American, 1899–1988, sculptor
Dawn's Wedding Chapel, 1959, 329, Fig. 12.20

Hepworth, Barbara, English, 1903–1975, sculptor
Figure for Landscape, 1960, 128, Fig. 6.15

Lawrence, Jacob, African-American, b. 1917, painter
Parade, 1960, 238, Fig. 9.27

Rockwell, Norman, American, 1894–1978, painter, illustrator
Triple Self-Portrait, 1960, 70, Fig. 4.1

Town, Harold, Canadian, 1924–1990, painter
Night Riders, 1960, 161, Fig. 7.13

Johns, Jasper, American, b. 1930, painter
Map, 1961, 327, Fig. 12.17

Smith, David, American, 1906–1965, sculptor
Cubi IX, 1961, 123, Fig. 6.8

Glarner, Fritz, American (born in Switzerland), 1899–1972, painter
Relational Painting #93, 1962, 168, Fig. 7.23

Lichtenstein, Roy, American, b. 1923, painter
Blam, 1962, 336, Fig. 12.28

Nevelson, Louise, American, 1899–1988, sculptor
Dawn, 1962, 36, Fig. 2.9

Warhol, Andy, American, 1928–1987, painter, printmaker
Marilyn Monroe's Lips, 1962, 229, Fig. 9.12

Burchfield, Charles, American, 1893–1967, painter
October Wind and Sunlight in the Woods, 1962–63, 223, Fig. 9.3

Loewy, Raymond, American (born in France), b. 1893, designer
Avanti, 1963, 74, Fig. 4.4

Poons, Larry, American, b. 1937, painter
Orange Crush, 1963, 158, Fig. 7.6

Bearden, Romare, African-American, 1914–1989, painter
Prevalence of Ritual: Baptism, 1964, 178, Fig. 7.37

Hampton, James, African-American, 1909–1965, sculptor
The Throne of the Third Heaven of the Nations' Millennium General Assembly, 1950–1964, 208, Fig. 8.28

Botero, Fernando, Colombian, b. 1932, painter
The Pinzon Family, 1965, 302, Fig. 11.33

Magritte, René, Belgian, 1898–1967, painter
The Blank Signature, 1965, 148, Fig. 6.46

Albers, Josef, German, 1888–1976, painter
Homage to the Square: Glow, 1966, 265, Fig. 10.26

Oldenburg, Claes, American, b. 1929, painter, sculptor
Shoestring Potatoes Spilling from a Bag, 1966, 286, Fig. 11.10

Sutej, Miroslav, Yugoslavian, b. 1936, lithographer
Ultra AB, 1966, 14, Fig. 1.10

Jessup, Georgia Mills, American, b. 1926, painter
Rainy Night, Downtown, 1967, 331, Fig. 12.23

Wright, Frank Lloyd, American, 1867–1959, architect
Stained-glass window, 1967, 259, Fig. 10.18

Carpenter, Miles Burkholder, American, 1889–1985, craftsperson, sculptor
Root Monster, 1968, 184, Fig. 7.40

Bak, Brunislaw M., American (born in Poland), 1922–1981, painter
Holocaust, 1969, 156, Fig. 7.3

Dodd, Lamar, American, b. 1909, painter
Night Before Launch, 1969, 19, Fig. 1.17

Fernandes, Julio, American, b. date unknown, painter
Apollo 11, 1969, 19, Fig. 1.16

Kingman, Dong, American, b. 1911, painter
Higher, Faster, and Farther, 1969, 19, Fig. 1.15

Twiggs, Leo F., African-American, b. 1934, batik painter
The Blue Wall, 1969, 29, Fig. 2.5

Catlett, Elizabeth, African-American, b. 1915, printmaker, sculptor, painter
Sharecropper, 1970, 13, Fig. 1.9

Hunt, Henry, Canadian Native American, Kwakiutl, 1923–1985, sculptor
K'umugwe' (Komokwa) Mask, 1970, 304, Fig. 11.34

Neel, Alice, American, 1900–1984, painter
Loneliness, 1970, 319, Fig. 12.8

Tichich, Leslie Mims, American, b. 1948, craftsperson
Body Adornment, 1970, 253, Fig. 10.6

Lawrence, Jacob, African-American, b. 1917, painter
Study for the Munich Olympic Games Poster, 1971, 114, Fig. 5.39

Artist Unknown, Ewe peoples, Volta region, Ghana
Wrapper, 1972, 242, Fig. 9.29

Johns, Jasper, American, b. 1930, painter
Cups 4 Picasso, 1972, 124, Fig. 6.10

Curnoe, Greg, Canadian, 1936–1992, painter
Mariposa 10 Speed, 1973, 96, Fig. 5.18

Ringgold, Faith, African-American, b. 1930, painter, soft sculptor
Mrs. Jones and Family, 1973, 306, Fig. 11.35

Andrews, Benny, African-American, b. 1930, painter, printmaker
The Scholar, 1974, 101, Fig. 5.28

1975–

Benton, Thomas Hart, American, 1882–1975, painter
The Sources of Country Music, 1975, 61, Fig. 3.29

Graves, Nancy Stevenson, b. 1940, sculptor
Rheo, 1975, 26, Fig. 2.2

Garcia, Rupert, American, b. 1941, painter
Political Prisoner, 1976, 126, Fig. 6.12

Jacquette, Yvonne, American, b. 1934, painter
East River Drive, 1976, 93, Fig. 5.6

Moore, Henry, English, 1898–1986, sculptor
Reclining Mother and Child, 1974–76, 142, Fig. 6.40

Houser, Allan, Native American, b. 1914, sculptor
Coming of Age, 1977, 233, Fig. 9.19

Dillon, Leo and Diane, American, both b. 1933, graphic artists
A Wrinkle in Time, 1979, 82, Fig. 4.13

Bak, Brunislaw M., American (born in Poland), 1922–1981, painter
Interpenetrations in Red, 1980, 316, Fig. 12.4

Bak, Hedi, American (born in Germany), b. 1924, painter
Grand Canyon #2, 1980, 194, Fig. 8.4

McKelvey, Lucy Leuppe, Native American, b. date unknown, ceramicist
Whirling Rainbow Goddesses, date unknown, 237, Fig. 9.25

Mitchell, Joan, American, 1926–1992, painter
Dirty Snow, 1980, 205, Fig. 8.25

Thiebaud, Wayne, American, b. 1920, painter
Apartment Hill, 1980, 342, Fig. 12.31

Miyawaki, Ayako, Japanese, b. 1905, appliqué artist
The Red Crab, 1981, 212, Fig. 8.30

Neel, Alice, American, 1900–1984, painter
Marisol, 1981, 42, Fig. 3.2

Dvorak, Lois, American, 1934–1993, mixed media
The Lizards, 1982, 318, Fig. 12.6

Graves, Nancy Stevenson, b. 1940, sculptor
Zaga, 1983, 17, Fig. 1.13

de Amaral, Olga, Colombian, b. 1937, fiber artist
Alquimia XIII, 1984, 203, Fig. 8.22

Steir, Pat, American, b. 1938, painter
The Brueghel Series (A Vanitas of Style), 1982–84, 180, Fig. 7.38

Torivio, Dorothy, Native American, b. 1946, ceramicist
Vase, 1984, 257, Fig. 10.14

Dvorak, Lois, American, 1934–1993, mixed media
Spirit Boxes I, 1985, 334, Fig. 12.27

Naranjo, Michael, Native American, b. 1944, sculptor
Spirits Soaring, 1985, 150, Fig. 6.47

Clements, Bob, American, b. 1937, sculptor
Evening Up the Score, 1986, 263, Fig. 10.24

Garrison, Elizabeth, American, b. 1914, quilter
Long May Our Land Be Bright, 1986, 256, Fig. 10.13

Hanson, Duane, American, b. 1925, sculptor, painter
Traveler with Sunburn, 1986, 65, Fig. 3.33

Clive, Carolyn, American, b. 1931, painter
Amplitude, 1987, 110, Fig. 5.37

Fish, Janet I., American, b. 1939, painter
Fallen Vase, 1987, 7, Fig. 1.2

Larraz, Julio, Cuban, b. 1944, painter
Papiamento, 1987, 8, Fig. 1.3

Marisol, Venezuelan (in America since 1950), b. 1930, sculptor
Poor Family I, 1987, 118, Fig. 6.1

Schapiro, Miriam, American, b. 1923, painter, sculptor
Anna and David, 1987, 280, Fig. 11.1

Xiong, Chaing, Laotian, b. 1953, craftsperson
Hmong Story Cloth, 1987, 220, Fig. 9.1

Artist Unknown, Mexican
Bird, 1988, 210, Fig. 8.29

Fish, Janet I., American, b. 1939, painter
Jonathan and Lorraine, 1988, 198, Fig. 8.13

Jacquette, Yvonne, American, b. 1934, painter
Town of Skowhegan, Maine V, 1988, 312, Fig. 12.1

Murray, Elizabeth, American, b. 1936, painter
Things to Come, 1988, 186, Fig. 7.41

Spear, Laurinda, American, b. 1951, architect
Centre for Innovative Technology, 1985–1988, 65, Fig. 3.34

Close, Chuck, American, b. 1940, painter
Janet, 1989, 246, Fig. 9.31

Twiggs, Leo F., African-American, b. 1934, batik painter
East Wind Suite: Door, 1989, 88, Fig. 5.1

Courtney–Clarke, Margaret, English, b. 1949, photojournalist
photo from *African Canvas,* 1990, 172, Fig. 7.30

Hoover, John, Native American, Aleut, b. 1919, sculptor
Loon Song, 1990, 202, Fig. 8.20

Jimenez, Luis, American, b. 1940, sculptor
Vaquero, 1990, 16, Fig. 1.12

Skoglund, Sandy, American, b. 1946, photographer, mixed media
The Green House, 1990, 214, Fig. 8.31

Smith, Jaune Quick-To-See, Native American, b. 1940, painter
Spotted Owl, 1990, 182, Fig. 7.39

Dick, Beau, Canadian Native American, b. 1955, printmaker
Sacred Circles, 1991, 272, Fig. 10.33

Wilson, Jane, American, b. 1924, painter
Solstice, 1991, 333, Fig. 12.26

Yancy, John, African-American, b. 1956, muralist
Celebration of Arts: Vibrations of Life, 1991, 340, Fig. 12.30

Bayless, Florence, American, b. 1922, craftsperson
Haori Coat, 1992, 326, Fig. 12.16

Namingha, Dan, Native American, b. 1950, painter
Blessing Rain Chant, 1992, 97, Fig. 5.21

Tafoya, Juan, Native American, b. 1949, ceramicist
Seed Pot, 1992, 203, Fig. 8.23

Romero, Annette, Native American, b. 1951, ceramicist
Storyteller Doll, 1993, 300, Fig. 11.32

Schapiro, Miriam, American, b. 1923, painter, sculptor
Yard Sale, 1993, 201, Fig. 8.18

Smith, Larry, American, b. 1949, painter
North Georgia Waterfall, 1993, 144, Fig. 6.44

GLOSSARY

This section contains the important words and phrases used in *ArtTalk* that may be new to you. You may want to refer to this list of terms as you read the chapters, complete the exercises, and prepare to create your own works of art. You can also use the Glossary to review what you have learned in *ArtTalk*. It will help you to know that the terms used in the glossary definitions that are themselves defined elsewhere in the Glossary are in *italic*. The numbers shown in parentheses indicate the chapter in which the word is introduced.

A

Abstract art Twentieth-century art containing shapes that simplify shapes of real objects to emphasize form instead of subject matter.

Abstract Expressionism Painting style developed after World War II in New York City that stressed elements and principles of art as subject matter and emotion rather than planned design. Abstract Expressionism is also called *action painting* because artists applied paint freely to huge canvases (3).

Academies Art schools that developed in western Europe after the French Revolution. They replaced the *apprentice* system.

Acrylic paint *Pigments* mixed with an acrylic vehicle. Available in different degrees of quality: school and artists' acrylics. School acrylics are less expensive than the professional acrylics, can be washed out of brushes and clothes, and are nontoxic.

Action Painting See *Abstract Expressionism*

Active Expressing movement. Diagonal and zigzag lines (5) and diagonally slanting shapes and forms (6) are active. Opposite of *static*.

Aesthetic experience Your personal interaction with a work of art (2).

Aesthetic judgment Values used in judging a work of art involving reasons for finding a work of art beautiful or satisfying.

Aesthetics The philosophy or study of the nature of beauty and art (2).

Afterimage Weak image of *complementary color* created by a viewer's brain as a reaction to prolonged looking at a color. After staring at something red, the viewer sees an afterimage of green.

Age of Faith See *Middle Ages*.

Air brush Atomizer operated by compressed air used for spraying on paint.

Alternating rhythm Visual rhythm set up by repeating *motifs* but changing position or content of motifs or spaces between them (9).

Analogous colors Colors that sit side by side on the color wheel and have a common hue (7). Violet, red-violet, and red are analogous colors. Analogous colors can be used as a *color scheme*.

Analysis In art criticism, the step in which you discover how the work is organized (2). In art history, the step in which you determine the style of the work and how it fits into an art movement (3).

Animation The art of moving cartoons (4). A series of drawings are photographed, and the figures seem to move when they are projected one after another.

Appliqué An art form in which cutout fabric decorations are fastened to a larger surface to create a new design.

Apprentice Student artist. In the *Middle Ages*, apprentices learned from master artists in *craft guilds*.

Approximate symmetry Balance that is almost *symmetrical* (10). This type of symmetry produces the effect of stability, as formal balance does, but small differences make the arrangement more interesting.

Arbitrary color Color chosen by an artist to express his or her feelings (7). Opposite of *optical color*.

Arch Curved stone structure supporting weight of material over an open space. Doorways and bridges use arches.

Architect A person who designs buildings that are well constructed, aesthetically pleasing, and functional (4).

Architecture Art form of designing and planning construction of buildings, cities, and bridges.

Armature Framework for supporting material used in sculpting.

Armory Show First large exhibition of modern art in America. It was held in the 69th Regiment Armory building in New York City in 1913. The *Ashcan School* artists, who were influenced by modern European art, helped organize this exhibit.

Art The use of skill and imagination to produce beautiful objects.

Art criticism An organized system for studying a work of art. It has four stages: description, analysis, interpretation, and judgment (2).

Artistic style See *style*.

Ashcan School Group of American artists working in the early twentieth century who used city people and city scenes for subject matter (7). Originally called "The Eight," they helped to organize the *Armory Show*.

Assemblage Three-dimensional work of art consisting of many pieces assembled together.

Asymmetrical balance Another name for *informal balance*, in which unlike objects have equal *visual weight* or eye attraction.

Atmospheric perspective Effect of air and light on how an object is perceived by the viewer (6). The more air between the viewer and the object, the more the object seems to fade. A bright object seems closer to the viewer than a dull object.

B

Background Part of the picture plane that seems to be farthest from the viewer.

Balance Principle of design concerned with equalizing visual forces, or elements, in a work of art (10). If a work of art has visual balance, the viewer feels that the elements have been arranged in a satisfying way. Visual imbalance makes the viewer feel that the elements need to be rearranged. The two types of balance are *formal* (also called *symmetrical*) and *informal* (also called *asymmetrical*).

Baroque Artistic style that emphasized movement, strong value contrast, and variety. It developed after the Reformation in the seventeenth century. Artists used movement of forms and figures toward the viewer, dramatic lighting effects, contrast between dark and light, ornamentation, and curved lines to express energy and strong emotions (3).

Bas-relief Sculpture in which areas project slightly from a flat surface. Bas-relief is also called *low relief.*

Binder A liquid that holds together the grains of pigment (7).

Blending Technique of *shading* through smooth, gradual application of dark value.

Block Piece of engraved wood or linoleum inked to make a print.

Brayer Roller with a handle used to apply ink to a surface (5).

Buttress Projecting brick or stone structure that supports an arch or *vault.* A flying buttress is connected with a wall by an arch. It reaches over the side aisle to support the roof of a *cathedral.*

Byzantine Artistic style that developed around the city of Constantinople (now Istanbul, Turkey) in the eastern Roman Empire. The style blended Roman, Greek, and Oriental art. It featured very rich colors, and figures that were flat and stiff. These works blended Greek, Roman, and Asian styles and usually had a religious theme (3).

C

Calligraphic lines Flowing lines made with brushstrokes similar to Oriental writing (5).

Calligraphy An Oriental method of beautiful handwriting (5).

Canvas Rough cloth on which an oil painting is made.

Caricature Humorous drawing that exaggerates features of a person to make fun of or criticize him or her. Caricatures are often used in editorial cartoons.

Carving Shaping wood, stone, or marble by cutting and chipping.

Cast Shaped by pouring melted material into a mold and letting it harden.

Catacombs Rock tunnels under the city of Rome that early Christians used as meeting places. Paintings on catacomb walls used secret symbols because Christianity was illegal until the fourth century.

Cathedral Main church in a district (3).

Central axis A dividing line that works like the point of balance in the balance scale. The central axis is used to measure *visual weight* in a work of art. It can be vertical (balance between sides is measured) or horizontal (balance between top and bottom is measured) (10).

Ceramics Art of making objects with clay to produce pottery and sculpture. Pottery is *fired* in a *kiln* to make it stronger.

Characters Chinese or Japanese line drawings that stand for letters, ideas, objects, or verbal sounds. They are formed by *calligraphic lines.*

Chiaroscuro The arrangement of light and shadow (6). This technique was introduced by Italian artists during the Renaissance and used widely by Baroque artists. Chiaroscuro is also called *modeling* and *shading.*

Cityscape Painting or drawing in which a city is the main feature.

Classical Referring to the art of ancient Greece and Rome. The Greeks created art based on the ideals of perfect proportion and logic instead of emotion. The Romans adapted Greek art and spread it throughout the civilized world.

Clay Stiff, sticky earth that is used in ceramics. It is wet, and it hardens after drying or heating.

Clustering Technique for creating a *focal point* by grouping several different shapes closely together (12).

Coil Long roll joined into a circle or spiral. Clay coils are used to make pottery.

Collage Two-dimensional work of art consisting of bits and pieces of textured paper and fabric pasted onto a painting (8).

Color An element of art that is derived from reflected light (7). The sensation of color is aroused in the brain by response of the eyes to different wavelengths of light. Color has three properties: *hue, value,* and *intensity.*

Color-Field Painting Twentieth-century style of painting using flat areas of color for the pure sensation of color. Artists creating color-field paintings are not trying to express emotion or use a precise design.

Color scheme Plan for organizing colors. Types of color schemes include *monochromatic, analogous, complementary, triad, split complementary, warm,* and *cool.*

Color spectrum The effect that occurs when light passes through a *prism*; the beam of white light is bent and separated into bands of color. Colors always appear in the same order, by wavelengths, from longest to shortest: red, orange, yellow, green, blue, violet. A rainbow displays the *spectrum* (7).

Color triad Three colors spaced an equal distance apart on the *color wheel* (7). The primary color triad is red, yellow, and blue; the secondary color triad is orange, green, and violet. A color triad is a type of *color scheme.*

Color wheel The *spectrum* bent into a circle (7).

Compass Instrument used for measuring and drawing arcs and circles.

Complementary colors The colors opposite each other on the *color wheel* (7). A complement of a color absorbs all the light waves the color reflects and is the strongest contrast to the color. Mixing a hue with its complementary color dulls it. Red and green are complementary colors. Complementary colors can be used as a *color scheme.*

Composition The way the principles of design are used to organize the elements (1).

Content The message the work communicates. The content can relate to the subject matter or be an idea or emotion. *Theme* is another word for content (1).

Continuation Technique for creating *unity* by arranging shapes so that the line or edge of one shape continues a line or edge of the next (12).

Contour drawing Drawing in which only *contour lines* are used to represent the subject matter (5). Artists keep their eyes on the object they are drawing and concentrate on directions and curves.

Contour lines Lines creating boundaries that separate one area from another (5). Contour lines define the edges and surface ridges of an object.

Contrast Technique for creating a *focal point* by using differences in elements (12).

Convergence Technique for creating a *focal point* by arranging elements so that many lines or shapes point to one item or area (12).

Cool colors Blue, green, and violet (7). Cool colors suggest coolness and seem to recede from a viewer. Cool colors can be used as a *color scheme.* Opposite of *warm colors.*

Craft guilds Groups of artists working in western European towns in the Middle Ages. Master artists taught *apprentices* their skills.

Crafts Art forms creating works of art that are both beautiful and useful. Crafts include weaving, fabric design, ceramics, and jewelry making.

Crayons *Pigments* held together with wax and molded into sticks.

Credit line A list of important facts about a work of art. A credit line usually includes the artist's name, the title of the work, year completed, *medium* used, size (height, width, and depth), location (gallery, museum, or collection and city), donors, and date donated (1).

Crewel Loosely twisted yarn used in *embroidery*.

Criteria Standards of judgment (2).

Crosshatching The technique of using crossed lines for *shading* (5).

Cubism Twentieth-century art movement that emphasizes structure and *design* (3). Three-dimensional objects are pictured from many different points of view at the same time.

Culture Behaviors, customs, ideas, and skills of a group of people. Studying art objects produced by a group of people is one way to learn about a culture.

Curved lines Lines that are always bending and change direction gradually (5).

D

Dadaists Early twentieth-century artists using fantastic and strange objects as subject matter.

Dark Ages See *Middle Ages*.

Decalcomania The technique of creating random *texture* patterns by pulling apart surfaces between which blobs of paint have been squeezed (8).

Dense Compact; having parts crowded together. Dense materials are solid and heavy. Opposite of soft.

Description A list of all the things you see in the work (2).

Design Plan, organization, or arrangement of elements in a work of art.

Design qualities How well the work is organized (2). This aesthetic quality is favored by *formalism*.

De Stijl Dutch for "the style." A painting style developed by Mondrian in Holland in the early twentieth century that uses only vertical and horizontal lines; black, white, and gray; and the three primary colors.

Diagonal lines Lines that slant (5).

Dimension Amount of space an object takes up in one direction (5). The three dimensions are height, width, and depth.

Distortion Deviations from expected, normal *proportions* (11).

Divine Proportion See *Golden Mean*.

Dome Hemispherical *vault* or ceiling over a circular opening. A dome rises above the center part of a building.

Dominant element Element of a work of art noticed first. Elements noticed later are called *subordinate*.

Dyes *Pigments* that dissolve in liquid. Dye sinks into a material and stains it (7).

Dynamism Term used by the *Futurists* to refer to the forces of movement.

Dynasty A period of time during which a single family provided a succession of rulers (3).

E

Edition A series of identical *prints* made from the same plate (1).

Elements of art Basic visual symbols in the language of art. The elements of art are *line, shape, form, space, color, value,* and *texture* (1).

Embroidery Method of decorating fabric with stitches.

Emotionalism Theory that requires a strong communication of feelings, moods, or ideas from the work to the viewer. One of the three theories of art, the others being *formalism* and *imitationalism* (2).

Emphasis Principle of *design* that makes one part of a work dominant over the other parts (12). The element noticed first is called *dominant;* the elements noticed later are called *subordinate*.

Engraving Method of cutting a *design* into a material, usually metal, with a sharp tool. A *print* can be made by inking an engraved surface.

Exaggeration Deviations from expected, normal *proportions* (11).

Expressionism Twentieth-century art movement in which artists tried to communicate their strong emotional feelings and which stressed personal feelings rather than *composition* (3).

Expressive qualities Those qualities that communicate ideas and moods (2).

Fabric Material made from *fibers*. Cloth and felt are fabrics.

Fauves French for "wild beasts." A group of early twentieth-century painters who used brilliant colors and bold distortions in an uncontrolled way. Their leader was Henri Matisse.

Federal Arts Project Government program established during the Depression to create jobs for American artists.

Fiber Thin, threadlike linear material that can be woven or spun into fabric.

Fiberfill Lightweight, fluffy filling material made of synthetic fibers.

Figure Human form in a work of art.

Fine art Works of art made to be enjoyed, not used, and judged by the theories of art. Opposite of *functional art*.

Fire To apply heat to harden pottery.

Flowing rhythm Visual rhythm created by repeating wavy lines (9).

Focal point The first part of a work to attract the attention of the viewer (12). Focal points are created by *contrast, location, isolation, convergence,* and use of the unusual.

Foreground Part of the *picture plane* that appears closest to the viewer. The foreground is usually at the bottom of the picture.

Foreshortening To shorten an object to make it look as if it extends backward into space (11). This method reproduces *proportions* a viewer actually sees, which depend on the viewer's distance from the object or person.

Form Objects having three dimensions (6). Like a *shape,* a form has height and width, but it also has depth. Forms are either *geometric* or *free-form*.

Formal balance Way of organizing parts of a *design* so that equal, or very similar, elements are placed on opposite sides of a *central axis* (10). Formal balance suggests stability. *Symmetry* is a type of formal balance. Opposite of *informal balance*.

Formalism Theory that places emphasis on the *design* qualities. One of the three theories of art, the others being *emotionalism* and *imitationalism* (2).

Found materials Natural objects (such as stones or leaves) and ordinary, manufactured objects (such as coins, keys, wire, or paper plates) found by chance that can be used to create a work of art.

Free-form shapes Irregular and uneven shapes (6). Their outlines are curved, or angular, or both. Free-form shapes are often natural. Opposite of *geometric shapes*.

Freestanding Work of art surrounded on all sides by space (6). A three-dimensional work of art is freestanding. Opposite of *relief* (1).

Frottage A method of placing a freshly painted canvas right-side-up over a raised *texture* and scraping the surface of the paint (8).

Functional art Works of art made to be used instead of only enjoyed. Objects must be judged by how well they work when used.

Futurists Early twentieth-century Italian artists who arranged angular forms to suggest motion (9). They called the forces of movement *dynamism*.

Gallery Place for displaying or selling works of art.

Genre painting Paintings that have scenes from everyday life as their subject matter.

Geometric shapes Precise shapes that can be described using mathematical formulas (6). Basic geometric shapes are the circle, the square, and the triangle. Basic geometric forms are the cylinder, the cube, and the pyramid. Opposite of *free-form shapes*.

Gestures An expressive movement (5).

Gesture drawing Line drawing done quickly to capture movement of the subject's body (5).

Glaze In ceramics, a thin, glossy coating fired into pottery. In painting, a thin layer of *transparent* paint.

Golden Mean A *line* divided into two parts so that the smaller line has the same *proportion*, or ratio, to the larger line as the larger line has to the whole line (11). Perfect ratio (relationship of parts) discovered by Euclid, a Greek Philosopher. Its mathematical expression is 1 to 1.6. It was also called the *Golden Section* and the *Golden Rectangle*. The long sides of the Golden Rectangle are a little more than half again as long as the short sides. This ratio was rediscovered in the early sixteenth century and named the *Divine Proportion*.

Gothic Artistic style developed in western Europe between the twelfth and sixteenth centuries. Gothic *cathedrals* used pointed arches and flying *buttresses* to emphasize upward movement and featured *stained-glass* windows. *Sculpture* and painting showed humans realistically (3).

Gouache *Pigments* ground in water and mixed with gum to form *opaque* watercolor. Gouache resembles school tempera or poster paint.

Grattage The technique of scratching into wet paint with a variety of tools, such as forks, razors, and combs for the purpose of creating different *textures* (8).

Grid Pattern of intersecting vertical and horizontal lines (9).

Hard-edge In two-dimensional art, shapes with clearly defined outlines. Hard-edge shapes look dense. Opposite of *soft-edge*.

Harmony The principle of *design* that creates *unity* by stressing similarities of separate but related parts (12).

Hatching Technique of *shading* with a series of fine parallel *lines*.

Hierarchical proportion When figures are arranged in a work of art so scale indicates importance (11).

Hieroglyphics Picture writing used by ancient Egyptians.

High-key painting Painting using many *tints* of a *color* (7). Opposite of *low-key painting*.

Highlights Small areas of white used to show the very brightest spots (6). Highlights show the surfaces of the subject that reflect the most light. They are used to create the illusion of *form*. Opposite of *shadows*.

High relief *Sculpture* in which areas project far out from a flat surface.

High-resolution Producing a sharp image.

Hologram Images in three dimensions created with a laser beam (6).

Horizon Point at which earth and sky seem to meet.

Horizontal line *Line* parallel to the horizon (5). Horizontal lines lie flat and are parallel to the bottom edge of the paper or canvas.

Hue The name of a spectral *color* (7). Hue is related to the wavelength of reflected light. The primary hues are red, yellow, and blue; they are called *primary* because they cannot be made by mixing other hues together. The secondary hues, made by mixing two primary hues, are orange, violet, and green. Hue is one of the three properties of color.

Hyper-Realism See *New Realism*.

Imitationalism An *aesthetic* theory focusing on realistic presentation. One of the three theories of art, the others being *emotionalism* and *formalism* (2).

Implied lines A series of points that the viewer's eyes automatically connect. Implied lines are suggested, not real (5).

Impression Mark or imprint made by pressure.

Impressionism Style of painting started in France in the 1860s (3). It captured everyday subjects and emphasized the momentary effects of sunlight.

Industrial designers People who *design* the products of industry (4).

Informal balance Way of organizing parts of a *design* so that unlike objects have equal *visual weight* or eye attraction (10). *Asymmetry* is another term for informal balance. Opposite of *formal balance*.

Intensity The brightness or dullness of a hue. A pure *hue* is called a high-intensity *color*. A dulled hue (a color mixed with its complement) is called a low-intensity color. Intensity is one of the three properties of color (7).

Interior Designer A person who plans the *design* and decoration of the interior spaces in homes and offices (4).

Intermediate color A *color* made by mixing a primary color with a secondary color. Red-orange is an intermediate color.

Interpretation The meaning or mood of the work (2).

Invented texture A kind of *visual texture* that does not represent a real texture but creates a sensation of one by repeating *lines* and shapes in a two-dimensional pattern (8). Opposite of *simulated texture*.

Isolation Technique for creating a *focal point* by putting one object alone to emphasize it (12).

Judgment In art criticism, the step in which you determine the degree of artistic merit (2). In art history, the step in which you determine if the work has made an important contribution to the history of art (3).

Kiln Furnace in which *clay* is fired in order to harden it. A kiln may be electric, gas, or wood-burning.

Kinetic sculpture A work of art that actually moves in space (9).

Landscape Painting or drawing in which natural land scenery, such as mountains, trees, rivers, or lakes, is the main feature.

Landscape architect A person who *designs* playgrounds, parks, and outdoor areas around buildings and along highways (4).

Layout The way items are arranged on the page (4).

Line A mark drawn with a pointed, moving tool. Although lines can vary in appearance (they can have different lengths, widths, *textures*, directions, and degree of curve), they are considered one-dimensional and are measured by length. A line is also considered the path of a dot through space and is used by an artist to control the viewer's eye movement. There are five kinds of lines: *vertical, horizontal, diagonal, curved,* and *zigzag* (5).

Linear perspective A graphic system that creates the illusion of depth and volume on a flat surface. In one-point linear perspective, all receding lines meet at a single point. In two-point linear perspective, different sets of lines meet at different points (6).

Literal qualities The realistic qualities that appear in the subject of the work (2).

Location The technique of using placement of elements to create a *focal point* (12). Items near the center of a work of art are usually noticed first.

Logos Identifying symbols (4).

Loom Machine or frame for *weaving*.

Low-key painting Painting using many *shades* or dark *values* of a color (7). Opposite of *high-key painting*.

Low-relief See *bas-relief*.

Lucite Trademark for an acrylic plastic molded into *transparent* sheets, tubes, or rods.

Mannerism European sixteenth-century artistic style featuring highly emotional scenes and distorted figures.

Manufactured shapes/forms Shapes or forms made by people either by hand or by machine. Opposite of *natural shapes/forms*.

Mat To frame a picture or drawing with a cardboard border.

Matte surface Surface that reflects a soft, dull light (8). Paper has a matte surface. Opposite of *shiny surface*.

Medallion Round, medal-like decoration (10).

Media See *medium*.

Medieval Related to the *Middle Ages*.

Medium Material used to make art. Plural is *media* (1).

Mexican muralists Early twentieth-century artists whose paintings on walls and ceilings used solid *forms* and powerful *colors* to express their feelings about the Mexican Revolution. Also called *Mexican Expressionists*.

Middle Ages Period of roughly one thousand years from the destruction of the Roman Empire to the *Renaissance*. Culture centered around the Church. The Middle Ages are also called the *Dark Ages* (because few new ideas developed) and the *Age of Faith* (because religion was a powerful force.)

Middle ground Area in a picture between the *foreground* and the *background*.

Mobile Moving *sculpture* in which shapes are balanced and arranged on wire arms and suspended from the ceiling to move freely in the air currents (3).

Modeling See *chiaroscuro*.

Modular sculpture *Freestanding* sculpture that joins *modules* (9).

Module A three-dimensional *motif* (9).

Monk's cloth Heavy cloth with a basket weave, often used for curtains.

Monochrome One *color*. A monochromatic *color scheme* uses only one *hue* and the *values*, *tints*, and *shades* of that hue for a unifying effect (7).

Mortar and pestle Ceramic bowl and tool for grinding something into a powder.

Mosaics Pictures made with small cubes of colored marble, glass, or tile and set into cement.

Motif A unit that is repeated in visual rhythm (9). Units in a motif may or may not be an exact duplicate of the first unit.

Movement Principle of *design* that deals with creating the illusion of action or physical change in position (9).

Mural Painting on a wall or ceiling.

Natural shapes/forms Shapes or forms made by the forces of nature. Opposite of *manufactured shapes/forms*.

Negative spaces Empty spaces surrounding *shapes* and *forms* (6). The shape and size of negative spaces affect the interpretation of *positive spaces*. Negative spaces are also called *ground*.

Neoclassicism New classic. French artistic style developed in the nineteenth century after the *Rococo* style. It used *classical* features and was unemotional and realistic.

Neutral colors Black, white, and gray. Black reflects no wavelengths of light, white reflects all wavelengths of light, and gray reflects all wavelengths of light equally but only partially.

New Realism Twentieth-century American artistic style in which subjects are portrayed realistically (3). Also called *Hyper-Realism, Photo-Realism,* and *Super-Realism*.

Nonobjective art Art that has no recognizable subject matter.

Oil paint Slow-drying paint made by mixing *pigments* in oil and usually used on *canvas*.

Opaque Quality of a material that does not let any light pass through. Opposite of *transparent*.

Op Art Optical art. Twentieth-century artistic style in which artists tried to create the impression of movement on the surface of paintings with hard edges, smooth surfaces, and mathematical planning.

Optical color *Color* perceived by the viewer due to the effect of atmosphere or unusual light on the actual color (7). Opposite of *arbitrary color*.

Outline A *line* that shows or creates the outer edges of a *shape* (5).

Paint *Pigments* mixed with oil or water. Pigment particles in paint stick to the surface of the material on which the paint is applied.

Palette Tray for mixing *colors* of *paints*.

Papier-mâché French for "mashed paper." Modeling material made of paper and liquid paste and molded over a supporting structure called the *armature*.

Parallel lines *Lines* that move in the same direction and always stay the same distance apart.

Pastels *Pigments* held together with gum and molded into sticks.

Paste-up Model of a printed page. It is photographed for the purpose of making a plate for the printing process.

Pattern Two-dimensional decorative visual repetition (9). A pattern has no *movement* and may or may not have *rhythm.*

Perception The act of looking at something carefully and thinking deeply about what is seen (1).

Perspective A graphic system that creates the illusion of depth and volume on a two-dimensional surface (6). It was developed during the Renaissance by architect Filippo Brunelleschi. Perspective is created by overlapping, size variations, placement, detail, *color*, and *converging lines.*

Photogram Image on blueprint paper developed by fumes from liquid ammonia.

Photography A technique of capturing optical images on light-sensitive surfaces (1).

Photojournalists Visual reporters (4).

Photo-Realism See *New Realism.*

Picture plane The surface of a painting or drawing.

Pigments Finely ground, colored powders that form paint when mixed with a liquid. Pigments are also used to make *crayons* and *pastels* (7).

Plaster Mixture of lime, sand, and water that hardens on drying.

Point of view Angle from which the viewer sees an object (6). The shapes and forms a viewer sees depend on his or her point of view.

Polymer medium Liquid used in *acrylic* painting as a thinning or finishing material.

Pop art Artistic style used in the early 1960s in America featuring subject matter from popular culture (mass media, commercial art, comic strips, and advertising) (3).

Portrait Image of a person, especially the face and upper body.

Positive spaces *Shapes* or *forms* in two- and three-dimensional art (6). Empty spaces surrounding them are called *negative spaces* or *ground.*

Post-Impressionism French painting style of the late nineteenth century that used basic structures of art to express feelings and ideas (3). The Post-Impressionism movement, which immediately followed *Impressionism*, was led by Paul Cézanne, Vincent van Gogh, and Paul Gauguin.

Prehistoric Period before history was written down.

Principles of design Rules that govern how artists organize the elements of art. The principles of design are *rhythm, movement, balance, proportion, variety, emphasis, harmony,* and *unity* (1).

Print *Impression* created by an artist made on paper or fabric from a *printing plate, stone,* or *block* and repeated many times to produce identical images.

Printing plate Surface containing the *impression* transferred to paper or fabric to make a *print* (1).

Printmaking A process in which an artist repeatedly transfers an original image from one prepared surface to another (1).

Prism Wedge-shaped piece of glass that bends white light and separates it into *spectral hues.*

Profile Side view of a face.

Progressive rhythm Visual rhythm that changes a *motif* each time it is repeated (9).

Proportion Principle of art concerned with the size relationships of one part to another (11).

Protractor Semicircular instrument used to measure and draw angles.

Proximity Technique for creating *unity* by limiting *negative spaces* between *shapes* (12).

Pyramids Tombs of Egyptian pharaohs, who were rulers worshiped as gods.

Radial balance Type of balance in which forces or elements of a *design* come out (radiate) from a central point (10).

Random rhythm Visual rhythm in which a *motif* is repeated in no apparent order, with no regular spaces (9).

Rasp File with sharp, rough teeth used for cutting into a surface.

Realism Mid-nineteenth-century artistic style in which artists turned away from the style of Romanticism to paint familiar scenes as they actually were (3).

Realists Artists in the nineteenth century who portrayed political, social, and moral issues (3).

Real texture Texture that can be perceived through touch. Opposite of *visual texture.*

Recede To move back or become more distant.

Reformation Religious revolution in western Europe in the sixteenth century. It started as a reform movement in the Catholic Church and led to the beginnings of Protestantism.

Regionalists Artists who painted the farmlands and cities of America realistically (3).

Regular rhythm Visual rhythm achieved through repeating identical *motifs* using the same intervals of *space* between them (9).

Relief Type of *sculpture* in which *forms* project from a flat background. Opposite of *freestanding* (1).

Renaissance The name given to the period of awakening at the end of the *Middle Ages* (3). French for "rebirth." Interest in *Classical* art was renewed. Important Renaissance artists are Leonardo da Vinci, Michelangelo, and Raphael.

Repetition Technique for creating *rhythm* and *unity* in which a *motif* or single element appears again and again (12).

Reproduction Copy of a work of art.

Rhythm *Principle of design* that indicates movement by the repetition of elements (9). Visual rhythm is perceived through the eyes and is created by repeating *positive spaces* separated by *negative spaces.* There are five types of rhythm: *random, regular, alternating, flowing,* and *progressive.*

Rococo Eighteenth-century artistic style that began in the luxurious homes of the French aristocracy and spread to the rest of Europe. It stressed free graceful movement, a playful use of *line*, and delicate *colors* (3).

Romanesque Style of *architecture* and *sculpture* developed during the Middle Ages in western Europe that featured massive size; solid, heavy walls; wide use of the rounded Roman *arch*; and many sculptural decorations (3).

Romanticism Early nineteenth-century artistic style that was a reaction against *Neoclassicism.* It featured dramatic scenes, bright *colors*, loose *compositions*, and exotic settings. It also emphasized the feelings and personality of the artist.

Rough texture Irregular surface that reflects light unevenly (8). Opposite of *smooth texture.*

Rubbing Technique for transferring textural quality of a surface to paper by placing paper over the surface and rubbing the top of the paper with *crayon* or pencil (8).

Safety labels Labels identifying *art* products that are safe to use or that must be used with caution.

Scale Size as measured against a standard reference. Scale can refer to an entire work of art or to elements within it (11).

Score To make neat, sharp creases in paper using a cutting tool.

Sculpture Three-dimensional work of art created out of wood, stone, metal, or clay by *carving*, welding, *casting*, or *modeling.*

Seascape Painting or drawing in which the sea is the subject.

Shade A dark *value* of a *hue* made by adding black to it. Opposite of *tint* (7).

Shading See *chiaroscuro*.

Shadows Shaded areas in a drawing or painting. Shadows show the surfaces of the subject that reflect the least light and are used to create the illusion of *form*. Opposite of *highlights*.

Shape A two-dimensional area that is defined in some way. While a *form* has depth, a *shape* has only height and width. Shapes are either *geometric* or *free-form* (6).

Shiny surface Surface that reflects bright light. Window glass has a shiny surface. Opposite of *matte surface*.

Sighting Technique for determining the proportional relationship of one part of an object to another (11).

Silhouette Outline drawing of a *shape*. Originally a silhouette was a *profile* portrait, filled in with a solid *color*.

Simplicity Technique for creating *unity* by limiting the number of variations of an element.

Simulated texture A kind of *visual texture* that imitates real *texture* by using a two-dimensional pattern to create the illusion of a three-dimensional surface (8). A plastic tabletop can use a pattern to simulate the texture of wood. Opposite of *invented texture*.

Sketch Quick, rough drawing without much detail that can be used as a plan or reference for later work.

Slip Creamy mixture of *clay* and water used to fasten pieces of clay together.

Smooth texture Regular surface that reflects light evenly. Opposite of *rough texture* (8).

Soft-edge In two-dimensional art, shapes with fuzzy, blurred outlines. Soft-edge shapes look soft. Opposite of *hard-edge*.

Soft sculpture *Sculpture* made with fabric and stuffed with soft material.

Solvent The liquid that controls the thickness or the thinness of the *paint* (7).

Space The element of *art* that refers to the emptiness or area between, around, above, below, or within objects. *Shapes* and *forms* are defined by space around and within them (6).

Spectral colors Red, orange, yellow, green, blue, violet.

Split complementary colors One **hue** and the hues on each side of its complement on the *color wheel* (7). Red-orange, blue, and green are split complementary colors. Split complementary colors can be used as a *color scheme*.

Stained glass Colored glass cut into pieces, arranged in a *design*, and joined with strips of lead.

Static Inactive (5). Vertical and horizontal lines and horizontal *shapes* and *forms* are static. Opposite of *active*.

Still life Painting or drawing of inanimate (nonmoving) objects.

Stippling Technique of *shading* using dots.

Stitchery Technique for decorating fabric by stitching *fibers* onto it.

Stone Age Period of history during which stone tools were used.

Storyboards A series of still drawings that show a story's progress for *animation*. Storyboards are an outline for the development of a film (4).

Style The artist's personal way of using the elements of *art* and *principles of design* to express feelings and ideas (3).

Subject The image viewers can easily identify in a work of art (1).

Subordinate element Element of a work of *art* noticed after the *dominant element*.

Super-Realism See *New Realism*.

Surrealism Twentieth-century artistic style in which dreams, fantasy, and the subconscious served as inspiration for artists (3).

Symbol Something that stands for, or represents, something else (1).

Symmetry A special type of *formal balance* in which two halves of a balanced *composition* are identical, mirror images of each other (10).

Synthetic Made by chemical processes rather than natural processes.

T

Tapestry Fabric wall hanging that is woven, painted, or embroidered.

Tempera Paint made by mixing *pigments* with egg yolk (egg tempera) or another liquid. School poster paint is a type of tempera.

Texture Element of art that refers to how things feel, or look as if they might feel if touched. Texture is perceived by touch and sight. Objects can have *rough* or *smooth textures* and *matte* or *shiny surfaces* (8).

Tint A light *value* of a *hue* made by mixing the hue with white. Opposite of *shade* (7).

Tonality Arrangement of colors in a painting so that one *color* dominates the work of *art* (7).

Transparent Quality of a material that allows light to pass through. Opposite of *opaque*.

Trompe l'oeil French for "deceive the eye." Style of painting in which painters try to give the viewer the illusion of seeing a three-dimensional object, so that the viewer wonders whether he or she is seeing a picture or something real.

U

Undercut A cut made below another so that an overhang is left.

Unity The quality of wholeness or oneness that is achieved through the effective use of the elements and principles of art (12). Unity is created by *simplicity, repetition, proximity,* and *continuation*.

Unusual Technique for creating a *focal point* by using the unexpected (12).

V

Value The art element that describes the darkness or lightness of an object (5). Value depends on how much light a surface reflects. Value is also one of the three properties of *color*.

Vanishing point Point on the horizon where receding parallel lines seem to meet (6).

Variety *Principle of design* concerned with difference or contrast (12).

Vault Arched roof, ceiling, or covering made of brick, stone, or concrete.

Vehicle Liquid, like water or oil, that *pigments* are mixed with to make *paint* or *dye*.

Vertical lines *Lines* that are straight up and down (5). Vertical lines are at right angles to the bottom edge of the paper or canvas and the horizon, and parallel to the side of the paper or canvas.

Viewing frame A piece of paper with an area cut from the middle. By holding the frame at arm's length and looking through it at the subject, the artist can focus on the area of the subject he or she wants to draw or paint.

Visual arts The arts that produce beautiful objects to look at.

Visual rhythm Rhythm you receive through your eyes rather than through your ears (9).

Visual texture Illusion of a three-dimensional surface based on the memory of how things feel. There are two types of visual texture: *invented* and *simulated*. Opposite of *real texture* (8).

Visual weight Attraction that elements in a work of *art* have for the viewer's eyes. Visual weight is affected by size, *contour*, *intensity* of colors, warmth and coolness of colors, contrast in *value*, *texture*, and position.

Warm colors Red, orange, and yellow (7). Warm colors suggest warmth and seem to move toward the viewer. Warm colors can be used as a *color scheme*. Opposite of *cool colors*.

Warp In *weaving*, lengthwise threads held in place on the loom and crossed by *weft* threads.

Watercolor paint *Transparent pigments* mixed with water.

Weaving Art of making fabric by interlacing two sets of parallel threads, held at right angles to each other on a *loom*.

Weft In *weaving*, crosswise threads that are carried over and under the *warp* threads.

Yarn Fibers spun into strands for *weaving*, knitting, or embroidery.

Zigzag lines *Lines* formed by short, sharp turns (5). Zigzag lines are a combination of diagonal lines. They can change direction suddenly.

BIBLIOGRAPHY

The following is an annotated listing of books dealing with various areas of art and art education. These books can provide valuable assistance to you as you study and work in the visual arts.

Architecture

American Heritage Publishing Co. *The Horizon Book of Great Cathedrals.* Edited by Jay Jacobs and the editors of Horizon Magazine. NY: American Heritage Publishing Co., 1984.

Brown, R. Allen. *Castles: A History and Guide.* NY: Greenwich House, Distributed by Crown Publishers, 1982.

Crouch, Dora P. *History of Architecture: Stonehenge to Skyscrapers.* NY: McGraw-Hill Book Co., 1985. Provides an analysis of architectural design in historical context.

Macaulay, David. *Pyramid.* Boston, MA: Houghton Mifflin Co., 1975.

McAlester, Virginia and Lee. *A Field Guide to American Houses.* NY: Alfred A. Knopf, Inc., 1984. An informative guide to the various architectural styles in American houses from the seventeenth century to the present. Lavishly detailed and profusely illustrated.

Computer Graphics

Jankel, Annabel, and Rocky Morton. *Creative Computer Graphics.* NY: Cambridge University Press, 1984. Explores the techniques used in creating computer graphic images and touches on modern computer graphic technology as well as a variety of applications.

Lewell, John. *Computer Graphics: A Survey of Current Techniques and Applications.* NY: Van Nostrand Reinhold Co., Inc., 1985. An illustrated volume that provides an overview of computer graphics.

Wilson, Mark. *Drawing with Computers.* NY: The Putnam Publishing Group, 1985. Describes the techniques of computer graphics, providing software and hardware information.

Design

Berger, Arthur Asa. *Seeing is Believing: An Introduction to Visual Communication.* Mountain View, CA: Mayfield Publishing Co., 1989.

Cheatham, Frank, Jane H. Cheatham, and Sheryl A. Haler. *Design Concepts and Applications.* Baltimore, MD: University Park Press, 1983.

Horn, George F. *Contemporary Posters: Design and Techniques.* Worcester, MA: Davis Publications, Inc., 1976. Explains effective poster design, including uses of color and various reproductive techniques.

Lauer, David A. *Design Basics.* 2d ed. NY: Holt, Rinehart and Winston, 1985.

Meilach, Dona Z., Jay Hinz, and Bill Hinz. *How to Create Your Own Designs: An Introduction to Color, Form and Composition.* NY: Doubleday and Co., Inc., 1975. An excellent introduction to the elements of design.

Ocvirk, Otto, et al. *Art Fundamentals Theory and Practice.* 6th ed. Dubuque, IA: William C. Brown, Publishers, 1990. A design resource book for teachers.

Drawing

Gatto, Joseph. *Drawing Media and Techniques.* Worcester, MA: Davis Publications, Inc., 1987. Suggestions for using a wide variety of drawing media.

James, Jane H. *Perspective Drawing: A Point of View.* 2d ed. Englewood Cliffs, NJ: Prentice-Hall, Inc., 1988. For students who want to know more about perspective.

Sheaks, Barclay. *Drawing Figures and Faces.* Worcester, MA: Davis Publications, Inc., 1987. A useful resource for students who wish to expand their drawing techniques.

Sheppard, Joseph. *Anatomy: A Complete Guide for Artists.* unabr. ed. NY: Dover Publications, Inc., 1992. A handbook of anatomy, including surface anatomy, with over 430 drawings in line and in tone.

Wilson, Brent, Al Hurwitz, and Marjorie Wilson. *Teaching Drawing from Art.* Worcester, MA: Davis Publications, Inc., 1987. Presents a unique approach to drawing. Masterworks of art are used to motivate drawing activities.

Fiber Arts

BATIK

Meilach, Dona Z. *Contemporary Batik and Tie-Dye: Methods, Inspiration, Dyes.* NY: Crown Publishers, Inc., 1973. A detailed work for beginning and experienced artists with information on many different techniques and projects and a thorough treatment of dyeing.

NEEDLECRAFT

Guild, Vera P. *Good Housekeeping New Complete Book of Needlecraft.* NY: Hearst Books, 1971. Directions for a variety of needlecraft techniques.

SILK-SCREENING

Termini, Maria. *Silkscreening.* Englewood Cliffs, NJ: Prentice-Hall, Inc., 1978. Well-rounded work on the mechanics of silk-screening with good advice for the beginner.

WEAVING

Brown, Rachel. *The Weaving, Spinning, and Dyeing Book.* 2d. ed., rev. and expanded. NY: Alfred A. Knopf, Inc., 1983. A good look at all phases of the weaving craft, including primitive and ethnic weaving.

Floral Arts

Cook, Hal. *Arranging: The Basics of Contemporary Floral Design.* NY: William Morrow & Co., Inc., 1985. A book that treats floral design as an art form. Extensively illustrated.

General Crafts

Sprintzen, Alice. *Crafts: Contemporary Design and Technique.* Worcester, MA: Davis Publications, Inc., 1987. An introduction to traditional and modern crafts, with instructions for beginners.

Stribling, Mary Lou. *Crafts From North American Indian Arts: Techniques, Designs and Contemporary Applications.* NY: Crown Publishers, Inc., 1975. Techniques and applications of many different crafts using a variety of materials.

Jewelry

Ferre, R. Duane. *How to Make Wire Jewelry.* Radnor, PA: Chilton Book Co., 1980. A good guide to beginning jewelry making using a variety of inexpensive and simple techniques.

Meilach, Dona Z. *Ethnic Jewelry: Design and Inspiration for Collectors and Craftsmen.* NY: Crown Publishers, Inc., 1981. An overview of ethnic jewelry from around the world, made from a variety of materials.

Painting

Cahill, James. *Chinese Painting.* Treasures of Asia. NY: Rizzoli International Publications, 1985.

Davidson, Abraham A. *The Story of American Painting.* NY: Harry N. Abrams, 1974.

Freedberg, Sydney J. *Painting in Italy, 1500–1600.* Pelican History of Art. NY: Penguin, 1975.

Gaunt, William. *The Great Century of British Painting: Hogarth to Turner.* London: Phaidon, 1971.

Grabar, André. *Byzantine Painting.* NY: Rizzoli International Publications, 1979.

Haak, Bob. *The Golden Age: Dutch Painters of the Seventeenth Century.* NY: Harry N. Abrams, 1984.

Levey, Michael. *Rococo to Revolution: Major Trends in Eighteenth-Century Painting.* NY: Oxford University Press, 1977.

Mayer, Ralph. *The Artist's Handbook of Materials and Techniques.* 5th ed., rev. and updated. NY: Viking-Penguin, Inc., 1991. An up-to-date reference.

Porter, Albert W. *Expressive Watercolor Techniques.* Worcester, MA: Davis Publications, Inc., 1982. A useful resource with valuable information on techniques and processes.

Sheaks, Barclay. *Painting with Acrylics: From Start to Finish.* Worcester, MA: Davis Publications, Inc., 1972. Information on techniques for teacher and student.

Terukazu, Akiyama. *Japanese Painting.* Treasures of Asia. NY: Rizzoli International Publications, 1977.

Paper

Betts, Victoria. *Exploring Papier-Mâché.* 4th ed., rev. Worcester, MA: Davis Publications, Inc., 1962. A classic technique book.

Johnson, Pauline. *Creating with Paper.* Seattle: University of Washington Press, 1975. A variety of approaches to paper sculpture.

Toale, Bernard. *The Art of Papermaking.* Worcester, MA: Davis Publications, Inc., 1983. A source of ideas for additional texture experiences.

Photography

FILM MAKING

Eastman Kodak Co. *Movies and Slides without a Camera.* Rochester, NY: 1972. A creative approach to film making.

Halas, John. *The Technique of Film Animation.* 4th ed. NY: Focal Press, 1976. A look at the history and techniques of film animation.

Laybourne, Kit. *The Animation Book.* NY: Crown Publishers, Inc., 1988. An informative discussion of animation assuming no previous training.

Linder, Carl. *Film Making: A Practical Guide.* Englewood Cliffs, NJ: Prentice-Hall, Inc., 1976. An interesting work that provides information for the amateur film maker.

Piper, James. *Personal Film Making.* Englewood Cliffs, NJ: Prentice-Hall, Inc., 1975. An excellent introduction to "super-S" film making with step-by-step instructions on all phases of film.

STILL PHOTOGRAPHY

Craven, George M. *Object and Image.* 3rd ed. Englewood Cliffs, NJ: Prentice-Hall, Inc., 1989. An approach to photography as a creative medium.

Feininger, Andreas. *The Complete Photographer.* rev. ed. Englewood Cliffs, NJ: Prentice-Hall, Inc., 1978. A good overview of basic photographic techniques.

Feininger, Andreas. *Darkroom Techniques.* Garden City, NY: Amphoto, 1974. An in-depth work covering the basic concepts of black-and-white development and printing.

Patterson, Freeman. *Photography and the Art of Seeing.* rev. ed. San Francisco, CA: Sierra Club Books, 1990. Good advice on creative photography of particular interest to the beginning photographer.

Printmaking

Ross, John and Clare Romano. *The Complete Relief Print.* NY: Free Press-Macmillan, 1974. A clear presentation of ideas and techniques for secondary students.

Sculpture

Hall, Carolyn Vosburg. *Soft Sculpture.* Worcester, MA: Davis Publications, Inc., 1981. Provides useful information for soft sculpture projects.

Hammacher, A. M. *Modern Sculpture: Tradition and Innovation.* NY: Harry N. Abrams, 1970.

Kleiner, Diane E. E. *Roman Sculpture.* New Haven, CT: Yale University Press, 1992.

Meilach, Dona Z. *Contemporary Art with Wood: Creative Techniques and Appreciation.* NY: Crown Publishers, Inc., 1968. Wood in art today including techniques of sculpture, selecting wood, and wood in architecture.

Meilach, Dona Z. *Soft Sculpture and Other Soft Art Forms.* NY: Crown Publishers, Inc., 1974. A thorough book with useful information for soft sculpture projects.

Meilach, Dona Z. and Melvin Meilach. *Box Art: Assemblage and Construction.* NY: Crown Publishers, Inc., 1975. Useful technique information.

Morris, John. *Creative Metal Sculpture: A Step-By-Step Approach.* NY: Bruce Publishing Co., 1971. Takes the novice metalworker through the process of creating various types of metal sculpture.

Pop-Hennessy, John. *Italian Renaissance Sculpture.* NY: Phaidon, 1971.

Richter, Gisela M. A. *The Sculpture and Sculptors of the Greeks.* 4th ed., rev. New Haven, CT: Yale University Press, 1970.

Art History

Armstrong, Tom, et al. *200 Years of American Sculpture.* Boston: David R. Godine, Publishers, Inc., 1976. An informative look at the evolution of American sculpture.

Arnason, H. H. *History of Modern Art: Painting, Sculpture, Architecture, Photography.* 3d ed. NY: Harry N. Abrams, 1986.

Barnicoat, John. *Posters: A Concise History.* NY: Thames and Hudson, 1985. The importance of the poster, including its role in various artistic movements.

Beaton, Cecil Walter Hardy and Gail Buckland. *The Magic Image: The Genius of Photography.* NY: Viking-Penguin, Inc., 1990. An assortment of the work of over two hundred photographers since 1839, with biographical sketches.

Broder, Patricia J. *American Indian Painting and Sculpture.* NY: Abbeville Press, Inc., 1981. A good introduction to contemporary Indian art with excellent illustrations.

Chadwick, Whitney. *Women, Art, and Society.* The World of Art Series. London: Thames and Hudson, 1989.

Driskell, David. C. *Two Centuries of Black American Art.* NY: Los Angeles County Museum of Art and Random House, 1976.

Dwyer, Jane Powell, and Edward B. Dwyer. *Traditional Art of Africa, Oceania, and the Americas.* San Francisco, CA: Fine Arts Museum of San Francisco, 1973.

Etthighausen, Richard, and Oleg Grabar. *The Art and Architecture of Islam: 650–1250.* New Haven, CT: Yale University Press, 1992.

Feldman, Edmund B. *Thinking About Art.* Englewood Cliffs, NJ: Prentice-Hall, Inc., 1985. Combines aesthetics, art criticism, and art history. For the academically gifted student.

Frisch, T. G. *Gothic Art 1140-ca.* 1450. Toronto, Canada: University of Toronto Press, 1987.

Gardner, Helen. *Art Through the Ages.* 9th ed. NY: Harcourt Brace Jovanovich, Inc., 1991. An art history resource book for teachers.

Handlin, Oscar. *Statue of Liberty.* NY: Newsweek Book Division, 1980. A history of the conception and building of the symbolic statue.

Highwater, Jamake. *Arts of the Indian Americas: Leaves from the Sacred Tree.* NY: Harper & Row Publishers, Inc., 1983. Provides an excellent view of the arts of North, South, and Central American Indians, with information on culture and history of Native Americans.

Hillier, Bevis. *The Style of the Century: 1900–1980.* Franklin, NY: Amsterdam Books, 1990. A survey of style in art and industrial design from the turn of the century to the present with a look at the social, political, and economic situations that influenced each decade's sense of style.

Janson, H. W. *History of Art for Young People.* 4th ed. NY: Harry N. Abrams, Inc., 1992. Can be used for art history reports by academically advanced students.

Johnson, Una E. *American Prints and Printmakers: A Chronicle of Over 400 Artists and Their Prints From 1900 to the Present.* NY: Doubleday and Co., Inc., 1980. A survey of artists involved in printmaking in this century.

Lassiter, Barbara Babcock. *American Wilderness: The Hudson River School of Painting.* NY: Doubleday and Co., Inc., 1978. A history of this American realistic landscape school of painting.

Lee, Sherman. *A History of Far Eastern Art.* 4th ed. NY: Harry N. Abrams, 1982.

Lewinski, Jorge. *The Camera at War: A History of War Photography From 1848 to the Present Day.* NY: Simon and Schuster, 1980. A look at combat photographers, the problems they face, and the work they produce.

Sandler, Martin W. *The Story of American Photography: An Illustrated History for Young People.* Boston: Little, Brown and Co., 1979. A survey of American photographers and their work.

Sayer, Chloe. *The Arts and Crafts of Mexico.* San Francisco, CA: Chronicle Books, 1990. An overview of Mexican crafts with good discussion of history and culture. Richly illustrated.

Shadwell, Wendy J., et al. *American Printmaking, the First 150 Years.* Washington, D.C.: Smithsonian Institution Press, 1969. A thorough retrospective on American printmaking.

Taylor, Joshua C. *Learning to Look: A Handbook for the Visual Arts.* 2d ed. Chicago: University of Chicago Press, 1981.

Wilmerding, John. *American Masterpieces from the National Gallery of Art.* NY: Hudson Hills Press, 1980.

Artists

Adams, Ansel. *The Portfolios of Ansel Adams.* Boston: Little, Brown and Co., 1981. Adams's seven limited-edition portfolios in one volume. A definitive collection of his stunning photographic work.

Brown, Jonathan. *Diego de Velázquez, Painter and Courtier.* New Haven, CT: Yale University Press, 1986.

Bruzeau, Maurice. *Alexander Calder.* Translated by I. Mark. NY: Harry N. Abrams, Inc., 1979. A picture book of Calder's work.

Chambers, D. S. *Patrons and Artists in the Italian Renaissance.* Columbia, SC: University of South Carolina Press, 1971.

Feaver, William. *Masters of Caricature: From Hogarth and Gillray to Scarfe and Levine.* NY: Alfred E. Knopf, Inc., 1981. Brief biographical sketches of caricaturists of the last three centuries. Illustrated.

Hoving, Thomas. *Two Worlds of Andrew Wyeth: A Conversation with Andrew Wyeth.* Boston: Houghton Mifflin Co., 1978. Includes many examples of Wyeth's work as well as a long interview.

Kelder, Diane. *The French Impressionists and Their Century.* NY: Praeger, 1970.

Levin, Gail. *Edward Hopper: The Art and the Artist.* NY: W. W. Norton and Co., Inc., 1986. A representative collection of Hopper's work, combined with text on Hopper's development and characteristic themes.

Lisle, Laurie. *Portrait of an Artist: A Biography of Georgia O'Keeffe.* Albuquerque, NM: University of New Mexico, 1986. A fascinating account of O'Keeffe's life and work.

Locher, J. L., ed. *The World of M. C. Escher.* NY: Harry N. Abrams, Inc., 1988. A catalog of the precise, visually intricate and often stunning work of the Dutch mathematician and artist.

Rewald, John. *Post-Impressionism: From Van Gogh to Gauguin.* 2d ed. NY: The Museum of Modern Art, 1962.

Rockwell, Norman. *Norman Rockwell: My Adventures As An Illustrator.* NY: Harry N. Abrams, Inc., 1988. Rockwell's own fascinating account of his life and career.

NDEX

B

C

D

E

F

G

N

O

P

R

S

T

U

V

Photography Credits

Art Resource 13, 16, 40, 108, 112, 124, 184, 200t, 208; Atlee Studio/Columbia S.C. 101bl; Bachmann/Photo Edit 236; Ian Berry/Magnum Photos 22; Bettmann 68; Leslye Borden/Photo Edit 296; Borromeo/Art Resource 46t; Courtesy of Chuck Close 248; Margaret Courtney-Clarke 172; Cris Eden/Eden Art 116; Tony Freeman/Photo Edit 75b, 78; Frank Fortune 29, 74, 76, 128b, 144, 203bl, 210(2), 256, 272, 300, 316; Giraudon/Art Resource 151, 285, 290; Glencoe Stock 72, 79, 81, 252; Jeff Greenberg/Photo Edit 77; Timothy Hursley 65b; Jerry Jacka Photography 201, 237, 257, 274(2); Mark Jasin/Stockworks 73; Barry Kornbluh 188; Lessing/Art Resource 83; Charles Moore/Black Star 38; © MTV Networks 314; Courtesy of Michael Naranjo 152; Robert Nix 90(6), 92, 118, 130(3), 192(6), 196(3), 197, 222(4), 227b, 232t, 282; Mark Nohl 150(3); Nick Pauloff 156(2); Sandak 62t, 126, 140, 254, 265, 330t; Scala/Art Resource 37, 43, 45, 49b, 52t, 277, 309; SEF/Art Resource 46b, 51; Courtesy of Sandy Skoglund 216; Courtesy of Wayne Thiebaud 344.

Selected student work photographed by Lee White Photography.